CLIENT/SERVER F

MW01703327

Visual Basic 5

THE
LEARNING
CURVE
JUST GOT
FLATTER

ANNE PRINCE
ED KOOP

MIKE MURACH & ASSOCIATES
2560 West Shaw Lane, Suite 101
Fresno, CA 93711-2765 • (209) 440-9071

Authors: Anne Prince
Ed Koop
Writer/editor: Joel Murach
Editor: Mike Murach
Design: Zylka Design
Production: Tom Murach

The next book in our client/server series

Client/Server Programming: Access 97 by Anne Prince and Joel Murach

© 1998, Mike Murach & Associates, Inc.
All rights reserved.

Printed in the United States of America.

10 9 8 7 6 5 4 3 2 1
ISBN: 1-890774-00-6

Library of Congress Cataloging-in-Publication Data
Prince, Anne.
Client/server programming : Visual Basic 5 / Anne Prince and Ed Koop.
p. cm.
Includes index.
ISBN: 1-890774-00-6 (pbk.)
1. Client/server computing. 2. Microsoft Visual BASIC. I. Koop, Edward. II. Title.
QA76.9.C55P75 1998
005.2'768--dc21 98-13129
CIP

Contents

Expanded Contents

Introduction

"I can't *believe* how steep the learning curve is!" That's what we said dozens of times as we learned how to use Visual Basic for developing client/server applications. We kept repeating that even after we bought a dozen of the best-selling Visual Basic books. And we didn't stop even after we hired a high-priced "expert" to help us answer the questions that weren't adequately addressed in any of those books.

That steep learning curve, of course, is one reason why so many client/server projects have failed during the last few years. It's also why most successful client/server projects have been for relatively simple applications with fewer than 100 users. Yet, even though the technology is inherently difficult, that's still no reason why the learning curve should be so steep.

And now, with the publication of this book, we believe that "the learning curve just got flatter," and that you'll be able to master client/server programming with less frustration and in less time than you thought possible. In the first two chapters, you'll learn the concepts that apply to all client/server systems. In the next two chapters, you'll learn how to create simple client/server applications of your own. And each chapter thereafter builds on that knowledge base until you have all the essential skills of a professional client/server programmer.

5 ways this book differs from all the others

- In this 480-page book, you can learn all the skills that you need for developing complete client/server applications with a Visual Basic front-end that gets data from a SQL Server database (or any other ODBC database) on the back-end. No other Visual Basic book has this practical emphasis on client/server applications right from page 1.
- The trick to learning Visual Basic is handling the relationships between the dozens of statements, functions, objects, properties, methods, and events that VB offers. So that's what this book focuses on. And to make sure that you understand which elements to use when and how they all work together, this book presents all the property settings and the complete code for six different projects.
- When you complete section 1 of this book…just 142 pages…you'll be able to develop true client/server applications of your own (talk about flattening the learning curve!). After that, you'll learn more quickly because you understand how Visual Basic programming works.
- As you page through the book, you'll see that all of the essential skills are presented in the figures, or illustrations, on the odd-numbered pages, while the text on the facing pages gives the perspective that you need for using the skills. We've been experimenting with this presentation method for about three years now; it works better than any other we've ever used; and you won't find anything like it anywhere else.
- After you use this book to learn Visual Basic programming, it becomes the best reference guide you've ever used. Why? Because all of the essential information is

presented in just the figures under headings that clearly identify the information chunks. This not only means that you can find what you're looking for faster, but also that you read less to get the information you need.

Who this book is for

This book is designed for anyone who wants to learn to develop client/server systems with Visual Basic. That includes mainframe developers like COBOL programmers as well as client/server developers who are currently using tools like PowerBuilder or Delphi. That also includes technical managers who need to better understand what the implications of using Visual Basic are (and section 1 will answer most of your questions).

This book does, however, assume that (1) you're already familiar with the Windows 95 interface, and (2) you have some programming experience. Being familiar with the Windows 95 interface just means that you have used one or more Windows programs (like Word, Excel, or Access). Having some programming experience means that you're familiar with the basic syntax and statements of one or more programming languages.

This book also assumes that you're a motivated learner because Visual Basic is inherently a formidable subject. So to master the relationships between the Visual Basic code and its objects, properties, methods and events, you're going to need to take some time after you finish reading each chapter—often two or more hours—to develop small applications on your own. That's especially true for chapters 3, 4, 6, and 12,which are the most difficult chapters in this book. The good news is that everything you need to know is between the covers of this book, so you will succeed if you stay with it.

What this book does

To get you started right, the first two chapters in section 1 present the client/server and database concepts that all Visual Basic programmers need to understand. Then, chapter 3 shows you how to develop a significant Visual Basic application, and chapter 4 shows you how to develop a true client/server application (one that gets data from a database server). By the time you finish this section (just 142 pages), you have reached a significant level of competence and you have a good idea of what you need to know to become proficient at Visual Basic programming.

In section 2, you build on this introduction by learning the essential skills for all client/server programmers. In chapter 6, for example, you learn how to enhance the chapter 4 application so it closely resembles a real-world application. In chapter 7, you learn how to enhance the database programming for this application so it gets the data more efficiently and without error. In chapter 8, you learn how to enhance the user interface by adding a splash screen, menus, toolbars, and help. By this time, your application starts to look thoroughly professional and ready for use. And all of these chapters are easier to follow because they keep adding features and code to the application that you started way back in chapter 4.

In section 3, you continue to build on what you've learned. Chapter 10 shows you how to use the Visual Data Manager that comes with Visual Basic to create simple databases that you can use for testing your programs. Chapter 11 shows you how to develop the reports for an application and run them from the Visual Basic interface (an essential skill that isn't included in most Visual Basic books). And chapter 13 shows how to deploy (or distribute) the finished application to the clients of a system.

The most exciting chapter in section 3, however, is chapter 12 because it takes you deeper into object-oriented programming. When you finish this chapter, you'll know how to create and use your own objects instead of just using those that come with Visual Basic. You'll also know how to deploy those objects as ActiveX components so they can be easily modified without changing the client software.

Because Visual Basic provides so many features and capabilities, they can easily become overwhelming. That's why this book makes no attempt to present *all* of them, but always focuses on the most practical. In particular, this book presents just the most commonly-used method for working with the data in a database (called DAO) instead of trying to cover all the available methods. And it doesn't present the file-handling features of Visual Basic because they aren't used in client/server applications. If you master the skills presented in this book, though, you'll be well prepared to learn new skills on your own.

Web site items that can help you learn more quickly

After you read the programming chapters in this book, you should take some time to develop applications of your own that are like those illustrated in the chapters. After you read chapter 4, for example, you should develop a Vendors maintenance application. After you read chapter 6, you should develop an AccountsPayable application. And after you read chapter 12, you should develop a book order application. That, of course, is the best way to turn your knowledge into skills.

To make this development process as efficient as possible, you can download nine of the applications used in this book from our web site. Then, you can review the applications to see how the forms, controls, database, and Visual Basic code work together. You can also enhance these applications and test the results as you continue to build your skills. This, of course, is an another way to learn, especially when you have this book to guide you through the complexities.

Whether or not you download the applications, you're going to need databases for testing the applications in this book or for testing applications of your own. As a result, our web site also provides two databases that you can download to your system. These are the databases that you need for testing the nine applications that you can download.

To find out more about what's available from our web site, please refer to the appendix at the back of this book. Or look us up at *www.murach.com*.

Please let us know how this book works for you

From the start, our goal has been to present client/server programming in a way that helps you learn more…faster. That's what we call "flattening the learning curve."

Now, if you have any comments about this book, we would enjoy hearing from you. That's why there's a postage-paid comment form at the back of this book. If this book helps you learn what you wanted to know, we'd be delighted to hear about it. And if the way we've organized and presented the material flattens the learning curve for you, we'd be even more delighted to hear about it.

Anne Prince
Author

Ed Koop
Author

SECTION ONE 1

Introduction to client/server programming

Chapter 1 in this section introduces you to the hardware and software of client/server systems. In particular, it introduces you to the three critical components of every client/server system: the user interface on the client, the database management system on the server, and the SQL query that communicates between the two. This chapter also introduces you to the Microsoft products for developing client/server systems including Access 97 and Visual Basic 5.

Then, chapter 2 takes a more detailed look at the relational database and relational database management system that make up the back end of a client/server application. In particular, this chapter focuses on how the tables in a relational database are organized and defined and how you can use SQL to manipulate the data in those tables. When you finish this chapter, you should understand what the server side of a client/server system can do.

Last, chapter 3 introduces you to Visual Basic programming, and chapter 4 introduces you to database programming in Visual Basic. In each of these chapters, you will learn how to develop a small, but complete, application. So when you finish these chapters, you should be able to develop simple applications of your own. You should also have a good sense of what client/server programming entails and what you need to know to become proficient at it.

Chapter 1

Client/Server concepts

Today, most new application development is being done for client/server systems. In addition, the current trend in application development is toward the use of Microsoft products. This chapter introduces you to client/server systems as well as the Microsoft products for developing client/server applications.

Introduction to client/server systems

In case you aren't familiar with client/server systems, this first topic introduces you to the essential hardware and software components of both the clients and the server. The end result is a collection of components that work together as a single system.

The hardware components of a client/server system

Figure 1-1 presents the three hardware components of a client/server system: the clients, the network, and the server. The *clients* are usually the PCs that are already available on the desktops throughout a company. And the *network* is the cabling, communication lines, network interface cards, hubs, routers, and other components that connect the clients and the server.

The *server* is a computer that has enough processor speed, internal memory (RAM), and disk storage to serve the clients of the system. This computer is usually a high-powered PC or a RISC system, but it can also be a mid-range system or even a mainframe system. To back up the files of a system, a server usually has a tape drive or some other form of off-line storage. It may also have one or more printers or specialized devices that can be shared by the users of the system. However, printers can also be attached directly to the network using network interface cards.

Because all of the PCs on the system depend on the server, the server should be fault tolerant and scaleable. *Fault tolerant* means that the server is able to correct most hardware errors without failing. *Scaleable* means that you should be able to enhance the server with more processing speed, internal memory (RAM), or disk storage as the number of clients or the usage of the system goes up.

In a simple client/server system, the clients and the server are part of a *local area network* (or LAN). However, two or more LANs can be connected as part of a *wide area network* (or WAN). Then, the clients that are on the LANs that are connected by the WAN can share data and communicate via services like e-mail.

The components of a client/server system

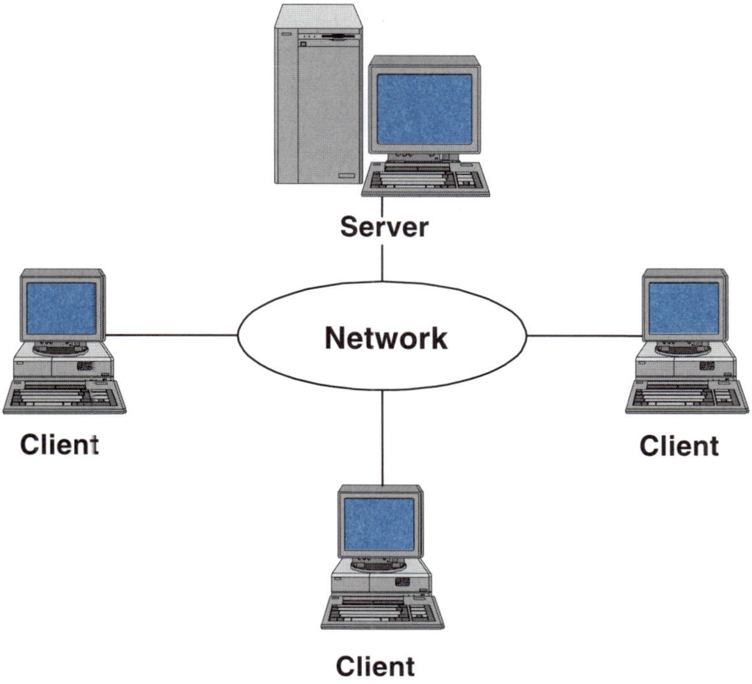

The three hardware components of a client/server system

- The *clients* are the PCs, Macintoshes, or workstations of the system.
- The *server* is a computer that stores the files and databases of the system and provides services to the clients.
- The *network* consists of the cabling, communication lines, and other components that connect the clients and the servers of the system. A *local area network* (*LAN*) connects clients in the same geographic area (usually, a department or building). A *wide area network* (*WAN*) connects two or more LANs.

Server requirements

- The server is a PC or other computer that has enough disk storage, internal memory (RAM), and speed to support the clients of the system. A server often includes a large-capacity tape drive for backing up the data on the system.
- The server should be *fault tolerant* because the entire client/server system fails if the server fails. To protect against power failures, for example, a server is often equipped with a backup power system.
- The server should also be *scaleable*. This means you should be able to add processing speed, RAM, and disk storage to the server as the number of users and the user requirements increase. You should also be able to add extra servers to the system to help share the client workload.

Figure 1-1 The hardware components of a client/server system

The software components of a client/server system

Figure 1-2 presents the software components of a typical client/server system. As you can see, the server requires a *network operating system* that manages the functions of the network. The current Microsoft product is Windows NT Server 4.0, but NT Server 5.0 is due to be released in the next few months.

The server also requires a *database management system* (*DBMS*) like Oracle or Microsoft SQL Server. This DBMS manages the databases that are stored on the server. For improved performance, some database management systems provide for databases that are spread over two or more servers.

In contrast to a server, each client requires an operating system and network access software. This network software may be part of the operating system or a separate component.

To perform useful work, the client also requires *application software*. This can be a purchased software package like a financial accounting package, or it can be custom software that's developed for a specific application. This book, of course, shows you how to develop custom software for a client/server system.

Although the application software is run on the client, it uses data that's stored on the server. To make this communication between client and server possible, the client requires an *Open Database Connectivity* (*ODBC*) *driver*. For instance, the ODBC driver for SQL Server lets the client communicate with a SQL Server database. And the ODBC driver for Oracle lets a client communicate with an Oracle database.

Once the software for both client and server is installed, the client communicates with the server via *SQL queries* (or just *queries*) that are passed to the DBMS through the ODBC driver. SQL, which stands for *Structured Query Language*, is an industry standard that makes communication between any application and any DBMS possible. After the client sends a query to the DBMS, the DBMS interprets the query and sends the results back to the client.

Client software, server software, and the SQL interface

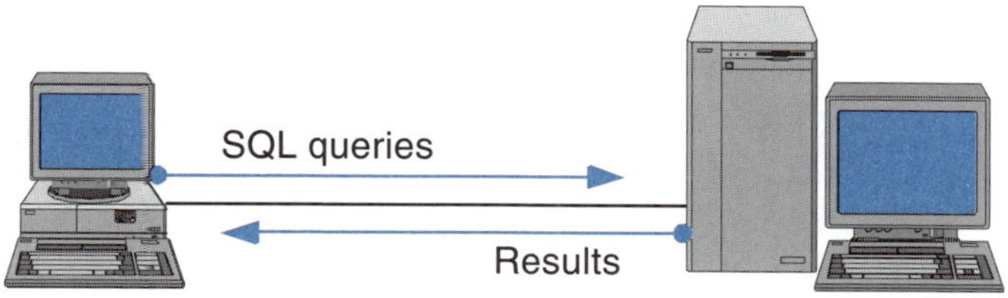

Client
Operating system
Network software
ODBC driver
Application software

Server
Network operating system
Database Management System (DBMS)

Server software

- Each server requires a *network operating system* like Windows NT Server, Novell NetWare, or UNIX.
- To store the databases of the client/server system, each server requires a *database management system* (*DBMS*) like Microsoft SQL Server, Sybase SQL Server, Oracle, or DB2.

Client software

- Each client requires an operating system like Windows NT Workstation, Windows 95, Windows 3.1, OS/2, DOS, or Macintosh.
- Each client also requires network software. With Windows 95 or Windows NT Workstation, the required software for use with Windows NT Server or Novell Netware is built into the operating system. Otherwise, the required network software must be installed on each client.
- The *application software* does the work that the user wants to do. This type of software can be purchased or developed.
- The *ODBC* (*Open Database Connectivity*) *driver* for the database lets the client application communicate with the database.

The SQL interface

- The application software communicates with the database management system by sending *SQL queries* through the ODBC driver. When the DBMS receives a query, it provides a service like returning the requested data (*results*) to the client.

Figure 1-2 The software components of a client/server system

The defining characteristics of a client/server system

Figure 1-3 presents the one defining characteristic of a client/server system that everyone agrees upon. Quite simply, the processing for an application must be divided between the client and the server. Theoretically, at least, this lets you balance the workload between the clients and server of a system and makes for a more efficient system.

In a *two-tier system* like the one in figure 1-3, all of the processing is done by the clients and the server. The processing done by each client can be referred to as *front-end processing*; the processing done by the server can be referred to as *back-end processing*. Today, most client/server systems are two-tier systems, but some of the processing can be moved to a second server in a three-tier system and to other servers in a multi-tier system. You'll learn more about this near the end of this chapter.

Client processing and server processing

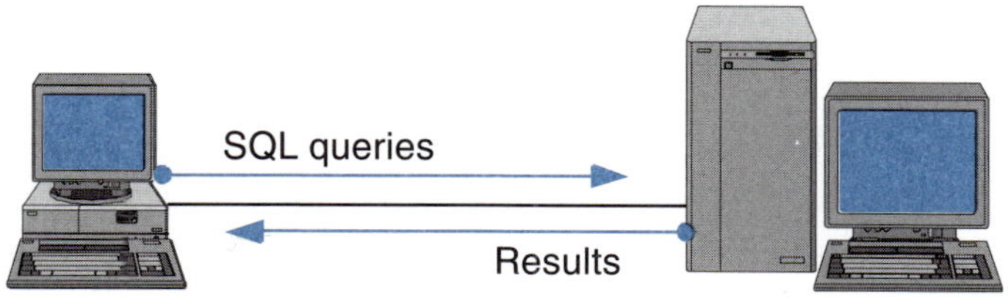

Client

Front-end processing

User interface

Server

Back-end processing

Database management services

The defining characteristic of a client/server system

- The processing is divided between client and server. The client always does the processing associated with the user interface (the *front-end processing*), and the server always does the processing associated with the database (the *back-end processing*).

Other characteristics of a modern client/server system

- The application software on the client uses a graphical user interface (GUI) like Windows 95.
- The application software communicates with the database management system on the server by sending *SQL queries*.
- The interface between the client and the server is based on the use of SQL and an Open Database Connectivity (ODBC) driver.
- In a *two-tier* physical system, the client and server do all of the processing. In a *multi-tier* (or *n-tier*) *system*, other servers do some of the processing.

Figure 1-3 The defining characteristics of a client/server system

The primary software components of a client/server system

From a developer's point of view, the primary software components of modern client/server systems are the user interface on the client, the database management system on the server, and the SQL query that communicates between client and server. The topics that follow give more information about each of these components.

The user interface

Figure 1-4 presents the characteristics of a *user interface*. On a modern client/server system, that interface is a graphical user interface (GUI) like Windows 95 or Windows 98. Because this is a standard interface, it should be easier to use than non-standard interfaces like those found on traditional mainframe, mid-range, and DOS systems.

The good news is that it's relatively easy to build a Windows interface when you use a development product like Access 97 or Visual Basic 5. To a large extent, you can design a *form* (window) for an application by dragging controls like text boxes and command buttons onto it. Then, to get the controls to look and act the way you want them to, you change some of the properties for the controls. That doesn't require any programming.

To complete a form, though, you must write the Visual Basic procedures that control the way the form and its controls work. For the form in figure 1-4, for example, the developer needs to write Visual Basic code that tells the application what to do when a user clicks on the Enter Invoices command button. This code will switch to a new form and let the user enter invoice data. That's the programming part of application development and that's what makes application development difficult.

The Windows 95 interface for an Accounts Payable application

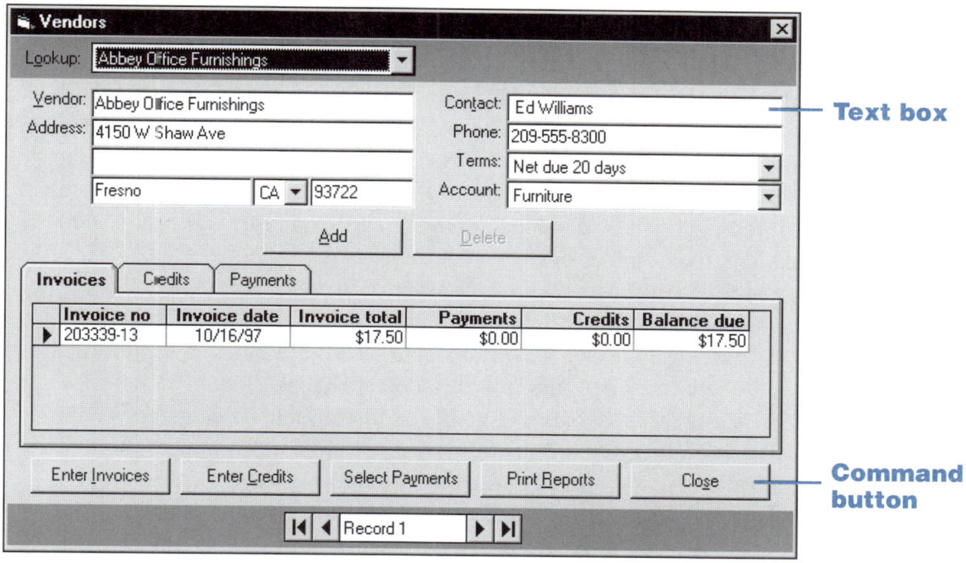

The characteristics of the Windows 95 user interface

- The *user interface* for any application developed for Windows 95 or Windows NT Workstation 4 has the same general look and feel as any other Windows 95 application.
- The primary interface for an application consists of one or more interrelated windows, which application developers refer to as *forms*. Each form contains controls that let the user interact with it.
- In general, the controls in a form or dialog box work the same way they do in other Windows applications. If, for example, you click in a text box, the focus is moved to that box. And if you click on a command button, its function is started.
- When you use modern application development products like Access 97 or Visual Basic 5, you can build a form and its controls without any programming.
- To complete a form, the application developer writes the Visual Basic code for those functions that require it.

Figure 1-4 The user interface

The database and database management system

Figure 1-5 presents the characteristics of a *relational database* and a *relational database management system* (*RDBMS*). If you've ever used a relational database, you know that it consists of related *tables*, and each table consists of *records* and *fields*.

When a client tries to access data from a database, the RDBMS (or just DBMS) must be running on the server because the DBMS manages the services for its databases. At the least, the DBMS interprets the SQL queries that are sent to it from the clients. Then, it returns the requested data to the clients or performs the requested actions (like adding, updating, or deleting records).

In addition, a DBMS enforces the rules that are defined for a database. This includes checking data for validity before adding or updating a record. This may also include checking data for integrity so, for example, you don't delete a vendor record if invoice records that are related to that vendor record still exist.

The DBMS is a critical component of a client/server system because it provides many of the benefits of the system. In contrast to traditional development methods, the DBMS makes it relatively easy for you to define a database, extract data from the database, and make modifications to the design of the database. In chapter 2, you'll learn more about databases and database management systems.

Three tables of a database in Access 97's relationships view

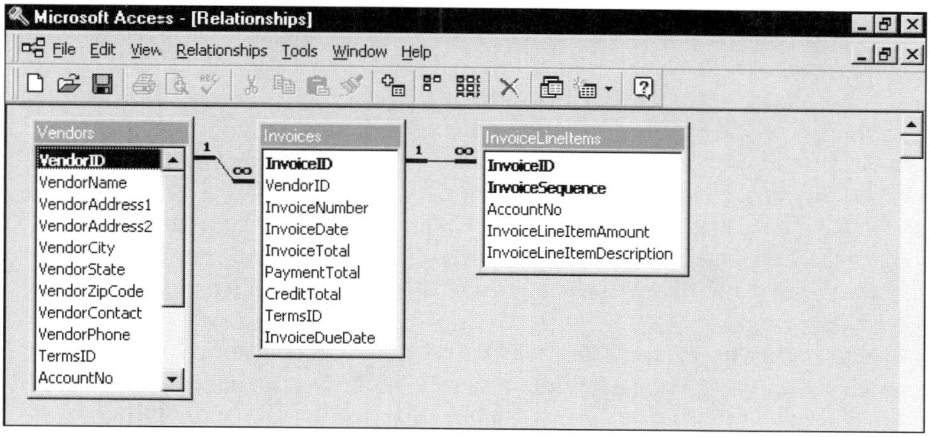

The characteristics of a relational database

- A *relational database* consists of two or more related *tables*. In the example above, the three tables are named Vendors, Invoices, and InvoiceLineItems, but the database could include other tables.
- The tables in a database consist of *records*, or *rows*, and they in turn consist of *fields*, or *columns*. The tables above list the fields in each record.
- The tables in a database are related by *key fields*. In the example above, the Vendors table is related to the Invoices table by the VendorID field, and the Invoices table is related to the InvoiceLineItems table by the InvoiceID field.

The characteristics of a database management system

- The DBMS must be running on the server when a client tries to access its data because it does the back-end processing for the client/server system.
- The DBMS receives SQL queries from the clients of the system and returns the requested data or performs the requested action (like updating or deleting a record).
- The DBMS helps insure the integrity of the data by enforcing the rules that have been defined for the database.

Notes

- Other types of databases may be used in a client/server system, but relational databases are commonly used for business systems.
- A DBMS for a relational database may also be referred to as a *relational database management system*, or *RDBMS*.

Figure 1-5 The database and database management system

The SQL query

Structured Query Language, or *SQL*, is the standard language that is used for database operations. In a typical client/server communication, the client sends an *SQL query* to the server where it is processed by the DBMS. The DBMS then returns the requested data or performs the requested action.

In the top part of figure 1-6, you can see a query that's created with the query tool of Access. In the query that's shown, data from two tables in a SQL Server database is requested, but only when the InvoiceTotal field in the Invoices table is greater than 1000 and the PaymentTotal field is equal to zero. This should give you some idea of how easy it is to extract data from a relational database…a major benefit of a modern client/server system.

As you create a query, it is converted by Access to Structured Query Language. Then, when the SQL query is sent from the client application to the server, the ODBC driver on the client converts the query to a form that can be used by the DBMS on the server. This means a client application can work with any database for which there's an ODBC driver. In chapter 2, you'll learn more about SQL.

An Access query that gets data from two SQL Server tables

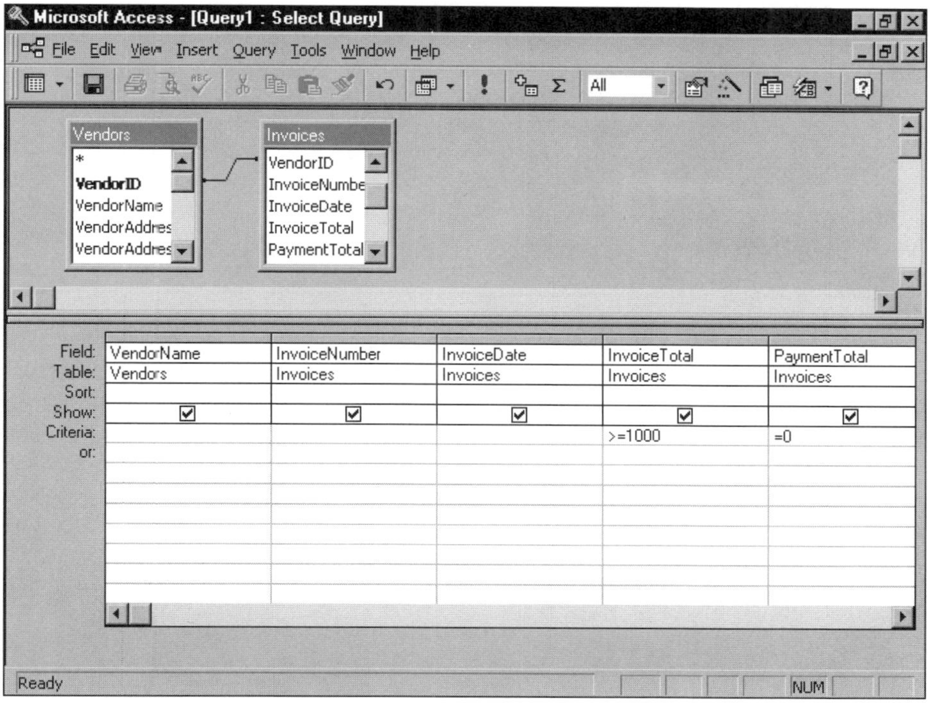

The Structured Query Language (SQL) for the query shown above

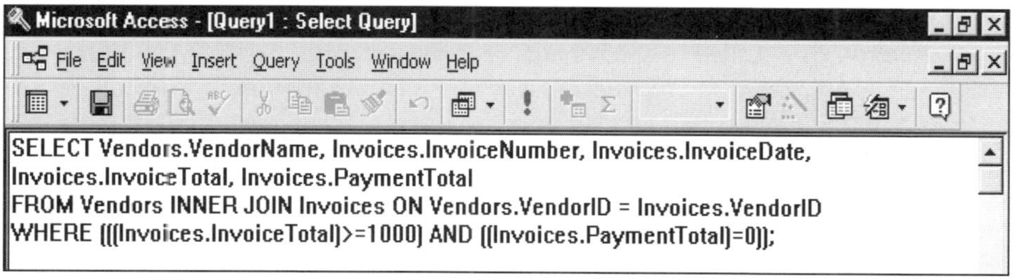

The characteristics of a query

- You can create a query in several ways when you work with a relational database. One way is to use a visual query tool like the one for Access shown at the top of this figure. Another way is to code the query directly using *Structured Query Language* (or *SQL*). This is a standard language with minor variations from one software vendor to another.
- When you use a visual tool to create a query, it is automatically converted to SQL. In conversation, SQL is usually pronounced *sequel* or S-Q-L.

Figure 1-6 The SQL query

How client/server systems differ from other systems

To help clarify the differences between client/server systems and other types of systems, it's worth comparing client/server systems with other types of systems. Two types that you're probably familiar with are (1) traditional mainframe or mid-range systems and (2) file server systems.

How mainframe and mid-range systems differ

Figure 1-7 presents a traditional computer system. In contrast to a client/server system, the system consists of only one mid-range or mainframe computer so all of the processing is done on that computer. As a result, that computer must provide all of the disk storage and all of the processing for all of the *terminals* of the system. In addition, the terminals aren't computers so they are considered "dumb" or at best "semi-intelligent" devices.

In a large company, a *mainframe computer* (or just *mainframe*) often supports hundreds of terminals. This means that the computer must be immensely powerful with enormous storage capacities. It must also be able to run many programs at the same time so each terminal user feels like he or she has complete control of the system.

One of the benefits of the traditional computer system was that all hardware and software came from the same vendor. As a result, the hardware and software worked together without many of the interface problems that are common in multi-vendor systems.

As PCs became popular in the 1980s, many office workers found the need for both a PC and a terminal attached to a mid-range or mainframe. But that was too much hardware for most desktops. The solution was to use PCs as terminals. That can be done by using PC software that emulates the operation of a terminal. Then, if you use a multi-tasking operating system like Windows, you can run the terminal emulation in one window and other applications like word processing or spreadsheet software in other windows.

The architecture of a traditional mainframe or mid-range system

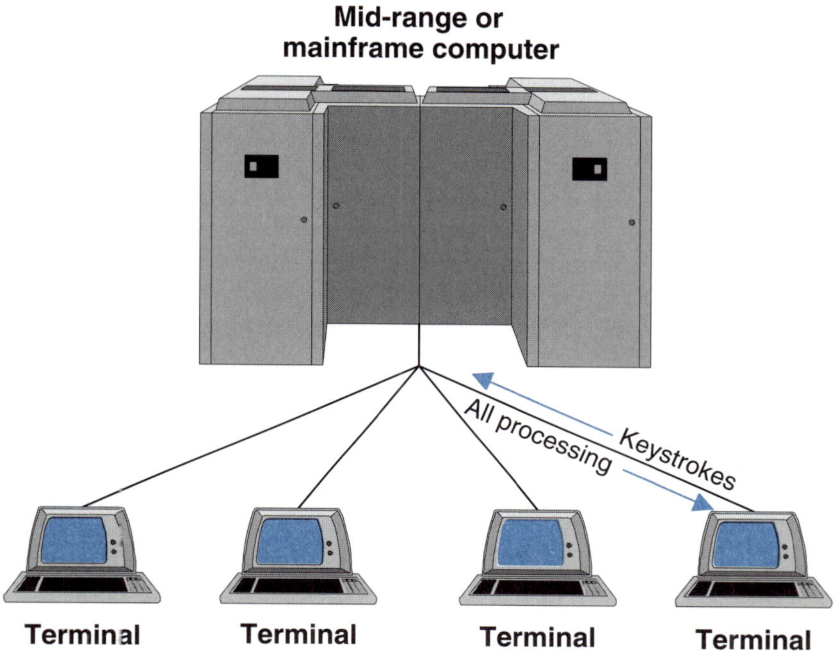

Why this isn't a client/server system

- The mainframe or mid-range computer does all the processing for the entire system including the processing for the user interface and the database management services.
- The terminals aren't computers and don't do any of the processing (they are "dumb" or "semi-intelligent" workstations). The terminals simply accept the keystrokes that are entered and send them to the computer when an attention key like the Enter key is pressed.

Notes

- Today, PCs are often used as the terminals in a mainframe or mid-range system. In that case, one window of the PC emulates a terminal. The other windows can be used for applications like word processing or spreadsheets.
- Today, PCs can be connected to a mid-range or mainframe computer in a client/server relationship. Then, the mid-range or mainframe computer becomes the database server for the client PCs.

Figure 1-7 How mainframe and mid-range systems differ from client/server systems

How file server systems differ

Figure 1-8 presents the architecture of a file server system. Like a client/server system, a file server system consists of clients and a server. Unlike a client/server system, though, the server doesn't do any processing. It just stores the files and databases that are used by the client. When a client opens a file, for example, the entire file (or at least a segment of it) is transferred to the client.

File servers became popular when the need for sharing data and printers between PCs became obvious. By connecting the PCs in a local area network and storing the shared data on the file server, the data could be shared. And by sending print files to the file server, the clients could print their documents on the network printers.

The architecture of a file server system

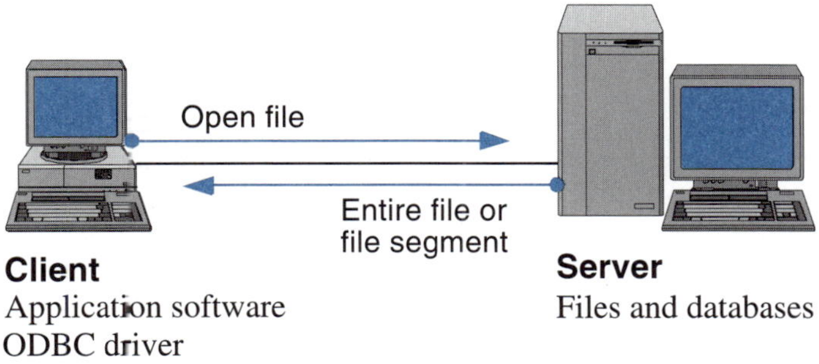

Why this isn't a client/server system

- The client does all the processing. The file server just stores the files and databases that are used by the clients.
- The application software on the client opens the file or database on the file server, and the entire file or at least a portion of it is sent to the client.

Figure 1-8 How file server systems differ from client/server systems

Microsoft products for developing client/server systems

As you have already seen, a client/server system consists of several interrelated software products. Although these products can come from more than one company, Microsoft is doing its best to provide all of the products you need for running and developing client/server systems. Figure 1-9 summarizes its primary products.

These products can be purchased separately or as part of one of the product suites mentioned in figure 1-9. BackOffice provides products for the server side of a system. Visual Studio provides products for developing the client side of a system. And Office 97 provides products for the end user including Word 97, Excel 97, and Access 97.

The first product in the BackOffice suite is Windows NT Server, which is a network operating system. It can be used with clients that are running a variety of operating systems. And it can be used in a wide area network with other servers that are running network operating systems like NetWare and UNIX.

To develop application software for client/server systems, Microsoft provides three products: Visual C++, Visual Basic, and Access. Although Visual C++ has been widely used in the past, Visual Basic and Access are the products of the future. These products can be used to develop front-ends for any DMBS that's supported by an ODBC driver.

Microsoft's database management system for client/server systems is called SQL Server, and it is supported by an ODBC driver. It can be the DBMS for either an Access or a Visual Basic front-end, and it is specifically designed for use with Windows NT Server.

Because the interfaces between many client/server products are standardized, you can use Access, Visual Basic, and SQL Server with a third-party operating system like Novell Netware. You can use Access and Visual Basic to develop front-ends for third-party databases like *Oracle* and *Sybase*. And you can use SQL Server with front-ends that are developed with third-party products like *PowerBuilder* and *Delphi*. This illustrates the many development options that have been made possible by standardization.

Products that are included in Microsoft BackOffice

Product	Description
Windows NT Server	A network operating system that supports a variety of client operating systems including Windows NT Workstation, Windows 95, Windows 3.1, DOS, UNIX, OS/2, and Macintosh.
Exchange Server	Provides e-mail capabilities for all the users of a network; replaces Mail Server.
SNA Server	A gateway that connects the clients on a network to an IBM AS/400 or mainframe computer.
Systems Management Server	Centralizes administrative tasks like keeping client hardware and software inventories, automating software distribution and installation, and solving problems on remote systems.
SQL Server	A database management system that's designed to take full advantage of the features of Windows NT Server.

Products that are included in Microsoft Visual Studio

Product	Description
Visual C++	An object-oriented programming language and development environment that can be used to develop client/server applications for any DBMS supported by an ODBC driver.
Visual Basic	A programming language and Integrated Development Environment that can be used to develop client/server applications for any DBMS supported by an ODBC driver.

Products that are included in Microsoft Office 97

Product	Description
Access	An application development package that integrates the development of the user interface and an Access database.

Figure 1-9 Microsoft products for developing client/server systems

Access 97 for application development

Figure 1-10 illustrates the *Integrated Development Environment* (*IDE*) for Access 97 and summarizes the features of Access when used for application development. The IDE makes it easy for you to drag fields from the field list and controls from the toolbox onto a form. This helps you build the user interface quickly and easily with minimal programming.

In general, you can develop database applications faster with Access than you can with Visual Basic because the database is an integral part of Access. This lets you *prototype* an application in just a few days or weeks so you can get early feedback from the eventual users of the system. Then, when the application is finished, you can convert the database to SQL Server...but you only need to do that if the performance of the Access database isn't satisfactory.

The programming language that's used with Access is called *Visual Basic for Applications*, or *VBA*. In contrast, the language that's used with the Visual Basic development environment is just *Visual Basic*, or *VB*. Since VBA isn't quite as powerful as VB, Visual Basic is often the preferred development environment for applications that require the extra functionality of VB.

When you complete an Access 97 application, you can deliver it to the clients in one of two ways. First, if Access 97 is available to those clients, you can simply deliver a copy of the application file to them. Second, you can create a run-time version of the application so that some of the functionality of Access is built right into the application. In that case, it's not necessary for each client to have Access 97. To create a run-time version of an application, though, you need to have the Developer Edition of Microsoft Office 97.

The Integrated Development Environment for Access 97

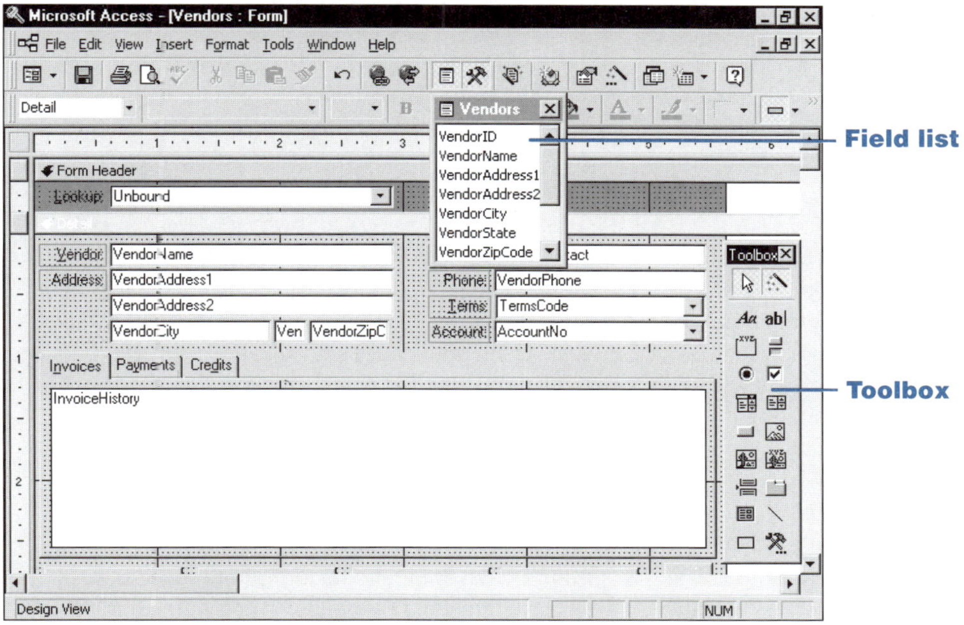

Access 97 characteristics

- Provides an integrated environment that lets you develop a complete application including the database tables, the SQL queries, the forms (the user interface), and the reports.
- Encourages prototyping and rapid application development by integrating the development of the database and the user interface.
- Lets you create Access databases that are run by the Jet database engine. If necessary, you can port these databases later on to any database that's supported by an ODBC driver (like SQL Server).
- The programming language that's used with Access is called *Visual Basic for Applications* (or *VBA*). It is similar but not the same as the *Visual Basic* (*VB*) language that's used with the Visual Basic development environment.
- Microsoft Office 97 Developer Edition lets you create a run-time version of an Access 97 application so you can run it on clients that don't have Access 97. Without the Developer Edition, Access 97 must be available on each client that will use the Access 97 application.

When to use Access for application development

- For systems with 100 or fewer simultaneous users
- For applications that extract and summarize data
- For prototyping systems that can later be implemented with Access or Visual Basic

Figure 1-10 Access 97 for application development

Visual Basic 5 for application development

Figure 1-11 illustrates the *Integrated Development Environment* (*IDE*) for Visual Basic 5 and summarizes its features. The IDE makes it easy for you to drag controls onto a form and to set the properties for those controls. Because Visual Basic isn't integrated with the database, though, you can't build a form and extract data from a database as quickly and easily with Visual Basic as you can with Access.

On the other hand, Visual Basic gives you more control over the database operations of an application. Its Visual Basic language is more powerful than the VBA language that's used with Access. And the resulting applications are executable files that can be run on any clients that use Windows 95, Windows 98, or NT Workstation 4 or 5. (Because Visual Basic 5 creates 32-bit applications, they can be run only on 32-bit operating systems.) That's why Visual Basic is the preferred development environment for operational systems that require careful control of data entry and database updating and for large enterprise systems.

Today, Visual Basic comes in a Professional and an Enterprise Edition. With the Enterprise Edition, you also get an add-in program called Visual Database Tools that lets you create and work with the objects in ODBC databases. For instance, you can use this program to create the tables for a database and to add data to those tables. Although the Visual Database Tools program can't completely replace the tools that come with the DBMS, it can be useful for performing some of the functions you'll need most often. And it's available from within the Visual Basic environment.

The Integrated Development Environment for Visual Basic 5

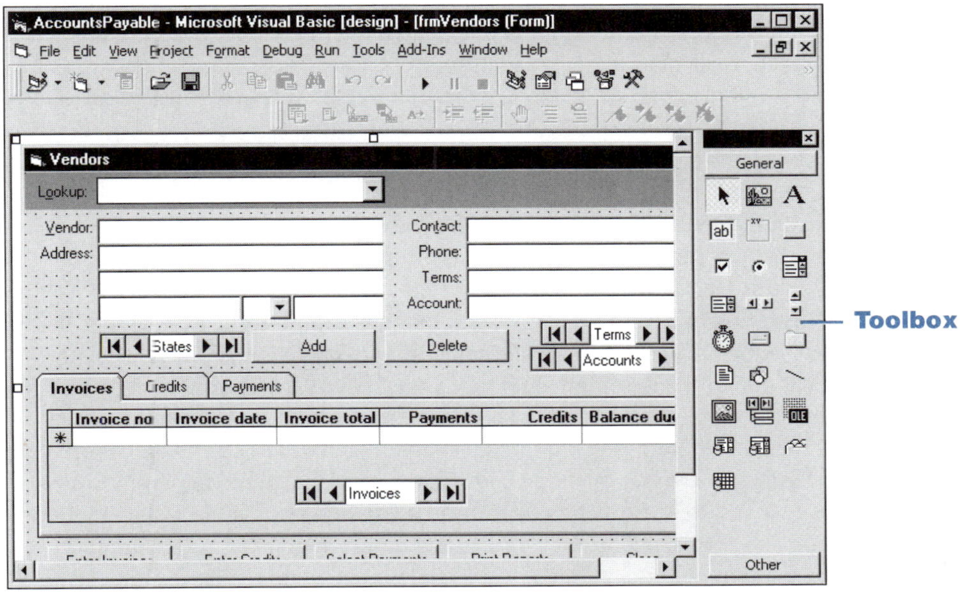

Visual Basic 5 characteristics

- Lets you develop powerful client/server applications for enterprise systems.
- Gives you more control over database operations than Access.
- Lets you create ActiveX components that can be used by more than one application.
- The programming language that's used with the Integrated Development Environment is called Visual Basic, which is more powerful than the Visual Basic for Applications language that's used with Access.
- Creates standalone executable (exe) files that can be run on clients that use Windows 95 or 98 or Windows NT 4 or NT 5.
- Lets you work with an ODBC database using an add-in program called Visual Database Tools (Enterprise Edition only).

When to use Visual Basic for application development

- For applications that require careful control of data entry and database operations
- For enterprise systems
- For developing ActiveX components

Figure 1-11 Visual Basic 5 for application development

Jet and SQL Server databases

When you use Access for developing client/server applications, you normally use the database management system that's built into Access. This DBMS uses a database engine called the *Jet engine*, so Access databases are often referred to as *Jet databases*.

When you use the Jet engine with a Jet database as shown by the first example in figure 1-12, the front-end software sends queries to the Jet engine, which opens the database file on the server. Then, the entire database (or at least a segment of it) is sent to the Jet engine, which processes the query. This means that the client does all the processing, so this isn't a true client/server system.

True client/server or not, though, a system like this can perform well with as many as 100 clients using the application at the same time. That's why you may as well think of this as one of the development options for a client/server system.

When the user requirements demand a true client/server system, you can use an Access or Visual Basic front-end with a SQL Server database as shown by the second example in figure 1-12. Here, the front-end still uses the Jet engine to pass the query to SQL Server. Then, SQL Server processes the query and returns the results to the Jet engine, which can perform additional processing on the query. This is a commonly-used implementation of a true client/server system, although one that may not be as efficient as the next alternative.

The third example in figure 1-12 shows another way that a Visual Basic front-end can work with a SQL Server back-end. Here, Visual Basic passes queries directly to SQL Server without using the Jet engine. This method of implementation works best when rapid response is required in a transaction processing system that serves many clients.

The focus of this book is on developing client/server systems using the second method of implementation shown in this figure. In that case, you use a data access model known as DAO (Data Access Objects), which works with Jet to perform the database processing. Today, this is the most commonly-used method for implementing client/server systems. In chapter seven of this book, however, you'll learn about some of the techniques you can use to implement the third method shown in this figure. Then, you can use these techniques when response time is critical. Note that you can use both of these methods in a single application.

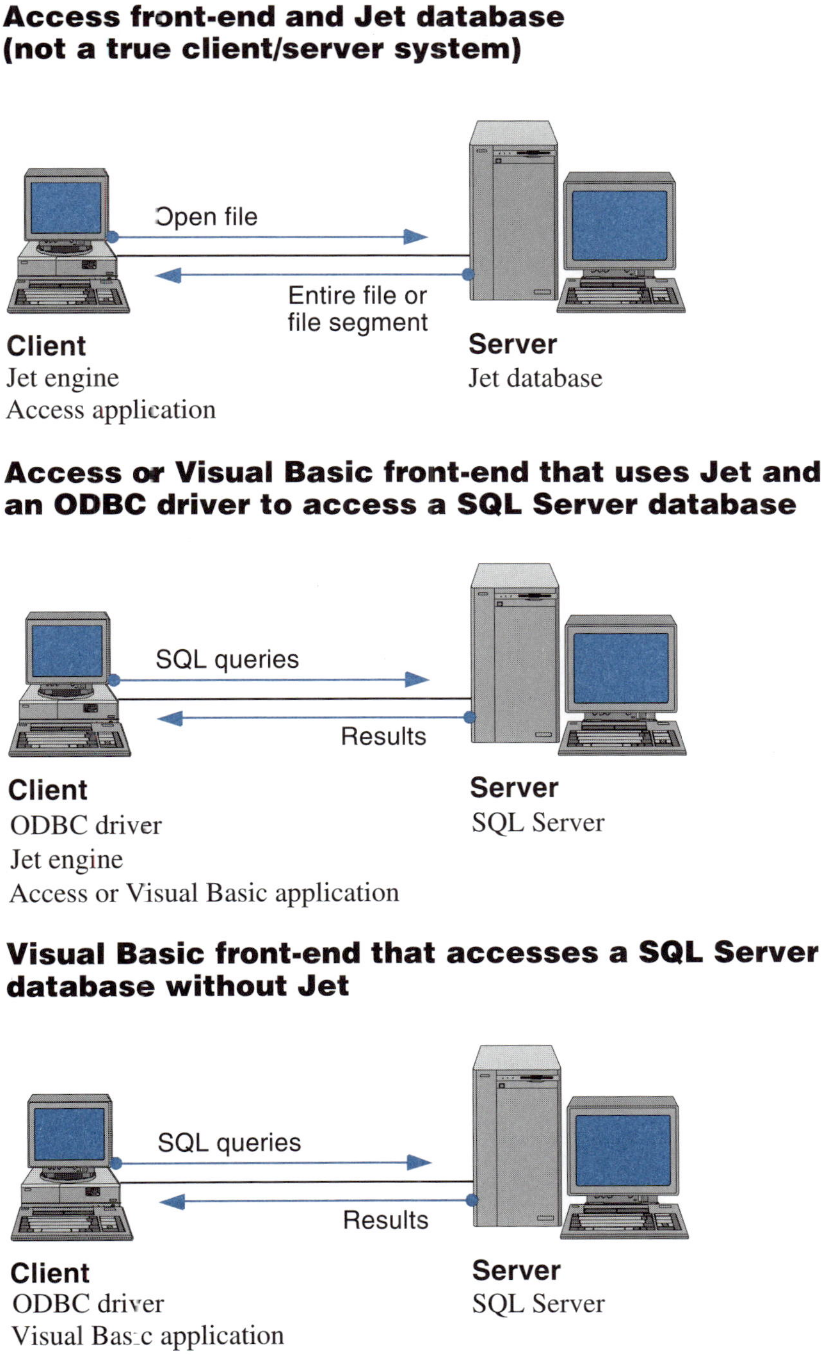

Figure 1-12 How Access and Visual Basic work with Jet and SQL Server databases

Client/Server complexities

If you refer back to figure 1-1, you can see the architecture of a simple client/server system: one server, two or more clients, and a local area network. In the real world, though, client/server systems are more complicated than that.

Mixed platforms

In the best of all client/server worlds, everyone is on the same platform. That means all clients run the same operating system (like Windows 95 or Windows 98), and all the servers of the system run the same operating system (like Windows NT Server or Novell Netware). Few companies, however, have the luxury of using just one platform.

Instead, most companies run a mix of client operating systems (like Windows 3.1, Windows 95, and Macintosh) and a mix of network operating systems (like Novell Netware, Windows NT, and UNIX). That makes it more difficult for an application like e-mail to work throughout the entire wide area network. That also means that you can't run the same client/server application on all clients. If, for example, you're using Access 97 or Visual Basic 5, the application can only run on clients that are running Windows 95, Windows 98, or Windows NT Workstation 4 or 5.

Enterprise systems

The term *enterprise system* refers to all of the computers of a large, often multinational, company. Today, an enterprise system is likely to consist of at least one mainframe, a number of mid-range systems like DEC or AS/400 systems, a number of client/server systems, and some file server systems. The problem, of course, is to connect these mixed platforms so all the people in the enterprise have access to the data they need. To complicate the problem, mid-range and mainframe systems weren't designed to communicate with PCs or PC networks.

To help standardize the communication between PCs, its mid-range computers, and its mainframes, IBM established a protocol called System Network Architecture (SNA). Today, that architecture can lead to communications between systems like those shown in figure 1-13. Here, the clients of a client/server system can get data from the mainframe of the enterprise as well as from the AS/400 for the branch. To make this possible, a second server on the system called an *SNA server* provides a *gateway* to the AS/400 and mainframe.

The purpose of this figure is just to show one way that client/server systems and the other computers in an enterprise can communicate. This enhances the value of client/server systems because it lets each client get the data it needs from whatever computer has that data. The real-world complexities of implementing this type of connectivity, though, are far beyond the scope of this book.

A client/server system for an enterprise

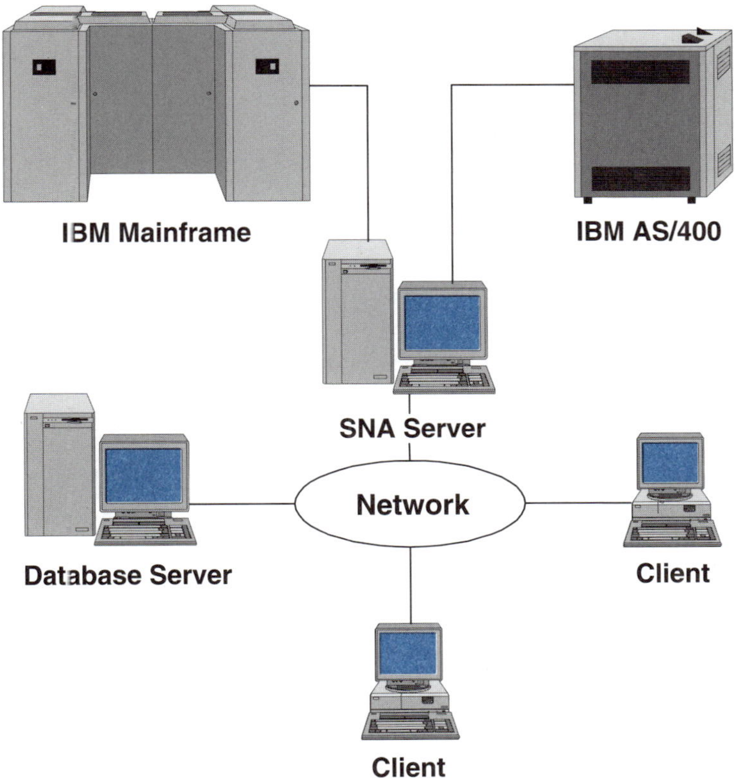

Concepts

- *Enterprise system* is a general term for the computer system of a large company with many geographic locations.
- Today, an enterprise system is likely to consist of file server systems, client/server systems running on more than one platform, mid-range systems like AS/400s, and a mainframe system.
- One of the major challenges of an enterprise system is providing the data that users need when they need it. This data may come from a database server on a local network, but it may also come from a database at a distant location on another network, a mid-range system, or a mainframe.
- IBM's System Network Architecture (SNA) makes it possible for the clients on a client/server system to communicate with AS/400s and mainframes. This communication is done through *gateways*. When you use Microsoft's SNA Server, the server becomes the gateway.

Figure 1-13 Enterprise systems

Multi-tier systems and ActiveX components

Today, most client/server systems are two-tier systems. The first tier is the client, which does the front-end processing. The second tier is the server, which does the back-end processing. And all of the processing is done by either the client or the server.

In contrast, figure 1-14 presents a three-tier client/server system. Here, the clients are the first tier; the database server is the second tier; and the *component server* is the third tier. In a *multi-tier* (or *n-tier*) *system*, you add more servers to this physical configuration.

In the three-tier system shown in figure 1-14, the component server is used to store and execute *ActiveX components*. When you implement functions as ActiveX components, the components can be re-used by any applications that need those functions, including applications developed in Access and Visual Basic. The use of ActiveX components and component servers can also simplify the maintenance of an application later on. Reusability and maintainability have, of course, been goals of software developers for many years, although the goals have been largely unrealized. In chapter 12, you'll learn how to use Visual Basic to create and use ActiveX components.

Although components can be stored on a single component server as shown in figure 1-14, they can also be stored on the clients, on database servers, on additional component servers, and on Internet servers. How they're deployed, of course, can have a significant effect on the performance of the system.

A three-tier physical implementation of a client/server application

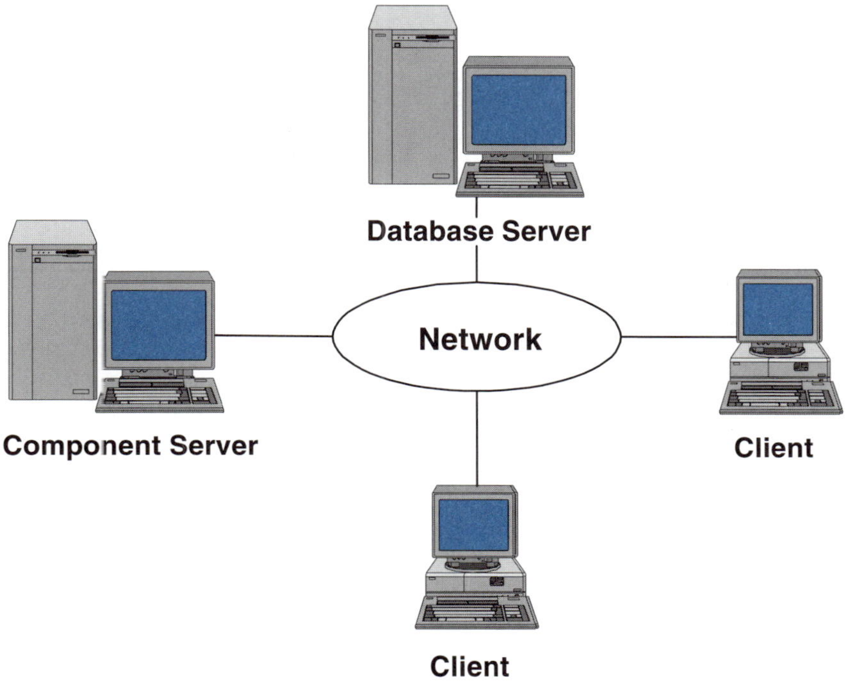

Concepts

- Visual Basic can be used to create *ActiveX components* that perform functions that can be used by more than one client/server application.
- One way to implement these components is to store them on a *component server* that's separate from the *database server*. The system then has three physical tiers so it can be called a *three-tier system*.
- The components do not have to be deployed as a third physical tier, however. They can be deployed on the clients, on the database server (still a two-tier system), on two or more component servers (an *n-tier*, or *multi-tier*, *system*), or on an Internet server.
- The primary benefits of using ActiveX components are (1) the components can be used by any applications that need their functions, and (2) the code is easier to maintain because it occurs in a single component rather than in every application that uses it.

Figure 1-14 Multi-tier systems and ActiveX components

The benefits and problems of client/server systems

Figure 1-15 summarizes the potential benefits and common problems of client/server systems. As you can see, the potential benefits are significant, but the development problems have all too often been overwhelming.

Potential benefits

With a powerful database on the back-end and a standard Windows interface on the front-end, a new client/server system should not only be easier to use, it should also help users do better work faster. In fact, you can think of client/server systems as one of the tools for re-engineering the corporation. The end result should be improved user productivity and business results.

From the developer's point of view, the Access and Visual Basic development environments should help you prototype applications for early and repeated user review. This should eliminate the gap between user expectations and the resulting system. In addition, the development environments should increase developer productivity and thus reduce software costs.

Beyond that, hardware costs may be reduced if you are able to replace a traditional mainframe or mid-range system with a client/server system. That, at least, was one of the hopes for early client/server systems. Since then, however, the cost per user of traditional systems has dropped, so hardware cost reductions are less likely today than they once were. And if you replace an existing network of PCs with modern 32MB or 64MB PCs that run the latest releases of Windows or NT Workstation, the hardware cost for the new system may even go up.

Typical problems

The main problem with client/server systems is that they have been anything but easy to develop. "Behind schedule and over budget" is the norm, just as it has been with mainframe and mid-range software projects. A surprisingly high percentage of client/server projects fail altogether. And most successful projects have been small systems that serve 100 or fewer users.

One of the contributing factors has been the shortage of trained client/server programmers. Another has been the relative immaturity of the development tools. With the release of Access 97 and Visual Basic 5, however, we believe that the development tools are coming of age. So the next step is to train the programmers. Once that's done, the success rate for client/server systems should go up dramatically.

Potential benefits

New applications that improve business results

- The client/server technologies make it possible to develop new systems that help users do more and do it better.

Applications that are easier to use

- The standard Windows interface should make client/server applications easier to use than traditional applications.

Rapid prototyping and application development

- With Access or Visual Basic, a developer can quickly prototype the user interface. With a Jet or SQL Server database, a developer can quickly prototype the database capabilities of an application. The end result should be systems that do what the user wants them to do.

Improved developer productivity and reduced software costs

- Productivity should certainly improve, if for no other reason than because traditional productivity levels have been so low. In the long run, that increase in productivity should reduce software development costs.

Reduced hardware costs

- Theoretically, at least, the hardware costs of a client/server system should be less than the hardware costs of a traditional mainframe or mid-range system.

Typical problems

Projects that are behind schedule and over budget

- This has been the norm for client/server projects just as it has been for traditional projects. Some of the underlying problems are a shortage of trained developers, a steep learning curve, continual hardware and software changes that undermine progress, and poor project management.

Projects that fail dismally and never get installed

- One early study of client/server projects reported a 70% failure rate. Another study showed that most successful projects were for small, departmental systems. This should change now that the development tools have been improved.

Figure 1-15 The benefits and problems of client/server systems

Perspective

This chapter has introduced you to the components of a modern client/server system and to the Microsoft products that you can use for developing client/server applications. Today, the trend in client/server systems is clearly away from the use of Unix and NetWare and toward the use of Windows NT Server. The trend is also away from the use of low-level languages like Visual C++ and toward the use of integrated development environments like Access 97 and Visual Basic 5.

In the next chapter, you'll learn more about the database and the database management system of a client/server system. Then, chapter 3 will introduce you to programming with Visual Basic 5, and chapter 4 will introduce you to database programming. By the time you complete those chapters, you should have a clear idea of how you develop and program client/server applications, both on the back-end and the front-end of a system.

Chapter 2

Database concepts

This chapter presents the concepts and terms you need for working with the database in a client/server application. You need this knowledge whether you're the one who designs the database or whether you're just developing the front-end for a database that has already been designed by someone else. Either way, you need to understand how a database works and what a database management system can do.

To illustrate database concepts, this chapter uses examples from both SQL Server and Access (Jet) databases. If you use a database other than SQL Server or Jet, the implementation details will vary somewhat, but the concepts will be the same.

How a relational database is organized

In 1970, Dr. E. F. Codd developed a model for a new type of database called a relational database. This type of database eliminated some of the problems that were associated with earlier types of databases like flat files and hierarchical databases. By using the relational model, you can reduce data redundancy, which saves disk storage and leads to efficient data retrieval. You can also view and manipulate data in a way that is both intuitive and efficient. Today, relational databases are the de facto standard for client/server applications.

How a relational table is organized

The model for a *relational database* states that data is stored in one or more *tables*. It also states that each table can be viewed as a two-dimensional matrix consisting of *rows* and *columns*. This is illustrated by the relational table in figure 2-1. Each row in this table contains information about a single vendor.

In practice, the rows and columns of a relational database table are often referred to by the more traditional terms, *records* and *fields*. In fact, some software packages use one set of terms, some use the other, and some use a combination. Throughout this chapter and book, these terms are used interchangeably.

If a table contains one or more columns that uniquely identify each row in the table, you can define these columns as the *primary key* of the table. For instance, the primary key of the Vendors table in figure 2-1 is the VendorID column. This column contains a number that is generated automatically by the DBMS. In SQL Server, this type of column is called an *identity column*. In Access, this type of column is called an *autonumber field*. A primary key is required for a Jet table and it's optional for a SQL Server table, although most of the SQL Server tables you create will include a primary key.

In addition to primary keys, some database management systems let you define additional keys that uniquely identify each row in a table. If, for example, the VendorName column in the Vendors table contains unique data, it can be defined as a *non-primary key*. In SQL Server, this is called a *unique constraint* or a *unique key*. The only difference between a unique key and a primary key is that a unique key can contain a null value and a primary key can't.

Indexes provide an efficient way to access the rows in a table based on the values in one or more columns. Because applications typically access table rows by referring to their key values, an index is automatically created for each key you define. But you can define indexes for other columns as well. Like a key, an index can include one or more columns.

Although indexes can improve the efficiency of retrieval operations, they reduce the efficiency of add, update, and delete operations. That's because the index has to be updated whenever a record is added or deleted or when the data in an index field is changed. So if you add indexes to a database, you'll want to make sure that they improve the overall efficiency of the database operations.

The Vendors table in the Accounts Payable database

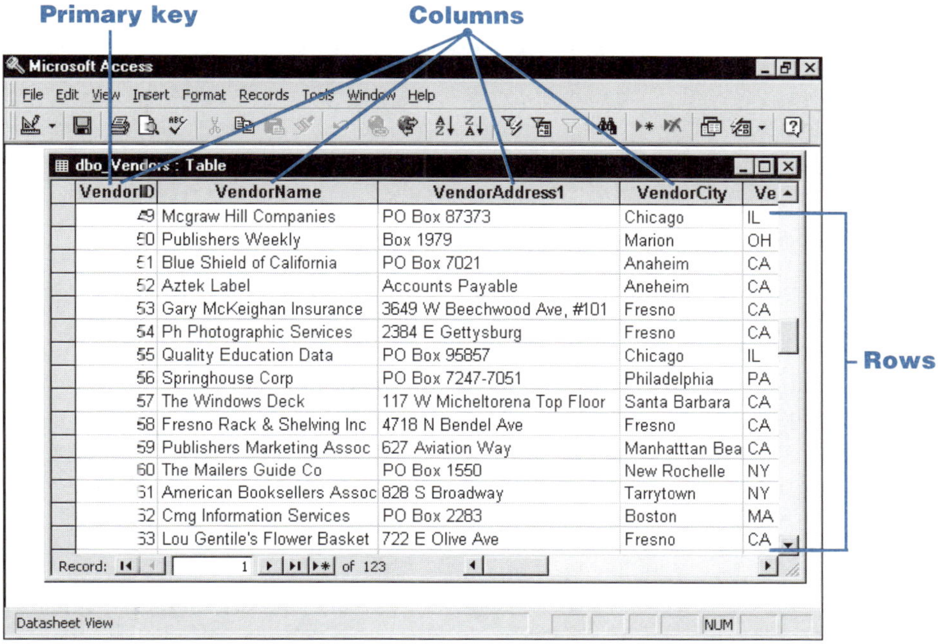

Concepts

- A *relational database* uses *tables* to store and manipulate data. Each table consists of one or more *records*, or *rows*, that contain the data for a single entry. Each row contains one or more *fields*, or *columns*, with each column representing a single item of data.
- Most tables contain a *primary key* that uniquely identifies each row in the table. The primary key often consists of a single field, but it can also consist of two or more fields.
- In addition to primary keys, some database management systems let you define one or more *non-primary keys*. In SQL Server, these keys are called *unique constraints* or *unique keys*. Like a primary key, a non-primary key uniquely identifies each row in the table.
- A table can also be defined with one or more *indexes*. An index provides an efficient way of accessing the data in a table. An index is automatically created for a table's primary and non-primary keys.

Figure 2-1 How a relational table is organized

How the tables in a relational database are related

The tables in a relational database can be related to other tables by values in specific columns. This is where the term *relational* comes from. The two tables shown in figure 2-2 illustrate this concept. Here, each row in the Vendors table is related to one or more rows in the Invoices table. This is called a *one-to-many relationship*.

Typically, relationships exist between the primary key in one table and the *foreign key* in another table. The foreign key is simply one or more columns in a table that refer to a primary key in another table. In SQL Server, relationships can also exist between a unique key in one table and a foreign key in another table. In Access, relationships can exist between a *unique index* in one table (an index whose column values are unique in each row) and a foreign key in another table. For simplicity, though, I'll just refer to primary keys when talking about relationships.

Although one-to-many relationships are the most common, two tables can also have a one-to-one or many-to-many relationship. If a table has a *one-to-one relationship* with another table, the data in the two tables could be stored in a single table. Because of that, one-to-one relationships are used infrequently.

In contrast, a *many-to-many relationship* is usually implemented by using an intermediate table that has a one-to-many relationship with the two tables in the many-to-many relationship. In other words, a many-to-many relationship can usually be broken down into two one-to-many relationships.

The relationship between the Vendors and Invoices tables

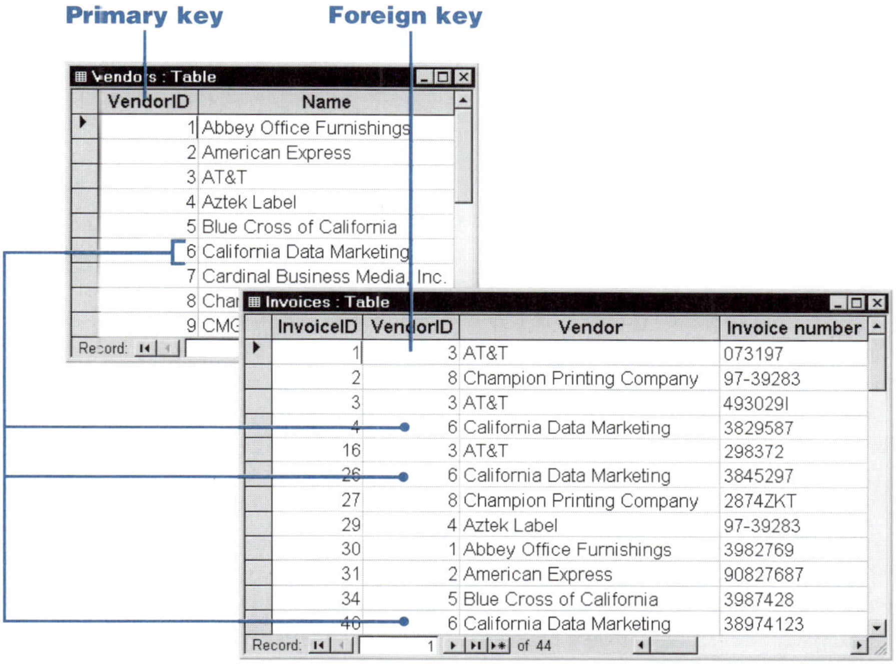

VendorID	Name
1	Abbey Office Furnishings
2	American Express
3	AT&T
4	Aztek Label
5	Blue Cross of California
6	California Data Marketing
7	Cardinal Business Media, Inc.
8	Char
9	CMC

InvoiceID	VendorID	Vendor	Invoice number
1	3	AT&T	073197
2	8	Champion Printing Company	97-39283
3	3	AT&T	4930291
4	6	California Data Marketing	3829587
16	3	AT&T	298372
26	6	California Data Marketing	3845297
27	8	Champion Printing Company	2874ZKT
29	4	Aztek Label	97-39283
30	1	Abbey Office Furnishings	3982769
31	2	American Express	90827687
34	5	Blue Cross of California	3987428
40	6	California Data Marketing	38974123

Concepts

- The tables in a relational database are related to each other through their key fields. For example, the VendorID field is used to relate the Vendors and Invoices tables above. The VendorID field in the Invoices table is called a *foreign key* because it identifies a related row in the Vendors table.
- Three types of relationships can exist between tables. The most common type is a *one-to-many relationship* as illustrated above. A table can also have a *one-to-one relationship* or a *many-to-many relationship* with another table.
- Key fields can be used to enforce *referential integrity* as shown in the next figure.

Figure 2-2 How the tables in a relational database are related

How to enforce referential integrity

Referential integrity means that records with foreign key values always have a matching primary key record. That means that you can't add a record with a foreign key value if a primary key record with that value doesn't already exist. It means that you can't change a primary key value without changing the foreign key values in related records. And it means you can't delete a primary key record without deleting related foreign key records.

To enforce referential integrity, you have to define the primary key and foreign key relationships within the database. In Access, you do that using the Relationships window and the Relationships dialog box shown at the top of figure 2-3. As you can see, the Relationships dialog box lets you select whether or not referential integrity is enforced. It also lets you select whether or not updates and deletes are *cascaded* to related fields and records. If you select the Cascade Update Related Fields option, a change to a primary key value will be applied to any matching foreign key values. If you select the Cascade Delete Related Records option, foreign key records will be deleted when the matching primary key record is deleted.

In SQL Server, relationships are defined by *foreign key constraints*. To define a foreign key constraint, you use the Foreign Keys tab of the Manage Tables dialog box as shown in this figure. When you define foreign key constraints, you are using what SQL Server calls *declarative referential integrity*, or *DRI*. This simply means that referential integrity is enforced automatically by the DBMS.

When you use DRI, you should be aware that you can't change a primary key value or delete a primary key record. That's because SQL Server doesn't provide for cascading changes and deletes like Access does. If you want to be able to cascade changes and deletes, you have to use triggers to enforce referential integrity (see figure 2-14).

How Access enforces referential integrity

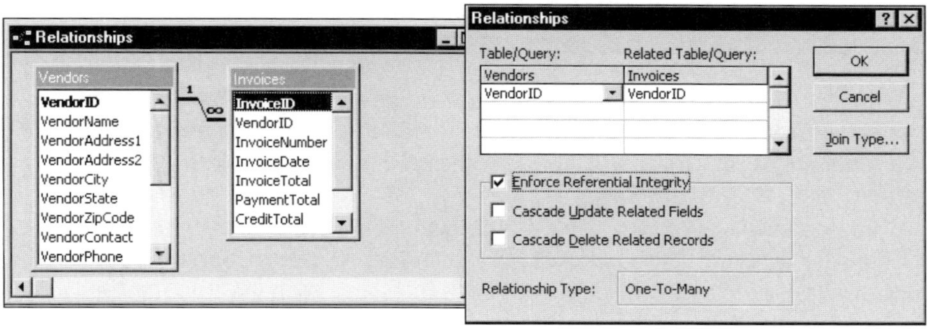

How SQL Server enforces referential integrity

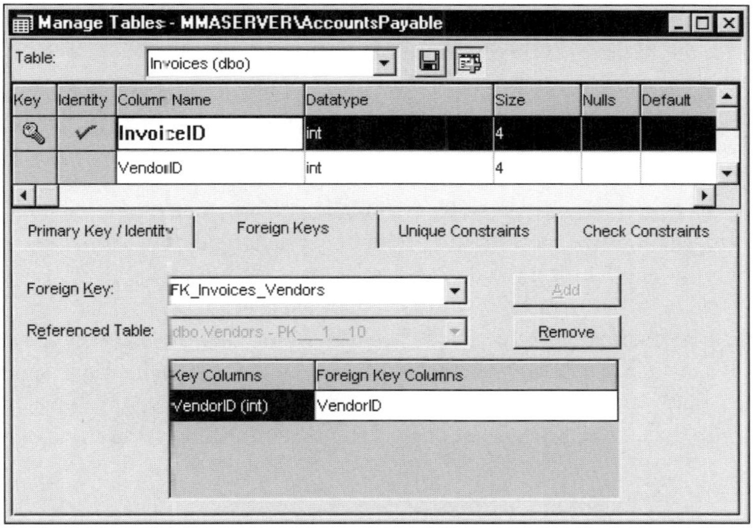

Concepts

- *Referential integrity* means that the relationships between the tables are maintained correctly. That means that a table with a foreign key can't have records with foreign key values that don't have matching primary key values in the related table.
- In Access, you enforce referential integrity by selecting the Enforce Referential Integrity option from the Relationships dialog box after you define a relationship. You can also select options that provide for cascading changes from the primary key field to the foreign key field and cascading deletes from primary key records to foreign key records.
- In SQL Server, you enforce referential integrity by defining *foreign key constraints*. When foreign keys are defined, you can't change a primary key value or delete a primary key record whether or not related records exist

Figure 2-3 How to enforce referential integrity

How to use data types to restrict the type of data that can be entered into a field

When you define a field in a database, you assign a *data type* to it. This data type determines what type of information can be stored in the field. In figure 2-4, you can see a summary of some of the data types that can be used with Microsoft SQL Server and Jet (Access).

Because each data type has a specific format, it's important to assign the correct data type to each field. This is especially critical when you're dealing with numeric fields. If you assign the wrong data type, the DBMS may round or truncate the data that it stores, which can lead to inaccurate results. Although you can change a data type and convert the related data after it has been entered into a database, it's better to define your fields right in the first place.

The data types that you assign can also affect system performance. For example, a SQL Server field with the *varchar* data type uses only as many bytes of storage as it needs. But a field with the *char* data type requires a fixed number of bytes no matter how many characters are actually stored in the field. So if a table has a large number of char fields and contains thousands of records, it will usually require more disk space than a table that uses varchar fields. This also affects the amount of data that is passed between the server and the client, which affects the performance of the client/server application. In general, then, you should use the char data type only when the data that will be stored in the field is a fixed size. A state code, for example, is always two characters so it can be stored in a field with the char data type.

In addition to the system data types like those listed in figure 2-4, SQL Server lets you create your own *user-defined data types* that are based on the system data types. This lets you create a data type for fields with special formats or special restrictions like social security numbers. In most cases, though, the standard data types are sufficient.

Common SQL Server data types

Type	Description
Bit	A value of 1 or 0 that represents a True or False value.
Char, Varchar	Any combination of letters, symbols, and numbers.
Datetime, Smalldatetime	Alphanumeric data that represents a date and time. Various formats are acceptable.
Decimal, Numeric	Numeric data that is accurate to the least significant digit. The data can contain an integer and a fractional portion.
Float, Real	Floating-point values that contain an approximation of a decimal value.
Int, Smallint, Tinyint	Numeric data that contains only an integer portion.
Money, Smallmoney	Monetary values that are accurate to four decimal places.
Timestamp	A counter whose value is always unique within a database.

Jet data types

Type	Description
Boolean (Yes/No)	A value of –1 or 0 that represents a True or False value.
Byte	Integers in the range of 0 to 255.
Currency	Monetary values that are accurate to four decimal places.
DateTime	Alphanumeric data that represents a date and time. The data must be enclosed in single quotes, and various formats are acceptable.
Hyperlink	A hyperlink address.
Integer, Long Integer	Numeric data that contains only an integer portion.
Single, Double	Single- and double-precision floating-point numbers.
Text, Long Text (Memo)	Any combination of text and numbers.

Figure 2-4 SQL Server and Jet data types

How to use defaults, constraints, and rules to restrict the values that can be entered into a field

As you define the fields in a database, you can specify defaults, constraints, and rules to help maintain the validity of the data. A *default* provides a default value for a field when the user or the program doesn't enter anything into the field. A *rule* or *constraint* defines the acceptable values for a field.

Figure 2-5 illustrates how defaults, rules, and constraints are implemented in SQL Server and Access. In SQL Server, you can specify a *default value* (or just *default*) for each field in a table. In addition, you can use *check constraints* to limit the values that can be entered into one or more fields. For instance, the constraint in this figure requires that the value in the InvoiceDueDate field be greater than the value in the InvoiceDate field. Because this constraint is specified at the table level, not the field level, it can refer to two or more fields. You can specify any number of constraints for a table.

You can also use rules in SQL Server to restrict the data that can be entered into a column. In SQL Server, a rule is a separate *object* that's defined at the database level. Then, that rule can be *bound* (applied) to any number of fields in the database. For example, you can define a rule that requires the value in a field to be greater than zero. Then, you can bind that rule to every numeric field in the database that you want to contain a positive value. Note, however, that you can only bind a single rule to each field in the database. For that reason, check constraints are used more commonly than rules.

Figure 2-5 also illustrates how you can use Access to define a default value and a *validation rule* for each field in a database. Although you can only specify one validation rule for each field, you can include compound conditions in the rule. You can also specify validation text that's displayed if a value doesn't meet the validation rule.

When you specify a validation rule at the field level in Access, you can't compare the value of the field with the values of other fields in the table as you can with a SQL Server check constraint. To do that in Access, you have to specify a validation rule at the table level. Although you can only specify a single validation rule for each table, you can include compound conditions in the rule just as you can for a field validation rule.

After you define the constraints and rules for a database, they're managed by the DBMS. If, for example, a user tries to add a record with data that violates a rule or constraint, the DBMS sends an appropriate error code back to the client without adding the record to the database. The client software can then respond to the error code.

Another way to provide for data validation is to check the field values in the code for an application. In that case, the client software makes sure that invalid data is never sent to the database. For many applications, this is the preferred way to work.

The SQL Server window for defining defaults and check constraints

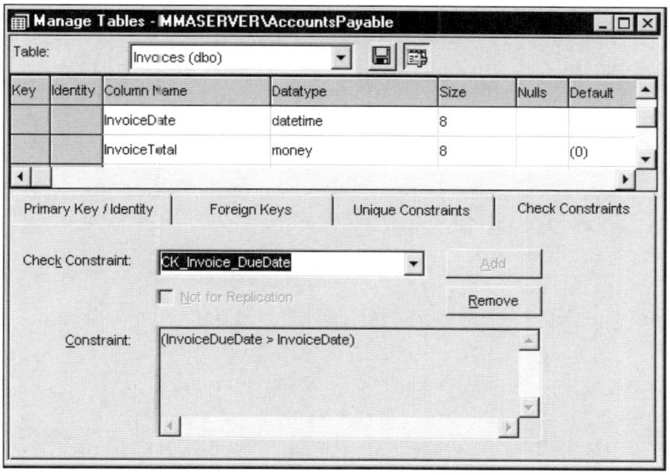

The Access screen for defining default values and validation rules

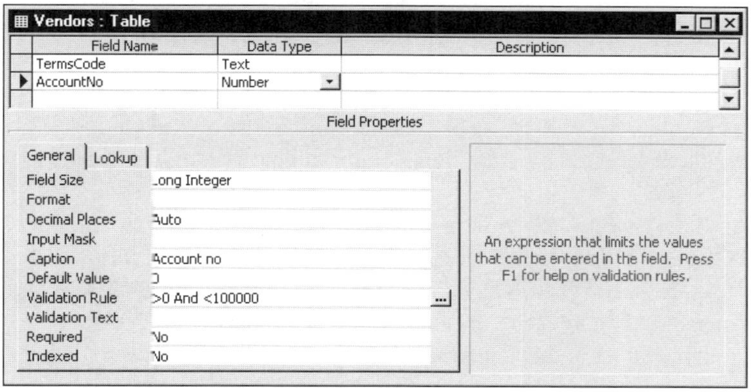

Concepts

- In SQL Server, *check constraints* are specified at the table level and can refer to one or more fields in the table, and *rules* are defined at the database level as separate objects. A rule object can be bound to any number of fields in the database. You can also use a rule or check constraint to restrict the format of a field.
- In Access, *validation rules* can be specified at the field or table level.
- A *default* is used for the value of a field if no value is specified for the field. In SQL Server, you can specify a default at the field level or at the database level as a separate object. A default object can be bound to any number of fields in the database

Figure 2-5 How to restrict the values that can be entered into a field

How to normalize the data in a database

Back in 1970, when Dr. E. F. Codd developed the relational database model, he also developed the concepts and rules of *data normalization*. These rules help you answer questions like these: How many tables does the database require? What fields should be included in each record? What fields will be used to define the relationships between the tables?

Figure 2-6 presents the first three rules for normalizing a database. When you apply them, your database is normalized to the *third normal form* (or *3NF*). When you apply one of these rules, the assumption is that you've already applied the previous rules. For a database to meet the requirements of the third rule, for example, it must also meet the requirements of the first and second rules. When a database meets the requirements of all three rules, it is said to be *normalized*. Although there are two more rules that lead to a database that is normalized to the *fifth normal form* (*5NF*), the first three rules are adequate for most business databases.

If you look at the unnormalized table in figure 2-6, you can see that it contains two sets of repeating fields so it violates the first rule. These fields represent the general ledger accounts and the invoice amounts that should be applied to these accounts. In the normalized tables in this figure, you can see that these paired fields are placed in separate rows of a new table that includes the invoice number. That satisfies the requirement of the first rule.

If you look again at the unnormalized table, you can see that it contains a vendor name field that isn't dependent on or subordinate to the primary key, which is the invoice number. This violates the second normalization rule. In the normalized tables, you can see that this rule is satisfied by creating a vendor table that includes the vendor name.

In practice, you probably won't apply the normalization rules one after another as implied by figure 2-6. Instead, you'll use common sense to divide the data into manageable tables from the start. Then, you can use the normalization rules as guidelines to make sure that the tables are normalized. This will help you design a database that's efficient, reliable, and expandable.

An unnormalized table

Invoice Number	Invoice Date	Vendor Number	Vendor Name	Acct 1	Amount 1	Acct 2	Amount 2	Invoice Total
38297	12/5/97	347	Jones Janitorial	1405	250.00			250.00
938473	12/10/97	162	American Express	1228	347.58	2297	538.57	886.15
939736	1/10/98	162	American Express	1402	125.79	3236	731.88	857.67
8372	1/15/98	275	Office Depot	3410	56.89	4417	128.76	185.65

The resulting tables when they're normalized to the third form

Invoice Number	Invoice Date	Vendor Number	Invoice Total
38297	12/5/97	347	250.00
938473	12/10/97	162	886.15
939736	1/10/98	162	857.67
8372	1/15/98	275	185.65

Vendor Number	Vendor Name
347	Jones Janitorial
162	American Express
275	Office Depot

Invoice Number	Account Number	Account Amount
38297	1405	250.00
938473	1228	347.58
938473	2297	538.57
939736	1402	125.79
939736	3236	731.88
8372	3410	56.89
8372	4417	128.76

The rules for the first three forms of database normalization

Form	Rule
First normal	No repeating fields in a table
Second normal	All fields in each table must be dependent on all the fields in the primary key
Third normal	All fields in each table must be dependent *only* on the primary key

Concepts

- *Normalization* is the process of decomposing database tables into logical, single subject tables. By normalizing a database, you eliminate redundant data and improve database efficiency.
- Normalization is based on the three rules shown above, with each rule dependent on the previous rule. A database in this state is said to be in the *third normal form*.
- Although higher normal forms are possible, a database is said to be normalized after the third rule has been applied.

Note

- The shaded fields in the tables above are the primary keys for the tables.

Figure 2-6 How to normalize the data in a database

How to use SQL to work with the data in a relational database

When you use a development environment like Visual Basic, you can often use a graphical interface to create SQL statements. And when you use an object model like DAO to work with the data in a database, the DAO methods are converted to the appropriate SQL statements. Eventually, though, every application developer has to write some SQL statements, so every developer should at least know the basic functions and syntax of the common SQL statements.

An introduction to the Structured Query Language

To communicate with a database, you use *Structured Query Language*, or *SQL*. Although SQL is a standard language, each database management system is likely to have its own extensions and variations, commonly called a *dialect*. So when you use SQL, you need to make sure that you're using the dialect that's supported by your DBMS. In this chapter and throughout this book, all of the SQL examples are based on Microsoft SQL Server's dialect of SQL, which is called *Transact-SQL*. In this version of SQL, Microsoft has extended the standard SQL language so you can use cursors, stored procedures, and triggers.

Figure 2-7 summarizes some of the most common SQL statements. As you can see, these statements can be divided into two categories. The statements that you use to work with the objects of a database are called the *data definition language*, or *DDL, statements*. These statements let you create databases, tables, indexes, rules, defaults, and other objects that you'll be introduced to in a moment.

In contrast, the statements that you use to work with the data in a database are called the *data manipulation language*, or *DML, statements*. These are the SELECT, INSERT, UPDATE, and DELETE statements, and these are the statements that the application programmer uses the most. Although the execution of any one of these statements can be referred to as a *query*, the term *query* is commonly used to refer to just the execution of SELECT statements, while *action query* is used to refer to the other DML statements.

Incidentally, SQL is pronounced either S-Q-L or *sequel* in conversation. In this book, we use the first pronunciation when we refer to "an SQL statement" and the second pronunciation when we refer to "a SQL Server database."

SQL statements for data definition

Statement	Description
CREATE DATABASE	Creates a new database.
CREATE TABLE	Creates a new table in the specified database.
CREATE INDEX	Creates a new index for the specified table.
CREATE TRIGGER	Creates a trigger for the specified table.
CREATE VIEW	Creates a view from the data in one or more tables.
CREATE RULE	Creates a rule that can be bound to one or more columns in the database.
CREATE DEFAULT	Creates a default that can be bound to one or more columns in the database.
CREATE PROCEDURE	Creates a stored procedure.
ALTER DATABASE	Increases the amount of space that's allocated to the specified database.
ALTER TABLE	Adds new columns or constraints to the specified table.

SQL statements for data manipulation

Statement	Description
SELECT	Retrieves data from one or more tables.
INSERT	Inserts one or more new rows into a table.
UPDATE	Updates existing rows in a table.
DELETE	Deletes existing rows from a table.

Concepts

- SQL statements can be divided into two categories: the *data definition language* (*DDL*) that lets you work with the objects in a database, like tables and views; and the *data manipulation language* (*DML*) that lets you work with the data in a database. Application programmers typically work with the DML statements.
- The execution of a SELECT statement is typically referred to as a *query*. In contrast, the execution of an INSERT, UPDATE, or DELETE statement can be referred to as an *action query*.
- Although SQL is a standard language, each vendor has its own *SQL dialect*, which may include extensions to the standards. SQL Server's SQL dialect is called *Transact-SQL*.

Figure 2-7 An introduction to the Structured Query Language

How to query a database

Figure 2-8 illustrates how to use a SELECT statement to query a database. Although the syntax of the SELECT statement presented in this figure has been simplified, it illustrates its basic function, which is to retrieve selected fields and records from a database.

The syntax summary at the top of this figure uses conventions that you're probably familiar with if you've worked with other languages. Here, the capitalized words are SQL words and the lowercase words indicate the location of variables that you must supply. The brackets [ ] indicate that a phrase is optional; the pipe (|) indicates a choice between the options on either side; and the ellipsis (...) indicates that you can code a series of like items. To separate the items in a statement, you can use one or more spaces, and you can use indentation whenever it helps you improve the readability of a statement.

If you study the SELECT statement below the syntax summary, you can see how you code this statement. Here, the SELECT statement retrieves fields from a table named Invoices. It selects a record from the Invoices table only if it has a balance due that's greater than zero. And it sorts the returned records by the balance due in descending sequence.

Please note in this SELECT statement that the last field in the query, BalanceDue, is calculated by subtracting PaymentTotal and CreditTotal from InvoiceTotal. In other words, a field by the name of BalanceDue doesn't actually exist in the database. This type of field is called a *calculated field*, and it exists only in the results of the query.

Figure 2-8 also shows the result set that is returned by the SELECT statement. A *result set* is a logical table that's created temporarily within the database. The current record in the result set is identified by the *current row pointer*, or *current record pointer*. When you make a change to a result set, the change is automatically reflected in the table that the result set was created from.

Although it's not indicated in the figure, you can select all of the fields in a table by coding an asterisk (*) in place of the field names. For example, this statement will select all of the fields from the Invoices table:

```
SELECT * FROM Invoices
```

As you might guess, queries can have a significant effect on the performance of a client/server application. The more fields and records that are returned by a query, the more traffic the network has to bear. When you design a query, then, you should try to keep the number of fields and records to a minimum.

Simplified syntax for the SELECT statement

```
SELECT field-1 [, field-2…]
FROM table-1
[WHERE selection-criteria]
[ORDER BY field-1 [ASC|DESC] [,field-2 [ASC|DESC]…]
```

A SELECT statement that retrieves and sorts selected fields and records from the Invoices table

```
SELECT InvoiceNumber, InvoiceDate, InvoiceTotal,
    InvoiceTotal - PaymentTotal - CreditTotal
        AS BalanceDue
FROM Invoices
WHERE BalanceDue > 0
ORDER BY BalanceDue DESC
```

The result set defined by the SELECT statement

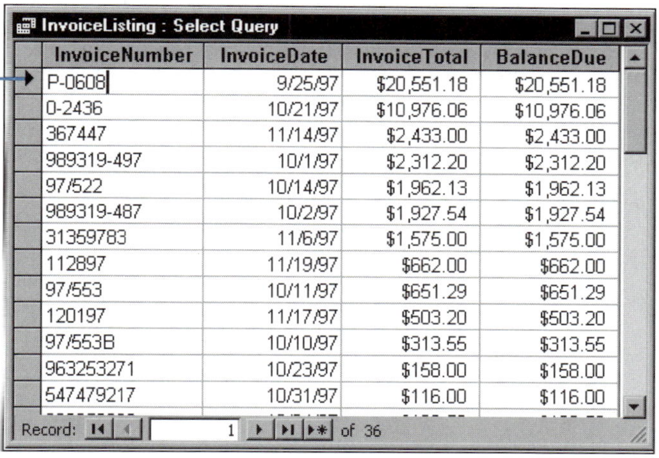

InvoiceNumber	InvoiceDate	InvoiceTotal	BalanceDue
P-0608	9/25/97	$20,551.18	$20,551.18
0-2436	10/21/97	$10,976.06	$10,976.06
367447	11/14/97	$2,433.00	$2,433.00
989319-497	10/1/97	$2,312.20	$2,312.20
97/522	10/14/97	$1,962.13	$1,962.13
989319-487	10/2/97	$1,927.54	$1,927.54
31359783	11/6/97	$1,575.00	$1,575.00
112897	11/19/97	$662.00	$662.00
97/553	10/11/97	$651.29	$651.29
120197	11/17/97	$503.20	$503.20
97/553B	10/10/97	$313.55	$313.55
963253271	10/23/97	$158.00	$158.00
547479217	10/31/97	$116.00	$116.00

Concepts

- The result of a SELECT query is a *result set* like the one shown above. A result set is a logical set of records that consists of all of the fields and records requested by the SELECT statement.
- The *current row pointer* identifies the current record in a result set. You can use this pointer to identify a record you want to update or delete from the result set. Any change to the result set is reflected in the table that the result set is based on.
- *Cursors* can be used to identify the individual records in a result set and provide for scrolling through those records as shown in the next figure.

Figure 2-8 How to use a SELECT statement to query a database

How to work with cursors

Figure 2-9 presents the four types of cursors that you can use to work with the results of a query. Because you use different techniques to choose a cursor type depending on the method you're using to access data, I won't try to show you how to choose a cursor in this chapter. But I will describe the four types of cursors so you understand how they work.

If you need to be able to add, modify, and delete records from a recordset, you'll want to use a *keyset cursor* or a *dynamic cursor*. Both of these cursors contain a set of keys that point to the records in the associated result set. That means that when you create one of these cursors, only the keys, and not the rest of the data in the result set, are passed from the server to the client. The rest of the data is passed to the client only when it's requested. As you can imagine, this can have a dramatic affect on the efficiency of an application.

Both the keyset and the dynamic cursor are fully scrollable. That means that you can use them to move forward and backward to any record in the result set. The difference between a keyset cursor and a dynamic cursor is that a keyset cursor doesn't reflect changes made by other users to the tables that the result set was created from, but a dynamic cursor does. So if it's important that the result set always reflects the most current data, you'll want to use a dynamic cursor. Note, however, that not all data access techniques provide for dynamic cursors.

The *static cursor* and the *forward-only scrolling cursor* provide less functionality than the keyset and dynamic cursors. In particular, they don't let you add, modify, and delete records from the associated result set. As a result, you'll want to use them when you need to access, but not change, the data in the result set. As its name implies, you can use a forward-only scrolling cursor only to scroll forward through the records in a result set.

It's important to note that both the static and the forward-only scrolling cursor contain all of the data from the associated result set. That means that all of the data in the result set is passed from the server to the client when the cursor is created. For efficiency, then, you'll want to use these cursors only if the number of records in the result set is limited.

So far in this discussion of cursors, I've assumed that the cursors are being created on and managed by the client. This type of cursor is called a *client-side cursor*. However, some database management systems like SQL Server let you create cursors on the server. This type of cursor, called a *server-side cursor*, is created on and managed by the server. When you use a server-side cursor, the overhead on the client and the network traffic is reduced, but the overhead on the server is increased. So you'll want to be sure that the server can handle the additional overhead before you use a server-side cursor.

The four types of cursors

Cursor type	Description
Keyset	A set of keys that point to the records in a result set. When the cursor is created, only the keys are passed to the client, not the other data in the result set. This type of cursor is fully scrollable, and you can use it to add, modify, and delete records from the result set.
Dynamic	Like a keyset cursor, but includes changes, additions, and deletions made by other users. When the cursor is created, only the keys are passed to the client, not the other data in the result set. This type of result set is not available when you use Jet.
Static	A copy of the records in a result set. When the cursor is created, all of the data in the result set is passed from the server to the client. This type of cursor is fully scrollable, but you can't use it to update records.
Forward-only scrolling	Like a static cursor, but you can only scroll forward through the records. When the cursor is created, all of the data in the result set is passed from the server to the client.

Concepts

- The type of cursor you use depends on the data you're accessing, the method you're using to access the data, and the processing you need to perform on the data. In general, you should choose the cursor with the least overhead that provides the functionality you need.
- When you use Jet to access data, you create *client-side cursors*, which reside on the client. If the data you're accessing resides on a server, that means that the cursor data must be sent over the network to the client when the cursor is built.
- If you're accessing SQL Server data without using Jet, you can create *server-side cursors*, which are created on the server and managed by the DBMS. When you use server-side cursors, the cursor data does not need to be sent to the client. SQL Server server-side cursors are always keyset-type cursors.

Note

- Jet implements cursors using *recordsets*, which you'll learn about in chapter 4.

Figure 2-9 How to work with cursors

How to join data from two or more tables

Figure 2-10 presents the syntax of the SELECT statement for retrieving data from two tables. This type of operation is called a *join* because the data from the two tables is joined together into a single result set. For example, the SELECT statement in this figure joins data from the Invoices and Vendors table into a single result set.

An *inner join*, or *equi-join*, is the most common type of join. When you use an inner join, records from the two tables in the join are included in the result set only if their related fields match. These matching fields are specified in the SELECT statement. In the SELECT statement in this example, records from the Invoices and Vendors tables are included only if the value of the VendorID field in the Vendors table matches the value of the VendorID field in one or more records in the Invoices table. If there aren't any invoices for a particular vendor, that vendor won't be included in the result set.

The second type of join is an *outer join*. With this type of join, all of the records in one of the tables are included in the result set whether or not there are matching records in the other table. In a *left outer join*, all of the records in the first table (the one on the left) are included in the result set. In a *right outer join*, all of the records in the second table are included. To illustrate, suppose that I had used a left outer join in the example in this figure. In that case, all of the records in the Vendors table would have been included in the result set even if no matching records were found in the Invoices table.

Although this figure shows only how to join data from two tables, you should know that you can extend this syntax to join data from additional tables. If, for example, I also wanted to include line item data from a table named InvoiceLineItems in the results shown in figure 2-10, I could have coded the FROM clause of the SELECT statement like this:

```
FROM Vendors
    INNER JOIN Invoices
        ON Vendors.VendorID = Invoices.VendorID
    INNER JOIN InvoiceLineItems
        ON Invoices.InvoiceID = InvoiceLineItems.InvoiceID
```

Then, I could include any of the fields in the InvoiceLineItems table in the field list of the SELECT statement.

If you're using SQL Server 6.0 or an earlier release, you should know that you can't join tables as illustrated in figure 2-10. Instead, you have to list the tables you want to join in the FROM clause, and you have to specify how the tables are to be joined in the WHERE clause. Although you can still use this syntax with SQL Server 6.5, the results of the query aren't updatable. If possible, then, you'll want to use the new syntax.

SELECT statement syntax for joining two tables

```
SELECT field-list
FROM table-1
    {INNER | LEFT OUTER | RIGHT OUTER} JOIN table-2
    ON table-1.field-1 {=|<|>|<=|>=|<>} table-2.field-2
[WHERE selection-criteria]
[ORDER BY field-list]
```

A SELECT statement that joins data from the Vendors and Invoices tables

```
SELECT VendorName, InvoiceNumber, InvoiceDate,
    InvoiceTotal
FROM Vendors INNER JOIN Invoices
    ON Vendors.VendorID = Invoices.VendorID
WHERE InvoiceTotal >= 500
ORDER BY VendorName, InvoiceTotal DESC
```

The result set defined by the SELECT statement

Vendors Query : Select Query

VendorName	InvoiceNumber	InvoiceDate	InvoiceTotal
IBM	Q545443	8/28/97	$1,083.58
Ingram	31359783	11/6/97	$1,575.00
Malloy Lithographing Inc	0-2058	10/22/97	$37,966.19
Malloy Lithographing Inc	P-0259	9/30/97	$26,881.40
Malloy Lithographing Inc	0-2060	10/22/97	$23,517.58
Malloy Lithographing Inc	P-0608	9/25/97	$20,551.18
Malloy Lithographing Inc	0-2436	10/21/97	$10,976.06
Pollstar	120197	11/18/97	$1,750.00
Reiter's Scientific & Pro Books	C73-24	10/1/97	$600.00
United Parcel Service	989319-457	10/8/97	$3,813.33
United Parcel Service	989319-447	10/8/97	$3,689.99
United Parcel Service	989319-437	10/8/97	$2,765.36
United Parcel Service	989319-467	10/8/97	$2,318.03

Record: 1 of 35

Concepts

- A *join* lets you combine data from two or more tables into a single result set. The type of join you choose determines how the data is combined.
- An *inner join*, also called an *equi-join*, returns records from both tables only if their related fields match. *An outer join* returns records from one table in the join (the LEFT or RIGHT table) even if the other table doesn't contain a matching record.
- Some database management systems support additional types of joins. For example, SQL Server 6.5 supports *cross joins* and *full outer joins*.

Note

- You can also join tables by listing the tables on the FROM clause and specifying the join condition on the WHERE clause. However, you can't update the results of this type of join.

Figure 2-10 How to join data from two or more tables

How to add, modify, and delete records from a database

Figure 2-11 presents the basic syntax of the SQL INSERT, UPDATE, and DELETE statements. You use the INSERT statement to insert one or more records into a table. As you can see, the syntax of this statement is different depending on whether you're adding a single record or selected records.

To add a single record to a table, you specify the name of the table you want to add the record to, the names of the fields you're supplying data for, and the values for those fields. The example in this figure adds a record to a table named Terms, which contains three fields: TermsID, TermsDescription, and TermsDueDays. Because the value of the TermsID field is generated automatically, though, it's not included in the INSERT statement. If you're going to supply values for all the fields in a table, you can omit the field names, but then you must be sure to specify the values in the same order as the fields in the table.

To add selected records to a table, you include a SELECT statement within the INSERT statement. Then, the SELECT statement retrieves fields from one or more tables based on the conditions you specify, and the INSERT statement adds those records to another table. In the example in this figure, the SELECT statement selects all the fields from the records in the Invoices table that have been paid in full and inserts them into a table named InvoiceArchive.

To change the values of one or more fields in a table, you use the UPDATE statement. In this statement, you specify the name of the table you want to update, expressions that indicate the fields you want to change and how you want to change them, and a condition that indicates the record or records you want to change. In the example in this figure, the UPDATE statement uses a Transact-SQL function named DATEADD to add a value of 1 to the InvoiceDate field in the Invoices table for each record with the invoice date that's specified.

To delete records from a table, you use the DELETE statement. In this statement, you specify the table you want to delete one or more records from and a condition that indicates the records you want to delete. The DELETE statement in this figure deletes all the records from the Invoices table that have been paid in full.

INSERT INTO statement syntax for adding a single record

```
INSERT INTO table-name [(field-list)]
VALUES (value-list)
```

A statement that adds a single record to a table

```
INSERT INTO Terms (TermsDescription, TermsDueDays)
    VALUES ("Net due 90 days", 90)
```

INSERT INTO statement syntax for adding selected records

```
INSERT INTO table-name (field-list)
SELECT-statement
```

A statement that adds selected records from one table to another table

```
INSERT INTO InvoiceArchive
    SELECT * FROM Invoices
    WHERE InvoiceTotal – PaymentTotal – CreditTotal = 0
```

UPDATE statement syntax

```
UPDATE table-name
SET expression-1 [,expression-2…]
WHERE selection-criteria
```

A statement that changes the invoice date for selected records

```
UPDATE Invoices
    SET InvoiceDate = DATEADD(Day, 1, InvoiceDate)
    WHERE InvoiceDate = "11/15/97"
```

DELETE statement syntax

```
DELETE FROM table-name
WHERE selection-criteria
```

A statement that deletes all paid invoices

```
DELETE FROM Invoices
    WHERE InvoiceTotal – PaymentTotal – CreditTotal = 0
```

Figure 2-11 How to add, modify, and delete records from a database

How to use views

A *view* is a pre-defined query that's stored in a database. In general, views are used to restrict the data that users have access to. If, for example, you want to restrict the access to payroll information, you can create a view that doesn't include sensitive salary information. Then, you can allow users to access the table only through that view.

You can also use views to present the data in a database in a format that the user is familiar with. Then, even if the structure of the database changes, the view can remain the same.

To create a view, you use the CREATE VIEW statement as shown in figure 2-12. This just stores the SELECT statement for the view with the database. This SELECT statement isn't executed until a client accesses the view.

To access a view, the client issues a SELECT statement that refers to the view as shown in this figure. Next, the SELECT statement that's stored in the view is executed, and a virtual table that contains the specified fields and records is created (a virtual table is just a temporary table that's created on the server). Once that table or view is created, the SELECT statement that referred to the view is executed on this virtual table to create the result set. Then, the results are sent to the client, usually in the form of a cursor.

In the example in this figure, you'll notice that the SELECT statement used by the client includes an ORDER BY clause that sorts the result set. Although you might think that you could include this clause in the view definition, you can't. This is one of the restrictions on view definitions.

When a user modifies the data in a result set that's created from a view, the data in the underlying tables is changed just as it is with any other result set. When a view joins data from two or more tables, though, you can change the data in only one table at a time. In most cases, that's not a problem.

Although views can be quite useful, it should be obvious from figure 2-12 that they require some additional overhead. That's because every time an application refers to a view, the view has to be created from scratch. If that's a problem, you can also restrict access to a database by using stored procedures.

A CREATE VIEW statement for a view named VendorsMin

```
CREATE VIEW VendorsMin As
    SELECT VendorName, VendorState, VendorPhone
    FROM Vendors
```

A SELECT statement from a client that uses the VendorsMin view

```
SELECT * FROM VendorsMin
    WHERE VendorState = "CA"
    ORDER BY VendorName
```

The view that's created when the client's SELECT statement is executed

VendorName	VendorState	VendorPhone
ComputerWorld	CA	(617) 555-0700
AT&T	AZ	(800) 555-1234
Blue Cross of CA	CA	(800) 555-0912
American Express	IL	(800) 555-3344
Federal Express	TN	(800) 555-4091
The Fresno Bee	CA	(209) 555-4442
Office Depot	CA	(209) 555-1711

The result set created from the view when the client's SELECT statement is executed

VendorName	VendorState	VendorPhone
Blue Cross of CA	CA	(800) 555-0912
ComputerWorld	CA	(617) 555-0700
Office Depot	CA	(209) 555-1711
The Fresno Bee	CA	(209) 555-4442

Concepts

- To create a *view*, you use the CREATE VIEW statement, which includes a SELECT statement. That SELECT statement is then stored on the server as the definition of the view.
- To access a view, the client issues an SQL statement that refers to the view. This creates a virtual table on the server that represents the view. Then, the result set is extracted from this view.
- Views can be used to restrict the data that a user is allowed to access or to present data in a form that's familiar to the user. In some databases, users may be allowed to access data only through views.

Figure 2-12 How to use views

How to use stored procedures

A *stored procedure* is a set of one or more SQL statements that are stored together in a database. Stored procedures provide an efficient way to store and execute commonly used SQL statements. These procedures can improve system performance because the system doesn't have to compile and check the SQL statements in the procedures each time they're executed. Instead, a stored procedure is compiled and optimized when it's created.

One use for stored procedures is to restrict access to the tables in a database. Instead of allowing users direct access to the tables in a database, for example, you can restrict their access to a set of stored procedures that provide all the functions they need. This is similar to using views, except that you can use stored procedures to add, update, and delete records as well as to retrieve data.

To create a stored procedure, you use the CREATE PROCEDURE statement as shown in figure 2-13. In the example in this figure, the stored procedure consists of just a single SELECT statement, but a procedure can contain as many SQL statements as it needs.

To use a stored procedure, the client must send a request for the stored procedure to be executed. Because that can be done in several different ways, the example in this figure uses *pseudocode* that gives the intent of the request but not the actual code for the request.

When the server receives the request, it executes the stored procedure, which in this example creates a result set based on the SELECT statement. Then, the results are sent to the client.

One advantage of using a stored procedure instead of a view is that you can include *parameters* in a stored procedure. A parameter acts as a variable within the procedure. Then, when you execute the procedure, you specify the value that you want to use for that variable. In figure 2-13, for example, the stored procedure uses a parameter named @State. When this procedure is executed, a value of "CA" is supplied for this parameter so only the records for vendors who live in California are included in the result set. If you compare this with the processing that's required to create a result set with the same data from a view, you'll see that using stored procedures is more efficient because a virtual table is never created.

Stored procedures that contain INSERT, UPDATE, and DELETE statements work similarly. Instead of creating a result set, though, they perform the appropriate processing on the selected records. When you need to perform an operation that affects several records, using a stored procedure can be considerably more efficient than using a cursor to update one record at a time.

In addition to SQL statements, stored procedures can contain *control-of-flow language*. This language lets you control the flow of execution within a stored procedure. For example, you can use If...Else language to determine the processing to be done based on specific conditions.

A CREATE PROCEDURE statement for a procedure named VendorsByState

```
CREATE PROCEDURE VendorsByState @State String As
    SELECT VendorName, VendorState, VendorPhone
        FROM Vendors
        WHERE VendorState = @State
        ORDER BY VendorName
```

Pseudocode for executing a stored procedure from the client

```
Execute VendorsByState for State = "CA"
```

The result set created by the client's request

VendorName	VendorState	VendorPhone
Blue Cross of CA	CA	(800) 555-0912
ComputerWorld	CA	(617) 555-0700
Office Depot	CA	(209) 555-1711
The Fresno Bee	CA	(209) 555-4442

Concepts

- A *stored procedure* is one or more SQL statements that have been compiled and stored with the database. A stored procedure can be started by application code on the client as indicated by the pseudocode above.
- Stored procedures can improve database performance because the SQL statements in each procedure are compiled and optimized the first time they're executed. In contrast, SQL statements that are sent from a client to the server have to be compiled and optimized every time they're executed.
- In addition to SELECT statements, a stored procedure can contain other SQL statements such as INSERT, UPDATE, and DELETE statements. It can also contain *control-of-flow language*, which lets you perform conditional processing within the stored procedure.
- In addition to the procedures you create (called *user-defined procedures*), you can use pre-defined procedures that come with your DBMS (called *system procedures*). These procedures allow you to perform system functions such as adding users, creating tables, and setting permissions.

Figure 2-13 How to use stored procedures

How to use triggers

A *trigger* is a special type of stored procedure that is executed automatically when an insert, update, or delete operation is executed on a table. This process is summarized in figure 2-14. In this example, when the client requests that a record in the Vendors table be updated, the DBMS does two things. First, it updates the record as requested. Then, if the record is successfully updated, it *fires* the Update trigger that's defined for the Vendors table.

In this example, the Update trigger checks to see if the primary key value in the Vendor record has changed. If it has, the trigger updates all the records in the Invoices table that have matching foreign keys so the relationship between the two tables is maintained. This enforces the referential integrity of the database. Note, however, that the pseudocode shown here is just a summary of what the trigger does, not the actual code, which would be far more complicated.

If the update is unsuccessful, though, the trigger is never fired. Because of that, you can't use triggers to enforce referential integrity if a foreign key constraint defines the relationship between the tables. That's because the foreign key constraint will not allow the primary key to be changed, so the update operation won't be successful. If you want to be able to change primary key values or delete primary key records, then, you need to enforce referential integrity by using triggers instead of foreign key constraints.

You can also use triggers to check the validity of data in a record that's being added to or changed in a table. Although you can do that to some extent using rules and constraints as described earlier in this chapter, triggers give you additional flexibility. In particular, you can refer to any column in any table from a trigger; you can use conditional processing and error handling within the trigger; and you can use a trigger to compare the state of a table before and after the operation that fired the trigger is executed.

Pseudocode for a trigger that fires when a record in the Vendors table is updated

```
If the primary key value has changed Then
    Change all records in the Invoices table with
    matching foreign keys
```

What happens when a client sends a request to update a Vendor record

- If the update isn't successful, nothing happens.
- If the update is successful, the trigger fires. Then, if the primary key value in the updated record has been changed, the trigger updates all records in the Invoices table that have matching foreign keys.

Concepts

- A *trigger* is a special type of stored procedure that is executed, or *fired*, when records are added, updated, or deleted from a table. You can create a trigger for each of these three operations for each table in a database.
- A trigger is fired only if the operation is successful. If an operation isn't successful, the trigger doesn't fire.
- A trigger can be used to enforce referential integrity as shown in the example above. In that case, however, you can't use foreign key constraints. If you use them, the update or delete operation on the primary key table will be unsuccessful, and the trigger will not be fired.
- Triggers can also be used to check the validity of the data in a record that's being updated or added to a table. In fact, triggers can be used to provide checking that can't be done through rules and check constraints.

Figure 2-14 How to use triggers

Data security and locking

Data security determines who can access the tables and fields in a database, while locking prevents two or more users from changing the same data at the same time. Although the database administrator usually establishes the security for a database and locking is implemented automatically, they can both affect the way you develop your client/server applications. That's why you should be familiar with how they work.

How data security is implemented by NT Server and SQL Server

Data security determines who can access the tables and fields in a database. When you use Windows NT Server as the network operating system and SQL Server for database management, you actually have two layers of data security. NT Server controls who can log in to the network. And SQL Server controls who can access the objects and data in a database and what operations they can perform. This security is summarized in figure 2-15.

To provide for network security, a network administrator sets up an account name and password for each user of the network. The administrator also determines what servers, files, and printers each user has access to. Then, when a user tries to connect to the network, NT Server asks for a valid name and password. If a user can't supply them, he or she isn't given access to the network and therefore can't access SQL Server data.

To provide for database security, a database administrator sets up a login ID and password for each user of a database. To do this with SQL Server, the administrator uses the Manage Logins dialog box shown in this figure. From this dialog box, the administrator can also grant access rights to individual databases.

After giving a user access to a database, the database administrator can use the Object Permissions dialog box shown in this figure to give the user specific capabilities and access rights. For instance, the database administrator can give the user permission to perform select, insert, update, and delete operations on the tables and views in the database; permission to select and update specific columns in a table or view; and permission to execute stored procedures or to add foreign key constraints to a table.

The Manage Logins and Object Permissions dialog boxes for SQL Server

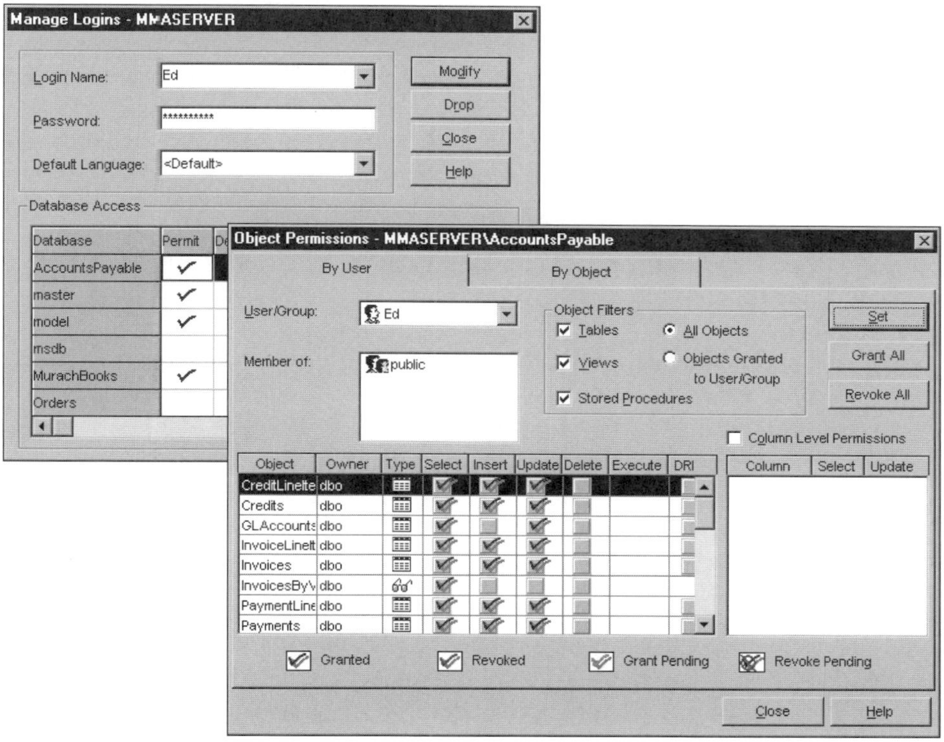

Concepts

- The *network security* provided by Windows NT Server determines what servers, files, and printers each user has access to.
- The *database security* provided by SQL Server determines who can log in to SQL Server, what databases and database objects (tables, views, etc.) each user has access to, and what operations each user can perform on the database and its objects.
- Both Windows NT Server and SQL Server require that users log in with a name or ID and a password. However, NT Server user accounts can be mapped to SQL Server login IDs so a user can connect to the network and log in to SQL Server at the same time.

Figure 2-15 How data security is implemented by NT Server and SQL Server

How locking is implemented by Jet and SQL Server

Locking prevents two or more users from changing the same data at the same time. To illustrate the need for locking, suppose user A accesses a record in the Vendors table to update the vendor's address. At the same time, user B accesses the same record to change the payment terms for the vendor. When user A finishes changing the address, the change is saved to the table. But when user B saves the same record with the updated payment terms, it replaces the record that user A just updated so the address returns to the old address. With a large database, of course, this type of problem should be rare, but it is nonetheless a problem that a business application must provide for.

SQL Server prevents this type of problem by automatically locking records. The type of lock that SQL Server uses depends on the type of access that's requested. The three types of SQL Server locks are presented in figure 2-16.

By default, SQL Server locks the page that contains the record being accessed. A page is a 4KB block of memory on the server that is used to hold the most recently-accessed records. However, SQL Server may also lock an entire table. That happens when a table reaches its *lock escalation level*. The lock escalation level determines at what point it's more efficient to lock the entire table than to lock additional pages in the table. The lock escalation level is typically set by the database administrator.

In contrast, Jet implements two types of locking: pessimistic and optimistic. *Pessimistic locking* is the default. With this type of locking, the page that contains a record is locked as soon as the user begins editing the record, and the lock isn't removed until the changes are saved or discarded. With *optimistic locking*, the page that contains a record isn't locked until the record is updated. If you use this type of locking, then, you need to be sure that the record you're updating hasn't changed since you retrieved it before you save any changes to it. If you don't and the record has changed, the update operation will be unsuccessful. These Jet locks, however, apply only to Jet databases because Jet has no control over the locking that's performed by a DBMS like SQL Server.

SQL Server lock types

Lock type	Description
Shared	Shared locks allow the data in a page or table to be accessed by other operations. They are used for statements like SELECT that don't change data.
Update	Update locks allow other operations to acquire shared access to the same data. They are used to lock a page that SQL Server intends to modify. An update lock is upgraded to an exclusive lock when data is actually updated.
Exclusive	Exclusive locks prevent other operations from accessing the same data. They are used at the page and table level for statements like UPDATE, INSERT, and DELETE and at the extent level when a new database extent is created in response to a query.

Jet lock types

Lock type	Description
Pessimistic	The page that contains a record is locked when the user begins to edit the record. This insures that other users don't change or delete the record while it's being edited. This is the default.
Optimistic	Locks the page that contains a record before changes to the record are saved. If another user changes or deletes the record while it's being edited, the update will fail.

Concepts

- *Locking* prevents one user from accessing data that is being modified by another user. Locking is implemented automatically by Jet and SQL Server.
- SQL Server's default lock size is a page. If many pages in the same table are locked at the same time, SQL Server will increase the lock size to the entire table. This is called *lock escalation*.
- With Jet, you can use either *pessimistic locks* or *optimistic locks*. Pessimistic locks are the default. You use Jet locks only with Jet databases. They have no effect on data stored in an external database like SQL Server.

Notes

- You can customize the locking that's provided by SQL Server by coding locking options on a SELECT statement. In most cases, however, this isn't necessary. For details, see the SELECT statement in the online *Transact-SQL Reference* manual.
- SQL Server 6.5 introduced a new level of locking called *insert row-level locking*. This type of locking allows multiple INSERT operations to be performed on the same page. For details, see the online *What's New in SQL Server 6.5* manual.

Figure 2-16 How locking is implemented by Jet and SQL Server

Tools for working with relational databases

Figure 2-17 presents four tools that you can use for working with databases. In chapter 10, you can learn how to use the Visual Data Manager that comes with both the Professional and Enterprise Editions of Visual Basic. But you should also be aware of the capabilities of the other database tools.

Access provides an easy-to-use interface for working with Jet and ODBC databases. To work with an ODBC database, you create *links* to the tables in that database. Then, you can work with the data in the database just as if it were stored in local tables. You can also use a visual interface to create queries. However, you can't modify the table structures or field properties of an ODBC database. To do that, you need to use one of the other database tools.

Like Access, the Visual Data Manager is most useful for working with Jet databases. However, you can also use it to define a connection to an ODBC database (called a *data source*), to create and manage the tables in the database, to work with the data in the database, and to create queries. Nevertheless, this program is extremely limited. When you add a new field to a table in an ODBC database, for example, you can't specify a default value or a validation rule. And once you add a field, you can't change its name, data type, or size. You also aren't able to work with any of the other objects in the database, like views and stored procedures. Because of that, you're usually better off using the tools that come with the DBMS. Or, if you have the Enterprise Edition of Visual Basic, you can use the Visual Database Tools program.

The Visual Database Tools program is new to Visual Basic 5. It was designed specifically for working with the objects in ODBC databases, especially SQL Server databases. It provides an easy-to-use interface for creating and managing tables, views, and stored procedures; for working with data; and for creating queries. You can also use it to define the connection to a database. If you have the Enterprise Edition of Visual Basic, it should be your tool of choice for working with databases.

One thing you can't do with the Visual Database Tools program is create the actual database and database device (a logical device) that it's stored in. To do that, you have to use the tools that come with the DBMS. For a SQL Server database, you use the SQL Enterprise Manager. You can also use the Enterprise Manager to work with database objects and create queries.

Access

- Lets you create and define Jet tables
- Lets you link to tables in an ODBC database
- Lets you add, modify, delete, sort, and filter records in Jet and linked tables
- Provides a graphical interface for creating a variety of queries, including select, insert, update, and delete, and lets you enter SQL-specific queries
- Provides a tool called the Upsizing Wizard that lets you convert a Jet database to SQL Server

Visual Data Manager (Professional and Enterprise Edition)

- Lets you define ODBC data sources
- Lets you create and manage tables, fields, and indexes in Jet and ODBC databases
- Lets you add, modify, delete, sort, and filter records
- Provides a graphical interface for creating simple select queries, and lets you enter more complex queries

Visual Database Tools (Enterprise Edition only)

- Lets you define ODBC data sources
- Lets you create and manage ODBC database objects, including tables, views, and stored procedures
- Lets you add, modify, and delete records
- Provides a graphical interface for creating a variety of queries, including select, insert, update, and delete, and lets you enter other types of queries

SQL Enterprise Manager (SQL Server only)

- Lets you create and manage database devices, databases, and database objects including tables, views, stored procedures, rules, defaults, and data types
- Lets you create SQL-specific queries

Note

- Although the Visual Data Manager lets you access and work with ODBC databases, it's specifically designed to be used with Jet databases. Because of that, you'll want to use the Visual Database Tools program or the program that comes with your DBMS to work with an ODBC database.

Figure 2-17 Tools for working with relational databases

Perspective

This chapter has introduced you to what takes place on the server side of a client/server application. That includes how a relational database is defined and organized, how SQL is used to communicate with a relational database, and how a DBMS protects a database by providing features for security and locking.

With that as background, you are now ready to learn how to develop the client software of a client/server application. In the next chapter, you'll be introduced to the Visual Basic skills that you need for all applications. And in chapter 4, you will be introduced to the specific programming skills that you need for working with a database.

Because the effective use of a database is so critical to the success of client/server applications in business, several of the later chapters also focus on database use. In chapter 6, for example, you'll learn more about database programming with DAO. In chapter 7, you'll learn how to use stored procedures from the client side and how to manage the processing of related transactions (*transaction processing*). And in chapter 10, you can learn how to use the Visual Data Manager for working with a database and creating queries.

Chapter 3

Introduction to Visual Basic programming

This chapter presents the most important concepts and techniques for developing applications in Visual Basic. It shows you how to work in the Visual Basic development environment; how to code in the Visual Basic language; and how to use the events, properties, and methods of the objects in this object-oriented language. In short, this chapter tells you everything you need to know for developing your first Visual Basic application.

When you finish this chapter, you should take the time to develop the small but complete application that's used for illustration. That will give you an even better idea of how Visual Basic programming works and what you need to know to become proficient at it. Then, the remaining chapters will help you develop that proficiency.

The basics of Visual Basic programming

To start, this chapter presents the basic concepts that you need for developing Visual Basic programs. In particular, you'll learn about objects and how you work with them as you design the user interface and develop the code for an application.

The user interface

The user interface for a Visual Basic program consists of forms like those shown in figure 3-1. The first form in this figure lets the user perform one of two different calculations depending on the option that's selected at the top of the form. The second form lets the user work with the records in a table of vendors.

If you've worked with other Windows applications, you can see that these forms are like the windows that you've used in those applications. Like those windows, forms contain *controls* that let the user interact with the application. To calculate a monthly investment using the first form shown in figure 3-1, for example, you click on the Monthly Investment option button and then enter values into the appropriate text boxes.

Option buttons and *text boxes* are only two of the many types of controls that you can use on forms. Two other common types of controls are *combo boxes* and *command buttons*. The second form also illustrates a *data control*, which is used to work with the data associated with the form. In chapter 6, you can learn more about the types of controls that are available and how you use them.

Forms and controls are two types of *objects* that you'll work with frequently as you develop Visual Basic applications. In a moment, you'll learn what these objects are and how you create and work with them. Then, in the next chapter, you'll learn how to work with database objects like tables and fields.

A form that calculates future values or monthly investment amounts

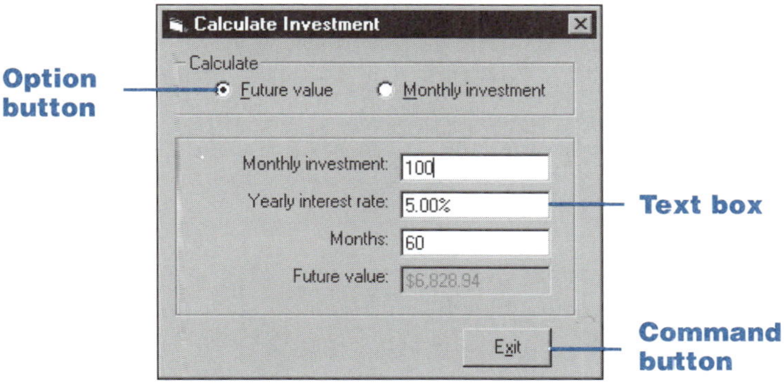

A form that maintains vendor information

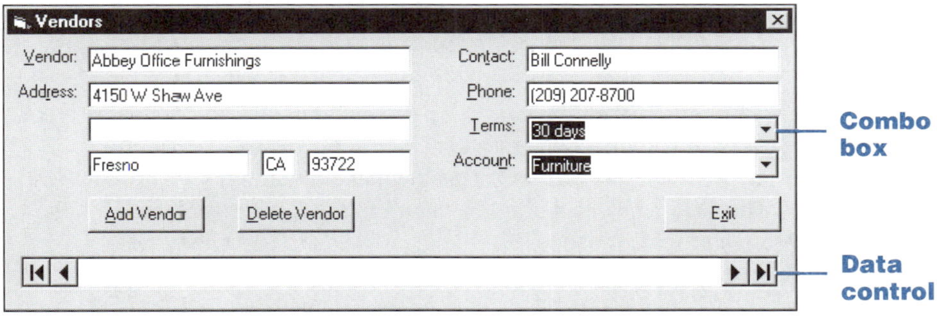

Concepts

- *Forms* provide the user interface for an application. A form contains *controls* that let the user interact with it by using the mouse or keyboard. Some of the most common controls are *command buttons*, *text boxes*, *list boxes*, and *combo boxes*, but many others are also available.
- A form can perform a variety of operations. Most forms, like the Vendors form shown above, provide access to the data in a database. Other forms, like the Calculate Investment form above, aren't tied to the data in a database.
- Forms and controls are two types of *objects* that you work with in Visual Basic. If a form accesses data, you also work with data objects like *databases*, *tables*, and *recordsets*.

Figure 3-1 The user interface

The concepts of object-oriented programming

Figure 3-2 presents the basic concepts of object-oriented programming. Here, you can see that an object is created from an object *class*. An object class is like a template that defines the properties, methods, and events for a particular type of object. When you create an object, it *inherits* the properties, methods, and events of the object class. As a result, each text box you create has the same properties, methods, and events as every other text box, which are different from the properties, methods, and events of other controls.

You use an object's *properties* to define how an object looks and acts. You can think of properties as variables that can contain different values. The values you choose determine how the object looks and acts. When you create a command button, for example, you can change the text that's displayed on it by changing the value of its Caption property. So, although all command buttons have the same properties, those properties can have different values that make the command buttons unique.

In many cases, you'll set an object's properties as you design an application. However, you can also change an object's properties while an application is running by referring to the property in program code. If you look back at the Calculate Investment form in figure 3-1, for example, you'll see that the Future Value text box is disabled so the user can't enter a value into it. If the user clicks on the Monthly Investment option, however, this text box is enabled and the Monthly Investment text box is disabled. This is done by changing the values of the Enabled properties in these two controls through program code.

You can use an object's *methods* to perform operations defined by that object's class. For example, you can use the Show method of a form object to display the form on the screen. To do that, you refer to the object's method through program code. You can think of a method as a segment of code, or a *procedure*, that's executed when you refer to the method.

You can use an object's *events* to respond to actions that occur on an object. For instance, the Click event occurs when the user clicks the left mouse button on an object like a command button. If the object recognizes the Click event, it can then be programmed to respond to that event.

Visual Basic 5 comes with many object classes. You'll learn how to find out about those object classes later in this chapter when I present the Object Browser. You can also use Visual Basic to create object classes of your own.

How an object is created from an object class

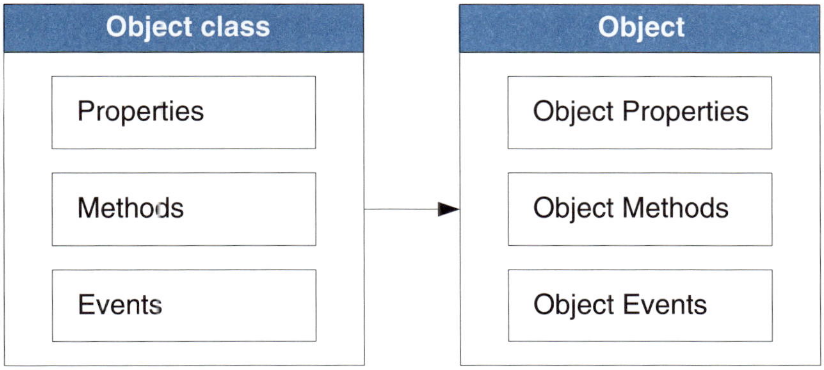

Concepts

- An *object* is a unique entity that consists of a set of properties, a set of methods, and a set of events. The properties, methods, and events that an object contains are determined by the object template, or *class*, that the object is based on.
- An object's *properties* define its attributes. By changing the values of an object's properties, you can change how that object looks and acts. For example, you can change the Caption property of a form to change what's displayed in the form's title bar. You can change an object's properties as you design the object or while an object is running using program code.
- An object's *methods* define the operations that can be performed on that object. For example, a form's Show method displays the form on the screen and its Hide method removes the form from the screen. You execute a method on an object by referring to the object and method in program code.
- An object's *events* define what actions are recognized by that object. Most objects, for example, recognize the Click event, which occurs when the user clicks the left mouse button on the object. When you want an application to perform some processing in response to an event, you add code to the application in the form of *event procedures*.
- To find out what classes are available to you as you develop an application and what properties, methods, and events they define, you can use the Object Browser that comes with Visual Basic (see figure 3-13).
- In programming terms, an object class is just program code from which the code for an object is derived. The properties of an object class are variables, and its methods are procedures. The objects that are derived from an object class *inherit* the properties, methods, and events of the object class.

Figure 3-2 The concepts of object-oriented programming

How an application responds to events

Programs developed in the Windows environment are *event-driven*. That means that they work by responding to events that occur on objects. This is considerably different from the way traditional applications work. In a mainframe program, for example, a top-down structure controls and limits the user's operations. In a Visual Basic application, the program is driven by the user's actions.

To respond to an event that occurs on an object, you write program code in the form of an *event procedure* as illustrated in figure 3-3. This figure shows the code that's executed when the user clicks on the Monthly Investment option button on the Calculate Investment form. This procedure consists of Visual Basic statements and references to properties, methods, and events. Don't worry if this code doesn't make sense to you right now, because you should understand it by the time you complete this chapter.

Although the user initiates most events, additional events can be initiated by program code. For instance, the SetFocus method that's executed as part of the Click event procedure in figure 3-3 causes two additional events to occur. The LostFocus event occurs on the control that loses the focus, and the GotFocus event occurs on the control that the focus is moved to. If you want additional processing to take place when either of these events occurs, you can code event procedures for them.

How an event is processed

Event: The user clicks on the Monthly Investment option button.

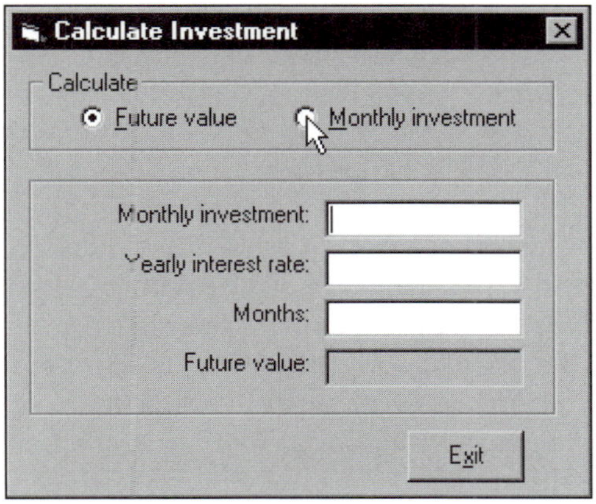

Response: The Click event procedure for that option button is executed.

```
Private Sub optMonthlyInvestment_Click()
    mskFutureValue.Enabled = True
    mskMonthlyInvestment.Enabled = False
    mskMonthlyInvestment.Text = ""
    mskInterestRate.Text = ""
    mskMonths.Text = ""
    mskFutureValue.Text = ""
    mskInterestRate.SetFocus
End Sub
```

Concepts

- Windows programs work by responding to events that occur on objects. To respond to an event, you code an *event procedure*.
- The code for an event procedure can consist of Visual Basic statements and functions, as well as references to objects, properties, methods, and events. Two Visual Basic statements (Sub and End Sub) are shown above. The rest of the code sets properties (Enabled and Text) and executes a method (SetFocus).
- Event procedures can also call *general procedures*. General procedures are typically used when a block of code needs to be executed from more than one location in an application.
- An event can be an action initiated by the user like the Click event shown above, or it can be an action initiated by the system or by program code. For instance, the SetFocus method shown above initiates the LostFocus event on the control that lost the focus and the GotFocus event on the control that the focus is moved to. You can then respond to either of those events with an event procedure.

Figure 3-3 How an application responds to events

How to code procedures

Most of the code that you write for a Visual Basic application will be part of a *procedure*. Besides event procedures, you can code *general procedures*, which can be called from event procedures and other general procedures. Typically, you code a general procedure if the code it contains needs to be executed from more than one procedure. That way, instead of repeating the code in each procedure, you can code it in a single general procedure.

In figure 3-4, you can see both an event procedure and a general procedure. A Sub statement at the start of each procedure indicates that it is a *Sub procedure*, and an End Sub statement ends each procedure. For the event procedure, the Sub statement identifies the object and the event that the procedure will respond to. In this case, the procedure responds to the LostFocus event on the control named mskFutureValue. In contrast, the Sub statement for the general procedure gives a procedure name created by the programmer, CalcMonthlyInvestment.

A general procedure can also be coded as a *Function procedure*, which is commonly referred to as a *function*. Unlike a Sub procedure, a function can return a value. You code a function using the Function and End Function statements.

In these coding examples and in all the examples in this book, three or more lowercase letters at the start of an object name identify the object type. For instance, the *msk* in *mskFutureValue* means that the object is a *masked edit control*. Although you're not required to use prefixes like this when you name objects, the prefixes make your code easier to read and understand.

When you create a procedure that's related to a form, it is saved in the *form module* for that form. However, you can also store procedures in *standard modules* and *class modules*. A standard module typically contains the general procedures that you need to access from two or more form modules. And a class module contains code that defines a new object class. In addition to procedures, each module can contain *declarations* that identify the variables and constants that can be used by all the procedures in a module.

In figure 3-4, the keyword *Private* that starts the Sub statements means that the procedures can't be called from other modules in the application. And the parentheses following the procedure name indicate that no arguments can be passed to the procedure. In chapter 5, you can learn more about Sub procedures, Function procedures, modules, and declarations, but this should be enough to get you started.

An event procedure that calls a general procedure

Object **Event**

```
Private Sub mskFutureValue_LostFocus()
    CalcMonthlyInvestment
End Sub
```

Procedure name

A general procedure that's called by the event procedure above

Procedure name

```
Private Sub CalcMonthlyInvestment()
    If Val(mskInterestRate.Text) > 0 _
            And Val(mskMonths.Text) > 0 _
            And Val(mskFutureValue.Text) > 0 Then
        mskMonthlyInvestment.Text = _
            Pmt(mskInterestRate.Text / 12, _
            mskMonths.Text, 0, mskFutureValue.Text, 1) * -1
    End If
End Sub
```

Concepts

- The code in a Visual Basic application is divided into *procedures*. Event procedures respond to specific events on specific objects. General procedures are called explicitly from other procedures.
- You can code two types of procedures: *Sub procedures* and *Function procedures* (or just *functions*). The only difference between a Sub procedure and a function is that a function returns a value and a Sub procedure doesn't. Event procedures can only be coded as Sub procedures.
- A Sub procedure begins with a Sub statement and ends with an End Sub statement. For an event procedure, the Sub statement identifies the object and event that the procedure will respond to. For a general procedure, the Sub statement specifies the name of the procedure.
- A function begins with a Function statement and ends with an End Function statement. The Function statement specifies the name of the function and the type of data that the function will return.
- When you write a procedure that relates to a specific form, you typically store it in the *form module* for that form. However, you can also store procedures in standard modules and class modules. A *standard module* contains code that can be accessed from any module in the application. And a *class module* contains code that defines a new object class.
- In addition to procedures, a module can contain *declarations* that identify the *variables* and *constants* that can be used by all the procedures within a module.

Figure 3-4 How to code procedures

How to refer to properties and methods

If you want to refer to a property or method in your program code, you need to use the syntax presented in figure 3-5. In general, you refer to a property or method by coding the object name, followed by a period, called a *dot operator*, followed by the property or method name. This syntax is illustrated by the examples presented at the top of figure 3-5.

The first example in the figure shows how to assign a new value to a property, and the second example shows how to extract the value of a property and assign it to a variable. These kinds of statements are called *assignment statements*.

The third example shows how you can test the value of a property using an If statement. Notice that no property or method is specified following the object name in this example. In that case, Visual Basic assumes that you want to refer to the *default property*. Since the default property of a text box is the Text property, which contains the current contents of the text box, this example checks to see if the text box is equal to zero.

The next two examples show how to refer to methods. The first example uses the SetFocus method to move the focus to a command button named cmdOK. The second example uses the AddItem method to add an entry to a list box named lstName, and it requires an argument that names the entry to be added to the list. In this case, the argument is the name of a text box that contains the entry.

When a method requires an argument, you can often code it as shown in this example. That is, you type one space after the method, then type the argument. And if the method requires more than one argument, you separate the items by commas.

Some methods, however, require that the argument or arguments be placed in parentheses with the arguments separated by commas. To find the proper syntax for the arguments of a method, you can look up the method in the online help feature or in the Language Reference manual that comes with Visual Basic. You can also look up the method in the Object Browser, which you'll learn about later in this chapter.

Statements that refer to properties

`cmdAccept.Enabled = False`	Assigns the value "False" to the Enabled property of the command button named cmdAccept so the button appears disabled.
`strName = lstName.Text`	Assigns the value of the Text property of the currently selected item in the list box named lstName to the variable named strName.
`If txtQuantity = 0 Then ...`	Tests the value of the text box named txtQuantity to see if it's zero. Because no property or method is specified, the default property, Text, is assumed.

Statements that refer to methods

`cmdOK.SetFocus`	Uses the SetFocus method to move the focus to the command button named cmdOK.
`lstName.AddItem txtName.Text`	Uses the AddItem method to add the contents of the text box named txtName to the list box named lstName.

Description

- To refer to a property or method of an object, you specify the name of the object and the name of the property or method, separated by a dot operator (a period). If the property or method is omitted as in the third example above, the default property is assumed.
- You can perform three basic types of operations with properties as shown by the examples above. You can assign a new value to the property, you can assign the value of a property to a variable or another object, or you can test the value of a property.
- When you refer to a method in Visual Basic code, that method is executed. If the method accepts arguments, you specify the arguments following the method as shown in the second example above. The syntax you use to specify arguments depends on the method. If the method returns a value (most don't), you can assign that value to a variable or another object.
- In the examples above, a lowercase prefix in an object's name indicates the object type, and a lowercase prefix in a variable name indicates the variable type. Although the use of prefixes isn't required, this is a worthwhile coding practice.

Figure 3-5 How to refer to the properties and methods of an object

A simple Visual Basic application

To help you see how a Visual Basic program works, the topics that follow present the Calculate Investment application in detail. The first topic explains how the application works from the user's point of view. The second one shows how the form and control properties have to be set as the application is designed. The third one presents the Visual Basic code for the entire application.

How the Calculate Investment application works

Figure 3-6 summarizes the operation of the Calculate Investment application. This application can perform two different calculations. First, it can calculate the future value of a monthly investment. Second, it can calculate the monthly investment that is needed to attain a specific future value.

The user can choose the calculation that's performed by selecting the appropriate option at the top of the form. When the form is first displayed, the Future Value option is selected. Because this calculation doesn't require an entry in the Future Value text box, this box is disabled as illustrated by the first form in figure 3-6. If the user selects the Monthly Investment option, the Future Value text box is enabled and the Monthly Investment text box is disabled. Clicking on the other option also clears out any values that have been entered into the text boxes.

To perform a calculation, the user must enter values into the appropriate boxes. If all three required values are entered, the calculation is performed when the user moves out of the last box. That usually occurs when the user presses the Tab key, but it can also happen if the user clicks on another control. Pressing the Enter key, however, has no effect in this application.

After the calculation is performed, the focus moves back to the first enabled text box. Then, the user can change any of the entered values. Each time the user changes a value and moves out of the box that contains that value, the investment is recalculated. If, for example, the user changes the monthly investment in the first form in figure 3-6 to $150, the future value is recalculated when the user presses the Tab key.

To end the application, the user clicks on the Close button at the top of the form, clicks on the Exit command button, or presses Alt+X to activate the Exit command button. In short, the application works the way an experienced Windows user would expect it to.

The two versions of the Calculate Investment form

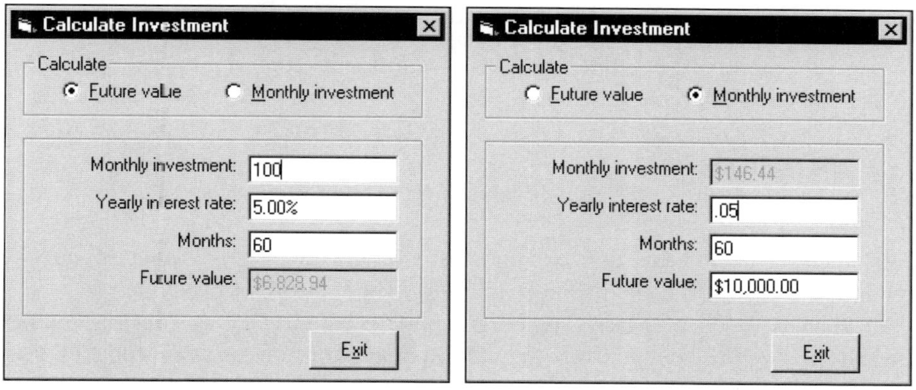

Description

- The Calculate Investment application can perform two operations. It can calculate the future value of a fixed monthly investment. Or it can calculate the monthly investment needed to attain a given future value. The operation that's performed depends on the Calculate option that's selected.
- The Future Value option is selected by default. When this option is selected, the user can enter a monthly investment, a yearly interest rate, and the life of the investment in months. For this operation, the control that lets you enter a future value is disabled since it will contain a calculated value.
- When the Monthly Investment option is selected, the user can enter a yearly interest rate, the life of the investment in months, and the future value to be attained. In this case, the control that lets you enter the monthly investment is disabled since it will contain a calculated value.
- Whenever the user enters a new value into one of the controls, the program checks to be sure that all of the values required to perform the appropriate calculation have been entered. If not, the focus automatically moves to the next control so the user can enter additional information. If all of the required fields have been entered, the calculation is performed.
- To end the application, the user can click on the Exit button in the lower right corner of the form or on the Close button in the upper right corner of the form.

Figure 3-6 How the Calculate Investment application works

The property settings for the application

Figure 3-7 presents the initial settings for the form and control properties of the Calculate Investment application. These are the settings that you have to make so the form looks and operates correctly. Some of the other properties, like those that affect the size and position of the form and its controls, are set as you design the layout of the form. And you can use the default values for the other properties of the form and its controls.

As you'll see later in this chapter, you usually set the properties as you design a form and its controls. When you create a new form or control, for example, you usually change its Name property to give it a more meaningful name. This is particularly helpful if you're going to refer to the form or control from program code. Figure 3-7 shows the names I used for the Calculate Investment form and its controls. A three-character prefix on each name indicates the type of object.

The other property settings for the form determine the type of border that's used for the form, the caption that's displayed in the title bar of the form, and whether the standard Minimize and Maximize buttons are included on the form. Because you usually design a form so it's the appropriate size for the controls that it contains, you'll want to change the BorderStyle property as shown in the figure so the user can't change the size. You'll also want to change the MaxButton and MinButton properties to False so the user can't maximize or minimize the form.

The other property settings don't require much explanation. The Caption property provides the text that's displayed on each control. The TabStop properties of the two option buttons and the command button are set to False so the focus doesn't move to them when the user presses the Tab key. The Value property of the Future Value option button is set to True so it is turned on when the application starts. And the Format properties of the four masked edit controls are set so the values entered by the user are displayed in appropriate formats.

Incidentally, I often refer to the masked edit controls as text boxes in this chapter because a masked edit control is a type of text box that formats the data it contains. If, for example, the user enters .12 into the masked edit control for the interest rate, 12% is displayed. If the user enters 100000 in the control for future value, $100,000 is displayed.

One other property that you may need to change when you design this form is the TabIndex property for each of the controls. It determines the sequence in which the controls receive the focus when the user presses the Tab key. By default, the sequence is the order in which the controls are added to the form, but you can use this property to change that. If the TabStop property of a control is set to False, however, you don't need to change the TabIndex property.

The required property settings for the Calculate Investment form

Form	Property	Setting
Calculate Investment form	Name BorderStyle Caption MaxButton MinButton	frmCalculateInvestment 1 - Fixed Single Calculate Investment False False

The required property settings for the controls on the form

Control	Property	Setting
Calculate frame	Caption	Calculate
Future Value option button	Name Caption TabStop Value	optFutureValue &Future value False True
Monthly Investment option button	Name Caption TabStop	optMonthlyInvestment &Monthly investment False
Monthly Investment masked edit control	Name Format	mskMonthlyInvestment $#,##0.00;($#,##0.00)
Yearly Interest Rate masked edit control	Name Format	mskInterestRate 0.00%
Months masked edit control	Name Format	mskMonths 0
Future Value masked edit control	Name Enabled Format	mskFutureValue False $#,##0.00;($#,##0.00)
Exit command button	Name Caption TabStop	cmdExit E&xit False

Notes

- This list includes only the properties that you have to change to get this application to work right.
- The four label controls that identify the masked edit controls aren't included in this list. For each of these controls, you have to set the Caption property to the identifying label and the Alignment property to Right Justify.
- An ampersand in a Caption name causes the next letter to be underlined when displayed on the control. The user can then press Alt plus the underlined letter to activate the control.

Figure 3-7 The property settings for the Calculate Investment application

The code for the application

Figure 3-8 presents all the code for the Calculate Investment application. As you can see, the code consists of seven event procedures and two general procedures. The event procedures respond to the user actions, and the general procedures perform the two calculations.

The first event procedure is executed when the user clicks on the Future Value option button. This procedure disables the Future Value text box (actually, a masked edit control) and enables the Monthly Investment text box. It also clears out the four text boxes by moving spaces to them and moves the focus to the first enabled text box, which is the Monthly Investment text box.

The second event procedure is executed when the user clicks on the Monthly Investment option button. It is similar to the first event procedure. It enables the Future Value text box, disables the Monthly Investment text box, clears out the four text boxes, and moves the focus to the Yearly Interest Rate text box.

The third event procedure is executed when the focus moves out of the Monthly Investment text box. Typically, that will happen when the user enters a value into this text box and then presses the Tab key. This event procedure simply calls the general procedure that calculates the future value.

The fourth event procedure is executed when the focus moves out of the Yearly Interest Rate text box. It uses a Visual Basic If statement to test the value of the Future Value option button. If this button is selected (its value is True), this procedure calls the procedure that calculates the future value. If the Future Value button isn't selected, this procedure calls the procedure that calculates the monthly investment.

The fifth event procedure is executed when the focus moves out of the Months text box. It uses another If statement, and it works like the procedure for the Yearly Interest Rate text box.

The event procedures for the Calculate Investment application

1
```
Private Sub optFutureValue_Click()
    mskFutureValue.Enabled = False
    mskMonthlyInvestment.Enabled = True
    mskMonthlyInvestment.Text = ""
    mskInterestRate.Text = ""
    mskMonths.Text = ""
    mskFutureValue.Text = ""
    mskMonthlyInvestment.SetFocus
End Sub
```

2
```
Private Sub optMonthlyInvestment_Click()
    mskFutureValue.Enabled = True
    mskMonthlyInvestment.Enabled = False
    mskMonthlyInvestment.Text = ""
    mskInterestRate.Text = ""
    mskMonths.Text = ""
    mskFutureValue.Text = ""
    mskInterestRate.SetFocus
End Sub
```

3
```
Private Sub mskMonthlyInvestment_LostFocus()
    CalcFutureValue
End Sub
```

4
```
Private Sub mskInterestRate_LostFocus()
    If optFutureValue = True Then
        CalcFutureValue
    Else
        CalcMonthlyInvestment
    End If
End Sub
```

5
```
Private Sub mskMonths_LostFocus()
    If optFutureValue = True Then
        CalcFutureValue
    Else
        CalcMonthlyInvestment
    End If
End Sub
```

Figure 3-8 The code for the Calculate Investment application (part 1 of 2)

The sixth event procedure is executed when the focus moves out of the Future Value text box. It calls the procedure that calculates the monthly investment.

The last event procedure is executed when the user clicks on the Exit button. It uses the Unload statement to remove the Calculate Investment form from the screen and the End statement to release the resources used by the application.

The first general procedure performs the future value calculation. It uses an If statement to check that appropriate values have been entered into the three enabled text boxes. To do that, it uses three Visual Basic Val functions, which extract the numeric values from these controls. Then, if all three values are greater than zero, this procedure uses the Visual Basic FV (Future Value) function to perform the required calculation and assign the resulting value to the Future Value text box.

The second general procedure performs the monthly investment calculation. It works like the first general procedure except that it uses the Visual Basic Pmt (Payment) function and assigns the result to the Monthly Investment text box.

If you have some programming experience, you should now understand the Visual Basic code in figure 3-8 and see how it interacts with the controls described in figure 3-7. If you have trouble with that, you may want to review some of the earlier figures in this chapter. If you haven't ever worked with an object-oriented language before, it may take you a while to get used to the Visual Basic code, but understanding the code in figure 3-8 is critical to your progress.

Later on, when you're actually using Visual Basic to enter code, you can use the help feature to get more information about the syntax or operation of a statement or function. For instance, you can use this feature to find out what the syntax of the If statement is. And you can use it to find out what the 0 and 1 at the end of the FV function mean and why you have to divide the interest rate by 12. Then, in chapter 5, you can learn more about the statements and functions that are provided by Visual Basic.

The event procedures for the Calculate Investment application (continued)

6
```
Private Sub mskFutureValue_LostFocus()
    CalcMonthlyInvestment
End Sub
```

7
```
Private Sub cmdExit_Click()
    Unload frmCalculateInvestment
    End
End Sub
```

The general procedures for the Calculate Investment application

1
```
Private Sub CalcFutureValue()
    If Val(mskMonthlyInvestment.Text) > 0 _
            And Val(mskInterestRate.Text) > 0 _
            And Val(mskMonths.Text) > 0 Then
        mskFutureValue.Text = _
            FV(mskInterestRate.Text / 12, _
            mskMonths.Text, mskMonthlyInvestment.Text, _
            0, 1) * -1
    End If
End Sub
```

2
```
Private Sub CalcMonthlyInvestment()
    If Val(mskInterestRate.Text) > 0 _
            And Val(mskMonths.Text) > 0 _
            And Val(mskFutureValue.Text) > 0 Then
        mskMonthlyInvestment.Text = _
            Pmt(mskInterestRate.Text / 12, _
            mskMonths.Text, 0, mskFutureValue.Text, 1) _
            * -1
    End If
End Sub
```

Figure 3-8 The code for the Calculate Investment application (part 2 of 2)

The Integrated Development Environment

Now that you understand how to work with objects, properties, methods, and events, you're ready to learn how to work in the Visual Basic development environment. You use this environment to perform all phases of application development, including designing forms and writing and debugging program code. That's why it's called the Integrated Development Environment, *or* IDE.

How to start a new project

In Visual Basic, the applications that you develop are called *projects*. When you first start Visual Basic, the New Project dialog box shown in figure 3-9 is displayed. This dialog box lets you start a new project, open an existing project, or open a recent project.

If you want to start a new project, you choose one of the options in the New tab of this dialog box. For most projects, you'll use the Standard EXE option. This starts a new project and displays a new form for it.

If you don't want the New Project dialog box displayed when you start Visual Basic, you can check the box at the bottom of the dialog box. After that, Visual Basic starts with its application window displayed and no dialog box. You can then use the File menu or toolbar buttons to start a new project or open an existing project.

The dialog box that's displayed when you start Visual Basic

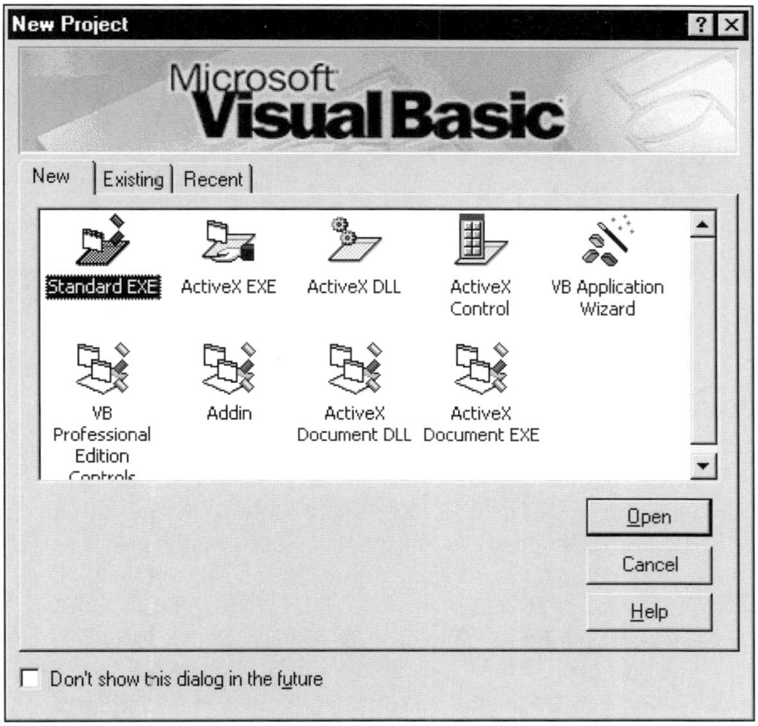

Operation

- Visual Basic lets you create several different types of projects. Most of the time, though, you choose the Standard EXE option to create a standard project.
- When you start Visual Basic, the New Project dialog box lets you open a new project, an existing project, or one that you worked on recently. However, if you display this dialog box later on by selecting the New command in the File menu, only the New options are available.

Figure 3-9 How to start a new project

How to develop the user interface

Figure 3-10 presents the Visual Basic application window. You use this window to perform all phases of application development. Like most Windows programs, Visual Basic provides menus and toolbars that you can use to perform its various operations. You can also right-click at appropriate places to get shortcut menus that provide context-sensitive options. Note, however, that this chapter makes no attempt to present all the ways that you can do a task so by all means do some experimenting.

To develop a form in Visual Basic, you work in the Form Designer window. When you start a new project, a blank form is displayed in this window. Then, you can add controls to this form by clicking on a control in the *toolbox* and then dragging in the form to size and place the control. In figure 3-10, for example, a command button is being added to the form. You can also double-click on a control in the toolbox to add a control in the center of the form.

If you need to change the size of a form, you can do that by clicking on the form to select it and then dragging one of the handles that appears around the outside of the form. You can work with the controls on a form in a similar manner. Just click on a control to select it and then drag one of its handles to size it. If you need to, you can also change the size of the Form Designer window by dragging its borders.

When you first start a new project, it consists of a single form. Most projects, however, will consist of many forms as well as other modules. To help manage these forms and modules, you can use the Project Explorer. To display another form, for example, just double-click on a form in the Project Explorer, or click on the form to select it and then click on the View Object button at the top of the Project Explorer window. You can also display the code for a module by selecting it and clicking on the View Code button. Most of the time, though, you'll leave the Project Explorer window closed so you have more room to work in the Form Designer window.

The IDE with the Form Designer, toolbox, and Project Explorer displayed

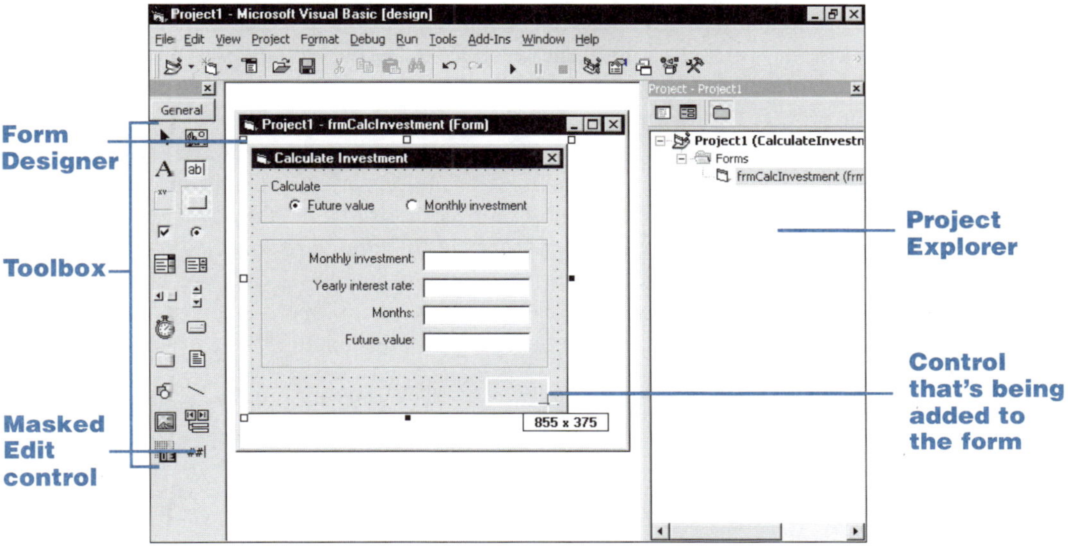

Operation

- When you start a new project, a single form is created by default and placed in the Form Designer window. To select the form, click on it. And to change the size of the form, drag the handles that appear around it.
- If the toolbox isn't displayed, select the Toolbox command from the View menu or click on the Toolbox button in the toolbar. To add a control to a form, click on the control in the toolbox. Then, drag the pointer in the Form Designer window to place and size the control. You can also add a control by double-clicking on it.
- To move a control, drag it. To select a control, click on it. And to size a control, drag the handles that appear around it when it's selected.
- When you start a new project, the toolbox contains a standard set of controls. To add other controls to the toolbox, use the Components command in the Project menu. For instance, the Masked Edit control has been added to the toolbox above.
- To display the Project Explorer, select the Project Explorer command from the View menu or click on the Project Explorer button in the toolbar. This window shows all the modules of a project.
- To save a project and its forms for the first time, click on the Save Project button in the toolbar. Visual Basic then asks you to provide a name for each form as well as a name for the entire project. Once saved, you can click on the Save Project button to save the updated versions of the forms and project.

Figure 3-10 How to develop the user interface

How to work with properties

As you design a form, you need to change some of the properties of the form and its controls. That way, they'll look and work the way you want them to when the form is initially displayed. Keep in mind, though, that you can also use program code to change the properties of a form or control as the program executes.

To work with the properties of a form or control as you design the form, you work in the Properties window shown in figure 3-11. To display the properties for a specific form or control, you click on that object or select it from the drop-down list at the top of the Properties window. To list these properties in either alphabetical order or by category, you can click on the appropriate tab in this window. When you click on a property in the properties list, a brief description of that property is given at the bottom of the window. To change that property, you just change the entry to the right of the property name.

The Properties window for a masked edit control

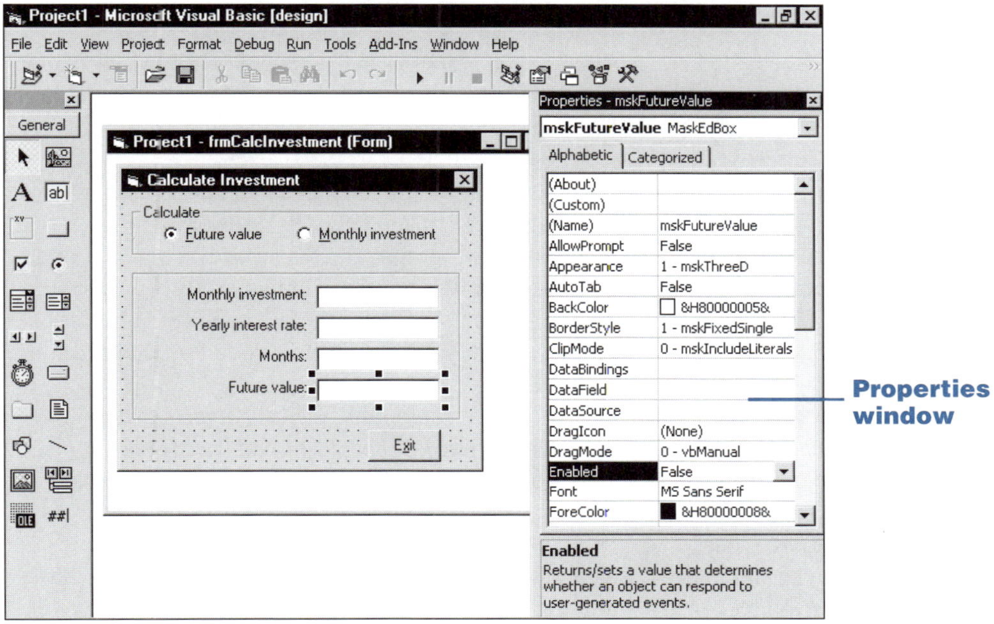

Operation

- To change an object's properties, you work in the Properties window. To display this window, select the Properties Window command from the View menu or click on the Properties Window toolbar button.
- When you first display the Properties window, the properties for the currently selected object are displayed. To display the properties for another object, click on the object in the form or select the object from the list at the top of the Properties window.
- To change a property, just enter a value into its text box or select a value from its drop-down list if it has one. If a button with an ellipsis (...) appears at the right side of a property's text box, you can click on this button to get help specifying the property.
- When you click on a property in the Properties window, a brief explanation of the property appears at the bottom of the window. For more information, press F1 to display the help information for the property.

Figure 3-11 How to work with properties

How to write the code for a procedure

To write the code for a procedure, you work in the Code window shown in figure 3-12. From this window, you can code event procedures for any object and event in the application. You can also code general procedures that can be called from other procedures.

One way to start an event procedure is to choose the object and event from the drop-down lists at the top of the window. When you choose the object, you'll see that Visual Basic selects the most common event for that object and adds a Sub and End Sub statement for that event procedure. If that's not the event you want, you can choose a different one from the drop-down list so the right Sub and End Sub statements are added to the Code window. Then, you can enter the code for that procedure between the Sub and End Sub statements.

Another way to start an event procedure is to double-click on a form or a control. This switches you to the Code window with the Sub and End Sub statements in place and a procedure name for the most common event for that object. If, for example, you double-click on a command button named cmdExit, a procedure is started with this name: cmdExit_Click.

One way to start a general procedure is to use the Add Procedure command in the Tools menu. When you select this command, a dialog box is displayed that asks you for the name of the procedure, the type of the procedure (Sub or Function), and the scope of the procedure (Public or Private). When you complete this dialog box, the appropriate Sub and End Sub or Function and End Function statements are added and you can enter the procedure code between them.

Another way to start a general procedure is to type the Sub or Function statement directly into the Code window. When you complete that statement, Visual Basic automatically adds the End Sub or End Function statement so you can enter the procedure code between these statements.

As you enter code, Visual Basic checks the syntax of each statement and displays an error message if the syntax is incorrect. As you enter the name of a Visual Basic function like FV, Visual Basic may display the syntax of the function below the function name. And as you enter the name of a property or method, Visual Basic may display a list of all the properties or methods for that object so you can select the name you want from the list. Features like these are easy to use, and they help you enter code quickly and accurately. In chapter 5, you can learn more about these features.

Although we're talking about forms and form modules at this point, you also use the Code window to write the code for other types of modules. If, for example, you want to add a general procedure to a standard module, you use the same procedure that you use for adding a general procedure to a form module. Before you do that, though, you need to add a standard module to your application by selecting the Add Module command from the Project menu.

The code for the Calculate Investment application

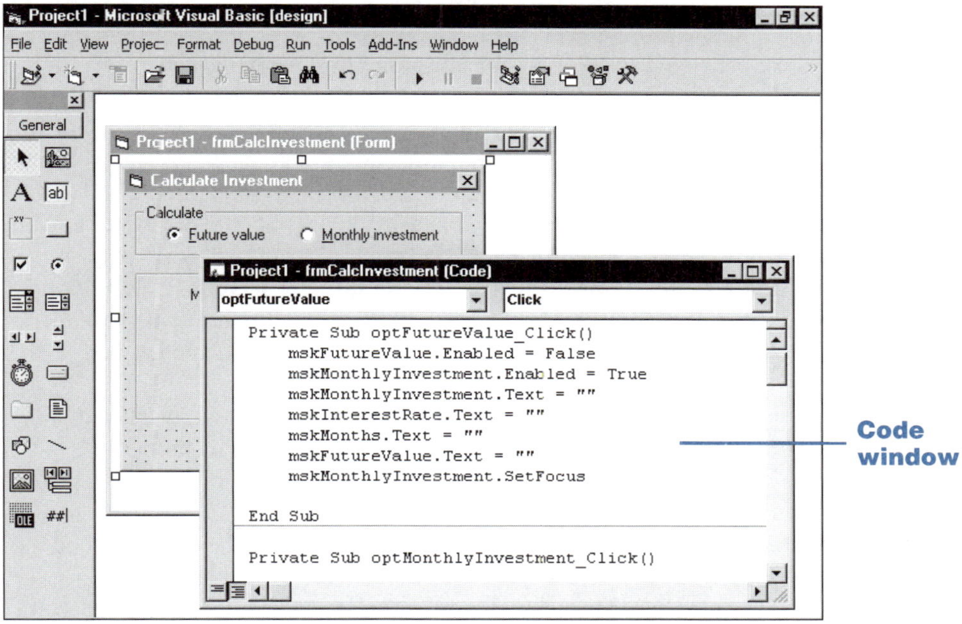

Operation

- You use the Code window whenever you write a procedure for an application. To display this window, select the Code command from the View menu or click on the View Code button in the toolbar of the Project Explorer.
- To code an event procedure, you can choose the object and event from the drop-down lists at the top of the window. Visual Basic then generates the Sub and End Sub statements, and you can write the code for the procedure between those statements.
- To code a general procedure, you can select the Add Procedure command from the Tools menu to display the Add Procedure dialog box. When you complete this dialog box, Visual Basic generates the Sub and End Sub or Function and End Function statements, and you can write the code for the procedure between those statements.
- You can also code procedures by typing the Sub or Function statement directly into the Code window. When you complete that statement, Visual Basic automatically drops down two lines and adds the End Sub or End Function statement.

Figure 3-12 How to write the code for a procedure

How to use the Object Browser

Because there are so many different objects, properties, methods, and events for developing applications in Visual Basic, it's impossible to remember all of them. Fortunately, though, Visual Basic provides an easy way to find out what the object classes are and what properties, methods, and events they contain. To do that, you use the Object Browser shown in figure 3-13.

To use the Object Browser, you begin by choosing a class library from the Project/Library list at the top of the Object Browser window. A *class library* is simply a collection of classes. For example, there's a class library for Visual Basic objects and a class library for Data Access Objects (which you'll learn about in the next chapter). The current project is also included in this list so you can look at its objects and modules.

When you select a class library, all of the classes in that library are displayed in the Classes list. Then, you can click on one of those classes to display its properties, methods, and events in the Members list. In addition, a brief description of the class is displayed in the Details pane at the bottom of the window.

In the Members list, the icon to the left of a member tells whether it's a method, property, or event. If you click on a member, an explanation of that member is displayed in the Details pane. Then, to get more information about that member, you can press F1.

By default, the items in the Members list are sorted alphabetically as shown in the figure. However, you can sort the members by type by right-clicking in the list and choosing the Group Members command from the shortcut menu that's displayed.

The Object Browser with the classes in the VB library displayed

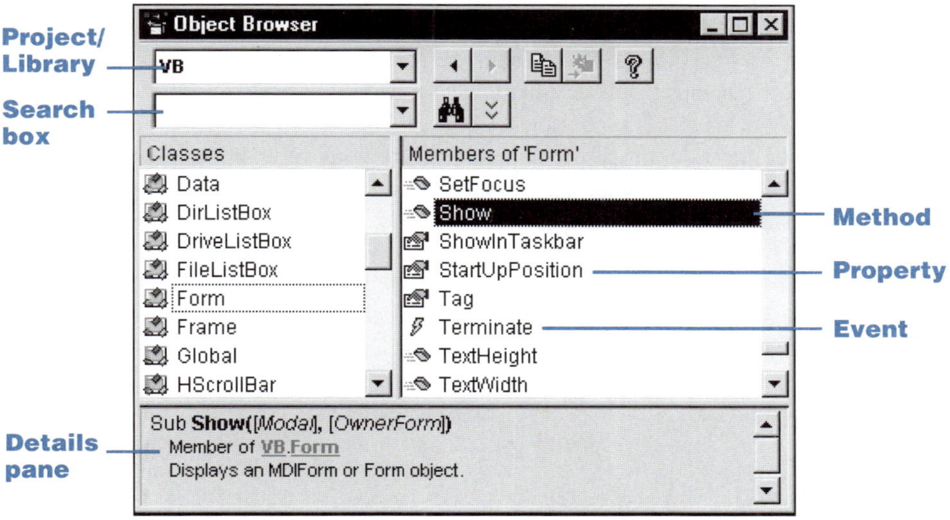

Description

- The Object Browser lets you display the objects, properties, methods, and events that are available to your application. To display the Object Browser, select the Object Browser command from the View menu or click on the Object Browser toolbar button.
- The classes that are available to an application are organized into *class libraries*. You can use the Project/Library drop-down list to choose the class library you want to display. For instance, the Visual Basic class library is shown above. This list also contains a reference to the current project.
- The Classes list displays all the classes that are available from the currently selected class library. You can select a class to display its *members*.
- The Members list contains all of the properties, methods, events, and constants that make up the currently selected class. These items can be listed alphabetically, as shown above, or they can be grouped by type using the shortcut menu. The icon to the left of each object indicates the type of object.
- The Details pane shows the definition and a description of the selected class or member. To get additional help on a selected class or member, click on the Help button or press F1.
- You can use the Search text box to search for classes or members that contain the text you enter. To run the search operation, click on the Search button or press the Enter key. The Show/Hide Search Results button lets you display or hide the results of the search.

Figure 3-13 How to use the Object Browser

How to test and debug an application

When you develop a Visual Basic application, it's a good practice to test and debug the code each time you add a new procedure or a few related procedures. Figure 3-14 shows how. Then, when you're sure that those procedures work correctly, you code a few more procedures.

As you enter the code for a procedure and before you test it, Visual Basic checks the syntax for each statement and displays a dialog box when it detects an error. This type of error is illustrated by the first dialog box in figure 3-14, and it is called a *compile-time error*. You correct this type of error as you enter code.

When you're ready to test the new procedures that you've added to the application, you start the test run by pressing F5 or using one of the other methods summarized in the figure. Visual Basic then compiles and tests the application one statement at a time. If it detects an error when it compiles a statement, a dialog box for a compile-time error is displayed. If it detects an error when it runs the compiled statement, a dialog box for a *run-time error* is displayed. This type of error is illustrated by the second dialog box in figure 3-14.

When you click on the Debug button in the dialog box for some types of run-time errors, Visual Basic switches you to the Code window and highlights the statement that couldn't be executed. This helps you figure out what the problem is so you can correct it. All too frequently, though, the message in the dialog box is of little or no help; the help information you can get by clicking on the Help button doesn't help; and the highlighted statement isn't even the statement that needs to be corrected.

Beyond that, many programming errors are logical errors that don't show up as run-time errors. You have to find and correct those errors yourself when you realize that the program isn't working the way it's supposed to. Visual Basic provides a variety of tools for locating these types of errors, though, and you can learn how to use them in chapter 9.

A dialog box for a compile-time error

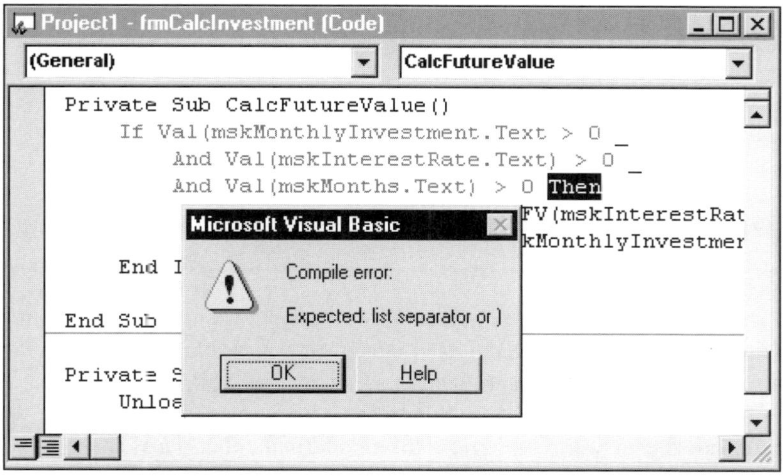

A dialog box for a run-time error

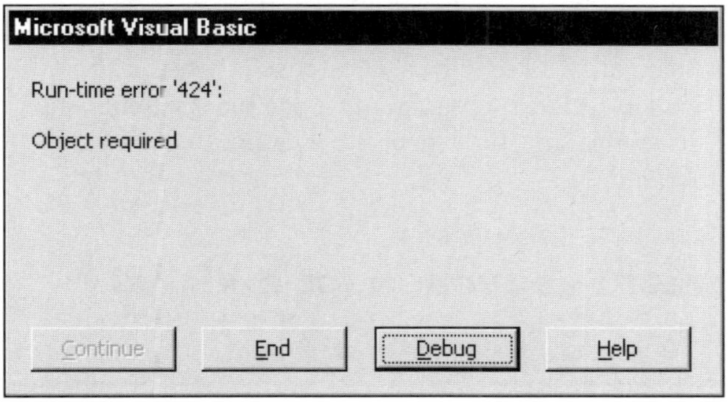

Description

- As you enter a statement, the syntax of that statement is checked. If an error is detected, a dialog box like the first one above is displayed so you can correct the error right away. This is one type of *compile, or compile-time, error.*
- To test an application, you can press the F5 key, click on the Start button in the toolbar, or choose Start from the Run menu. This compiles and tests the application one statement at a time. This can lead to either a compile-time or a *run-time error*. When an error is detected, an appropriate dialog box is displayed.
- When a run-time error is detected, a dialog box like the second one above is displayed. This means that the statement compiled okay, but an error occurred when the statement was executed. Then, if you click on the Debug button, you are switched to the statement that caused the error.

Figure 3-14 How to test and debug an application

How Visual Basic programming differs from traditional programming

Now that you've been introduced to Visual Basic programming, you can reflect upon how it differs from traditional programming.

What's different about Visual Basic programming

Figure 3-15 summarizes some of the obvious differences between Visual Basic and a traditional business language like COBOL. Perhaps most noticeable is that a Visual Basic application consists of many short procedures that are initiated by user events, while a typical COBOL program consists of hundreds of lines of code that are controlled by a top-down programming logic. This should make the Visual Basic application easier to code, debug, and maintain.

As the number of procedures in a Visual Basic application grows, however, it becomes more and more difficult to debug and maintain the application. In addition, the syntax of an object-oriented language like Visual Basic is essentially more complicated than the syntax of a language like COBOL. As a result, Visual Basic programming is at least as difficult as COBOL programming, and the reliability and maintainability of a Visual Basic application still depends to a large extent on the knowledge and skills of the programmer.

A typical development sequence for a Visual Basic programmer

Due to the nature of Visual Basic, the way an application developer works is different from the way a COBOL programmer works. This is summarized in the second portion of figure 3-15. Instead of separating the design, coding, and debugging phases of application development, a Visual Basic developer can easily overlap these phases. This encourages prototyping, which can improve communications with the eventual users of the application. This also encourages the coding, testing, and debugging of a few procedures at a time, which can reduce debugging problems and improve programmer productivity.

The downside of this working style is that it encourages a lack of planning and discipline that can cause problems later on. Before you can develop an effective Visual Basic application, for example, you need to (1) plan the database tables and relationships, (2) plan the user interface including the flow of the application from one form to another, (3) agree on naming conventions for forms, controls, data objects, and general procedures, and (4) plan the general procedures that are going to be available to all programmers. If you skip planning steps like these, your applications are likely to be just as difficult to code, debug, and maintain as traditional applications.

What's different about Visual Basic programming

- The Visual Basic language consists of a syntax and statements just like any other programming language. In addition to those statements, though, you can use the methods of any of the objects to perform functions. This, in effect, adds a large, variable number of verbs to the language, and it's relatively difficult to find out what those methods are and what they do.
- When you work with an object-oriented language like Visual Basic, you need to start thinking in terms of objects first, methods and properties later. If, for example, you want to move the focus to a control, you first identify the object, then use its SetFocus method (if it has one).
- A Visual Basic application consists of many, relatively short, event procedures, and many of those are started by a user event like clicking on a command button or pressing the Tab key to move to the next control. These event procedures are relatively easy to code, debug, and maintain.
- Much of the business processing of an application is done in general procedures that are called by event procedures or other general procedures. As the number of general procedures and the number of relationships between these procedures grows, the application becomes more and more difficult to code, debug, and maintain.
- The development environment for Visual Basic 5 tends to blur the lines between design, coding, and testing so you don't design the entire application, code it, and then test it. Instead, you're likely to design, code, and test one part of an application at a time. Although this is an excellent way to prototype an application, it also encourages a lack of planning and discipline that can lead to reliability and maintenance problems later on.

A typical development sequence for a Visual Basic programmer

1. Design the first form for the application by adding the required controls to it.
2. Set the properties for the form and its controls so they work the way you want them to.
3. Write the code for a few procedures, test the form, and correct any errors. Then, do the same for a few more procedures. Continue in this way until the form is fully tested and debugged.
4. Add the other forms to the application in this same general way, including the procedures that move the user from one form to another.
5. Add the reports that are going to be prepared by the application.
6. Add a startup form, toolbars, menus, and help information to the application.
7. Test and debug the entire application.

Figure 3-15 How Visual Basic programming differs from traditional programming

Perspective

If you haven't used an object-oriented programming language before, this chapter may have been somewhat overwhelming. If so, you may want to read it again before going on to your next chapter. Better yet, you should try to develop the Calculate Investment application that's described in this chapter. Although that may take an hour or two, it will give you a clear idea of what it takes to design, code, and test a Visual Basic application.

Remember, though, that a client/server application processes data that's stored in a database on a server. As a result, the Calculate Investment application is a Visual Basic application, but not a client/server application. To develop a client/server application, you need some additional skills, and the next chapter introduces you to those skills. When you complete it, you'll be able to develop your first client/server application.

Chapter 4

Introduction to database programming

In chapter 3, you learned how to develop a Visual Basic application that uses the properties and methods for form and control objects. When you develop a client/server application, though, you also need to use the properties and methods of data objects. These objects let you access and maintain the data that's stored in the database on a server. In this chapter, you'll learn how to work with these objects, properties, and methods, and you'll learn how to do the database programming for a simple client/server application.

When you complete this chapter, you should be able to develop simple client/server applications of your own. In fact, you should take the time to develop an application like the one that's illustrated in this chapter. That will give you a better idea of what database programming is and what you need to know to become proficient at it. Then, the remaining chapters in this book will help you develop that proficiency.

How to work with DAO

Visual Basic provides several different methods for working with a database. These methods are summarized at the end of this chapter. The most commonly-used method, though, is DAO, and that's the method that's presented in this chapter.

The Data Access Object model

Figure 4-1 presents the basic structure of the Data Access Object (*DAO*) model. This object model defines a hierarchy of data objects that you can use to interact with the data in a database. When you open a database, for example, a Database object is created within the specified Workspace object. And when you create a result set from a database, a recordset object is created within the specified Database object.

Like the form and control objects that you're already familiar with, data objects define properties and methods that you can use for working with them. That means that you can use the same object syntax that you use for working with forms and controls to work with data objects like tables and fields. Note, however, that none of the objects in the DAO model define events.

A *collection* in this model is just two or more of the same type of object. In the DAO model in figure 4-1, all of the plural objects can be collections. For instance, there can be a collection of TableDefs (tables) within a database, and there can be a collection of fields within a table. In chapter 5, you'll see some special coding techniques that can be used with collections.

Recordset is the DAO term for a result set, and a *recordset object* is the way the Jet engine implements a *cursor*. As you may remember from chapter 2, a cursor is used to identify and scroll through the records in a result set. When you use DAO, you use a recordset object to perform these functions.

To work with the objects in the Data Access Object model, you can use two different techniques. First, you can work with data objects by using a special control that you add to a form called a *data control*. Because the most common data processing functions are built into the data control, it provides a quick and easy way to develop simple forms that process data. Second, you can work with data objects through program code that uses the properties and methods of those objects. This technique gives you more direct control over the data processing that occurs in an application. In this chapter, you'll learn how to use both techniques.

Some of the objects in the Data Access Object model

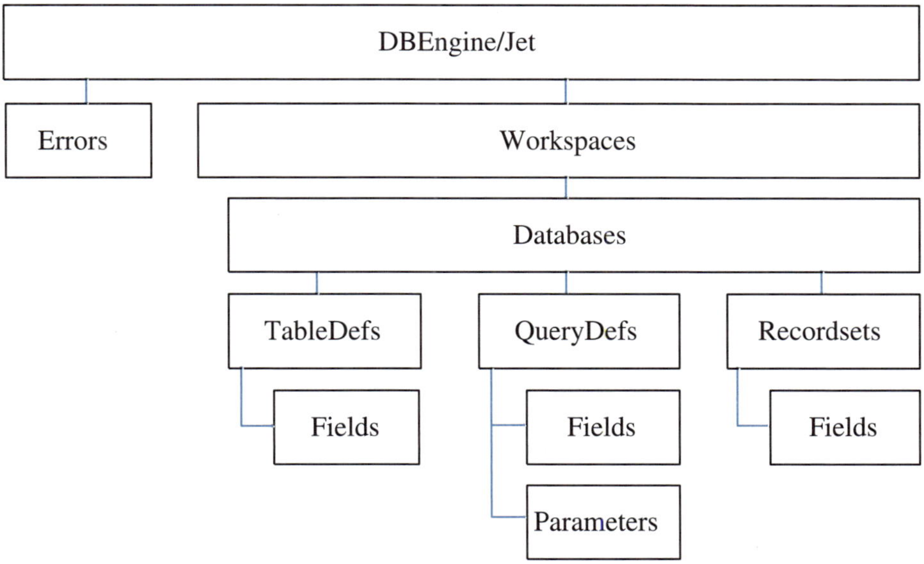

Concepts

- The Data Access Object (DAO) model consists of a variety of *collections* and objects. A collection is simply a set of objects of the same type. Some of the most common objects and collections are shown above.
- At the top of the DAO model is the DBEngine object, which represents the Jet engine. All data processing requests that use DAO go through the Jet engine.
- The Errors collection contains information about data access errors related to the most recent DAO operation. You can use the objects in this collection to determine what errors occurred.
- A Workspace object defines a session for a user and contains the databases used during that session.
- A Database object represents an open database and lets you work with the objects in that database. The objects you'll work with most often are tables, represented by TableDef objects; queries, represented by QueryDef objects; and cursors, represented by Recordset objects.
- The DAO model lets you access a database using an object-oriented interface. That means that you can use the same syntax to access data objects like tables and fields that you use to access application objects like forms and controls. The DAO model also provides a variety of properties and methods for working with the data access objects.
- You can work with data access objects directly by using program code. You can also work with data access objects by using the built-in functionality of a special control called a *data control.*

Figure 4-1 The Data Access Object model

Common DAO methods

Figure 4-2 presents the DAO methods that you're most likely to use in an application. As you can see, some of these methods can be used with several different objects. For instance, when you use the OpenRecordset method to create a new recordset, you can define the recordset based on a database, another recordset, a query, or a table.

The function of most of the methods shown in figure 4-2 should be relatively obvious. Three that may cause some confusion, however, are AddNew, Edit, and Update. All three of these methods work with a special buffer area called the *copy buffer*. The AddNew method, for example, doesn't add a record to the recordset as you might think. Instead, it clears the copy buffer so a new record can be added. Then, after the data for the new record is moved to the copy buffer, the Update method is used to save the new record to the recordset.

You use a similar technique to edit an existing record. First, you use the Edit method to copy the current record from the recordset to the copy buffer. Then, after you change the data for the record in the copy buffer, you use the Update method to save the edited record.

Even if you understand the function of the methods presented in figure 4-2, it may not be obvious when and how you use these methods. So, later in this chapter, you'll see how you can use some of these methods in an actual application. And you'll see additional examples in section 2 of this book.

Method	Object	Description
OpenDatabase	Workspace	Opens a database and returns a reference to the Database object.
OpenRecordset	Database Recordset QueryDef TableDef	Creates a new recordset and returns a reference to the Recordset object.
CreateQueryDef	Database	Creates a new query and returns a reference to the QueryDef object.
Execute	Database QueryDef	Executes a SQL statement or a QueryDef that contains a SQL statement.
AddNew	Recordset	Clears the copy buffer so a new record can be added.
Edit	Recordset	Copies the current record to the copy buffer for editing.
Update	Recordset	Saves the contents of the record in the copy buffer to the recordset object.
Delete	Recordset	Deletes the current record from a recordset.
MoveFirst MoveLast MovePrevious MoveNext	Recordset	Moves to the first, last, previous, or next record in the recordset.
FindFirst FindLast FindPrevious FindNext	Recordset	Finds the first, last, previous, or next record in the recordset that matches the criteria you specify and makes it the current record.
Requery	Recordset	Re-executes the query that a recordset is based on to reflect changes made to the underlying data.
Clone	Recordset	Creates a copy of the recordset. This can be useful if you need to maintain a current record pointer in two locations in the same recordset.
Close	Workspace Database Recordset QueryDef TableDef	Closes the object. If you don't close an object explicitly, it's closed automatically when the module that creates it is closed.

Figure 4-2 Common DAO methods

Common DAO properties

Figure 4-3 presents some of the most common DAO properties. As you can see, you won't work with nearly as many DAO properties as you will methods, and most of the properties you work with apply to Recordset objects. You'll see how to use a couple of these properties later in this chapter, and you'll see how to use others later in this book.

The BOF and EOF properties indicate whether you have reached the beginning or end of the recordset. When you use these properties, you should realize that they're not set to a True value until you try to move past the beginning or end of the recordset. If the current record pointer is on the last record in the recordset and you execute the MoveNext method, for example, the EOF property is set to True.

When the BOF or EOF property is True, the current record is undefined. Before you can continue processing the recordset, then, you have to move the current record pointer. If both the BOF and EOF properties are True, the recordset contains no records.

If you use the RecordCount property for a recordset, you should realize that it indicates the number of records in the recordset that have been accessed, not the total number of records in the recordset. When you first open a recordset, for example, the value of the RecordCount property will be 1 because only one record, the first record in the recordset, has been accessed. The only exception is if the recordset doesn't contain any records. In that case, the value of the RecordCount property is zero.

If you need to find out how many records are in the recordset, you can *populate* the recordset. The easiest way to do that is to use the MoveLast method to move to the last record in the recordset. Then, the RecordCount property will indicate the total number of records in the recordset. Keep in mind, however, that using the MoveLast method in a large file can be time-consuming, so you shouldn't use this method carelessly.

Property	Object	Description
Updatable	Database Recordset TableDef QueryDef	A true or false value that indicates if the object can be changed. For a recordset, this property determines if the records in the recordset can be changed.
AbsolutePosition	Recordset	The relative record number of the current record. The first record in a recordset has a relative record number of zero.
BOF EOF	Recordset	A true or false value that indicates whether or not the beginning or end of the recordset has been reached.
Bookmark	Recordset	Contains a value that uniquely identifies the current record.
EditMode	Recordset	A value that indicates if an editing operation is in progress and, if so, whether the Edit or AddNew method was invoked.
LastModified	Recordset	The bookmark of the last record that was added or modified.
LockEdits	Recordset	A true or false value that indicates whether pessimistic locking will be used. A false value indicates that optimistic locking will be used. This property is ignored if an ODBC database is being accessed.
NoMatch	Recordset	A true or false value that indicates if a Find operation was successful.
RecordCount	Recordset TableDef	The number of records that have been accessed in a recordset, or the total number of records in a table object.
DataUpdatable	Field	A true or false value that indicates if a field in a Recordset or QueryDef object can be updated.
SQL	QueryDef	Contains an SQL statement that defines the query that's executed by the QueryDef object.

Figure 4-3 Common DAO properties

How to build a form using a data control

Now that you understand the basics of working with data access objects, you'll learn how to build a form using a data control. First, you'll learn how to use a data control to process data. Next, you'll learn how to use the properties of the data control and bound controls as you work with data access objects. Then, you'll see the property settings and the actual code for a form that maintains records in a table of vendors. When you finish this topic, you should be able to create a simple maintenance form of your own.

How to use a data control to process data

Figure 4-4 shows how a *data control* is used for processing data. As you can see, the data control provides built-in functions for navigating through the records in the recordset defined by the data control and for displaying, adding, and updating the records in the recordset. That makes it easy to create a form that lets the user maintain records.

To display the individual fields in the recordset that's defined by a data control, you use *bound controls*. As the name implies, a bound control is bound to a specific field in the recordset. Each of the text boxes on the Vendors form in figure 4-4, for example, is bound to a field in the recordset defined by the data control shown at the bottom of the form. Then, when you use the data control to move to a different record in the recordset, the fields in the record are automatically displayed in the controls that are bound to those fields. And when you change the data in a bound control, the data is automatically saved to the recordset when you move to another record or close the form.

By default, a data control doesn't let the user add records to the recordset. To do that, you have to change the EOFAction property of the data control to Add New. Then, if the user clicks on the navigation button to move to the next record and the last record is already displayed, a new, blank record is added to the recordset and displayed on the form. When the user moves to another record or closes the form, the new record is saved to the recordset.

Because the delete function isn't built into a data control, the Vendors form in figure 4-4 includes a command button for this function. Then, an event procedure for the Click event of that command button must implement the function. Within that procedure, you use the Recordset property of the data control. When you use that property, you have access to all of the properties and methods of the Recordset object, including those shown in figures 4-2 and 4-3. In figure 4-4, for example, you can see the code that executes the Delete method of the Recordset property of the datVendors data control. In a moment, you'll see all the code for this event procedure.

You can also use the Recordset property to assign a recordset that you create through code to a data control. In most cases, though, there's no need to do that. You'll learn how to create a recordset through code without using a data control later in this chapter.

A form that uses a data control to maintain vendor records

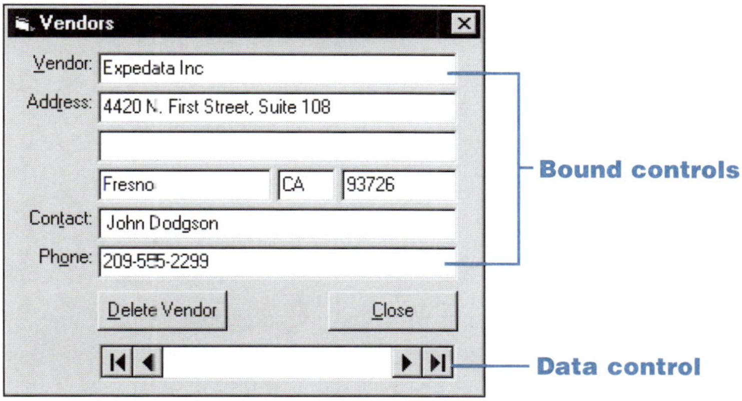

Code that deletes a record from the data source associated with a data control named datVendors

```
datVendors.Recordset.Delete
```

Description

- A *data control* defines the recordset for a form and provides functions for navigating, displaying, adding, and updating records. Because these functions are built into the data control, it isn't necessary to add code for these functions to the application.
- You can use *bound controls* to work with the fields in the current record of the recordset that's defined by a data control. Then, the field values are displayed automatically in the bound controls.
- A data control contains the four navigation buttons shown above. From left to right, these buttons let you move to the first, previous, next, and last records in the underlying recordset.
- You can also use the data control to add records to the recordset. To do that, just set the EOFAction property of the data control to Add New (see figure 4-5). Then, when the user clicks on the navigation button to move to the next record and the last record is already displayed, a new record is added.
- When the user clicks on one of the navigation buttons to move to another record, the current record is automatically updated if the data in any of the bound controls has been changed. The current record is also updated when the user closes the form.
- Some functions, like deleting records, aren't built into the data control. To provide for these functions, you use Visual Basic code. For instance, the statement above is executed when the user clicks on the Delete button in the form. This statement uses the Recordset property of the data control, which gives you access to all the properties and methods of the recordset object defined by the data control.

Figure 4-4 How to use a data control to process data

Data control and bound control properties

Figure 4-5 presents the properties that you'll work with when you use a data control and bound controls. The data control properties define the database and recordset you want to access as well as some of the properties of the Recordset object. The bound control properties identify the field that the control is bound to.

The Connect and DatabaseName properties of a data control identify the database you want to access. These properties are coded somewhat differently for an ODBC database than for other databases. For a Jet database, you just use the word *Access* as the Connect property, and you use the path and file name for the DatabaseName property.

For an ODBC database, the DatabaseName property gives the data source name (DSN) that defines the connection to the database. The Connect property consists of a string that identifies the database. This string includes the type of database (like ODBC) and the database name.

Before you can access an ODBC database, though, you must define a DSN for it. To do that, you can use the 32Bit ODBC program in the Windows Control Panel, or you can use one of the tools that come with Visual Basic. In chapter 10, for example, you'll learn how to create a DSN with the Visual Data Manager, which is similar to the procedure for creating a DSN from the Windows Control Panel.

Once you identify the database you're going to use, you use the RecordSource property of a data control to identify the recordset you want. If the recordset will contain all of the fields and records in a single table, the RecordSource property can simply be the name of the table. More likely, though, the RecordSource property will be the name of a view that's defined by an ODBC database, the name of a query for a Jet database, or an SQL SELECT statement that specifies the tables, fields, and records that you want to include in the recordset.

The RecordsetType property determines the type of recordset that's created. If you need to modify the data in the recordset, you need to create a *dynaset-type recordset* (or *dynaset*). Otherwise, you can create a *snapshot-type recordset* (or *snapshot*). If you're accessing a Jet database, you can also create a *table-type recordset*. This type of recordset lets you modify the data in a single Jet table.

After you set the data properties of the data control, you can create the bound controls for the form. For each control, you use the DataSource and DataField properties to identify the data control and the field in the recordset that you want to bind to the control. That's easy to do once you've got the data control set up properly.

The data properties of the data control

Property	Description
Connect	For an ODBC database, a connect string that identifies the database. The string can include the type of database (ODBC), the database name, the user id, and the user password. For a Jet database, use the Access option.
DatabaseName	For an ODBC database, a data source name that identifies the connection to the database. For a Jet database, use the complete path and file name for the file.
RecordSource	Identifies the fields and records to be retrieved from the underlying database. For an ODBC database, this can be a table, view, or SQL SELECT statement. For a Jet database, this can be a table, query, or SELECT statement.
RecordsetType	Determines the type of recordset to be created. Use Dynaset if you want to be able to modify the records in the recordset; use Snapshot if you want a static set of records that can't be modified. You can also use Table to modify the records in a single Jet table.
Exclusive	Determines whether the database can be accessed by other users.
ReadOnly	Determines whether the data in the database can be changed.
Options	Specifies the characteristics of the recordset object to be opened. See the help information for a complete list of acceptable values.
EOFAction	Determines what happens when the user tries to move to the next record when the last record is already displayed.
BOFAction	Determines what happens when the user tries to move to the previous record when the first record is already displayed.

The data properties of a text box that's bound to a data control

Property	Description
DataSource	Identifies the data control that defines the recordset you want the control bound to.
DataField	Identifies the field in the recordset that you want the control bound to.

Note

- You can also bind other Visual Basic controls, like a list box, combo box, or check box, to a data source using the DataSource and DataField properties.

Figure 4-5 Data control and bound control properties

Property settings for the bound version of the Vendors form

Figure 4-6 presents the critical property settings for the bound version of the Vendors form in figure 4-4. Here, the Connect property indicates that an ODBC database named AccountsPayable is being accessed, and the DatabaseName property indicates that the data source name is also AccountsPayable.

In the RecordSource property, you can see the name of the table that's going to be used by this application (*dbo* is a prefix used by SQL Server to indicate that this is a database object.) Once you specify the Connect and DatabaseName properties, you can drop down the list for the RecordSource property to display the names of all of the tables in the database. This list will also include any views that are defined by the database. If a password isn't included in the Connect property, though, SQL Server displays a dialog box that asks you for logon information (user id and password) when you drop down the list. That's part of the security that SQL Server provides.

Because you need to be able to modify the data in the recordset, the RecordsetType property in this figure is set to Dynaset (this is the default). Also, the Options property is changed from its default value of zero to the value 512. Because the Vendors table contains an identity field and because the application will modify this table, this option is required. To get a full listing of the acceptable options, you can look up the Options property in the online help information or in the Visual Basic Language Reference manual.

In contrast to the property settings for a SQL Server database, the settings for an Access (or Jet) database are relatively simple, and you don't have to create a data source name for the database before you use it. For the Connect property, you use the word Access. For the DatabaseName property, you use the complete path and file name. For the RecordSource property, you can drop down the list and select the table you want to work with, or you can enter the name of a query or the text of an SQL statement. And you can leave the other properties at their default settings.

Once you've defined the data properties for a data control, you can set the Name property to an appropriate name starting with the prefix *dat* like datVendors. Then, you can bind all of the text boxes on the Vendors form to the fields in the recordset that is defined by the data control.

To bind a text box control, you set its DataSource property to the name of the data control, datVendors. Then, you can drop down the list for the DataField property and select the name of the field that the control should be bound to. The text box that contains the vendor name, for example, should be bound to the field named VendorName, and the text box that contains the name of the contact person should be bound to the field named VendorContact.

The data properties for the data control on the Vendors form

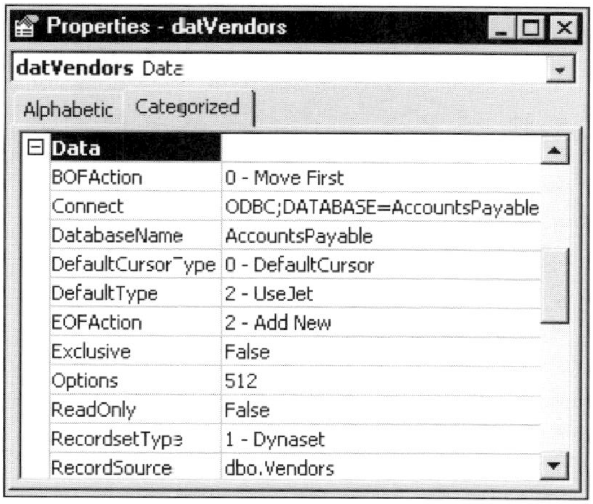

The property settings for an ODBC database (shown above)

- The Connect property specifies an ODBC database named AccountsPayable as shown above. This property can also include a user id and password using this format:

```
ODBC;DATABASE=AccountsPayable;UID=id;PWD=password
```

- The RecordSource property specifies that the source of data for the data control is the Vendors table. The RecordsetType property is set to Dynaset, which allows the records in the recordset to be updated.
- The BOFAction property is set to MoveFirst, which means that the focus will stay on the first record if the user tries to move past the beginning of the recordset. The EOFAction property is set to Add New, which means that a new record will be added if the user tries to move past the end of the recordset.
- The Options property is set to 512. This option causes an error to be generated if another user is editing the same data. This option is required for tables that have an identity field (a field that contains a number generated by the database engine).
- The DefaultType and DefaultCursorType properties determine the type of workspace and cursor to be used. You need to change these properties only if you're accessing data with a method called *ODBCDirect* (see figure 4-15).
- All of the text boxes on the Vendors form are bound to the data control shown above through the DataSource property of the control. Then, each control is bound to a different field in the data source through the DataField property.

The changes in the property settings for a Jet database

- The Connect property is Access; the DatabaseName property is the complete path for the file; the RecordSource property is the Vendors table; and the Options property is the default value (0).

Figure 4-6 Property settings for the bound version of the Vendors form

Code for the bound version of the Vendors form

Figure 4-7 presents the code for the bound version of the Vendors form. As you can see, the code consists of two event procedures that provide functions for deleting a record from the recordset and unloading the form. These are the only two functions that aren't provided by the data control.

The first event procedure is executed when the user clicks on the Delete command button. This procedure starts by using the MsgBox function to display a dialog box to confirm that the current record should be deleted. If the user confirms the delete operation by clicking on the Yes button, the Delete method is used to delete the record. Then, the MoveNext method is used to move to the next record in the recordset so the deleted record is no longer displayed on the form.

After the MoveNext method is executed, the EOF property of the recordset is checked to be sure that the current record pointer hasn't been moved beyond the end of the recordset. That would happen if the last record in the recordset were deleted. In that case, the MoveLast method is used to move to the last record in the recordset (the one before the deleted record). After the record pointer is moved, the SetFocus method is used to move the focus to the control named txtVendor, which is the first modifiable control on the form.

Because the Delete method deletes the current record, a user can cause problems by clicking on the Delete command button while entering a new record. That's because the new record hasn't actually been added to the recordset yet. As a result, the current record pointer is still positioned on the record that was displayed before the new record was started. And that's the record that's deleted when the Delete button is clicked. In the next topic, you'll see how you can avoid this problem by disabling the Delete button while a record is being added.

The second procedure in figure 4-7 is the one for the Click event of the Close command button. Like the procedure in chapter 3, this one just unloads the current form and issues the End statement to release the resources used by the application.

If you have any trouble following the code in these procedures, many of your questions will be answered when you read chapter 5. There, you'll get detailed information about the syntax of the Visual Basic language, the use of Visual Basic functions like the MsgBox function, and the use of Visual Basic statements like the Dim and If statements. What's important now is that you understand the use of the data objects, properties, and methods.

Visual Basic code for the bound Vendors form

1

```
Private Sub cmdDelete_Click()
    Dim strResponse As String
    strResponse = MsgBox("Are you sure you want to" _
        & " delete this record?", _
        vbYesNo + vbDefaultButton2, _
        "Delete Confirmation")
    If strResponse = vbYes Then
        datVendors.Recordset.Delete
        datVendors.Recordset.MoveNext
        If datVendors.Recordset.EOF Then
           datVendors.Recordset.MoveLast
        End If
        txtVendor.SetFocus
    End If
End Sub
```

2

```
Private Sub cmdClose_Click()
    Unload frmVendors
    End
End Sub
```

Notes

- The Dim statement is used to define variables. In the example above, it defines a string variable named *strResponse*.
- The MsgBox function displays a dialog box and receives a response from the user. In the example above, this function displays "Are you sure you want to delete this record?" in the dialog box; it offers Yes and No command buttons for the user's response (vbYesNo); it places the focus on the No button (vbDefaultButton2) so pressing the Enter key activates this button; it displays "Delete Confirmation" as the title of the dialog box; and it returns the value of the user's response to the variable named *strResponse*.
- The words that start with *vb* are Visual Basic constants. For instance, vbYes represents the value of a Yes response.
- In chapter 5, you can learn more about the use of variables, constants, functions, and the Visual Basic statements that are used in this chapter. Until then, you should focus on the use of DAO objects, properties, and methods.

Figure 4-7 Code for the bound version of the Vendors form

How to build a form without using a data control

The trouble with a data control is that its built-in functions limit the way the user interface works. To get around these limitations, though, you can build a form without using a data control. Then, you can code all the functions of the user interface so it works just the way you want it to. When you complete this topic, you should be able to create simple forms of your own without using a data control.

How to process data without using a data control

When a form doesn't use a data control, it can be referred to as an *unbound form*. When you create an unbound form, you use Visual Basic code for all the functions that are required. That means you have to use code to provide the functions that are automatically supplied by the data control. Before you can do that, though, you have to add a reference to the Microsoft DAO 3.5 object library so that you have access to all of the objects, properties, and methods in the DAO object model. To do that, select the References command from the Project menu and add a check mark to this option. (This reference is included in a project automatically when you add a data control to a form.)

Figure 4-8 lists the basic functions that the code has to provide for when you don't use a data control. It also indicates what methods and statements you use to perform these functions and when each of these functions is performed by a data control. Later in this chapter, when I show you how the sample form works, you'll see how these functions are actually implemented.

Figure 4-8 also shows you the basic techniques for working with a recordset when using code. The main point here is that you use *object variables* to refer to the database and recordset that the program accesses. An object variable is a special type of variable that holds a reference to an object.

To declare an object variable, you can use the Dim statement. In the first example in this figure, the Dim statement defines a Database object named dbAP and a Recordset object named recVendors.

After you declare an object variable, you use the Set statement to assign an object reference to the variable. In the example in this figure, two Set statements are used. The first one uses the OpenDatabase method to open the AccountsPayable database and assign its reference to the database variable named dbAP. If you refer back to figure 4-2, you can see that OpenDatabase is a method of the Workspace object. Since the name of the workspace object is omitted from this statement, the default workspace is used.

The second Set statement in this figure uses the OpenRecordset method to open the Vendors table. As you can see, this method is executed from the object variable dbAP, which represents the Database object.

Data control functions you must provide through code

Function	Method or statement	When it's executed by a data control
Open database	OpenDatabase method	Before the form is displayed.
Open recordset	OpenRecordset method	Before the form is displayed.
Recordset navigation	MoveFirst, MovePrevious, MoveNext, and MoveLast methods	When the user clicks on a navigation button.
Move values from fields to controls	Assignment statements	When the current record pointer is repositioned.
Clear control values	Assignment statements	Before a new record is entered.
Start a new record, move values from controls to record buffer, and update the recordset	AddNew method, assignment statements, Update method	When the user accepts a new record.
Move values from controls to record buffer, and update the recordset	Edit method, assignment statements, Update method	When the user accepts changes to an existing record.

Code that opens an ODBC database and creates a recordset

```
Dim dbAP As Database, recVendors As Recordset
Set dbAP = OpenDatabase("AccountsPayable", 0, 0, _
    "ODBC;DATABASE=AccountsPayable")
Set recVendors = dbAP.OpenRecordset("Vendors", _
    dbOpenDynaset)
```

Code that saves changes to the current record

```
recVendors.Update
```

Description

- When you use code to process data, you must provide for the same functions that are provided by the data control. That includes opening the database and recordset, navigating through and displaying the records in the recordset, adding new records to the recordset, and updating existing records.
- To define an *object variable*, you use the Dim statement as shown in the first example. Then, to assign a database or recordset to an object variable, you use a Set statement with the OpenDatabase or OpenRecordset method. After that, you can use those variables to refer to the properties and methods of the objects. To save changes to the current record in a recordset, for example, you use the Update method of the Recordset object as shown in the second example.

Figure 4-8 How to process data without using a data control

Once you open the recordset and assign its reference to an object variable, you can refer to the properties and methods of the Recordset object through the object variable. This is illustrated by the second example in this figure, which uses the Update method of the Recordset object. All of this will make more sense when you see the code for an entire application in figure 4-13.

How to use the OpenDatabase method

Figure 4-9 presents the syntax of the OpenDatabase method. You use this method to open a database in a workspace and return a reference to the database. The reference is stored in the object variable that's specified in the Set statement.

Although OpenDatabase is a method of a Workspace object, you don't usually need to specify the workspace when you use this method. If you omit the workspace as shown in the examples in this figure, the default workspace is used. This workspace is created automatically the first time you refer to one of its properties or methods. Although you can create additional workspaces, that's usually not necessary.

You can also code several arguments on the OpenDatabase method. Two of these arguments identify the database and provide connection information. The other two arguments determine whether the database will be opened for shared or exclusive use and whether the database will be opened for read-only or read/write access. Note that if you code a value for one argument, you must code a value for all preceding arguments.

In the first coding example in this figure, True is specified for the read-only argument. When you include this argument, you also have to include the options argument, which in this example is set to False so the database can be shared with other users.

In the second example, the connect argument includes a user id and password. Often, you will want to include these arguments while you're testing an application so you don't have to supply them each time you connect to a database. When you're ready to deploy the application, though, you'll probably want to remove these arguments so each user must enter an acceptable id and password before accessing the database.

In the third example in this figure, you can see a simple Set statement that provides the connection to a Jet database. Here, the name argument consists of the path and file name for the Access database.

The syntax of the OpenDatabase method

```
Set database = [workspace.]OpenDatabase(name, options,
    read-only, connect)
```

Argument	Description
database	The name of the object variable that represents the database you're opening.
workspace	The name of the object variable that represents the Workspace object that will contain the database. You can omit this variable if you want to use the default workspace.
name	For an ODBC database, a string that gives the data source name (DSN) of an ODBC data source. For a Jet database, a string that gives the full path and file name for the database.
options	Indicates whether the database is opened for exclusive use or shared use. For shared use, specify False or 0. For exclusive use, specify True or a non-zero value.
read-only	Indicates whether or not the database is opened with read-only access. Specify False or 0 for read/write access. Specify True or a non-zero value for read-only access.
connect	For an ODBC database, a string that gives the connection information, including the type of database, the database name, a user-id, and a password.

A statement that opens an ODBC database for shared use with read-only access

```
Set dbAP = OpenDatabase("AccountsPayable", False, True, _
    "ODBC;DATABASE=AccountsPayable")
```

A statement that includes a user-id and password in the connect argument

```
Set dbAP = OpenDatabase("AccountsPayable", 0, 0, _
    "ODBC;DATABASE=AccountsPayable;UID=sa;PWD=password")
```

A statement that opens a Jet database

```
Set dbAP = OpenDatabase("c:\Access\Payables.mdb")
```

Notes

- If the connect argument is specified on the OpenDatabase method, you must code values for the options and read-only arguments.
- You'll typically use Workspace objects other than the default when you want to create an ODBCDirect workspace.

Figure 4-9 How to use the OpenDatabase method

How to use the OpenRecordset method

Figure 4-10 presents the syntax of the OpenRecordset method. You use this method to open a recordset from a Database, QueryDef, TableDef, or another Recordset object. For a Database object, you include the source argument to indicate the table, view, or SELECT statement you want to use to create the recordset. For a QueryDef, TableDef, or Recordset object, the recordset is created from the object you specify so the source argument isn't required.

The type argument of the OpenRecordset method indicates the type of recordset you want to open. For an ODBC data source, the default is a dynaset-type recordset. Although this type of recordset provides the greatest functionality, it's usually the least efficient.

If you don't need to add, delete, or change records in the recordset, you may want to use a snapshot-type or forward-only-type recordset. With a snapshot-type recordset, you can still use all of the move and find methods for moving the current record pointer. With a forward-only-type recordset, you can only use the Move and Move Next methods.

For the options argument, you can specify a variety of constants that specify characteristics of the recordset object you're creating. Most of these options don't apply to data retrieved from an ODBC data source. If you're creating a dynaset-type recordset that includes an identity column, though, you need to specify the dbSeeChanges option so the program will know when another user is changing the same data. And if you want to send a pass-through query to an ODBC data source (see chapter 7), you need to use the dbSQLPassThrough option.

The lockedits argument determines what type of locking is used for the recordset. If you specify dbReadOnly, the data in the recordset can't be changed, so locking isn't necessary. If you're accessing an ODBC data source, the dbOptimistic and dbPessimistic options have no effect since Jet has no control over the locking in an external database.

The first example in figure 4-10 shows how to use the OpenRecordset method with a Database object. Here, a SELECT statement that's assigned to a string variable is used for the source argument. The other arguments indicate that a dynaset-type recordset will be created and optimistic locking will be used.

The second example shows how to use the OpenRecordset method with a QueryDef object. This statement creates a snapshot-type recordset using the SELECT statement that's stored in the QueryDef. You'll learn more about working with QueryDefs in chapter 6.

The syntax of the OpenRecordset method for Database objects

```
Set recordset = object.OpenRecordset(source, type,
    options, lockedits)
```

The syntax of the OpenRecordset method for QueryDef, Recordset, and TableDef objects

```
Set recordset = object.OpenRecordset(type, options,
    lockedits)
```

Argument	Description
recordset	The name of the object variable that represents the recordset you're opening.
object	The name of the object variable that represents the Database, QueryDef, Recordset, or TableDef object you want to create the recordset from.
source	A string that gives the table, view, or SQL SELECT statement that you want to use to create the recordset.
type	A constant that indicates the type of recordset you want to open. For an ODBC data source, the valid options are dbOpenDynaset, dbOpenSnapshot, and dbOpenForwardOnly.
options	One or more constants that specify the characteristics of the new recordset. The valid options are dbAppendOnly, dbSQLPassThrough, dbSeeChanges, dbDenyRead, dbDenyWrite, dbConsistent, and dbInconsistent.
lockedits	A constant that determines how a recordset is locked. The valid options are dbReadOnly, dbOptimistic, and dbPessimistic (the default). This option is ignored if an ODBC database is accessed. (If you code this argument, you must also include a value for the options argument as in the first example below.)

Statements that open a dynaset-type recordset with optimistic locking from a database named dbAP using a SELECT statement

```
strSQL = "SELECT * FROM Vendors ORDER BY VendorName"
Set recVendors = dbAP.OpenRecordset(strSQL, _
    dbOpenDynaset, 0, dbOptimistic)
```

A statement that opens a snapshot-type recordset from a QueryDef named qdfInvoices

```
Set recInvoices = qdfInvoices.OpenRecordset(dbOpenSnapshot)
```

Figure 4-10 How to use the OpenRecordset method

How to use a control array for the navigation functions

If two or more controls on a form perform similar functions, you may want to implement them as a *control array*. For instance, the command buttons that provide for scrolling through the records on an unbound maintenance form are perfect candidates for a control array. As you'll see in a minute, using a control array can simplify your code.

Figure 4-11 shows how to create and use a control array. To create an array, you just give two or more controls the same name. When you do that, Visual Basic assumes that you want to create an array and gives each control a different index number starting with zero. In this example, you can see that both command buttons are named cmdNavigate, but their Index properties have different values.

Although the controls in an array appear as individual controls on the form, they're treated as a group. That means that when you click on a command button in an array, an event occurs on the array, not on the individual control. However, the index value of the control that the event actually occurred on is passed to the event procedure. That way, you can use the index value within the procedure to determine what processing takes place. You'll soon see how to do that.

The properties for two controls in an array

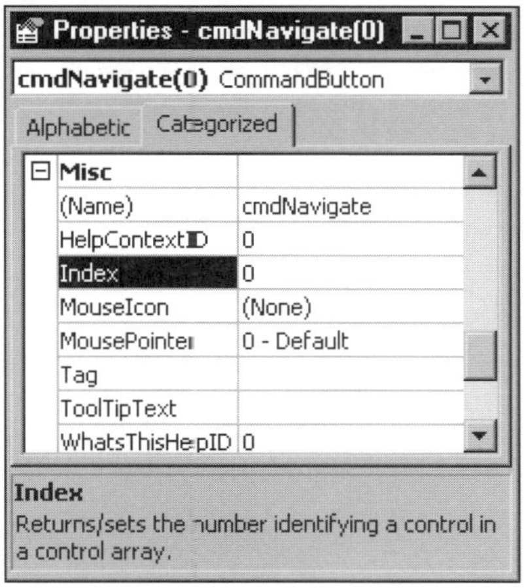

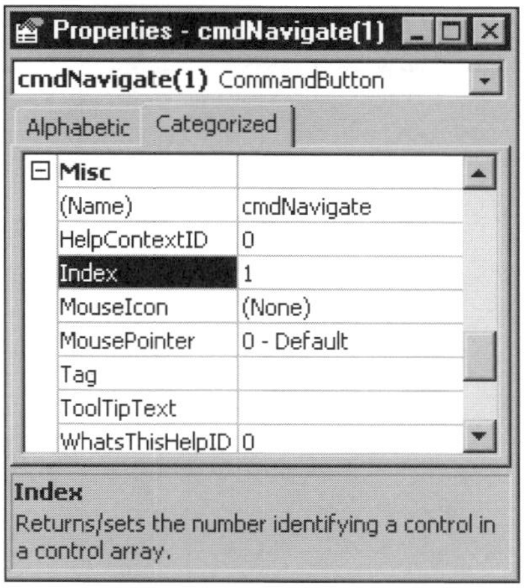

Description

- To create a control array, you add two or more controls of the same type to the form. Then, you change the names of the controls so they're all the same. When you change the name of the second control to match the first one, Visual Basic warns you that the form already contains a control with that name. If you continue with the name change, Visual Basic sets the Index property of the control so it's unique.
- To refer to a control in an array, you use the control name followed by its index number in parentheses, starting with zero for the first control in the array as in this example:

```
cmdNavigate(0)
```

- When you create a control array, the controls in the array are treated as a group. That means that you code a single event procedure for the entire array rather than coding an event procedure for each control in the array.
- When an event occurs on a control in an array, Visual Basic passes an argument to the event procedure that contains the index of the control that the event occurred on. Then, you can use that index to determine the processing that's done.
- The easiest way to test the value of an index in an event procedure is to use the Select Case statement. For a navigation procedure, you can use this statement to determine which Move method to use on the Recordset object.

Figure 4-11 How to use a control array for the navigation functions

How the unbound version of the Vendors form works

Figure 4-12 shows you what the unbound version of the Vendors form looks like and describes how it works. As you review this figure, you'll notice that the form provides some functions that weren't provided by the bound form. For example, the unbound form lets the user cancel out of an add or modify operation. It also displays an error message if the update of a new or existing record can't be done for any reason. Although you could probably figure out a way to implement these functions in a bound form, it wouldn't be easy.

To provide for navigation from one record to another, four command buttons at the bottom of this unbound form replace the data control of the bound form. These buttons are treated as a control array. Note, however, that they don't provide for the add and update functions that are built into a data control. Instead, these functions are implemented as separate command buttons on the form. That makes the form more intuitive for the user, and it simplifies the logic of the program.

To further improve the interface, the Add, Update, Delete, and navigation command buttons are enabled only when it makes sense. For example, the Update button isn't enabled in the form shown in the figure because none of the data in the form has been changed. As soon as the user changes any of this data, however, this button becomes available. By enabling and disabling these command buttons as the user works with the form, you limit what the user can do and maintain better control over the use of the form.

A form that uses code to maintain vendor records

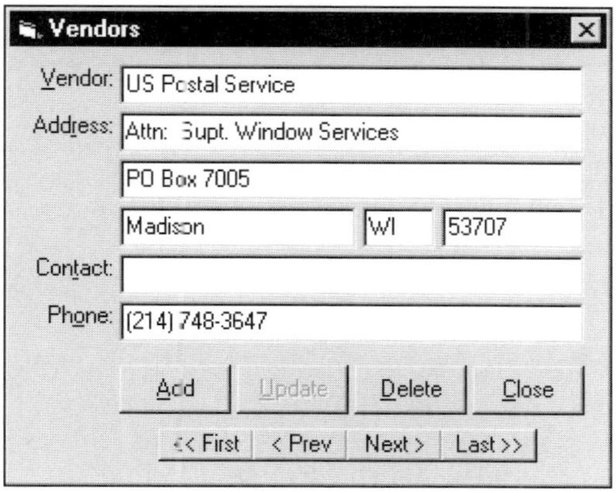

Description

- Unlike the bound version of the Vendors form, the navigation buttons in the unbound version shown above provide only for navigating through the recordset. They do not control the addition of new records or the updating of existing records.
- When an existing record is first displayed, the Update button is disabled as shown above. As soon as the user makes a change to the data in the form, however, the Update button is enabled and the Add button and all of the navigation buttons are disabled. To save the changes, the user must click on the Update button or press the Enter key to activate the Update button (it's set as the default). To cancel the changes, the user can press the Escape (Esc) key.
- When the user clicks on the Add button, the text boxes are cleared, the Update button is enabled, and the Add, Delete, and navigation buttons are disabled. After the data for the new record is entered into the form, the user can save the record by clicking on the Update button or pressing the Enter key. After the new record is saved, the controls are cleared so another new record can be added. To cancel the addition, the user can press the Esc key.
- If the user clicks on the Update button to add a new record or modify an existing record and all of the required fields in the record haven't been entered, a dialog box is displayed indicating that the record couldn't be saved. After acknowledging the error, the user can enter the required data and click on the Update button again or press the Esc key to cancel the operation.
- When the user presses the Delete key, a dialog box is displayed to confirm the delete operation. If the user confirms the operation, the record is deleted and the next record in the recordset is displayed.

Figure 4-12 How the unbound version of the Vendors form works

The events that control the logic of the Vendors form

The key to developing a form like the one in figure 4-12 is knowing what events you need to respond to and what processing needs to be done in response to those events. Figure 4-13 summarizes these events and the processing that they initiate.

Before the form can be displayed the first time, the program must open the database and recordset and display the current record on the form. These functions can be coded for the Load event of the form. This event occurs when the application starts.

The other events in this figure are started by user actions. When the user clicks on a navigation button, for example, the procedure moves the current record pointer to the record indicated by the navigation button and displays that record on the form. Since the controls on the form aren't bound to a data control, you have to provide the code for moving the data from the current record to the controls. Conversely, when the user changes the data in the controls, you have to provide for moving the data from the controls to the current record.

When the user clicks on the Update button or presses the Enter key, the current record is updated. To make this work correctly, you have to set the Default property of the Update button to True. That causes the Click event of the button to be executed when the user presses the Enter key.

When a user changes the data in one of the controls on the form, the Change event occurs on that control. To keep track of when a record has been changed, the Change event procedure changes the value of a variable that indicates that the record has been changed. Although it's not documented in this figure, this procedure should also enable the Update button on the form so the user can save the changes, disable the Delete button if a record is being added, and disable the navigation buttons.

If the user presses the Esc key, the current record is redisplayed. If a record was being edited, that record is the current record and it's redisplayed with its original values. If a record was being added, the current record is the record that was previously displayed, edited, or added.

The event that detects when the user has pressed the Esc key is the KeyDown event of the form. Within the event procedure for this event, the program can check to see what key was pressed and respond accordingly. In order to detect this event on the form object, though, the KeyPreview property of the form must be set to True. Otherwise, the event will occur on the control that has the focus.

The events that the Vendors form must respond to

Description

- Most of the logic of the Vendors form is controlled by the event procedures that are executed when the user clicks on a command button, changes the data in a form, or presses the Enter or Esc keys.
- The only other event procedure opens the database and recordset when the form is loaded.

Figure 4-13 The events that control the logic of the Vendors form

Code for the unbound version of the Vendors form

Figure 4-14 presents the complete code for the Vendors form. Although this code is five pages long, it's worth taking the time to understand every procedure in it. Once you understand it, you'll be able to start developing applications of your own.

If you have any trouble understanding this code, remember that chapter 5 gives detailed information about the syntax, functions, and statements of Visual Basic. So for now, your focus should be on the objects, properties, methods, and events that are used in this code.

The *Declarations section* of the form module (1) contains the definitions of four variables that are used throughout the form. The first two variables are used to refer to the Accounts Payable database and the Vendors recordset. The third variable is used to determine whether changes have been made to the current record. And the fourth variable is used to indicate whether a new record is being added to the recordset. These last two variables can be set to either True or False values.

In the event procedure for the Load event of the form (2), the database is opened and the recordset is created. Then, a procedure named LoadControls (3) is called, which moves the values from the fields in the current record in the recordset to the associated controls on the form. Here, the bang operator (!) is used to separate each field name in the record from the recordset object. This operator is typically used when referring to user-defined objects like fields.

Next, the Load procedure (2) calls another procedure named EnableNavigation (4), which enables all four of the navigation buttons. Then, the Load procedure calls a procedure named InitializeCommandButtons (5), which disables the Update button and enables the Add button. These procedures have to be called because the Change event occurs for each text box when the LoadControls procedure is executed, and the resulting Change event procedures (13) call other procedures that disable the navigation buttons and Add button and enable the Update button. As a result, the Load procedure has to reset these buttons to their initial state by calling the InitializeCommandButtons procedure. The last two statements in the Load procedure set the values of the blnRecordEdited and blnAddMode variables to False.

Visual Basic code for the unbound Vendors form Page 1

1

```
Option Explicit
Dim dbAP As Database
Dim recVendors As Recordset
Dim blnRecordEdited As Boolean
Dim blnAddMode As Boolean
```

2

```
Private Sub Form_Load()
    Set dbAP = OpenDatabase("AccountsPayable", 0, 0, _
      "ODBC;DATABASE=AccountsPayable")
    Set recVendors = dbAP.OpenRecordset("Vendors", _
      dbOpenDynaset, dbSeeChanges)
    LoadControls
    EnableNavigation
    InitializeCommandButtons
    blnRecordEdited = False
    blnAddMode = False
End Sub
```

3

```
Private Sub LoadControls()
    txtVendor = recVendors!VendorName
    txtAddress1 = recVendors!VendorAddress1
    txtAddress2 = recVendors!VendorAddress2
    txtCity = recVendors!VendorCity
    txtState = recVendors!VendorState
    txtZipCode = recVendors!VendorZipCode
    txtContact = recVendors!VendorContact
    txtPhone = recVendors!VendorPhone
End Sub
```

4

```
Private Sub EnableNavigation()
    cmdNavigate(0).Enabled = True
    cmdNavigate(1).Enabled = True
    cmdNavigate(2).Enabled = True
    cmdNavigate(3).Enabled = True
End Sub
```

5

```
Private Sub InitializeCommandButtons()
    cmdUpdate.Enabled = False
    cmdUpdate.Default = False
    cmdAdd.Enabled = True
    cmdDelete.Enabled = True
End Sub
```

Figure 4-14 Code for the unbound version of the Vendors form (part 1 of 5)

When the user clicks on a navigation button, the Click event procedure for the cmdNavigate control array (6) is executed. This procedure uses a Select Case statement to determine which button was clicked and then executes the appropriate Move method on the recordset. In this statement, each case provides for one index value for the array of navigation buttons. When the index value is zero, for example, that means that the user clicked on the First button so the MoveFirst method is executed. And when the index value is one, that means that the user clicked on the Prev button so the MovePrevious method is executed. But if that method moves the current record pointer to zero (the BOF property is True), the MoveFirst method is executed. In this way, the Select Case statement provides for all four buttons in the array.

After the Select Case statement repositions the current record pointer, the LoadControls procedure (3) is called to display the current record. Then, the EnableNavigation (4) and InitializeCommandButtons (5) procedures are called to reset the state of the command buttons; the blnRecordEdited variable is set to False to indicate that the current record hasn't been edited; and the focus is moved to the control named txtVendor, which is the first editable control on the form.

When the user clicks on the Add button, the Click event procedure for this control (7) is executed. This procedure starts by setting the blnAddMode variable to True to indicate that a record is going to be added to the recordset. Next, the ClearControls procedure (8) is called, which moves spaces to the controls on the form so that the user can enter the data for the new record into them. Then, the ChangeCommandButtons procedure (9) is called. This procedure enables the Update button so the user can update the record after entering the required data. It also disables the Add and Delete buttons.

Visual Basic code for the unbound Vendors form Page 2

6

```
Private Sub cmdNavigate_Click(Index As Integer)
    Select Case Index
        Case 0
            recVendors.MoveFirst
        Case 1
            recVendors.MovePrevious
            If recVendors.BOF = True Then
                recVendors.MoveFirst
            End If
        Case 2
            recVendors.MoveNext
            If recVendors.EOF = True Then
                recVendors.MoveLast
            End If
        Case 3
            recVendors.MoveLast
    End Select
    LoadControls
    EnableNavigation
    InitializeCommandButtons
    blnRecordEdited = False
    txtVendor.SetFocus
End Sub
```

7

```
Private Sub cmdAdd_Click()
    blnAddMode = True
    ClearControls
    ChangeCommandButtons
    txtVendor.SetFocus
End Sub
```

8

```
Private Sub ClearControls()
    txtVendor = ""
    txtAddress1 = ""
    txtAddress2 = ""
    txtCity = ""
    txtState = ""
    txtZipCode = ""
    txtContact = ""
    txtPhone = ""
End Sub
```

Figure 4-14 Code for the unbound version of the Vendors form (part 2 of 5)

When the user clicks on the Update button, the Click event procedure (10) for that button is executed. This is the most complicated procedure in the form. If you understand how the AddNew, Edit, and Update methods work, however, you shouldn't have too much trouble understanding this code.

The update procedure starts by using an On Error statement to enable an error-handling routine that's coded at the end of the update procedure. This routine will be executed any time an error occurs during the execution of the procedure. Although an error shouldn't occur, a professional business application should provide for that rare occasion when one does occur. Within the error-handling routine, the code uses two string variables and a MsgBox function that uses two Visual Basic constants. Because these language features are explained in detail in chapter 5, please don't worry if you don't understand this code right now.

After the On Error statement, the update procedure checks the blnAddMode variable to determine if a record is being added or edited. If this variable is True, the AddNew method is executed to clear the copy buffer. If this variable is False, the Edit method is used to copy the current record in the recordset to the copy buffer. After this If statement, the LoadBuffer procedure (11) is executed, which moves the values from the form controls to the copy buffer.

If you study the code in the LoadBuffer procedure (11), you may question why the statements refer to the fields in the recordset when the control values are supposed to be moved to the copy buffer, not the recordset. The explanation is that once the AddNew or Edit method is executed, any references to the fields in the current record in the recordset are actually made in the copy buffer. This continues until a statement is issued that resets or moves the current record pointer.

After the LoadBuffer procedure is executed, the Update method is used to save the record in the copy buffer to the recordset. Then, if a record was added, the update procedure sets the Bookmark property of the recordset to the LastModified property of the recordset. The LastModified property identifies the last record that was updated, in this case, the new record. By setting the Bookmark property to the LastModified property, the new record becomes the current record. That's necessary because after a new record is added to a recordset, the record that was current before the AddNew method was executed becomes current again. After the Bookmark property is set, the ClearControls procedure is called so another record can be added.

If a record was changed, the update procedure calls the EnableNavigation and InitializeCommandButtons procedures to change the state of the buttons on the form. Then, the blnRecordEdited variable is set to False. Notice that this procedure does not move the current record pointer. Although you could move to the next record in the recordset, it makes more sense in this case to leave the same record displayed and let the user decide what to do next.

The update procedure ends by moving the focus to the first editable field on the form. Then, the Exit Sub statement ends the procedure and prevents the error-handling routine that follows from being executed.

Visual Basic code for the unbound Vendors form   Page 3

9

```
Private Sub ChangeCommandButtons()
    cmdUpdate.Enabled = True
    cmdUpdate.Default = True
    cmdAdd.Enabled = False
    If blnAddMode = True Then
        cmdDelete.Enabled = False
    End If
End Sub
```

10

```
Private Sub cmdUpdate_Click()
    On Error GoTo UpdateError
    If blnAddMode = True Then
        recVendors.AddNew
    Else
        recVendors.Edit
    End If
    LoadBuffer
    recVendors.Update
    If blnAddMode = True Then
        recVendors.Bookmark = recVendors.LastModified
        ClearControls
    Else
        EnableNavigation
        InitializeCommandButtons
        blnRecordEdited = False
    End If
    txtVendor.SetFocus
    Exit Sub
UpdateError:
    Dim strMessage1 As String, strMessage2 As String
    strMessage1 = "The record could not be updated."
    strMessage2 = "Press Esc to cancel operation."
    MsgBox strMessage1 & vbCrLf & strMessage2, _
        vbOKOnly, "Update error"
    txtVendor.SetFocus
End Sub
```

11

```
Private Sub LoadBuffer()
    recVendors!VendorName = txtVendor
    recVendors!VendorAddress1 = txtAddress1
    recVendors!VendorAddress2 = txtAddress2
    recVendors!VendorCity = txtCity
    recVendors!VendorState = txtState
    recVendors!VendorZipCode = txtZipCode
    recVendors!VendorContact = txtContact
    recVendors!VendorPhone = txtPhone
End Sub
```

Figure 4-14 Code for the unbound version of the Vendors form (part 3 of 5)

When the user clicks on the Delete command button, the Click event procedure for the control (12) is executed. This procedure is similar to the event procedure you saw for the bound version of the Vendors form. It uses the MsgBox function to confirm the delete operation and executes the Delete method if it's confirmed. Then, it moves to the next record, checks the EOF property, and moves to the last record if this property is True. Finally, this procedure loads the form controls, initializes the navigation command buttons, sets the blnRecordEdited variable to False, and moves the focus to the first editable field on the form.

When the user changes any of the data in the text boxes on the form, the Change event procedure for the changed control is executed. Although only three of these procedures are shown in this figure (13), the complete code must include one Change procedure for each text box. Each procedure starts by checking the blnRecordEdited variable to see if any of the other fields have already been changed. If not, the ChangeCommandButtons and DisableNavigation procedures are executed and the blnRecordEdited variable is set to True. The DisableNavigation procedure (14) disables all of the command buttons so the user can't move to another record until the changes to the current record have been saved or canceled.

Visual Basic code for the unbound Vendors form Page 4

12

```
Private Sub cmdDelete_Click()
    Dim strResponse As String
    strResponse = MsgBox("Are you sure you want to " _
        & "delete this record?", _
        vbYesNo + vbDefaultButton2, "Delete Confirmation")
    If strResponse = vbYes Then
        recVendors.Delete
        recVendors.MoveNext
        If recVendors.EOF = True Then recVendors.MoveLast
        LoadControls
        EnableNavigation
        InitializeCommandButtons
        blnRecordEdited = False
        txtVendor.SetFocus
    End If
End Sub
```

13

```
Private Sub txtVendor_Change()
    If blnRecordEdited = False Then
        ChangeCommandButtons
        DisableNavigation
        blnRecordEdited = True
    End If
End Sub

Private Sub txtAddress1_Change()
    If blnRecordEdited = False Then
        ChangeCommandButtons
        DisableNavigation
        blnRecordEdited = True
    End If
End Sub
.
.
.
Private Sub txtPhone_Change()
    If blnRecordEdited = False Then
        ChangeCommandButtons
        DisableNavigation
        blnRecordEdited = True
    End If
End Sub
```

Figure 4-14 Code for the unbound version of the Vendors form (part 4 of 5)

Anytime the user presses a key, the KeyDown event procedure for the form (15) is executed. (Remember, the KeyPreview property of the form must be set to True for this to work properly.) This procedure checks to see if the Esc key was pressed, which indicates that the user wants to cancel the current operation. If this key was pressed, the LoadControls procedure is called to move the field values from the current record in the recordset to the controls on the form. If the user pressed the Esc key while adding a record, the last record that was displayed is redisplayed. If the user was modifying a record, that record is redisplayed with its original values.

Next, this procedure resets the state of the command buttons by calling the EnableNavigation and InitializeCommandButtons procedures. The last two statements in this procedure set the blnRecordEdited and blnAddMode variables to False.

The last event procedure (16) occurs when the users clicks on the Close button. This procedure unloads the form and releases the resources of the application.

Now that you've browsed through all the procedures in the program, you may want to review them to see how they work together. If you do, you'll find seven general procedures: LoadControls, LoadBuffer, ClearControls, EnableNavigation, DisableNavigation, InitializeCommandButtons, and ChangeCommandButtons. The name of each procedure is designed to give a clear indication of what each procedure does, and you need similar procedures whenever you develop a maintenance application.

The event procedures, of course, call the general procedures whenever they are needed. So once you code the general procedures, it's relatively easy to code most of the event procedures. The only difficult ones are those that use the DAO methods: the one for the Click event of the cmdNavigate array; the one for the Click event of the cmdUpdate button; and the one for the Click event of the cmdDelete button.

When you start developing a program, of course, you may not know what general procedures you're going to need. As you code the event procedures, though, you'll discover functions that are needed by more than one event procedure. Then, you can move the code for those functions from the event procedures into general procedures.

Visual Basic code for the unbound Vendors form Page 5

14

```
Private Sub DisableNavigation()
    cmdNavigate(0).Enabled = False
    cmdNavigate(1).Enabled = False
    cmdNavigate(2).Enabled = False
    cmdNavigate(3).Enabled = False
End Sub
```

15

```
Private Sub Form_KeyDown(KeyCode As Integer, _
    Shift As Integer)
    If KeyCode = vbKeyEscape Then
        LoadControls
        EnableNavigation
        InitializeCommandButtons
        blnRecordEdited = False
        blnAddMode = False
    End If
End Sub
```

16

```
Private Sub cmdClose_Click()
    Unload frmVendors
    End
End Sub
```

Figure 4-14 Code for the unbound version of the Vendors form (part 5 of 5)

Other data access models and techniques

Although DAO is the most common method used for accessing data, Visual Basic also provides several other methods for working with a database like SQL Server. These methods are summarized in figure 4-15. The method you choose depends on the type of database you're using, the location of the database, and the type of processing you need to perform.

When you use DAO, your data requests are typically processed by the Jet engine before they're passed on to ODBC. Because Jet was originally designed to be used with databases created in Access, though, it doesn't support some of the features of the most popular client/server databases, such as SQL Server. And even with recent improvements that have been made to Jet, it can still reduce program efficiency.

One alternative to using DAO is to use *RDO*, or *Remote Data Objects*. Like DAO, RDO is an object model that uses an object syntax for working with data. When you use RDO, you can use a data control called a *remote data control*. Or, you can use code to access data from unbound forms. Unlike DAO, RDO doesn't use Jet, so it can take advantage of many of the advanced features provided by client/server databases, like asynchronous queries, server-side cursors, and multiple result sets. That's why RDO is well-suited for working with these databases.

To use RDO directly, you need the Enterprise Edition of Visual Basic. If you don't have this edition, though, you can still use RDO through an extension of DAO called *ODBCDirect* (not shown in this figure). When you use ODBCDirect, you bypass the Jet engine and communicate with RDO through DAO. Even though you're using both DAO and RDO, though, you don't have access to all of the features of either object model.

The *Visual Basic Library for SQL Server*, or *VBSQL*, was the first native interface to SQL Server. To use it, you issue DB-Lib DECLARE statements from your application, which communicate with the DB-Lib DLL. The DB-Lib DLL, in turn, communicates directly with SQL. Today, most applications that would have been developed with VBSQL are developed with ODBC API.

ODBC API (*application programming interface*) is a low-level interface to the ODBC driver manager. To use it, you issue API DECLARE statements from your applications. Although ODBC API is quite efficient for accessing ODBC databases, the programming required to use it can be cumbersome. In general, you should consider using this API only when the other access methods don't provide the capabilities you need.

ADO, or *ActiveX Data Objects*, is a relatively new programming interface. Because it's still in its development stage, it's not used much yet for application programming. At some point in the future, though, it may become more popular than most of the other data access methods.

In this book, you'll only learn how to use DAO. Once you learn one data access method, though, it's a lot easier to learn another method like RDO.

Options for accessing SQL Server data

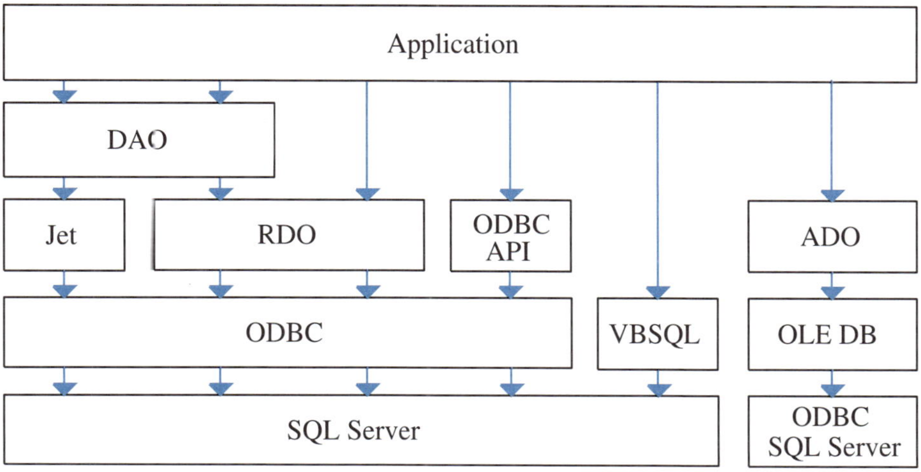

Description

- Today, using DAO is the most common way to access data from a Visual Basic application. However, Visual Basic also provides several other ways to access data, each with its own strengths and weaknesses.
- When you use DAO, your data requests are usually processed by Jet before they're sent to the ODBC Driver and the SQL Server Driver. Because Jet can make the process less efficient and because Jet doesn't support some of the features of SQL Server, there are times when you need to use one of the data access options that don't require Jet.
- *Remote Data Objects* (*RDO*) is an object model similar to DAO. Like DAO, you can access RDO through a data control, called a *remote data control*, or through Visual Basic code. Unlike DAO, RDO bypasses Jet and communicates directly with ODBC. RDO also provides a variety of features that aren't available when you use DAO. However, RDO is available only with the Enterprise Edition of Visual Basic.
- If you don't have the Enterprise Edition of Visual Basic, you can use an extension of DAO called *ODBCDirect* (not shown above) to communicate with RDO and ODBC and to bypass Jet. Although ODBCDirect uses both DAO and RDO, this access method doesn't provide for all of the features of either object model.
- Two other data access methods, VBSQL and ODBC API, provide low-level interfaces to SQL Server data. They communicate with SQL using DECLARE statements. Although these methods can be the most efficient access methods, they are the most cumbersome to use.
- *ADO*, or *ActiveX Data Objects*, is a new object model that's still in its development stage. Some experts believe this method will eventually supersede the others.

Figure 4-15 Other data access models and techniques

Perspective

Although the forms presented in this chapter are relatively simple, you can see that the database coding can quickly get complicated. It's essential, then, that you have a good idea of how you want a program to work and what functionality you want it to have before you start coding. To make sure that you do, you may want to create a diagram like the one in figure 4-13 to help you plan the logic of a program before you start coding.

It's also essential that you develop a consistent interface for your programs. That means that your programs should not only have a consistent look, but should work the same way too. This makes it possible for you to use the same basic coding structures that you develop for one form in new forms.

Now that you've completed this first section of this book, you should have a good understanding of what client/server programming is and what you have to do to become proficient at it. To improve that understanding, though, take a few hours to develop a simple client/server application of your own. First, use a data control to build a form so you can see how easy that is. Then, build an unbound form to see how much more control that gives you...and how much more difficult that is.

If you need a test database to work with, you can use one of the Access databases (Biblio and Nwind) that comes with Visual Basic. You can use the Visual Data Manager to develop a small database of your own as described in chapter 10. Or, you can download the AccountsPayable database that's used in our examples from our web site as described in the appendix.

Once you've created a simple application or two, you can go on to whatever chapters interest you the most. You don't have to read the chapters in sequence. If, for example, you're relatively new to programming, you may want to learn more about the Visual Basic language (chapter 5) and testing and debugging (chapter 9). Otherwise, you may want to learn how to build more complicated forms with DAO (chapter 6), how to enhance the user interface (chapter 8), or how to create a practice database (chapter 10). No matter what path you take through this book, though, you should eventually read all of the chapters because each one presents information that the client/server programmer should at least be aware of.

SECTION TWO 2

The essential programming skills

This section expands upon the introduction to programming in section 1 by presenting the skills that every programmer needs. When you complete this section, you should be able to develop complete client/server applications in Visual Basic 5 using the techniques of the best professional programmers.

Chapter 5 in this section presents the essentials of the Visual Basic language itself. Chapter 6 expands on what you learned in chapter 4 so you can build more complicated forms with DAO. Chapter 7 shows you how to further enhance the database programming by using a variety of query techniques and by providing for transaction and error processing. Chapter 8 shows you how to enhance the user interface by providing menus, toolbars, and help. And chapter 9 presents the best techniques for testing and debugging an application.

To make this section as easy to use as possible, all of the chapters are written as independent modules. This means that you can read them in whatever sequence you prefer. So if you want to learn how to test and debug an application, you can skip to that chapter next. And if you want to learn more about building forms with DAO, you can skip to that chapter. No matter what sequence you use, though, be sure to read all of the chapters because each one presents some of the essential programming skills.

Chapter 5

Visual Basic essentials

In the last two chapters, the emphasis has been on the use of the properties and methods for the form, control, and data objects that an application requires. In those chapters, the assumption was that you already knew how to work with a language like Visual Basic. If you've never worked with a language like this before, though, you'll need to learn the essential skills this chapter presents. Even if you have worked with a language like Visual Basic, you'll want to read this chapter to learn the specifics of working with the Visual Basic language.

Coding rules and guidelines

When you use Visual Basic, you must obey its coding rules. You should also follow some practical coding guidelines that will make your code easier to understand and maintain.

Basic coding rules

Figure 5-1 presents the basic coding rules (or *syntax*) for Visual Basic. If, for example, a Visual Basic statement continues from one line to the next, you must type a *continuation character* (a space followed by an underscore) at the end of the line that's continued. In the coding example at the top of this figure, you can see that these characters are used to continue the If statement to a second and third line. You can also see that these characters are used to continue the FV function to a second and third line.

To add a *comment* to a block of code, you just type an apostrophe followed by the text for the comment. In the coding example at the top of this figure, you can see one comment that describes what the If statement that follows is doing and another comment that describes what the FV function that follows is doing. When you review the code of others, you will often find comments interspersed throughout the code to help document what the code is doing.

When you review the code of others, you may also see two statements coded on a single line. To do that, you type a colon between the statements. You won't see that in this book, however, because we recommend that you code each statement on a separate line to make your code easier to read.

You can also make your code easier to read by using indentation and by capitalizing the first letter of each major word in names you create like variable names and procedure names. This too is illustrated by the coding example in the figure. Note, however, that the use of capital letters and indentation has nothing to do with the rules of Visual Basic. That's because Visual Basic treats capital letters the same as small letters, and it treats two or more spaces as if they were a single space.

A procedure that uses continuation characters and comments

```
Private Sub CalculateFutureValue()
    ' Check input values to make sure they're > zero
    If Val(mskMonthlyInvestment.Text) > 0 _
            And Val(mskInterestRate.Text) > 0 _
            And Val(mskMonths.Text) > 0 Then
    ' Use the FV function to calculate the future value
        mskFutureValue.Text =
            FV(mskInterestRate.Text / 12, _
            mskMonths.Text, _
            mskMonthlyInvestment.Text, 0, 1) * -1
    End If
End Sub
```

How to continue a statement

- Type the *continuation character*, which is a space followed by an underscore (_), at the end of the line you want to continue.

How to code a comment

- Type an apostrophe (') followed by the comment. A comment can be coded to the right of a statement or on a line with no statement. However, a comment can't be coded to the right of a continuation character.
- You can also code a comment by typing the keyword Rem (short for Remark) followed by a space and the comment, but it's easier to use the apostrophe.

How to code more than one statement on a line

- Separate the statements with a colon. Normally, though, you should start each statement on a new line.

Notes

- Although indentation and capitalization have no effect on the operation of the code, you can use them to make the code easier to read.
- As you enter code, Visual Basic may adjust the capitalization that you've used.

Figure 5-1 Basic coding rules

How to refer to properties and methods

In chapters 3 and 4, you learned how to refer to the properties and methods of form, control, and data objects. Now, figure 5-2 summarizes and expands upon that syntax. For most references, you use the period (*dot*) to separate the object from the property or method. And to refer to the default property of an object, you can omit the property name. Figure 5-2 presents the default properties for some common objects.

To refer to the current form object, you can use the word *Me* instead of the object name. This is illustrated by the fourth example for referring to a property, but it can also be used to refer to a method of the current form. The current form is the one that is active when a statement that uses this shortcut is executed.

To refer to an object, or *member*, that's part of a *collection*, you can use the three different formats shown in figure 5-2. Of these, we normally use the first format, particularly when referring to the members of the Fields collection for a recordset. In that format, a *bang* (!) is used to separate the recordset name from the field name as illustrated in all three examples for this format. Because the Fields collection is the default for a Recordset object, the collection name can be omitted as illustrated in the second example for this format. The third example shows that you can also code brackets around a field name. This is required if a field name, or any other database object name, contains spaces. Since SQL Server doesn't allows spaces in object names, you don't need to worry about using brackets if you're accessing SQL Server data. In fact, if you use brackets in a SQL statement that you send directly to SQL Server, you'll get an error. If you're using a Jet database, though, it's okay to use spaces and brackets.

How to refer to a property or method of an object

Syntax	Examples
Objectname.Property	`mskInterestRate.Text`
	`mskInterestRate`
	`frmVendors.KeyPreview`
	`Me.KeyPreview`
Objectname.Method	`mskInterestRate.SetFocus`

The default properties of some common objects

Object type	Default property
Text box	Text
Masked edit control	Text
Label	Caption
Data control	Caption
Field	Value

Three ways to refer to an object in a collection

Syntax	Examples
Collection!Objectname	`recVendors.Fields!VendorName`
	`recVendors!VendorName`
	`recVendors![VendorName]`
Collection("Objectname")	`recVendors.Fields("VendorID")`
Collection(Indexnumber)	`recVendors.Fields(2)`

Description

- To refer to a property or method of an object, just enter a period (called a *dot*) after the object name followed by the property or method name. When you refer to the default property of an object, you can omit the property name. When you refer to the current form, you can use *Me* as the object name.
- If an object is contained in a collection, it is a *member* of the collection. Then, you can refer to a member using one of the three formats shown above.
- In the first format for referring to a member, an exclamation point (called a *bang*) separates the collection name from the object name. Because Fields is the default collection for a recordset, it can be omitted. To code the name of a Database object that contains spaces, you must enclose the name in brackets [ ]. You can also refer to an object in a collection by name using the second format. In the third format, an index number (starting from 0) is used to identify the object.

Figure 5-2 How to refer to properties and methods

Recommended prefixes for objects, variables, and constants

As you develop a Visual Basic application, you create many different types of names including form names, control names, variable names, constant names, and procedure names. To help distinguish one type of name from the others, we recommend that you add a lowercase prefix to most names like *frm* for a form, *txt* for a text box control, and *int* for an integer variable. That way, your code will be easier to understand because you'll be able to tell what each name refers to. The only names that shouldn't start with prefixes are Sub and Function procedure names.

Figure 5-3 presents a starting set of prefixes that you can use as you develop applications. Or, if you like, you can develop your own set of prefixes. What's most important is that all the members of a programming staff use the same prefixes. That way, you'll be able to understand other people's code more easily, and they'll be able to understand yours.

In a moment, you'll learn how to define the variables and constants that a procedure or module requires. In the meantime, figure 5-3 summarizes some of the most common data types along with some one-letter and three-letter prefixes for each. In general, we recommend one-letter prefixes because that makes it easier to distinguish a variable or constant from an object. In the examples that follow, you'll see both one- and three-character prefixes.

In case you're not familiar with the terms that describe the data types, a *Boolean* value is either True or False, which is normally stored as –1 or +1 for true and 0 for false. An *integer* value is a whole number (no decimal positions). A *floating-point* number can represent a large number of digits both before and after the decimal point, and a *double-precision* number can hold about twice as many digits as a *single-precision* number. A *string* value can be made up of any characters. A *variant* variable, which is the default, can hold either a number or a string, but you're better off using a specific data type. And a Date data type stores a date as a floating-point number that can represent dates from January 1, 100 through December 31, 9999 and times from 0:00:00 through 23:59:59. Within the date value, the number to the left of the decimal point represents the date, while the number to the right represents the time.

Recommended prefixes for the names of some common objects

Type	Object	Prefix
Form	Form	frm
Control	Check box	chk
	Combo box	cbo
	Command button	cmd
	Data control	dat
	Data-bound combo box	dbc
	Data-bound grid	dbg
	Label	lbl
	Text box	txt
Menu	Menu	mnu
Toolbar	Toolbar	tlb
Report	Report	rpt

Recommended prefixes for common variables and constants

Data type	Prefix	Data type description
Boolean	bln or b	True or false
Byte	byt or t	Integer from 0 to 255
Currency	cur or c	Number with two decimal places
Date (Time)	dtm or d	Date and time
Double	dbl or p	Double-precision, floating-point number
Integer	int or n	Integer from –32,768 to +32,767
Long	lng or l	Long integer from –2 billion to +2 billion
Object	obj or o	Address that refers to an object
Single	sgl or f	Single-precision, floating-point number
String	str or s	Any characters
Variant	vnt or v	Either string or numeric data (the default)

Extra prefix letter to indicate the scope of variables and constants

Scope	Prefix	Example
Procedure	None	blnSwitch or bSwitch
Module	m	mintIndex or miIndex
Global	g	gblnSwitch or gbSwitch

Figure 5-3 Recommended prefixes for objects, variables, and constants

How to code expressions

Figure 5-4 presents examples and rules for coding three different types of *expressions*. To code an *arithmetic expression*, you can use any of the operators summarized in the arithmetic order of precedence. Besides the common numeric operators (+, -, *, and /), you can also use a caret (^) for exponentiation ("raising to a power of"), a backslash (\) for integer division, and the word *Mod* to get the remainder of an integer division.

To evaluate an arithmetic expression that doesn't include parentheses, Visual Basic performs the operations from left to right based on the *order of precedence*. This order says that all the exponentiation is done first; followed by the evaluation of minus signs before variables (called *negation*); followed by multiplication and division; and so on. Since most arithmetic expressions are relatively short, it's usually not difficult to understand how an expression will be evaluated.

If there's any chance for confusion, though, you should use parentheses to specify how you want an expression evaluated. Then, the expression in the innermost set of parentheses is evaluated first, followed by the operations in outer sets of parentheses. When all of the expressions in parentheses have been evaluated, the evaluation continues using the normal order of precedence on a left to right basis.

To code a *string expression*, you connect, or *concatenate,* two or more strings or string variables with ampersands (&). In the first example in figure 5-4, a string that contains the words "Switch value = " is concatenated to the string variable named sSwitch. So if the variable contains a value of Yes, the string expression evaluates to:

```
Switch value = Yes
```

Similarly, the second example concatenates a string variable, a Visual Basic constant that represents a carriage return and line feed (vbCrLf), and another string variable.

A *conditional expression* evaluates to either True or False. You use conditional expressions in Visual Basic statements like If and Select Case that test the value of the expression. You'll learn how to code these and other statements for conditional processing later in this chapter.

The first conditional expression in the figure tests a variable named sSwitch to see if it contains a value of Yes. If it does, the expression is true; otherwise, the expression is false. Similarly, if the Boolean variable in the second example has a value of True, the conditional expression is true; otherwise, the expression is false. The third conditional expression is just another way of coding the second example. In other words, if the condition is just a Boolean variable (or a Boolean property), Visual Basic assumes that the condition is true if that variable is equal to True.

If you review the order of precedence for conditional expressions, you can see that arithmetic operations are done first. Then, the relational operations are evaluated. Last, the logical operations are done. Although you can use six *logical operators* with Visual Basic, the ones you'll use the most are Not, And, and Or. You can see these operators used in the last three examples of conditional expressions, and you shouldn't have much trouble understanding how they're evaluated. When in doubt, however, you can use parentheses to make sure the expression gets evaluated correctly.

Arithmetic expressions

```
mskInterestRate.Text * 12
(cThisYTD - cLastYTD) / cLastYTD
iDividendValue Mod iDivisorValue
```

Order of precedence for arithmetic expressions

1. Exponentiation (^)
2. Minus sign before a value (negation)
3. Multiplication and division (* or /)
4. Integer division (\)
5. Mod operation (remainder of integer division)
6. Addition and subtraction (+ or -)

String expressions

```
"Switch value = " & sSwitch
sMessage1 & vbCrLf & sMessage2
```

Conditional expressions

```
sSwitch = "Yes"
bNewCustomer = True
bNewCustomer
iValue = 1
iValue Not > 99
cInterestRate > 0 And cMonthlyInvestment > 0
cThisYTD > cLastYTD Or _
    (cLastYTD <= 0 And cThisYTD >= 1000)
```

Order of precedence for conditional expressions

1. All arithmetic operations in the usual order of precedence
2. Relational operations (=, <>, >=, >, <=, <)
3. Logical operations in this order: Not, And, Or, Xor, Eqv, Imp

Use of parentheses

- Use parentheses whenever there's any doubt about the sequence in which the operations will be performed. Then, the operations in the inner parentheses are done first, followed by the operations in the outer sets of parentheses.

Figure 5-4 How to code expressions

Coding guidelines

When you compile and run an application, Visual Basic makes sure that your code follows all of its rules. But even if it does, your code may be difficult to understand if you don't adhere to some practical coding guidelines like the ones presented in figure 5-5. If you follow guidelines like these, it will be easier for you and others to understand, debug, and maintain your code.

To create names that are easy to interpret, you should start the names of objects, variables, and constants with standard prefixes and use long, meaningful names that clearly indicate what each object, variable, or constant represents. In the coding example in this figure, you can see that three-character prefixes are used for controls and single-character prefixes are used for variables. In contrast, the procedure name doesn't have a prefix, and its name starts with a verb to indicate the function of the procedure.

To make your code easier to read and understand, we recommend that you group all the Dim statements at the start of a procedure so they're easy to find (Visual Basic doesn't require that). We also recommend that you use indentation to show the structure of the statements that you use and that you write your code in a straightforward way that someone else will be able to follow.

Our last recommendation is to avoid the use of comments, even though many people recommend their use. The trouble with comments is that they may not accurately represent what the code does. This often occurs when you change the code, but not the comments. Besides that, if you follow our other naming and coding guidelines, your code should be easy to understand without comments. That's why we recommend that you use comments only to describe blocks of code that are unusually difficult to understand.

Now that you know our guidelines, you can modify and expand them to create your own. If you're working on a team project, what's important is that everyone on the team first agree on a set of coding guidelines…and then follow them.

A structured procedure

```
Private Sub CalculateFutureValue()
    Dim iMonths As Integer
    Dim fInterestRate As Single
    Dim cMonthlyInvestment As Currency
    Dim cFutureValue As Currency
    Dim iIndex As Integer
    If Val(mskMonthlyInvestment.Text) > 0 _
            And Val(mskInterestRate.Text) > 0 _
            And Val(mskMonths.Text) > 0 Then
        iMonths = Val(mskMonths.Text)
        fInterestRate = Val(mskInterestRate.Text) / 12
        cMonthlyInvestment = Val(mskMonthlyInvestment)
        cFutureValue = 0
        iIndex = 1
        Do Until iIndex > iMonths
            cFutureValue = (cFutureValue _
                         + cMonthlyInvestment) _
                         * (1 + fInterestRate)
            iIndex = iIndex + 1
        Loop
        mskFutureValue.Text = cFutureValue
    End If
End Sub
```

Naming recommendations

- Start the names of objects, variables, and constants with standard prefixes.
- Use meaningful names after the prefixes, even though that usually means long names.
- Use consistent names. Don't, for example, use curFutureValue to refer to a variable and mskFV to refer to a masked edit control when both are used for the future value of an investment.
- Start the names of Sub procedures with a verb (as in CalculateFutureValue), but omit the verb in the names of Function procedures (as in FutureValue).

Coding recommendations

- Group related variable and constant declarations, and code all declarations at the start of the procedure.
- Use indentation to make the code easier to understand.
- Write the code in a straightforward way, not a clever or cryptic way.
- Use comments only when the code is difficult to understand. Then, make sure that the comments are correct and up-to-date.

Figure 5-5 Coding guidelines

The Integrated Development Environment

In chapter 3, you were introduced to the Integrated Development Environment (IDE) *for Visual Basic. Since then, if you've created an application or two of your own, you've seen how easy this IDE is to work with, and you've probably discovered a few features on your own. Just in case you've missed a few, the topics that follow present some of the best features for coding in Visual Basic.*

How to work in the Code window

Figure 5-6 presents some of the features for working in the *Code window* of the IDE. After you enter the name of an object, for example, the Auto List Members feature lets you select a valid property or method from a members list. Then, to enter the member that you've selected into the code, you just press the Tab key.

In addition to the Auto List Members feature, Visual Basic provides other features that help you enter accurate code. For example, if you enter a property or method that requires arguments, Visual Basic displays the syntax of those arguments for you when you enter a space or a left parenthesis following the name of the property or method. Similarly, Visual Basic displays the syntax of a function or Sub procedure when you enter a Call statement for it. This applies to Visual Basic functions as well as functions and Sub procedures you code yourself. These features, and others, make entering Visual Basic code quick and easy.

After you've entered several procedures into a module, you may want to display a procedure that you've entered earlier. To find that procedure, you can use the drop-down lists at the top of the Code window.

If you haven't yet used the Edit toolbar, you'll find that its buttons provide some useful functions. For instance, they let you turn *bookmarks* on or off and move from one bookmark to another. (A bookmark simply flags a line a code.) This is useful when you're coding two or more closely related procedures.

Four of the other buttons on the toolbar let you get quick information about an object, function, or parameter in your code. As a result, it's worth taking the time to experiment with these buttons to see how helpful they can be, even though they don't always provide the information that you're looking for.

To switch between the Design window and the Code window, you can of course use the View menu or the Window menu or you can click on any visible window to switch to it. When you're typing code, though, it's often quicker to use the keystrokes shown in figure 5-6. These are the same keystrokes that you use for switching from one window to another when you use other Windows applications.

A Code window that contains a bookmark and a completion list

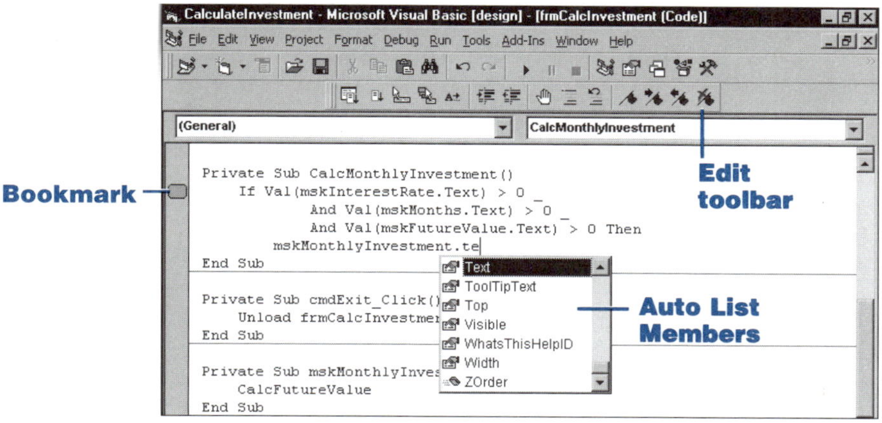

How to complete a property or method entry from a list

- As you enter a property or method, an automatic list of properties and methods may appear as shown above. To highlight the correct entry, type the first letter or two of the entry or select an entry from the list. Then, to insert the entry into your code, press the Tab key.

How to find a procedure

- Choose General or an object name from the first drop-down list at the top of the Code window. Then, choose an event or procedure name from the second drop-down list.

How to use the Edit toolbar

- To display or hide the Edit toolbar, right-click in the toolbar area and choose Edit in the shortcut menu. The buttons in this toolbar make it easy for you to turn a *bookmark* on or off, move to the next or previous bookmark, clear all bookmarks, indent or outdent selected lines of code, and change selected lines of code to comments or vice versa.
- To display information about an object, function, or parameter, move the insertion point into it. Then, click on one of these buttons: List Properties/Methods, List Constants, Quick Info, or Parameter Info. If a list of more information is available, Visual Basic will display it immediately.

Three ways to switch between the Design and Code windows

- Use the View or Window menu.
- Press Ctrl+F6 to move to the next window or Ctrl+Shift+F6 to move to the previous window.
- Click on any part of a visible window to switch to it.

Figure 5-6 How to work in the Code window

How to use the Project Explorer and Object Browser

Although you were introduced to the Project Explorer and Object Browser in chapter 3, figure 5-7 presents these features again because they can be so useful when you're coding. As you add more form modules and perhaps a standard module to a project, the Project Explorer helps you manage them. In the Project Explorer window in this figure, for example, you can see at a glance that the project consists of two form modules and one standard module. Then, you can use the Project Explorer, its toolbar, and its shortcut menus to move from one module's Code window to another, to rename a module, or to add a new module.

In contrast, the Object Browser provides a quick way to get information about a property, method, event, or constant. This is valuable because one of the difficulties of Visual Basic programming is figuring out what events, properties, and methods are available for each object. However, you can also get this information from the online help feature.

By default, the Project Explorer window is docked to the right side of the Visual Basic window. When a window is docked, you can size it and move it to any edge of the screen. However, you can't display it in the middle of the screen, and you can't maximize or minimize it. To do that, you have to undock the window by changing its *docking* option. To change the docking option, choose the Dockable command from the Project Explorer's shortcut menu or change the Docking option that's available from the Options dialog box that you access from the Tools menu. As you'll see in this dialog box, you can also dock and undock other components like the Object Browser and the toolbox.

A Project Explorer window

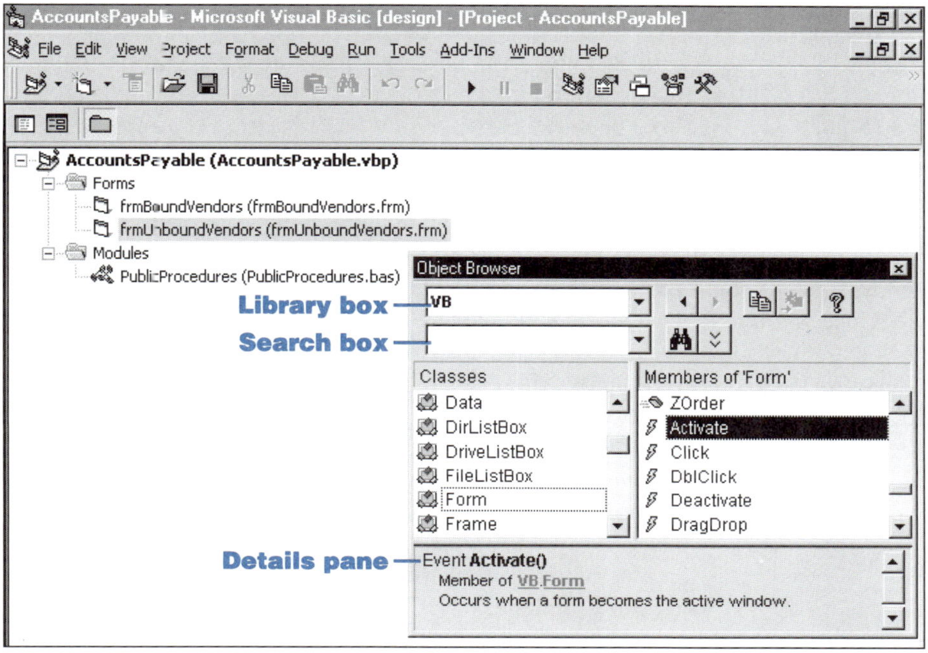

How to use the Project Explorer

- To display the Project Explorer, click on the Project Explorer button in the Standard toolbar or choose Project Explorer from the View menu. To hide the Project Explorer, click on its Close button or choose Hide from its shortcut menu.
- Use the buttons in the toolbar at the top of the Explorer to move to the design or Code window for the selected module. Or double-click on a module name to move to its Code window.
- Right-click on a module to display a shortcut menu that offers related functions like renaming a module (Properties) or adding a new module (Add).

How to use the Object Browser

- To display the Object Browser, click on the Object Browser button in the Standard toolbar or choose Object Browser from the View menu. To hide the Object Browser, click on its Close button or choose Hide from its shortcut menu.
- To get information about a property, method, event, or constant, select a library from the Library list, select a class from the Classes list, and select a property, method, event, or constant in the Members list. The Details pane then gives a description of the selected member, and you can get more information by pressing F1 or clicking on the Help button.
- To search for classes or members, enter the text you're looking for in the Search box. Then, press the Enter key or click on the Search button. To hide or display the search results, click on the Hide or Show Search Results button.

Figure 5-7 How to use the Project Explorer and Object Browser

How to get help information

Figure 5-8 shows how to get online help information for the statements, functions, and objects that you use when writing Visual Basic code. The quickest way to get that information is to press F1 while the insertion point is in a statement keyword, function name, object name, or other coding element. This usually delivers the help information for that element.

Otherwise, you can access the help information through the Help menu or by pressing F1 when the insertion point isn't in a word that the help feature recognizes. Then, you can use the Contents, Index, or Find tab to look for the information that you need. Once you find it, you can click on the underlined words to get still more information. In figure 5-8, for example, you see the help information for the Masked Edit control, and you can get information about its properties, methods, and events by clicking on those underlined words.

If you choose Books Online in the Help menu, you get access to all the information that's in the manuals that come with Visual Basic. If, for example, you look through the contents for the Programmer's Guide, you'll find the topic "Visual Basic Coding Conventions." Then, you can click on that topic to get the Microsoft guidelines for coding. By combining those recommendations with our starting set, you can build a complete set of your own coding guidelines.

The Help menu also offers Microsoft on the Web. Then, if your PC has an Internet connection, you can use that option to get information from Microsoft's web site. This can help you get recent information that isn't available in the help topics or the online books.

Because Visual Basic programming requires the use of so much detailed information, you will spend much of your time using the help information. In addition, the Edit toolbar and Object Browser will help you get certain types of quick information. You can also purchase the Visual Basic manuals in printed format.

The help information for the Masked Edit control

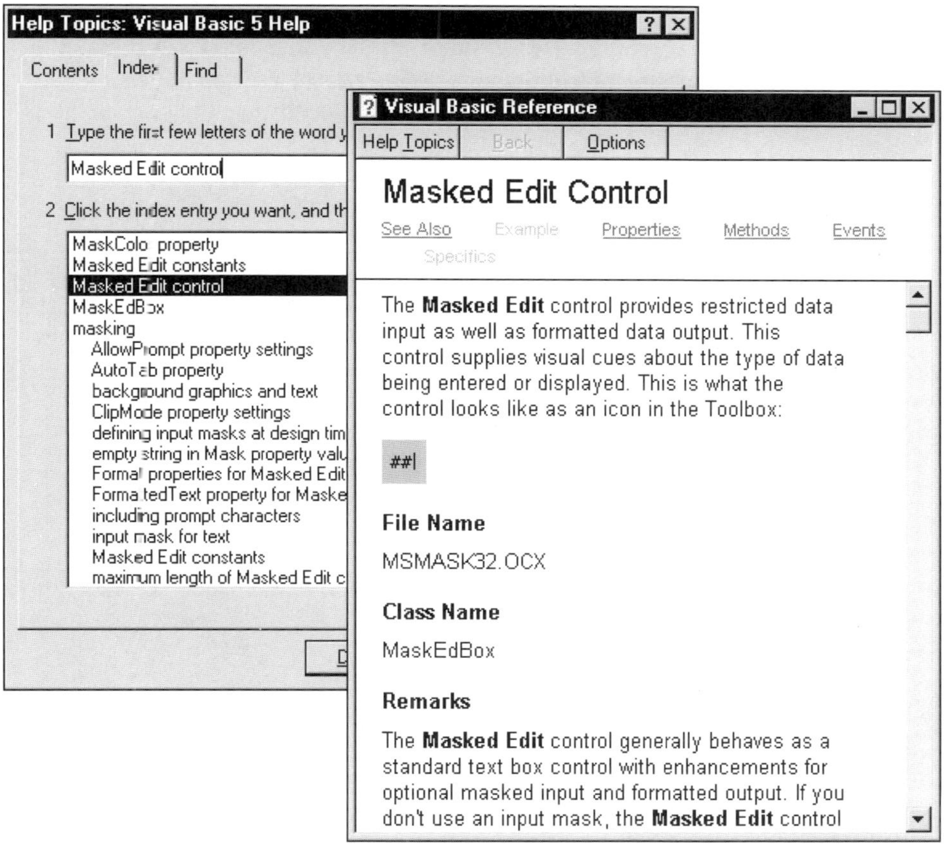

Description

- To display context-senstive help information, press F1 at any time. This is usually the best way to get help information.
- Another way to get help information is to choose Microsoft Visual Basic Help Topics from the Help menu. This opens the Help Topics dialog box shown above. The Contents, Index, and Find tabs in this dialog box let you access information in three different ways.
- Once you reach the Help window, you can use the Help Topics button to return to the Help Topics dialog box, the Back button to return to the previous Help topic, and the Print Topic command in the Options menu to print the current topic. You can also use the shortcut key or the Copy command in the Options menu to copy a topic to the clipboard so you can paste it into another document.
- A third way to get help information is to choose Books Online from the Help menu. This opens a window that presents an online version of the Microsoft manuals for Visual Basic. Depending on how you installed Visual Basic, this feature may require that you place the Visual Basic CD in your CD-ROM drive.

Figure 5-8 How to get help information

Variables and constants

Many Visual Basic procedures require the use of variables and constants. Before you can use a variable, you should declare it. After it's declared, you can assign a value to it. When you use constants, you declare and assign a value to them at the same time.

How to declare variables and constants

Figure 5-9 provides the information that you need for declaring *variables* and *constants*. In addition, you may want to refer back to figure 5-3 to review the common data types for variables and constants. Note that if you declare a variable without specifying a data type, it's defined as a variant. If you declare a constant without specifying a data type, it's assigned to the data type that's most appropriate for the value that is assigned to it.

In the examples of typical variable declarations, you can see how the Dim statement is used to declare various types of variables. In the second example, you can see how a string variable can be declared with a fixed length. And in the third example, you can see how two or more variables can be declared in a single Dim statement. If you use these examples as guides, you should be able to define the variables that you need in your procedures.

If you need to use a variable only within a single procedure, you can declare the variable within that procedure using the Dim or Static keyword. A variable that's declared within a procedure is called a *procedure-level*, or *local, variable*. If you need to use a variable in more than one procedure, you can declare it in the Declarations section using the Dim, Private, or Public keyword. If you use Dim or Private, the variable is available only to the procedures within the module and is called a *module-level variable*. (Dim is the same as Private when coded in the Declarations section.) If you use the Public keyword, the variable is available to the procedures in all the modules in the application and is called a *global variable*. You typically declare global variables in a standard module. Then, those variables are created when the application starts and are available throughout the execution of the application. In contrast, if you declare a global variable in a form module, it isn't created until the form is loaded.

To define an *object variable*, you specify the object type in the As clause. Two of the most-commonly used object variables are Database and Recordset variables, and you saw these used in chapter 4. You can also define a generic object variable using the Object data type. If you know what type of object the variable will refer to, though, you should declare it with that data type instead of using Object.

To define a constant, you use the keyword Const as shown in the typical constant declarations in figure 5-9. In addition, you use the equal sign followed by an expression to supply a value for each constant. Once declared, the value of a constant can't be changed by the statements that refer to it.

To define an *array*, you use parentheses to specify the dimensions of the array. In the first of the typical array declarations, for example, an array of 10 integer variables is declared. Then, you can refer to any one of the variables in the array by using an index number from 0 through 9. In contrast, the second example declares an array with ten variables that can be referred to by index values from 1 through 10. And the

Keyword meanings

Keyword	Meaning
Dim	The variable is available only within the procedure or module that declares it. When declared within a procedure, it's known as a *procedure-level variable* or a *local variable*. When declared within the Declarations section of a module, it's know as a *module-level variable*.
Private	The variable is available only to the procedures within the module that declares it.
Public	The variable is available to the procedures in all of the modules in the project. This is known as a *global variable*.
Static	The variable is available only within the procedure that declares it but retains its value from one execution of the procedure to another.

Typical variable declarations

```
Dim strErrorMessage As String
Dim strUserName As String * 25
Dim intIndex As Integer, dblInterestRate As Double
Private blnAddMode As Boolean
Public intUserStatus As Integer
Static intRunningValue As Integer
```

Typical object variable declarations

```
Dim dbAP As Database
Dim recVendors As Recordset
```

Typical constant declarations

```
Const blnAddMode As Boolean = False
Private Const intMonths As Integer = 60
Public Const sglInterestRate As Single = .125 / 12
```

Typical array declarations

```
Dim intValues (9) As Integer        'Index values are 0-9
Dim intValues (1 To 10) As Integer 'Index values are 1-10
Dim intValues (14, 29) As Integer  'A 2-dimensional array
```

Initial values

- When a variable is declared, it is given an initial value. A numeric variable is initialized to zero (0); a variable-length string to a zero-length string (""); and a fixed-length string to all zeros. In contrast, a Variant variable is initialized to Empty, which means it has no beginning value, but it is as treated as zero in a numeric context or as a zero-length string in a string context.

Figure 5-9 How to declare variables and constants

third example declares a two-dimensional array with 15 variables in one dimension (0 to 14) and 30 in the other (0 to 29). In figures 5-18 and 5-19, you can see some examples that use arrays, although you'll rarely need them in business applications.

In general, you should define your variables and constants so they have the smallest possible *scope*. That means that most of your variables should be local variables so they can't be used by other procedures. In contrast, a module-level variable should only be used if it's needed by more than one procedure in a module, and a global variable should only be used if it's needed by more than one module. By limiting the scope of your variables, you simplify your code and reduce the likelihood of errors.

How to assign values to variables

Once you declare variables, you can assign values to them as shown in figure 5-10. To do that, you use a Let statement, but the keyword Let is optional and usually omitted. As a result, you just code an equal sign after the variable name followed by an expression for the value. This type of statement is also known as an *assignment statement*.

Note in the first two examples of assignment statements that you can use the same variable name on both sides of the equal sign. In the first example, one is added to the starting value of intIndex so the new value is one more than it was. In the second example, a space and the value of a variable named strLastName are added to end of the string that is already stored in the variable named strName.

To assign a specific date to a date variable, you must code the date as a string within number signs (#). Then, the string date is converted to the correct numeric value before it is stored in the variable.

To assign a value to an object variable like a Database or Recordset object, you use the Set statement as shown in the two examples in this figure. Since the methods used in these statements were presented in chapter 4, you can refer back to that chapter if you want to analyze the expression that's assigned to each variable.

Whenever you use variables, you should make sure that the Option Explicit statement is coded at the start of the module. Then, you have to declare a variable before you can assign a value to it. In contrast, if the Option Explicit statement isn't coded, a variable is "implicitly" declared whenever you use a new variable name to the left of the equal sign in an assignment statement. As a result, a simple misspelling of a variable name that has already been declared can lead to the implicit declaration of a new variable and debugging problems later on. Fortunately, the Option Explicit statement is automatically entered into each module if you turn on the Require Variable Declaration option...so make sure this option is on.

Typical assignment statements

```
intIndex = intIndex + 1
strName = strName & " " & strLastName
curSalesTax = curProductTotal * .0775
curInvoiceTotal = curProductTotal + curSalesTax
curIncreasePct = (curThisYTD - curLastYTD) / _
                 curLastYTD * 100
blnNewCustomerSwitch = True
strMessage = "Invalid field entry"
strMessage = "Are you sure you want to delete" & _
             vbCrLf & "the record for " & _
             txtVendorName.Text & "?"
dtmYear2000 = #January 1, 2000#
```

The Option Explicit statement

- This statement should be coded in the Declarations section of each module in an application:

  ```
  Option Explicit
  ```
- When the Option Explicit statement is coded, you have to declare each variable that you use in an assignment statement. Otherwise, Visual Basic implicitly declares new variables that are used in assignment statements. This means that a misspelled variable name leads to a new variable declaration and a program bug.
- The Option Explicit statement is entered automatically in each module when the Require Variable Declaration option is on. To turn this option on, choose Options from the Tools menu and click on the Editor tab.

Typical assignment statements for object variables

```
Dim dbAP As Database, recVendors As Recordset
Set dbAP = OpenDatabase("AccountsPayable", 0, 0, _
    "ODBC;DATABASE=AccountsPayable")
Set recVendors = dbAP.OpenRecordset("Vendors", _
    dbOpenDynaset, dbSeeChanges)
```

Notes

- You use the Let statement to assign values to numeric and string variables. The keyword *Let* is optional, though, and it is normally omitted.
- You use the Set statement to assign values to object variables.
- False and True are keywords that can be used in assignment statements. They represent the Boolean values 0 (for false) and –1 or + 1 (for true).

Figure 5-10 How to assign values to variables

How to use Visual Basic constants

Besides the constants you declare, you can use any of the dozens of constants that are defined by Visual Basic. The names of these constants all start with the prefix *vb*, and figure 5-11 presents a few of the commonly-used constants. When you use one of the Visual Basic constants, your code becomes easier to read because you substitute a meaningful name for a cryptic code.

To find what Visual Basic constants are available, you can use the List Constants button in the Edit toolbar, the help information for a function or event, or the Object Browser. As you progress through this chapter and book, you'll see some of the more common uses of these constants.

In addition to the Visual Basic constants, you can use other types of constants like the ones listed in figure 5-11. When you use DAO, for example, you can use DAO constants to specify various options for some of the data access objects' properties and methods. You saw a few of these constants in the last chapter, and you'll see more later in this book. You can also use constants with the data-bound controls that you'll learn about in the next chapter.

Some of the constants that can be used in string variables

Constant	Equivalent	Description
vbCr	Chr(13)	Carriage return character
vbLf	Chr(10)	Linefeed character
vbCrLf	Chr(13) + Chr(10)	Carriage return and linefeed combination
vbTab	Chr(9)	Tab character

Some of the constants for key codes

Constant	Hex value	Description
vbKeyEscape	0x1B	Esc key
vbKeyReturn	0xD	Enter key
vbKeyF1	0x70	F1 key
vbKeyF2	0x71	F2 key

Typical uses of the Visual Basic constants

- To check the parameters that are passed to event procedures
- To check the response codes that are returned by functions
- To set a property for a form or control

Other types of constants that you can use with Visual Basic

- DBList control constants (dbl)
- DBCombo control constants (dbc)
- DBGrid control constants (dbg)
- DAO constants (db)
- RDO ccnstants (rd)

How to find the constants that you need

- Click on the List Constants button in the Edit toolbar when the insertion point is in code that you think has related constants.
- Use the help index to get the help information for a function or event. This information usually includes a summary of the related constants.
- Use the Object Browser to view the constants you can use with methods and properties.

Figure 5-11 How to use Visual Basic constants

Procedures and functions

In chapters 3 and 4, you learned how to code and call procedures. You also learned how to use two of the Visual Basic functions. Now, you can learn more about the coding and use of procedures and functions.

How to code and call a Sub procedure

Figure 5-12 shows the syntax for coding and calling a *Sub procedure*. In a syntax summary like this, the boldfaced words are *keywords* that must be spelled exactly as shown, while the other words represent elements that are coded by the programmer. In addition, elements that are coded within brackets are optional, and the vertical bar indicates a choice between two elements.

In the Sub statement, this syntax means that you have a choice between the keywords Private and Public. When you use Private to start the statement, the procedure can be called only by another procedure in the same module. When you use Public, the procedure can be called by any procedure in any of the modules of the project.

After the name of the procedure in the Sub statement, the syntax shows that you must always code parentheses. Within those parentheses, an argument list is optional. You only need to code it if one or more arguments needs to be passed to the procedure when it's called. The argument list defines the variables that will hold the values of those arguments.

To call a Sub procedure, you use the Call statement. Its syntax shows that the keyword Call is optional. Then, after you code the name of the procedure that's going to be called, you can code an argument list in parentheses. This list is required if the procedure that's being called is defined with an argument list.

The examples after the syntax summaries show how these statements can be used with and without argument lists. In the Sub statement for the procedure that requires four arguments, you can see that four values are expected when the procedure is called. Then, in the Call statement that calls this procedure, you can see that four variables are passed to the called procedure in the same sequence and with the same data types specified in the Sub statement for the procedure.

By default, the arguments that are passed to a Sub procedure are passed by reference, which means that the address of the argument, not its value, is passed. When you pass an argument by reference, the procedure has access to the actual variable and can change its value. If you do not want a procedure to change the value of the variable, you can pass it by value. When you pass an argument by value, a copy of the variable is passed so that if the procedure changes that value, it doesn't affect the value of the variable used by the calling procedure. To pass an argument by value, you use the ByVal keyword on the Sub statement like this:

```
ByVal Months As Integer
```

To pass an argument by reference, omit the ByVal keyword or use the ByRef keyword.

The syntax of the Sub and End Sub statements

```
[Private|Public] Sub name([argumentlist])
    statements
End Sub
```

The syntax of the Call statement

```
[Call] name[(argumentlist)]
```

A Sub statement with no arguments

```
Private Sub CalculateFutureValue()
```

A Call statement with no arguments

```
Call CalculateFutureValue
```

A procedure named CalculateFutureValue that requires four arguments

```
Private Sub CalculateFutureValue(Months As Integer, _
            InterestRate As Single, _
            MonthlyInvestment As Currency, _
            FutureValue As Currency)
    Dim iIndex As Integer
    FutureValue = 0
    iIndex = 1
    For iIndex = 1 To Months
        FutureValue = (FutureValue + MonthlyInvestment) _
            * (1 + InterestRate)
    Next iIndex
End Sub
```

A portion of a procedure that calls the CalculateFutureValue procedure

```
Dim iMonths As Integer
Dim fInterestRate As Single
Dim cMonthlyInvestment As Currency
Dim cFutureValue As Currency
If Val(mskMonthlyInvestment.Text) > 0 _
        And Val(mskInterestRate.Text) > 0 _
        And Val(mskMonths.Text) > 0 Then
    cMonthlyInvestment = Val(mskMonthlyInvestment.Text)
    fInterestRate = Val(mskInterestRate.Text) / 12
    iMonths = Val(mskMonths.Text)
    Call CalculateFutureValue(iMonths, fInterestRate, _
        cMonthlyInvestment, cFutureValue)
    mskFutureValue.Text = cFutureValue
End If
```

Figure 5-12 How to code and call a Sub procedure

By passing arguments from one procedure to another, you limit the scope of the variables that are used. In this example, all of the variables in both the called procedure and the calling procedure are local variables. The alternative is to code the variables as module-level variables so the variables don't have to be passed from one procedure to another. Remember, though, that you should always try to limit the scope of your variables because that makes your procedures easier to understand and debug.

How to code and call a Function procedure

Figure 5-13 presents the syntax for coding and calling a *Function procedure*, or *function*. The main difference between a Sub procedure and a function is that a function returns a value to the calling procedure. To specify the value to be returned, you assign it to the function name within the function. To specify the type of data to be returned, you include the As type clause on the Function statement.

After the syntax summaries, you can see code that creates and calls a function. This function requires three arguments and returns the future value of an investment. Since this function is called within an assignment statement, the future value that's calculated by the function is stored in the text property of a control named mskFutureValue.

If you compare this function example with the procedure example in the preceding figure, you can see how similar the function and procedure are. In fact, both accomplish the same purpose. In general, though, you should use a function when you need a calculated value returned, and you should use a procedure for other purposes.

The syntax of the Function and End Function statements

```
[Private|Public] Function name([argumentlist]) [As type]
    statements
    name = expression
End Function
```

The syntax of the Call statement

```
[Call] name[(argumentlist)]
```

A function named FutureValue that requires three arguments

```
Private Function FutureValue(Months as Integer, _
                InterestRate as Single, _
                MonthlyInvestment as Currency) _
                As Currency
    Dim iIndex As Integer
    FutureValue = 0
    iIndex = 1
    For iIndex = 1 To Months
        FutureValue = (FutureValue + MonthlyInvestment) _
            * (1 + InterestRate)
    Next iIndex
End Function
```

A procedure that calls the FutureValue function

```
Private Sub CalculateFutureValue()
    Dim iMonths As Integer
    Dim fInterestRate As Single
    Dim cMonthlyInvestment As Currency
    If Val(mskMonthlyInvestment.Text) > 0 _
            And Val(mskInterestRate.Text) > 0 _
            And Val(mskMonths.Text) > 0 Then
        iMonths = Val(mskMonths.Text)
        fInterestRate = Val(mskInterestRate) / 12
        cMonthlyInvestment = Val(mskMonthlyInvestment)
        mskFutureValue.Text = FutureValue(iMonths, _
            fInterestRate, cMonthlyInvestment)
    End If
End Sub
```

Notes

- If you use the keyword *Call* to call a function, the return value is discarded. Normally, though, you need to use the return value so you omit the word *Call*.
- You can use the ByVal and ByRef keywords when you define the arguments for a function just as you can for a Sub procedure. The default is ByRef.

Figure 5-13 How to code and call a Function procedure

How to use Visual Basic functions

Before you create a new function, you should check whether Visual Basic provides a built-in function that you can use. In figure 5-14, for example, you can see a few of the many functions that Visual Basic provides. In particular, Visual Basic provides most of the functions that you're likely to need for working with dates and strings and for performing math and financial calculations. One of the functions that you'll use the most is the MsgBox function, which is presented in the next figure.

Some of the date and time functions

Function	Description
Date	Returns the current date.
Now	Returns the current date and time.
Time	Returns the current time.
DateValue	Receives a date string and returns a date numeric value.

Some of the string functions

Function	Description
InStr	Returns the position of the first occurrence of one string within another.
Left	Finds or removes a specific number of characters from the start of a string.
Len	Returns the length of a string.
LTrim	Removes spaces from the start of a string.
Mid	Returns a specific number of characters from a string starting from a specific location in the string.

Some of the math and finance functions

Function	Description
Int	Returns the integer portion of a number.
Val	Returns the number contained in a string as a numeric value.
Rnd	Returns the next random number as a decimal fraction between 0 and 1.
FV	Calculates the future value of a periodic payment amount.
SLN	Calculates a straight-line depreciation amount.
SYD	Calculates a sum-of-years' digits depreciation amount.

Two dialog box functions

Function	Description
MsgBox	Displays a message in a dialog box, waits for the user to click a button, and returns an integer indicating which button the user clicked.
InputBox	Displays a message in a dialog box, waits for the user to enter text or click a button, and returns a string that contains what the user entered.

How to find the functions that you need

- Use the help index to get the help information for a type of function like math, string, or financial functions. Then, choose a function from the list that's displayed.

Figure 5-14 How to use Visual Basic functions

How to use the MsgBox function

In the syntax for the MsgBox function in figure 5-15, you can see that its arguments can include a *prompt* (a message that's displayed in the dialog box); buttons (values for how the command buttons in the dialog box should be displayed); and a title (a title for the dialog box). Then, when this function is executed, the dialog box is displayed so the user can respond to it by clicking on a button. When the user clicks on a button, the value associated with that button is returned to the program.

In the first example of a MsgBox function in this figure, a simple message is displayed in the dialog box. Note, here, that the argument isn't enclosed by parentheses as shown in the syntax, and there's a space between the function name and the argument. That's the way a MsgBox function that isn't used to return a value is normally coded. In fact, Visual Basic generates a compiler error if you use parentheses with some combinations of arguments. In this example, only the prompt argument is used so the default options are used for the buttons and for the title. As a result, just an OK button is displayed in the message box, and the name of the application is displayed in the title bar.

In the second example, the function does return a value to a variable named intResponse, and the arguments are enclosed in parentheses. These arguments include two Visual Basic constants to indicate (1) that the dialog box should contain both Yes and No buttons and (2) that the second button (No) should be the default. That means that the user can press the Enter key to select the No button instead of clicking on it. Notice that you use a plus sign (+) to combine the two constants. That's because the constants represent numeric values as indicated in the figure, and these constants are actually added together to determine the value of the buttons argument. This MsgBox function also displays "Delete Confirmation" as the title of the dialog box.

When the MsgBox function in the second example is executed, it displays this message in the dialog box:

```
Are you sure you want to
delete this record?
```

Because the processing that follows the MsgBox function in this example depends on the user's response to this message, the value that's returned by the MsgBox function is assigned to a variable. This variable is then tested in an If statement to see if the response is equal to the Visual Basic constant vbYes. If it is, the current record is deleted.

Because of the many ways that this function can be coded, it is widely used to display user messages. For that reason, you should become familiar with all of the constants that can be used with it. For a complete list, you can access the help information for the function.

The syntax of the MsgBox function

```
MsgBox(prompt[, buttons][, title])
```

A simple call to the MsgBox function

```
MsgBox "No record exists for that ID"
```

Part of a procedure that calls the MsgBox function and checks the response value

```
Dim intResponse As Integer
intResponse = MsgBox("Are you sure you want to" _
                    & vbCrLf & "delete this record?", _
                    vbYesNo + vbDefaultButton2, _
                    "Delete Confirmation")
If intResponse = vbYes Then
    recVendors.Delete
End If
```

Some Visual Basic constants for the buttons argument

Constant	Value	Description
vbOKOnly	0	Display OK button only.
vbOKCancel	1	Display OK and Cancel buttons.
vbAbortRetryIgnore	2	Display Abort, Retry, and Ignore buttons.
vbYesNoCancel	3	Display Yes, No, and Cancel buttons.
vbYesNo	4	Display Yes and No buttons.
vbRetryCancel	5	Display Retry and Cancel buttons.
vbCritical	16	Display Critical Message icon.
vbInformation	64	Display Information Message icon.
vbDefaultButton1	0	First button is default.
vbDefaultButton2	256	Second button is default.
vbDefaultButton3	512	Third button is default.

Some Visual Basic constants for return values

Constant	Value	Description
vbOK	1	User chose the OK button.
vbCancel	2	User chose the Cancel button.
vbAbort	3	User chose the Abort button.
vbRetry	4	User chose the Retry button.
vbIgnore	5	User chose the Ignore button.
vbYes	6	User chose the Yes button.
vbNo	7	User chose the No button.

Figure 5-15 How to use the MsgBox function

Visual Basic statements

As you code the procedures for a Visual Basic application, you use relatively few Visual Basic statements. In contrast, you're likely to use many different objects and methods. In the topics that follow, you'll be introduced to the Visual Basic statements that you'll use the most.

How to code If statements

When you use Visual Basic, the syntax of the If statement varies just slightly from what you might have used with another language. This syntax is shown in figure 5-16. Notice in the one-line If statement that the statement doesn't end with the words *End If* as it does in the block format. That's because the end of a one-line If statement is indicated by the end of the line. The block format also provides for ElseIf clauses. Notice that both the If and the ElseIf clauses must end with the word Then.

You can see how ElseIf clauses can be used in the second coding example in this figure. Here, the assumption is that the user clicked on one of the command buttons in an array so an index value has been returned to the procedure. The If statement then directs the coding for each of the four index values (from 0 to 3). In this case, the index values determine whether to move to the first, previous, next, or last record in a recordset. If none of these index values are returned, a message is displayed. This coding is an acceptable alternative to the use of the Select Case statement that's shown in the next figure.

Within the first two ElseIf clauses in the second coding example, you can see nested If statements that determine the processing when the BOF or EOF properties for the recordset are true. When you use *nested If statements*, you must make sure that you complete the inner statement before you go back to the outer statement. Otherwise, Visual Basic will detect an error and interrupt your coding. This automatic checking helps you code error-free If statements.

The syntax of the one-line If statement

```
If condition Then statements [Else statements]
```

The syntax of the block If statement

```
If condition Then
    statements
[ElseIf condition-n Then
    statements] ...
[Else
    statements]
End If
```

A simple If...Then...Else statement

```
If optFutureValue = True Then
    Call CalcFutureValue
Else
    Call CalcMonthlyInvestment
End If
```

An If statement with ElseIf clauses that implement a case structure

```
If Index = 0 Then
    recVendors.MoveFirst
ElseIf Index = 1 Then
    recVendors.MovePrevious
    If recVendors.BOF Then
        recVendors.MoveFirst
    End If
ElseIf Index = 2 Then
    recVendors.MoveNext
    If recVendors.EOF Then
        recVendors.MoveLast
    End If
ElseIf Index = 3 Then
    recVendors.MoveLast
Else
    MsgBox "Invalid index number"
End If
```

The structure of nested If statements

```
If condition-1 Then
    statement-group-1
Else
    If condition-2 Then
        statement-group-2
    Else
        statement-group-3
    End If
End If
```

Nested If statement

Figure 5-16 How to code If statements

How to code Select Case statements

Figure 5-17 shows the syntax for the Select Case statement and two of the ways this statement can be used. The first example is the alternative to the nested If statement in the previous figure. It determines the processing to be done by testing the value of an index.

In the second example, a discount percentage is determined from a variable named intQuantityOrdered, which contains the number of items that a customer has ordered. If the quantity is 1 or 2, the discount is zero. If the quantity is from 3 to 9, the discount is .1. If the quantity is from 10 to 24, the discount is .2. If the quantity is greater than or equal to 25, the discount is .3. And if none of those conditions is true (Else), the MsgBox function displays an error message. Note the variety of ways that these values can be specified in a Select Case statement.

The benefit of using the Select Case statement is that your code is easier to read and understand. To appreciate that benefit, compare the first example in this figure to the alternative If statement coding in the previous figure. Then, consider how the second example in this figure would be coded if you had to use nested If statements. To say the least, the coding would be longer and more complicated.

The syntax of the Select Case statement

```
Select Case testexpression
[Case expressionlist
    statements] ...
[Case Else
    statements]
End Select
```

A Select Case statement that tests a variable named Index

```
Select Case Index
    Case 0
        recVendors.MoveFirst
    Case 1
        recVendors.MovePrevious
        If recVendors.BOF Then
            recVendors.MoveFirst
        End If
    Case 2
        recVendors.MoveNext
        If recVendors.EOF Then
            recVendors.MoveLast
        End If
    Case 3
        recVendors.MoveLast
    Case Else
        MsgBox "Invalid index number"
End Select
```

A Select Case statement that sets discount percentages

```
Select Case intQuantityOrdered
    Case 1, 2
        dblDiscount = .0
    Case 3 To 9
        dblDiscount = .10
    Case 10 To 24
        dblDiscount = .20
    Case Is >= 25
        dblDiscount = .30
End Select
```

Coding note

- In the expression list for a case, you can code a series of specific values separated by commas, you can use the word *To* to specify a range of values, you can use the word *Is* with a conditional expression, or you can use a combination of these methods to identify the values for the case.

Figure 5-17 How to code Select Case statements

How to code Do statements

A Do statement can be used to repeat a series of statements while a condition is true or until a condition is true. This is called a *Do loop*. In figure 5-18, you can see the syntax for the two versions of this statement. In the first version, the condition is tested before the series of statements is executed. In the second version, the condition is tested after the series of statements is executed.

In the first two examples after the syntax, you can see how both versions of the statement can be used to calculate a future value from the values in three investment variables. In both cases, the statements in the loop are executed once for each value of the variable named intIndex. This variable starts with a value of 1 and ends with a value equal to the value in the variable named intMonths.

The third example in this figure shows how a Do loop can be used for working with an array. Here, the first Dim statement declares an array that contains 10 values with index values from 0 through 9. Then, the Do loop uses the Visual Basic Int and Rnd functions to put a random integer value in each variable in the array. To refer to each of the 10 array variables, an index variable is coded in parentheses after the array name. This index variable starts with the default value zero that's assigned to it when the variable is declared.

The Randomize statement in this example is used before the Do loop to make sure that the Rnd function starts with a new first value each time this procedure is executed. To learn more about the Randomize statement and the Rnd function, you can get help information about them. Of course, that isn't necessary unless you intend to do some work with random numbers.

The fourth example in this figure is similar to the third example. The difference is that it puts random numbers in all the variables of a two-dimensional array. To reference each of the variables in this array, two index values are given in parentheses:

```
intNumber(intFirstIndex, intSecondIndex)
```

To vary these values, the code uses one Do loop within another, called *nested Do loops*.

The syntax for the Do statement with the test first

```
Do [{While|Until} condition]
    statements
Loop
```

The syntax for the Do statement with the test last

```
Do
    statements
Loop [{While|Until} condition]
```

A Do loop with the test first that calculates future value

```
intIndex = 1
Do Until intIndex > intMonths
    curFutureValue = (curFutureValue + _
        curMonthlyInvestment) * (1 + sglInterestRate)
    intIndex = intIndex + 1
Loop
```

A Do loop with the test last that calculates future value

```
intIndex = 1
Do
    curFutureValue = (curFutureValue + _
        curMonthlyInvestment) * (1 + sglInterestRate)
    intIndex = intIndex + 1
Loop While intIndex <= intMonths
```

A Do loop that puts random numbers in an array

```
Dim intNumber(9) As Integer
Dim intIndex As Integer
Randomize
Do Until intIndex > 9
    intNumber(intIndex) = Int(10 * Rnd + 1)
    intIndex = intIndex + 1
Loop
```

Nested Do loops that put random numbers in a two-dimensional array

```
Dim intNumber(9, 19) As Integer
Dim intFirstIndex As Integer
Dim intSecondIndex As Integer
Randomize
Do While intFirstIndex <= 9
    Do While intSecondIndex <= 19
        intNumber(intFirstIndex, intSecondIndex) _
            = Int(10 * Rnd + 1)
        intSecondIndex = intSecondIndex + 1
    Loop
    intFirstIndex = intFirstIndex + 1
Loop
```

Figure 5-18 How to code Do statements

How to code For...Next statements

Figure 5-19 presents the syntax for the two versions of the For...Next statement, which are used to implement *For...Next loops*. The first version lets you repeat a series of statements for each value of an index or other variable. By default, the value of the index or variable is incremented by one each time the statements are repeated. If you want to increment the index or variable by a value other than one, you can include the Step clause on this statement.

The second version of the For...Next statement lets you repeat a series of statements for each element in a group. For example, you could repeat the statements for each Control object in a Controls collection.

In the first three examples in this figure, you can see how a For...Next loop can be used to perform the same functions that are done by the Do loops in the previous figure. This illustrates that the For...Next loop generally leads to simpler code that's easier to understand.

In the fourth example, you can see how a For Each statement can be used to work with all of the objects in a collection. Here, the For...Next loop is executed once for each control on the current form (which is referred to as Me). Then, for each control that's a command button, the Enabled property is set to True.

The syntax of a For...Next statement

```
For counter = start To end [Step step]
    statements
Next [counter]
```

The syntax of a For Each...Next statement

```
For Each element In group
    statements
Next [element]
```

A For...Next statement that calculates a future value

```
intIndex = 1
For intIndex = 1 To intMonths
    curFutureValue = (curFutureValue + _
        curMonthlyInvestment) * (1 + dblInterestRate)
Next intIndex
```

A For...Next loop that puts random numbers in an array

```
Dim intNumber(9) As Integer
Dim intIndex As Integer
Randomize
For intIndex = 0 To 9
    intNumber(intIndex) = Int(10 * Rnd + 1)
Next intIndex
```

Nested For...Next loops that put random numbers in a two-dimensional array

```
Dim intNumber(9, 19) As Integer
Dim intFirstIndex As Integer
Dim intSecondIndex As Integer
Randomize
For intFirstIndex = 0 To 9
    For intSecondIndex = 0 To 19
        intNumber(intFirstIndex, intSecondIndex) _
            = Int(10 * Rnd + 1)
    Next intSecondIndex
Next intFirstIndex
```

A For Each...Next statement that enables all command buttons in a form

```
Dim objControl As Control
For Each objControl In Me.Controls
    If TypeOf objControl Is CommandButton Then
        objControl.Enabled = True
    End If
Next objControl
```

Figure 5-19 How to code For...Next statements

How to code On Error statements

The On Error statement can be used to trap errors that are detected by Visual Basic while a program is running. These errors are referred to as *trappable errors*. If, for example, an arithmetic expression tries to divide a value by zero, a trappable error occurs. If one of these errors occurs and you haven't provided for it in your application, an error message is displayed and execution of the application stops. Since that's not what you want, you should provide for errors whenever there's a possibility that one will occur.

Figure 5-20 presents the On Error statement and other statements related to error processing. You code the On Error statement at the start of a procedure as shown in the example in the figure. If you want to perform some special processing when an error occurs, you use the GoTo *label* format of this statement. Then, if an error occurs when a subsequent statement in the procedure is executed, the procedure is interrupted and processing continues with the statement after the label. In the example in this figure, processing continues with the Dim statement after the ErrorRoutine: label. Notice that the label must end with a colon.

If you don't want to perform any special processing when an error occurs but you want normal processing to continue, you can use the Resume Next format of the On Error statement. You can also use the GoTo 0 format of the On Error statement to disable the error-handling routine. If you do that, though, and an error occurs, program execution will stop.

After the label, the first two statements in this example prepare a string variable that contains an error message. These statements get the number and description of the error by referring to the Number and Description properties of the Err object that are set by Visual Basic when an error is detected. The string variable is then used as an argument in a MsgBox function that displays the message.

Often, when an error-handling routine ends, the program should continue with the procedure that called the procedure that contains the error-handling routine. That's what happens in the example in figure 5-20. If that's not what you want, you can use one of the Resume statement formats to return to the statement that caused the error (Resume), the first statement after the statement that caused the error (Resume Next), or the statement identified by the label (Resume *label*).

If a procedure contains an error-handling routine, you'll want to be sure that the routine isn't executed following the normal processing statements. To do that, you code an Exit Sub or Exit Function statement at the end of the normal processing statements as shown in the figure. These statements cause control to be returned to the calling procedure before the error-handling routine is executed.

Besides the Visual Basic Err object, you can use the DAO Error object to get information about trappable Jet and DAO errors. This is illustrated by the last example in the next figure, and you can learn more about these errors in chapter 7.

The statements for error handling

Syntax	Meaning
On Error GoTo *label*	If an error occurs in one of the statements that follow, go to the line identified by the label.
On Error Resume Next	If an error occurs in one of the statements that follow, resume processing with the first statement after the statement that caused the error.
On Error GoTo 0	Disable the error-handling code.
Resume	Use this in an error-handling routine to resume processing with the statement that caused the error.
Resume Next	Use this in an error-handling routine to resume processing with the first statement after the one that caused the error.
Resume *label*	Use this in an error-handling routine to resume processing at the line identified by the label.

A Function procedure that contains an error-handling routine

```
Private Function PercentIncrease(ThisYTD As Double, _
        LastYTD As Double) As Single
    On Error GoTo ErrorRoutine
    PercentIncrease = (ThisYTD - LastYTD) / LastYTD * 100
    Exit Function
ErrorRoutine:
    Dim strMessage As String
    strMessage = "Error Number = " & Err.Number & vbCrLf
    strMessage = strMessage & Err.Description
    MsgBox strMessage, vbOKOnly, "Error Message"
End Function
```

The Err object

- When a trappable error occurs in Visual Basic, you can use the properties of an object named Err to get information about the error. Two of the most useful properties are Err.Number, which gives the number of the error, and Err.Description, which gives a description of the error.
- See the help information for “Trappable Errors” for a complete list of these errors.

The Error object in the Errors collection for DAO

- When a program does a DAO operation, one or more errors may occur. As each error occurs, an Error object is placed in the Errors collection of the DBEngine object. Then, the program can use a For Each...Next statement to analyze each of the Error objects (see figure 5-21). Two of the must useful properties of the Error object are Error.Number and Error.Description.

Figure 5-20 How to code On Error statements

How to code With statements

The With statement doesn't provide any new capabilities. Its purpose is to let you write code without repeating the name of a specific object. In figure 5-21, you can see its syntax and three coding examples.

The first example shows an If statement that uses either the AddNew or Edit method of the recVendors recordset. For both methods, the object name (recVendors) is repeated. In contrast, the second example shows how this duplication of the object name can be eliminated by using the With statement. (Notice that you still code the dot operator when you omit the object name.) In this case, the With statement just eliminates one repetition of the object name so using it doesn't make much sense. But some routines require many repetitions of the object name. Then, using the With statement can simplify the code.

The third example in this figure shows how the With statement can be used in an error-handling routine. Then, the code that follows refers to the Number, Description, and Source properties of the Error object without using the object name. This routine ends with a Resume Next statement so processing continues with the first statement after the statement that caused the error.

The syntax of the With statement

```
With object
    statements
End With
```

An If statement without a With statement

```
If AddMode = True Then
    recVendors.AddNew
Else
    recVendors.Edit
EndIf
```

The same If statement with a With statement

```
With recVendors
    If AddMode = True Then
        .AddNew
    Else
        .Edit
    EndIf
End With
```

An error routine that uses a With statement

```
ErrorRoutine:
    Dim strMessage As String
    Dim objError As Error
    For Each objError in Errors
        With objError
          strMessage = "Number = " & .Number & vbCrLf & _
             "Description = " & .Description & vbCrLf & _
             "Source = " & .Source
        End With
    Next
    MsgBox strMessage, vbOKOnly, "Error Message"
    Resume Next
```

Figure 5-21 How to code With statements

A summary of other Visual Basic statements

Although you've just been introduced to the Visual Basic statements that you'll use most of the time, you should know that there are many others. Some of these are summarized in figure 5-22. As you can see, there are statements for loading and unloading forms; statements for working with strings (in addition to the functions for working with strings); statements for processing the records in sequential and ISAM files (not databases); statements that control program execution; and some miscellaneous statements.

To learn more about the Visual Basic statements, you can use the help information. The Contents tab gives you access to each of the statements in alphabetic order. The Index tab lets you look up a specific statement when you know its name. For the applications presented in this book, though, you'll only need to use a few of these statements.

Statements for working with forms	
Load	Loads a form into memory.
Unload	Unloads a form from memory.

Statements for working with string variables	
Lset	Left aligns a string within a string variable.
Mid	Replaces a specified number of characters in a string variable with characters from another string.
Rset	Right aligns a string within a string variable.

Statements for file processing	
Open	Opens a file.
Close	Closes a file.
Get	Reads a record from a file.
Put	Writes to a disk file.
Seek	Positions a file for the next read or write operation.
Lock	Locks a range of records in a file.
Unlock	Unlocks a range of records in a file.

Statements for controlling program execution	
End	Terminates program execution immediately and releases all resources.
Stop	Sets a breakpoint in the code that suspends execution.
Exit	Provides a way to prematurely exit from a Do loop, For loop, Sub procedure, or function when used in these forms: Exit Do, Exit For, Exit Sub, or Exit Function.

Miscellaneous statements	
Beep	Sounds a tone through the computer's speaker.
Date	Sets the current system date.
Type	Lets you define a user-defined data type that contains one or more elements. Often used to define the fields within the records of a file.

Figure 5-22 A summary of other Visual Basic statements

Perspective

The goal of this chapter has been to improve your knowledge of the syntax, statements, and functions of the Visual Basic language. If you have some programming experience, you should now see that Visual Basic is much like other languages that you've used. What's different is the use of objects, methods, properties, and events, not the language itself.

If you had any difficulty understanding this chapter, you should now take some time to experiment with the statements that you just learned. To start, for example, you can revise the application that you created for chapter 3 by replacing the use of the FV function with your own Sub or Function procedure for calculating future value. First, do this by passing variables between the calling and called procedures. Then, do it by using module-level variables that you don't have to pass. When you're done experimenting with that application, you can experiment with some of the other new statements by rewriting some of the code for the application that you created for chapter 4.

Once you're confident that you understand how the Visual Basic language works, you're ready to go on to the other chapters in this section. These chapters will show you how to build enhanced forms with DAO, how to enhance the database programming, how to enhance the user interface, and how to test and debug a program. When you're done with these chapters, you should be able to develop complete client/server applications of your own.

Chapter 6

How to build forms with DAO

In chapters 3 and 4, you learned the basic skills for building forms and for working with data using DAO. Now, you'll learn some additional skills for building forms with DAO. In particular, you'll learn how to use some of the special Visual Basic controls for working with data. When you finish this chapter, you should be able to develop forms at a professional level for a wide variety of client/server applications.

Basic skills for building forms

This topic focuses on the basic skills for building forms that weren't presented in chapter 3. Here, you'll learn how to add another form to a project, how to use the various controls that come with Visual Basic, and how to work with two or more open forms.

How to add a form to a project

When you start a new project, a single blank form is opened for you. Most projects, however, consist of two or more forms. To add other forms to a project, you can use the techniques presented in figure 6-1.

The Add Form dialog box shown in this figure provides a variety of options for adding forms. If you want to create a new form, you can select one of the options in the New tab. Most of these options create forms that provide specific functions. If you need to create a form that provides one of these functions, these options can be useful. For most of the forms you create, though, you'll use the Form option to create a form from scratch.

If you want to add an existing form to a project, you can use the Existing tab of the Add Form dialog box to identify the form. This can be useful if you want to use the same form in two different projects or if you want to create a form that's similar to an existing form. Before you modify an existing form, though, you must save the form with a new name or in a new folder. Otherwise, the changes you make will be applied to the original form.

By default, the first form that's added to a project is the form that will be displayed when you run the application. If that's not what you want, you can change the Startup Object property of the project to the correct form. This property is available from the General tab of the Project Properties dialog box.

If you don't want a form to be displayed when an application starts, or if you want to execute code before a form is displayed, you can code a special Sub procedure named Main. Note that this procedure must be coded in a standard module, not a form module. Then, to execute this procedure when the application starts, choose the Sub Main option for the Startup Object property.

The dialog box that's displayed when you add a form

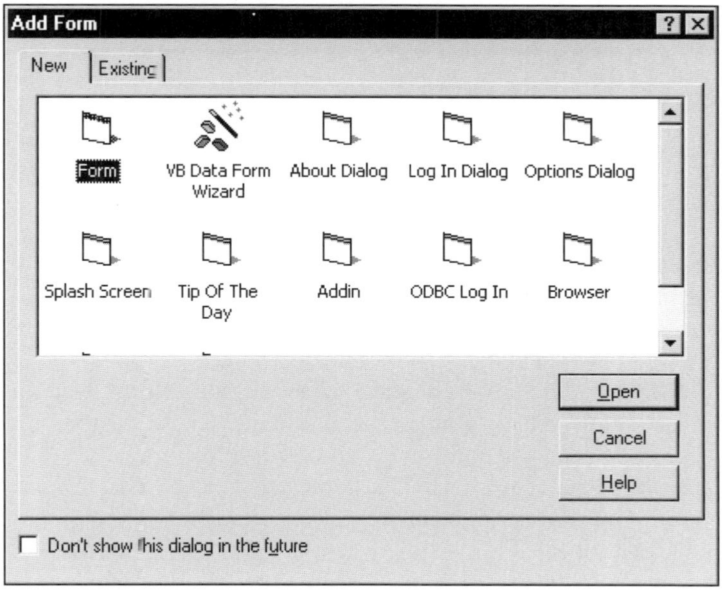

Description

- To add a new form to a project, select the New Form command from the Project menu to display the dialog box shown above. You can also display this dialog box by clicking on the arrow on the right side of the Add button in the toolbar and selecting the Form option.
- To create a new, blank form, select the Form option from the New tab of the dialog box. This is the default.
- The New tab provides a variety of other options that you can use to create specific types of forms. You can use the VB Data Form Wizard option, for example, to create a form that lets you manipulate data using a data control. This can provide a good starting point for the forms that you create.
- You can also add an existing form to a project by selecting it from the Existing tab of the dialog box.
- If a project contains more than one form, you'll want to be sure that the Startup Object property of the project is set to the form you want to be displayed when the application starts. By default, this property is set to the first form that's added to the project. To change this property, select the Properties command from the Project menu.

Figure 6-1 How to add a form to a project

The controls that are available from the standard toolbox

Figure 6-2 summarizes the controls that are available from the standard toolbox. Since many of them are standard Windows controls, you're probably already familiar with some of them. For instance, the DriveListBox control let's you select a disk drive, and the DirListBox control lets you select a directory (folder). Those controls are useful when you're working with files, but they're not needed when you're developing client/server applications that get data from databases.

The controls you use most often in business applications are the label, text box, command button, check box, option button, combo box, list box, and data controls. You'll see most of these controls used in the examples in this chapter.

You can experiment with the other toolbox controls whenever you find the need for them. If, for example, you want to add a graphic image to a form, you can use the PictureBox or Image control. If you want to develop a form that starts actions at certain times, you can use the Timer control, a hidden control that can be used to initiate Timer events. And if you want to insert an object from another program into a form, you can use an OLE control.

The only control in the toolbox that's not listed in figure 6-2 is the Pointer control. This is the control in the upper left corner of the standard toolbox with a picture of an arrow on it, and this control is selected by default. Unlike the other controls in the toolbox, it's not used to create a control on a form. Instead, it's used to select an existing control so you can work with it.

Control	Name	Description
	PictureBox	Displays a graphic
	Label	Displays descriptive information
	TextBox	Lets the user enter or modify a value
	Frame	Groups controls or defines areas of a form
	CommandButton	Performs an operation when clicked
	CheckBox	Turns an option on or off
	OptionButton	Turns an option on and turns off other options in the group
	ComboBox	Lets the user enter a value or select an item from a list
	ListBox	Displays a list that the user can select from
	HScrollBar	Provides horizontal navigation
	VScrollBar	Provides vertical navigation
	Timer	Executes code at a specified interval
	DriveListBox	Lets the user select a disk drive from a list
	DirListBox	Lets the user select a directory from a list
	FileListBox	Lets the user select a file from a list
	Shape	A graphical shape
	Line	A line
	Image	Displays a graphic
	Data	Lets the user navigate the records in a recordset
	OLE	Contains an OLE object

Figure 6-2 The controls in the standard toolbox

How to add controls to the toolbox

When you start a new project, the toolbox contains only the standard controls shown in figure 6-2. However, Visual Basic provides a variety of other controls that you can use in your applications. To add any of those controls to the toolbox, you can use the techniques summarized in figure 6-3.

The Controls tab of the Components dialog box lists all of the controls that can be added to a project. These can be controls that came with Visual Basic or controls that you purchased from other vendors or created yourself. In either case, you can add a control to the toolbox simply by selecting the check box for the control. Then, the new control is added to the bottom of the toolbox. (If you can't see the new control because there are too many controls in the toolbox, drag the edge of the toolbox to enlarge it.)

By default, the toolbox contains a single tab named General. If you add controls to the toolbox, however, you may want to place them on a separate tab. To create a new tab, just right-click on the toolbox, select the Add Tab command from the menu that's displayed, and enter a name for the tab. Then, the tab appears as a button at the bottom of the toolbox, and you can display the tab by clicking on that button. To add a control to the tab, just select the control in the Component dialog box while the tab is displayed.

The dialog box that lets you add controls to the toolbox

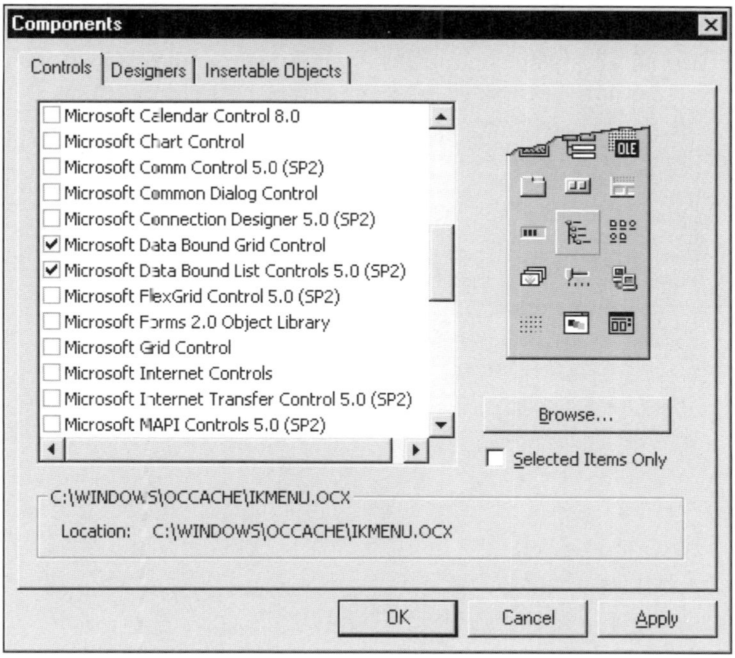

Description

- If you want to use a control other than those that are available from the standard toolbox, you can add the control to the toolbox using the dialog box shown above. To access this dialog box, choose the Components command from the Project menu.
- To add a control to the toolbox, click on its check box to select it. To remove a control from the toolbox, click on its check box to deselect it.
- Some of the options in the Controls tab of the Components dialog box add more than one control to the toolbox. The Microsoft Data Bound List Controls option, for example, adds both the data-bound combo box and the data-bound list box.
- Most of the controls were developed by third parties. These controls provide functions that aren't available when using the standard controls. In addition, you can buy other controls from various third-party vendors.
- By default, the Controls tab contains only the controls that come with Visual Basic. If you buy other controls, or if you develop controls of your own, you can add them to the Controls tab by clicking on the Browse button and identifying the OCX files for the controls.
- When you add a control to the toolbox, it's added to the tab that's currently displayed. By default, the toolbox contains a single tab named General. To add another tab, use the Add Tab command in the shortcut menu for the toolbox.

Figure 6-3 How to add controls to the toolbox

How to work with the controls on a form

Figure 6-4 shows how to work with controls. After you add controls to a form, you can select one or more controls using the Pointer control. When this control is selected, as it is by default, the mouse pointer appears as an arrow. Then, you can click on a control to select it, or you can hold down the Shift or Ctrl key as you click to select two or more controls.

After you select a control, you can move and size it using the mouse. You can also use the commands in the Format menu to work with controls. And you can change the properties of a control by using the Properties window.

The Format menu for a selected control

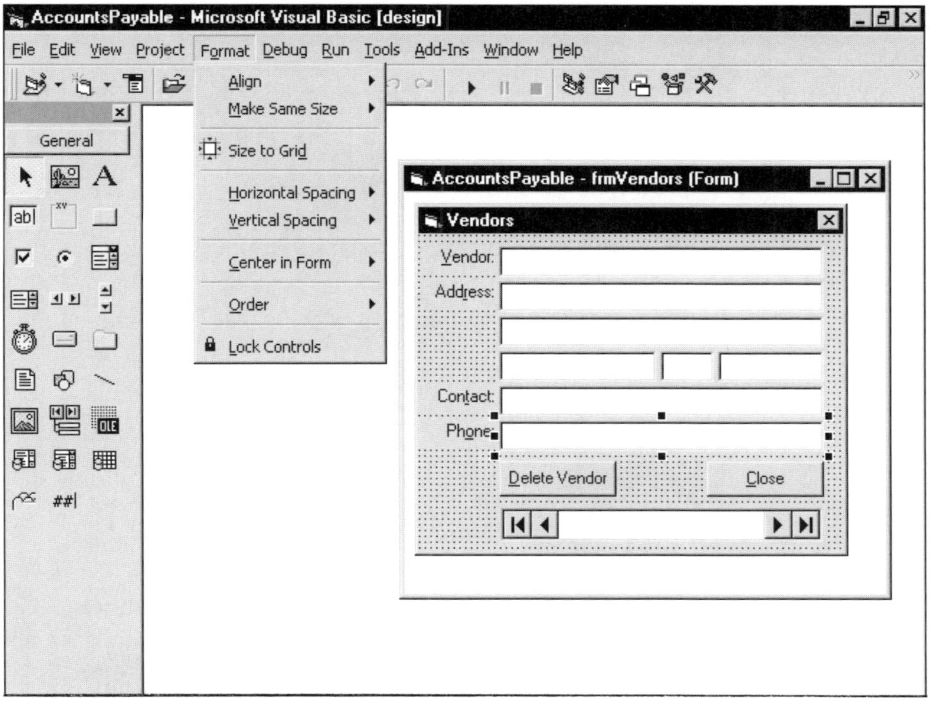

Description

- To add a control to a form, select the control in the toolbox and then drag the mouse pointer in the form where you want the control. You can also double-click on a control in the toolbox to add it to the center of the form.
- Before you can work with a control, you have to select it. To do that, click on the control. To select two or more controls, hold down the Shift or Ctrl key as you click on them. You can also select a group of controls by dragging around them with the mouse pointer.
- To move a control, drag it. To size a control, drag one of its handles. You can also change the size and position of a control by changing the appropriate properties of the control.
- You can also work with controls using the commands in the Format menu shown above. The first six items on this menu let you size and position controls using various techniques. The commands on the Order submenu let you control which objects appear on top of other objects when the objects are layered. And the Lock Controls command lets you lock all the controls on the form in their current position so that they can't be moved inadvertently.

Figure 6-4 How to work with the controls on a form

How to work with two or more open forms

While an application is running, two or more forms can be open at the same time. To work with these forms during development, you can use the techniques presented in figure 6-5. To display a second form while the first form is running, for example, you can use the Show method that's illustrated by the first example in this figure.

The Show method for a form loads that form if it hasn't already been loaded, and then displays it. The argument that's coded for the Show method specifies whether the form is *modal* (code 1) or *modeless* (code 0). When a modal form is displayed, the user can't interact with any other forms in the program until that form is closed or hidden. Otherwise, the user can interact with other forms while that form is still displayed.

To refer to the controls on an open form from another open form, just include the form name in the reference as shown in the second example in figure 6-5. This code refers to two fields in the recordset that are associated with the data control on another form. That code is used to synchronize the operation of two forms. Specifically, as an Invoices form is loaded, its load procedure accesses the invoice data that has the same VendorID as the current vendor on the Vendors form. Then, the Invoices recordset is positioned to the same record as the Invoices recordset for the Vendors form.

By default, the first form that's displayed when an application starts is positioned in the upper left corner of the screen. Then, when another form is displayed, it's positioned slightly down and to the right of the upper left corner of the first form. This is called a *cascaded* layout, and it's the Windows default.

You can change the default starting position of a form in one of two ways. First, you can change the StartupPosition property of the form. If you always want a form to be displayed in the center of the screen, for example, you can set this property to CenterScreen. Second, you can use the Form Layout window to position your forms manually. This window displays a representation of each form that's currently open in the project. Then, you can drag each form to an appropriate starting position.

A procedure that displays another form

```
Private Sub cmdInvoices_Click()
    frmInvoiceDetail.Show 1
End Sub
```

A procedure that refers to a control on another form

```
Private Sub Form_Load()
    Dim strSQL As String
    strSQL = "SELECT * FROM InvoicesByVendor " _
        & "WHERE VendorID = " _
        & frmVendors.datVendors.Recordset!VendorID
    datInvoices.RecordSource = strSQL
    datInvoices.Refresh
    datInvoices.Recordset.FindFirst "InvoiceID = " _
        & frmVendors.datInvoices.Recordset!InvoiceID
End Sub
```

Description

- To display another form, use the Show method of the form as shown in the first procedure above. This method will automatically load the form if it hasn't already been loaded.
- The Style argument on the Show method indicates whether the form is modal or modeless. To display a modal form, code 1 for the Style argument as shown above. To display a modeless form, code 0 or omit the Style argument.
- If you display a modal form, no actions can take place on other forms until the modal form is closed or hidden. Dialog boxes, for example, are usually displayed as modal forms. If you display a modeless form, the user can switch between the open forms.
- If two or more forms are open at the same time, you can refer to the controls on one form from another form. To do that, you include the name of the form in the reference as shown in the second procedure above. This procedure refers to two data controls on the form named frmVendors.
- To set the starting position for one or more forms, you can use the Form Layout window. To open this window, you can use the View menu or click on the Form Layout Window button in the Standard toolbar. Then, you can drag each form that you're using to an appropriate starting position. You can also set the starting position for a form by changing its StartupPosition property.
- To remove a form from the screen, use the Hide method of the form. This method has no arguments.

Note

- The SELECT statement that's constructed in the second example above retrieves data from a view named InvoicesByVendor. This view contains information from the Vendors, Invoices, and Terms tables of the AccountsPayable database.

Figure 6-5 How to work with two or more open forms

How to work with bound forms

The Vendors form presented in chapter 4 uses text boxes for all of the bound data. However, you can also use some special data-bound controls for working with data. In the topics that follow, you'll learn how to use those controls in an enhanced version of the bound Vendors form.

An enhanced version of the bound Vendors form

Figure 6-6 presents the enhanced version of the bound Vendors form. This form lets you add, modify, and delete records in a table of vendors. It also displays the invoices, credits, and payments for the current vendor; and it lets you display related forms for entering invoices, entering credits, selecting invoices for payments, and printing reports. To look up a vendor by name, you can use the Lookup box at the top of the form.

To implement these functions, the Vendors form uses three combo boxes that let the user select a state, terms, or an account from a list and another combo box to let the user look up a vendor name. This form also uses three grid controls on top of a tab control to display the invoice, credit, and payment records for each vendor. In addition, this form uses a separate button for the add function (instead of using the built-in function of the data control), and it includes the number of the current record in the display portion of the data control.

The combo boxes and grid controls on the Vendors form are special controls called *data-bound controls*. Each of these controls uses a separate data control as the source of its data, and all of the data controls except the Vendors control are hidden. The combo box that displays the state codes, for example, gets its data from a hidden data control that uses a table named States as its source of data. These controls along with the tab control are non-standard controls that you have to add to the toolbox (see figure 6-3).

When you use two or more data controls on the same form, you have to make sure that the controls are *synchronized*. When you display the record for a vendor, for example, you want to be sure that the correct terms description is displayed in the Terms combo box. As you'll see in a moment, you can use properties of the data controls and the data-bound controls to synchronize the data.

The enhanced version of the bound Vendors form

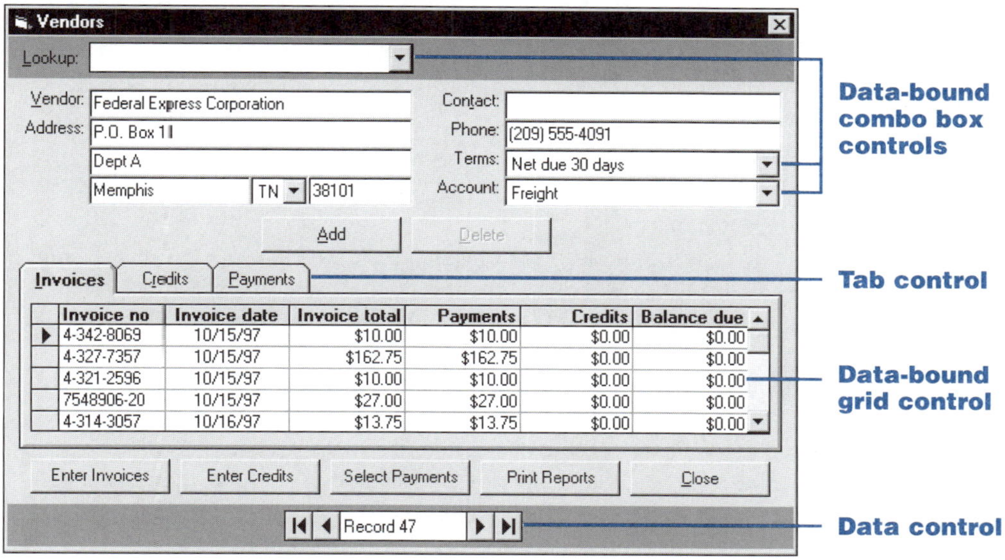

Description

- The main function of the Vendors form shown above is to maintain records in the Vendors table. The source of data for the data control on this form is the Vendors table sorted by vendor name.
- The user can add a record to the Vendors table by clicking on the Add button.
- The user can delete a record by clicking on the Delete button. This button is only enabled if the Vendor does not have any invoices, payments, or credits.
- Data-bound combo boxes are used to work with the state, terms, and account data. These combo boxes are bound to the Vendors data control, but they display data from three other recordsets that are defined by hidden data controls.
- The Vendors form uses three grid controls on top of a tab control to display the invoices, credits, and payments for the current vendor. These transactions are stored in three different tables.
- The first four buttons at the bottom of the Vendors form let the user display forms for entering invoices and credits, selecting payments, and printing reports.
- The combo box at the top of the Vendors form lets the user choose the name of a vendor from the drop-down list. Then, the data for that vendor is displayed.

Figure 6-6 An enhanced version of the bound Vendors form

How to use the Validate event of a data control

When the user clicks on one of the navigation buttons on a data control, the Validate event occurs before the recordset is repositioned. This event also occurs before an Update, Delete, or Close method is executed on the recordset associated with the data control and before the form that contains the data control is unloaded. In figure 6-7, you can see how you can use this event to control the processing that's performed by the data control.

The Validate event is used most often to validate the data the user has entered into bound controls. This is illustrated by the first event procedure in this figure, which checks to be sure that a phone number has been entered for each record before it is saved.

When the Validate event occurs, Visual Basic passes two arguments to the Validate procedure: the Action and Save arguments. The Action argument indicates what operation caused the Validate event to occur, and this figure summarizes the Visual Basic constants that represent the 12 possible operations. In contrast, the Save argument indicates whether any bound data has changed and, as a result, whether the related record will be updated. This is either a True or False value.

You can use the Action argument to adjust the processing based on what operation caused the Validate event. You can also change this argument so a different operation is performed or the current operation is canceled. In the first example in figure 6-7, this argument is changed to the VB constant vbDataActionCancel so the operation is canceled if a phone number isn't entered. If the user clicks on the navigation button to move to the next record and the phone number in the current record is blank, for example, the move operation is canceled.

Similarly, you can change the Save argument to cancel an update operation. In the first example in this figure, this argument is set to False if the phone number is blank so the related record isn't updated.

One of the limitations of using a data control is that it doesn't provide a way to cancel out of an add or change operation. Instead, when you click on one of its navigation buttons, the changes are saved automatically. With a little extra code, though, you can change the way records are updated. One way to do that is by using the Validate event of the data control as illustrated by the second example in figure 6-7.

In this example, the updating of a record is canceled if the user clicks on one of the navigation buttons on the data control or closes the form. That makes it possible for the user to use the navigation buttons or the Close button to cancel the changes made to an existing record or to cancel the addition of a new record. In this case, of course, the form has to provide another way for the user to update records. For example, the form could include an Update button that the user can click to save a record. For most people, that makes more sense than clicking a navigation button to save a record.

If you study the list of actions that you can use with the Validate event, you can probably think of some other uses for this event. When you use a data control, this is the event that helps you control its processing so it works the way you want it to.

A procedure that validates the data in a bound control

```
Private Sub datVendors_Validate(Action As Integer, Save As Integer)
    If txtPhone = "" Then
        MsgBox "You must enter a phone number", , "Data entry error"
        Action = vbDataActionCancel
        Save = False
    End If
End Sub
```

A procedure that cancels updating

```
Private Sub datVendors_Validate(Action As Integer, Save As Integer)
    If Save = True Then
        Select Case Action
            Case 1 to 4, 11
                Save = False
        End Select
    End If
End Sub
```

Values for the Action argument of the Validate event

Constant	Value	Operation
vbDataActionCancel	0	Cancel the operation
vbDataActionMoveFirst	1	Move to the first record
vbDataActionMovePrevious	2	Move to the previous record
vbDataActionMoveNext	3	Move to the next record
vbDataActionMoveLast	4	Move to the last record
vbDataActionAddNew	5	Execute the AddNew method
vbDataActionUpdate	6	Execute the Update method
vbDataActionDelete	7	Execute the Delete method
vbDataActionFind	8	Execute the Find method
vbDataActionBookmark	9	Set the Bookmark property
vbDataActionClose	10	Execute the Close method on the recordset object
vbDataActionUnload	11	Unload the form

Description

- The Validate event occurs before another record becomes the current record, before an Update, Delete, or Close method is executed, and before the form is unloaded.
- The Action argument indicates the operation that caused the Validate event to occur.
- The Save argument indicates whether data in bound controls has changed, and as a result, if the record will be saved. This argument can have a True or False value.

Figure 6-7 How to use the Validate event of a data control

How to synchronize the data on a form

When another record in the recordset associated with a data control becomes the current record, the Reposition event occurs on the data control. Then, you can use this event to perform operations like synchronizing the data in related recordsets with the current record.

The first example in figure 6-8 shows how you can display the current record number in the data control. This procedure uses the AbsolutePosition property of the recordset to determine the absolute position of the current record. Because the absolute position of the first record in a recordset is zero, this procedure adds one to the absolute position to get the record number of the current record. This value is then assigned to the Caption property of the data control, which causes it to be displayed in the middle of the data control.

The second example shows how you can synchronize the data in one data control with the current record in another data control. Here, the data control named datVendors defines a recordset that contains all of the records in a table of vendors. In addition, a second data control named datInvoices defines a recordset that contains all of the records in a table of invoices that are related to the current vendor.

When the current vendor changes, the Reposition event is used to update the recordset associated with the datInvoices data control so it displays the invoices for the current vendor. To do that, the event procedure constructs an appropriate SELECT statement in a string variable and then changes the RecordSource property of the data control to the value in that variable. After the RecordSource property is changed, the Refresh method is executed on the data control to rebuild the recordset based on the new property.

A procedure that displays the current record number in the data control

```
Private Sub datVendors_Reposition()
    datVendors.Caption = "Record " & _
        datVendors.Recordset.AbsolutePosition + 1
End Sub
```

A procedure that synchronizes the data in a data control with the current record in another data control

```
Private Sub datVendors_Reposition()
    Dim strSQL As String
    strSQL = "SELECT InvoiceID, VendorID, " _
        & "InvoiceNumber, InvoiceDate, InvoiceTotal " _
        & "FROM Invoices " _
        & "WHERE VendorID = " _
        & datVendors.Recordset!VendorID
    datInvoices.RecordSource = strSQL
    datInvoices.Refresh
End Sub
```

Description

- The Reposition event occurs after the current record pointer is moved. This event is typically used to synchronize data that's related to the recordset defined by the data control.
- The AbsolutePosition property returns the absolute position of the current record in the recordset. Because the absolute position of the first record is zero, one must be added to it to get the record number of the current record.
- The Refresh method rebuilds the recordset associated with a data control. You can use this method to update the recordset after you change the RecordSource property of the data control.

Figure 6-8 How to synchronize the data on a form

How to work with a data-bound combo box control

Three of the fields in the Vendors table contain values taken from records in related tables. The VendorState field contains a value from a record in the States table. The TermsID field contains a value from a record in the Terms table. And the AccountNo field contains a value from a record in the GLAccounts table.

To work with related tables like these, you can use the *data-bound combo box control*. This control lets you populate the combo box list with a field in a recordset defined by one data control and bind the control to a field in a recordset defined by another data control. It also provides for synchronizing the data in the two data controls when another record is displayed and for updating the data in the bound field when a different item is selected from the combo box list. And all of this can be done without any code.

Figure 6-9 presents the properties of the data-bound combo box control that you need to use. The DataSource and DataField properties work just like they do for any other bound control. They identify a data control and a field in the recordset associated with that data control. This binds the combo box to the data control. In the Vendors form, for example, the DataSource property for the Terms combo box is the name of the data control that defines the Vendors recordset: datVendors. And the DataField property is the name of the field that contains the terms code: TermsID.

In contrast, the RowSource property identifies the data control that defines the recordset used to populate the combo box list, and the ListField property identifies the field in that recordset that's displayed in the list. In the Vendors form, for example, the RowSource property for the Terms combo box is the name of the data control that defines the Terms recordset: datTerms. And the ListField property is the name of the field that populates the list for the combo box: TermsDescription.

Last, the BoundColumn property identifies the field in the recordset defined by the RowSource property that is passed to the field identified by the DataField property. The BoundColumn property for the Terms combo box, for example, specifies the TermsID field, and that's the field common to both the Vendors and Terms tables.

Once you've got these properties set up right, the combo box works the way you want it to. When the Vendors form in figure 6-6 is executed, for example, the first Vendors record is displayed and the Terms combo box displays the terms description for that vendor. That description, however, doesn't come from the Vendors table; it comes from the Terms table. Then, if the user selects a new description from the Terms combo box, the value in the TermsID field is passed back to the Vendors table so it can be used to update the current record. In figure 6-6, you can see that the TermsID value isn't even displayed on the Vendors form.

For the Terms combo box, one field is used for the ListField property and another is used for the BoundColumn property, but that isn't always the case. For the State combo box, for example, both of these properties should be set to the same field, StateCode.

When you use a data-bound combo box, it is usually bound to one data control, while another data control is used to populate its list. In some cases, though, you can use a data-bound combo box that isn't bound to a data control. You'll see how that works in just a moment.

Property	Description
DataSource	The name of the data control that the combo box is bound to.
DataField	The name of the field in the data control defined by the DataSource property that the combo box is bound to.
RowSource	The name of the data control that provides the data for the items in the combo box list.
ListField	The name of the field in the data control defined by the RowSource property that is displayed in the combo box list.
BoundColumn	The field in the data control defined by the RowSource property that is used to pass data to the field defined by the DataSource and DataField properties. This can be the same field specified in the ListField property.
BoundText	The value of the field specified by the BoundColumn property.
MatchEntry	Determines how the list portion of the combo box is searched as text is entered into the text portion of the combo box.
Style	Determines whether the list portion of the combo box drops down or is fixed and whether text can be entered into the text portion of the combo box.

Description

- The properties for a data-bound combo box let you bind the control to a field that's defined by one data control (the data control specified by the DataSource property) but list data from a field that's defined by another data control (the data control specified by the RowSource property). The field specified in the BoundColumn property is the field that is common to both recordsets that are defined by the data controls.
- The value of the field specified by the DataField property determines which entry in the combo box list is selected. This is also the field that is updated if a different entry is selected from the combo box list.
- To display the custom properties for a control, choose the Properties command from the shortcut menu. This displays the Property Pages dialog box. You can also display this dialog box from the Properties window by clicking on the Custom item and then clicking on the ellipsis (...) button that's displayed. Some properties are displayed in both the Properties window and the Property Pages dialog box, but it's usually best to work from the Property Pages dialog box.

Figure 6-9 Some of the properties of a data-bound combo box control

How to create and format a data-bound grid control

If you want to display more than one record from a recordset on a form at the same time, you can use a grid control like the one shown in the form in figure 6-6. This grid control is called a *data-bound grid control* because it's bound to a recordset defined by a data control. In this case, the recordset contains all of the invoices for the current vendor, and each column in the grid is bound to a different field in the recordset.

Figure 6-10 shows how to create this type of grid control. After you add a grid control to a form, you have to set its DataSource property to identify the data control that it's bound to. Once you've done that, you can use its shortcut menu to work with the grid control. To start, you can use the Retrieve Fields command to retrieve all the fields from the recordset that's defined by the data control. When you do that, each of the fields appears as a column in the grid as shown in this figure.

To edit the columns in the grid, you use the Edit command in the shortcut menu for the grid control. When you select this command, the grid enters *UI-active mode*. From this mode, you can use the commands in the shortcut menu (which is somewhat different from the one shown) to add, copy, delete, and move columns. You can also change column widths or the row heights while you're in this mode. To change the properties of the grid control, you can use either standard mode or UI-active mode.

The shortcut menu for a data-bound grid control

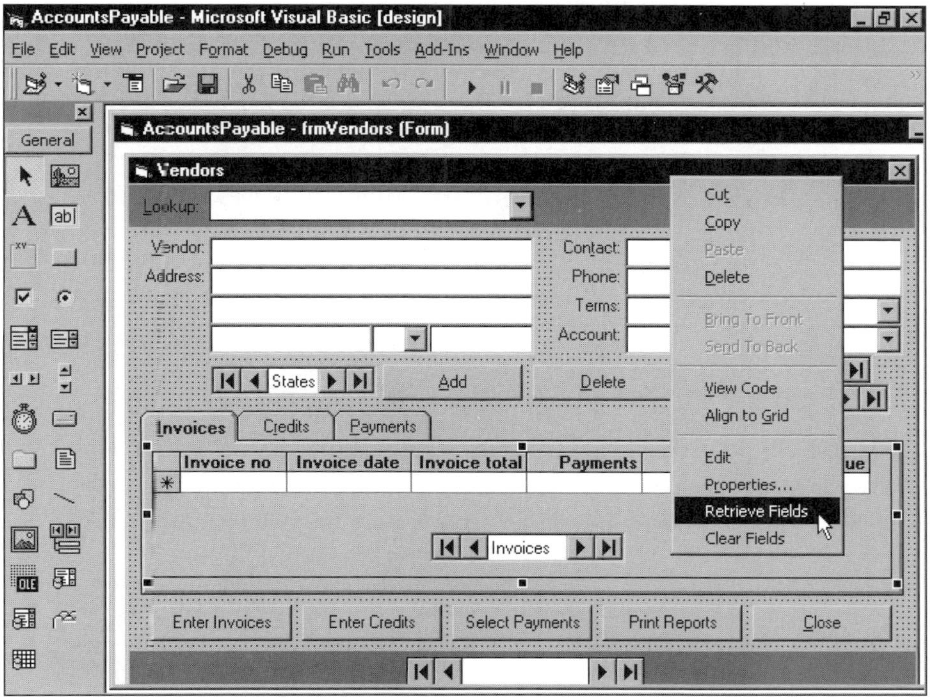

Description

- You use the DataSource property of a data-bound grid (DBGrid) control to establish the source of data for the control. The DataSource property specifies the name of the data control that the DBGrid control is bound to.
- Once you bind the DBGrid control to a data control, you can retrieve the fields from the data control using the Retrieve Fields command in the shortcut menu for the DBGrid control. Each of the fields in the recordset defined by the data control becomes a column in the DBGrid control as shown above.
- If you choose the Edit command from the shortcut menu for the DBGrid control, the grid enters into *UI-active mode*. From this mode, you can use the commands in the UI-active shortcut menu to change the layout of the columns and rows in the grid.
- The Cut, Copy, Paste, Delete, Insert, and Append commands in the UI-active shortcut menu let you manipulate the columns in a DBGrid control. To select the column you want to work with, click on the column header. To select two or more columns, drag over the column headers.
- You can also change individual column widths in UI-active mode by dragging the column dividers. And you can change the height of all the rows by dragging a row divider.
- To exit from UI-active mode, click anywhere outside the DBGrid control.

Figure 6-10 How to create and format a data-bound grid control

Some of the properties of a data-bound grid control

Figure 6-11 presents some of the properties of the data-bound grid control. These properties are displayed on the tabs of the Property Pages dialog box that you can display by selecting the Properties command from the shortcut menu for the control. Some of these properties are also available from the Properties window.

In addition to the three tabs referred to in this figure, four other tabs are available in the Property Pages dialog box. These tabs let you set properties that affect how the Tab and arrow keys work, what colors and fonts are used, and how splits work if the grid is split into two or more panes. For most grid controls, though, you won't need to change these properties.

The AllowAddNew, AllowDelete, and AllowUpdate properties in the General tab determine what you can do with the data in the grid. By default, you can update records but you can't add or delete records.

In contrast, the Columns tab provides properties for each column in the grid. Although the initial values of these properties are set when you retrieve the fields from the data control, some of these values change when you change the grid in UI-active mode. For each column, the Caption property contains the text that's displayed at the top of the column, which by default is the field name, and the NumberFormat property determines the format in which fields are displayed. As a result, you will frequently want to change the default values for these properties.

The Layout tab also provides properties for each column. Three of the properties in this tab that you might want to change are Locked, AllowSizing, and Alignment. If you change the Locked property to True, the user won't be able to change the data in the column even if updating is allowed.

Property	Tab	Description
AllowAddNew	General	Determines whether records can be added to the grid. By default, records cannot be added.
AllowDelete	General	Determines whether records can be deleted from the grid. By default, records cannot be deleted.
AllowUpdate	General	Determines whether records in the grid can be modified. By default, records can be modified.
DataMode	General	Determines whether the data in the grid is bound or unbound. The default is bound.
Caption	Columns	The caption that's displayed in the column header for the selected field. The default is the name of the field.
DataField	Columns	The field that the selected column is bound to.
DefaultValue	Columns	The value that's inserted into the selected column of a new record if a value isn't entered by the user.
NumberFormat	Columns	The format that's used to display the data in the selected column.
Locked	Layout	Determines whether or not data in the selected column can be edited. By default, columns are not locked.
AllowSizing	Layout	Determines whether the selected column can be sized. By default, columns can be sized.
Alignment	Layout	The alignment of the data in the selected column. The default is left-aligned.

Note

- To access the properties shown above, click on the indicated tab of the Property Pages dialog box. To access that dialog box, select the Properties command from the shortcut menu for the grid control.

Figure 6-11 Some of the properties of a data-bound grid control

The property settings for the data controls on the enhanced version of the bound Vendors form

Now that you've been introduced to the data-bound combo box and data-bound grid controls, you can see how they're used in the enhanced Vendors form shown in figure 6-6. First, figure 6-12 presents the primary property settings for five of the data controls that are used (the data controls for the Credits and Payments tab of the form aren't included, but their property settings are similar to the ones for the Invoices data control). Then, the next figure presents the primary property settings for the combo box and grid controls.

In figure 6-12, you can see the property settings that define the recordsets that are created for five of the data controls. In addition to these properties, you need to set the Connect and DatabaseName properties to identify and connect to the database that you're accessing just as you did for the database in chapter 4. You also need to set the Visible property of all of the data controls except datVendors to False so these controls aren't displayed when the form is run. (You only need to display a data control when you need access to its navigation buttons.)

Because the recordset that's defined by the Vendors data control is the only recordset that can be modified by the program, it is the only dynaset-type recordset. For all of the other data controls, the RecordsetType property is set to Snapshot. Because the recordsets defined by these data controls will contain a limited amount of data, this should be the most efficient setting.

The RecordSource property for each of the data controls is a SELECT statement. Except for the Invoices data control, the SELECT statements retrieve all of the records and fields from the appropriate tables and sort them by the appropriate fields. To improve the efficiency of the program, though, you can specify just the fields that are used by the program.

The SELECT statement for the Invoices data control retrieves all of the records in the Invoices table, but only the fields in each record that are used in the Invoices grid. Later, when you retrieve the fields for the grid, Visual Basic will use this SELECT statement to determine what columns to include in the grid. Then, after you define the grid, you can delete this statement from the RecordSource property. That's because this property is set in the code for the program, as you'll see in a moment.

If you don't delete this property setting after you design the grid, the form will still work, but it won't be as efficient. That's because all of the records in the Invoices table will be retrieved unnecessarily when the form is loaded. Then, before the form is displayed, the Invoices recordset is refreshed so it contains just the records for the current vendor.

Properties for the Vendors data control	
Name	datVendors
RecordsetType	Dynaset
RecordSource	Select * From Vendors Order By VendorName
Options	512

Properties for the States data control	
Name	datStates
RecordsetType	Snapshot
RecordSource	Select * From States Order By StateCode

Properties for the Invoices data control	
Name	datInvoices
RecordsetType	Snapshot
RecordSource	Select InvoiceNumber, InvoiceDate, InvoiceTotal, PaymentTotal, CreditTotal, InvoiceTotal – PaymentTotal – CreditTotal From Invoices

Properties for the Accounts data control	
Name	datAccounts
RecordsetType	Snapshot
RecordSource	Select * From GLAccounts Order By AccountDescription

Properties for the Terms data control	
Name	datTerms
RecordsetType	Snapshot
RecordSource	Select * From Terms Order By TermsDescription

Notes

- The Connect property for all of the data controls is set to "ODBC;DATABASE = AccountsPayable" and the DatabaseName property is set to AccountsPayable.
- The Visible property for all the data controls except for datVendors is set to False so that they're not visible when the form is displayed.
- The option 512 that's specified for the Vendors data control causes a trappable error to occur if another user is modifying the same data. This option is required if you're accessing a SQL Server 6.0 table (or later) for update and the table contains an identity field.

Figure 6-12 Property settings for the data controls on the Vendors form

The property settings for the data-bound controls on the enhanced version of the bound Vendors form

Figure 6-13 shows the primary property settings for the data-bound combo boxes and one of the data-bound grid controls used on the Vendors form. Although the settings for the Credits and Payments grid controls aren't included, they're similar to ones for the Invoices grid control.

For the State combo box, the DataSource and DataField properties bind this combo box to the VendorState field that's defined by the datVendors data control. Then, the RowSource and ListField properties are set so this box displays the values in the StateCode field in the recordset defined by the datStates data control. Last, the BoundColumn property says that the StateCode field in the States table should be passed to the field that the control is bound to (the VendorState field) whenever the StateCode field is changed. In other words, if the user selects a new state code from the combo box, the value in the Vendor record should be changed.

The Style property for this combo box (and all the other combo boxes on the form) is set to dbcDropdownList, which prevents the user from entering text into the text portion of the combo box that doesn't match an item in the list. That way, the user can't enter an invalid state code.

The Terms and Accounts combo boxes are similar to the States combo box. The main difference is that the same field isn't used for the ListField and BoundColumn properties. That's because the field that's displayed in the combo box list is not the same as the field that the control is bound to. If, for example, a user selects a new terms description from the Terms combo box list, it's the TermsID field that's passed to the field in the Vendors table that the control is bound to.

In contrast to the State, Terms, and Accounts combo boxes, the Lookup combo box isn't bound to a data control. Instead, its RowSource and ListField properties specify that the combo box list should display the values in the VendorName field that's in the recordset defined by the data control named datVendors (the same data control that's used to populate the text boxes on the form). Then, even though this control isn't bound to another data control, the VendorID field is specified for the BoundColumn property so it can be used to locate a vendor when a vendor name is selected from the list. As you'll see in a moment, you do that by using code. In addition, since the combo box isn't updated automatically when records are added to or deleted from the datVendors recordset, you need to do that through code.

The last properties in figure 6-13 are for the Invoices grid control. These just name the grid control and identify the data control that's used to get the data for the grid control. Besides these properties, though, you need to change some of the properties for the individual columns. To display the grid data as shown in figure 6-6, for example, you need to change the Caption property for each column, the Currency and Alignment properties for the four numeric fields, and the Alignment property for the InvoiceDate field. On the other hand, you don't have to change the default AllowUpdate setting, even though you don't want the user to be able to change the data in the grid. That's because the source of data for the grid is a snapshot-type recordset, which doesn't allow changes.

Properties for the Lookup combo box control	
Name	dbcLookup
Style	dbcDropdownList
DataSource	
DataField	
RowSource	datVendors
ListField	VendorName
BoundColumn	VendorID

Properties for the State combo box control	
Name	dbcStates
Style	dbcDropdownList
DataSource	datVendors
DataField	VendorState
RowSource	datStates
ListField	StateCode
BoundColumn	StateCode

Properties for the Terms combo box control	
Name	dbcTerms
Style	dbcDropdownList
DataSource	datVendors
DataField	TermsID
RowSource	datTerms
ListField	TermsDescription
BoundColumn	TermsID

Properties for the Accounts combo box control	
Name	dbcAccounts
Style	dbcDropdownList
DataSource	datVendors
DataField	AccountNo
RowSource	datAccounts
ListField	AccountDescription
BoundColumn	AccountNo

Properties for the Invoices grid control	
Name	dbgInvoices
DataSource	datInvoices

Note

- The properties for the individual columns in the Invoices grid are not shown in this figure. However, the DataField property for each column is set to the associated field in the Invoices data control; the Caption property is set as shown in figure 6-6; the NumberFormat property for the four numeric columns is set to Currency; the Alignment property for the four numeric fields is set to Right; and the Alignment property for the date column is set to Center.

Figure 6-13 Property settings for the data-bound controls on the Vendors form

Code for the enhanced version of the bound Vendors form

Once you set the properties for the data controls, combo boxes, and grid controls right, coding the enhanced version of the bound Vendors form is relatively easy. As you can see in figure 6-14, just 10 event procedures are required.

The main procedure for this form is the event procedure for the Reposition event of the Vendors data control (1). This event occurs when a different vendor is displayed on the form. Then, the data controls that are used as the source of data for the Invoices, Credits, and Payments grids have to be refreshed so they show the records for the current vendor. Although this procedure shows only the code for refreshing the Invoices data control, the code for refreshing the Credits and Payments data controls is similar.

The procedure starts by checking the EOF property of the Vendors recordset. This property is true only when the MoveNext method in the Click event procedure for the Delete command button is executed after the last record in the recordset has been deleted. In that case, it isn't necessary to execute the rest of the code in the procedure since there is no current record. Otherwise, the code that follows is executed.

That code starts by assigning the right value to a variable named intVendorID so the SELECT statement that uses it later on works correctly. To set that value right, an If statement uses the IsNull function to test whether the current VendorID field is a null value. If it is, the intVendorID variable is assigned a value of –1; otherwise, it's assigned the value of the VendorID field in the current record.

This code is necessary because the VendorID field is null when the Reposition event occurs after the AddNew method is executed. Then, if the null value were used in the WHERE clause of the SELECT statement in the procedure, an error would occur. With this code, though, the intVendorID variable is used in the WHERE clause with its value set to -1. But since the VendorID field will never contain a value of -1, the Invoices recordset will contain no records, which is what you want for a new record. On the other hand, if the VendorID isn't null, this procedure sets the intVendorID variable to the value of the VendorID field in the current record and updates the Caption property of the Vendors data control so it indicates the current record number.

Instead of using a variable for the VendorID field in the SELECT statement, you might think that you could just use the VendorID field and set its value to -1. If you do that, though, you'll get an error when you try to save the new record. That's because this field is an identity field, which means that its value must be generated by SQL Server.

After the If statement, this procedure assigns the SQL statement in the string variable named strSQL to the RecordSource property of the Invoices data control. Then, it uses the Refresh method to refresh the data in that data control. Last, this procedure checks the record count for this recordset. If it's zero, the Delete command button on the form is enabled so that the user can delete the Vendor record. If this recordset contains records, however, the Delete button is disabled so the Vendor record can't be deleted.

Visual Basic code for the bound Vendors form **Page 1**

```
Option Explicit
```

1

```
Private Sub datVendors_Reposition()
    If Not datVendors.Recordset.EOF Then
        Dim intVendorID As Integer, strSQL As String
        If IsNull(datVendors.Recordset!VendorID) Then
            intVendorID = -1
        Else
            intVendorID = datVendors.Recordset!VendorID
            datVendors.Caption = "Record " _
              & datVendors.Recordset.AbsolutePosition + 1
        End If
        strSQL = "SELECT VendorID, InvoiceNumber, " _
            & "InvoiceDate, InvoiceTotal, PaymentTotal, " _
            & "CreditTotal, " _
            & "InvoiceTotal - PaymentTotal - CreditTotal " _
            &     "AS BalanceDue " _
            & "FROM Invoices " _
            & "WHERE VendorID = " & intVendorID
        datInvoices.RecordSource = strSQL
        datInvoices.Refresh
        If datInvoices.Recordset.RecordCount = 0 Then
            cmdDelete.Enabled = True
        Else
            cmdDelete.Enabled = False
        End If
    End If
End Sub
```

Figure 6-14 Code for the bound Vendors form (part 1 of 3)

Before a new or existing record in the Vendors recordset is updated, the Validate event occurs on the data control (2). For this form, the procedure for the Validate event is used to verify that a valid zip code has been entered into the zip code field. To do that, the entered zip code is compared with the FirstZipCode and LastZipCode fields in the States table record for the state that's entered by the user. However, this is done only if the user has changed the state or zip code, which is determined by checking the DataChanged property of those fields.

If the state or zip code has been changed, the procedure uses the FindFirst method to locate the correct state record in the recordset associated with the datStates data control. That's necessary because the recordset is not repositioned when a different item is selected from the States combo box as you might think. Then, the code uses Val and Left functions to check whether the entered zip code falls within the range of zip codes for that state. If it doesn't, an error message is displayed by the MsgBox function; the Action argument of the procedure is assigned a value of vbDataActionCancel to cancel the operation that caused the Validate event to occur; and the Save argument is set to False so the record isn't updated.

In practice, the procedure for the Validate event can also be used to validate other fields that have been changed. Also, the code for checking a specific field like a zip code field can be placed in a Public procedure in a standard module. Then, that procedure can be called by any module in the project.

To add a Vendor record, the user clicks on the Add command button. Then, the Click event procedure for this button (3) executes the AddNew method for the recordset so a new, blank record is displayed in the form. This procedure also disables the Delete button, and it moves the focus to the first modifiable field on the form.

To delete a Vendor record, the user clicks on the Delete button. Then, the Click event procedure for this button (4) starts by displaying a message box so the user can verify the delete operation. If the user clicks on the Yes button, the procedure deletes the record and repositions the current record pointer. In addition, it refreshes the Vendors recordset so the deleted record is no longer included in the Lookup combo box. Last, because the Refresh method resets the current record pointer to the beginning of the recordset, the FindFirst method is used to move the record pointer back to its previous position.

Visual Basic code for the bound Vendors form Page 2

2
```
Private Sub datVendors_Validate(Action As Integer, _
    Save As Integer)
    If dbcStates.DataChanged Or txtZipCode.DataChanged Then
        Dim strLookupText As String
        strLookupText = "StateCode = '" & dbcStates & "'"
        datStates.Recordset.FindFirst strLookupText
        If         Val(Left(txtZipCode, 5)) < _
                     datStates.Recordset!FirstZipCode _
                Or Val(Left(txtZipCode, 5)) > _
                     datStates.Recordset!LastZipCode Then
            MsgBox "The zip code is invalid", , _
                   "Data entry error"
            txtZipCode.SetFocus
            Action = vbDataActionCancel
            Save = False
        End If
    End If
End Sub
```

3
```
Private Sub cmdAdd_Click()
    datVendors.Recordset.AddNew
    cmdDelete.Enabled = False
    txtVendor.SetFocus
End Sub
```

4
```
Private Sub cmdDelete_Click()
    Dim strResponse As String
    Dim intVendorID As Integer, strLookupText As String
    strResponse = MsgBox("Delete this record?", _
        vbYesNo + vbDefaultButton2, "Delete Confirmation")
    If strResponse = vbYes Then
        datVendors.Recordset.Delete
        datVendors.Recordset.MoveNext
        If datVendors.Recordset.EOF Then
            datVendors.Recordset.MoveLast
        End If
        intVendorID = datVendors.Recordset!VendorID
        datVendors.Refresh
        strLookupText = "VendorID = " & intVendorID
        datVendors.Recordset.FindFirst strLookupText
        txtVendor.SetFocus
    End If
End Sub
```

Figure 6-14 Code for the bound Vendors form (part 2 of 3)

If the user selects a vendor from the Lookup combo box, the Change event for that control occurs. Then, the Change event procedure (5) uses the FindFirst method to locate the selected vendor. To do that, it looks for the Vendor with the VendorID that's equal to the BoundText property of the combo box control. This property contains the value of the field specified in the BoundColumn property of the control, which in this case is VendorID. That's why the BoundColumn property was specified for this control even though the control isn't bound to a data control.

Because the user is only allowed to select a Vendor from the list of existing vendors, you can be sure that the FindFirst method will always work. In a situation where the FindFirst or another Find method may not find the specified record, though, you can use the NoMatch property of the recordset to determine if the operation was successful. If the value of this property is True, the specified record couldn't be found. In that case, the current record pointer will be undefined. If you want to be able to return to the previous record when that happens, you can save the bookmark of that record before you use the Find method. To do that, just assign the Bookmark property of the recordset to a variant-type variable. Then, if the find operation fails, you can restore the bookmark property.

The next five procedures (6) occur when the user clicks on one of the command buttons at the bottom of the form. The first four procedures use the Show method to display another form. Because the Style argument is omitted from the method in each procedure, the forms are modeless so more than one form can be open at a time.

The last of these procedures uses the Unload statement to close the Vendors form and the End statement to release the resources used by the application. Notice that this Unload statement uses the Me keyword rather than the name of the form to indicate that the form that contains the statement is to be closed.

Now that you've browsed through all of the procedures for this form, you may want to reflect on the coding and development process. Although you get a lot done with a minimal amount of code when you work with bound forms, you can't always get the application to work the way you want it to. In addition, you often have to establish and maintain some intricate relationships between the code and the property settings for the data and data-bound controls. This in turn can make an application difficult to debug and maintain.

Visual Basic code for the bound Vendors form Page 3

5

```
Private Sub dbcLookup_Change()
    Dim strLookupText As String
    strLookupText = "VendorID = " & dbcLookup.BoundText
    datVendors.Recordset.FindFirst strLookupText
End Sub
```

6

```
Private Sub cmdInvoices_Click()
    frmInvoices.Show
End Sub

Private Sub cmdCredits_Click()
    frmCredits.Show
End Sub

Private Sub cmdPayments_Click()
    frmPayments.Show
End Sub

Private Sub cmdReports_Click()
    frmReports.Show
End Sub

Private Sub cmdClose_Click()
    Unload Me
    End
End Sub
```

Figure 6-14 Code for the bound Vendors form (part 3 of 3)

How to work with unbound forms

As you have just seen in the bound version of the Vendors form, a minimum amount of code is required when you build forms with data controls. Often, though, it's easier and better to build forms without data controls. That way, you can develop applications that are more robust, more efficient, easier to use, and easier to maintain.

Keep in mind, though, that you can use data controls for some functions but not for others. For instance, you can use data controls to get the data for the combo boxes and grids of a form, even though you don't use a data control to work with the records in the Vendors table. But here again, you'll often find that you have more control over all of the data if you don't use any data controls.

An enhanced version of the unbound Vendors form

Figure 6-15 presents an enhanced version of the unbound Vendors form presented in chapter 4. This form provides the same basic functions as the bound form presented in figure 6-6. However, all of its functions are implemented without the use of data controls.

Like the bound form, the unbound form uses combo boxes that let the user select states, terms, and accounts. It also uses a combo box for the lookup function. And it uses grids to display the invoice, credit, and payment information.

Unlike the bound form, though, this form uses standard combo boxes instead of data-bound combo boxes, and it uses Microsoft FlexGrid (MSFlexGrid) controls instead of data-bound grid controls. That means you have to use Visual Basic code to populate each of these controls with the appropriate data and to synchronize them with the current vendor record. To populate the three grid controls, this form uses QueryDef objects, which you'll soon learn about.

This version of the Vendors form also keeps track of the position of the current record in the Vendors recordset so the appropriate navigation buttons can be disabled when the first or last record is displayed. And when a record is added to or deleted from the Vendors recordset, this version updates the list of vendors in the Lookup combo box. Because this combo box isn't bound to a data control, this function is easier to implement in this unbound form than it is in a bound form.

The enhanced version of the unbound Vendors form

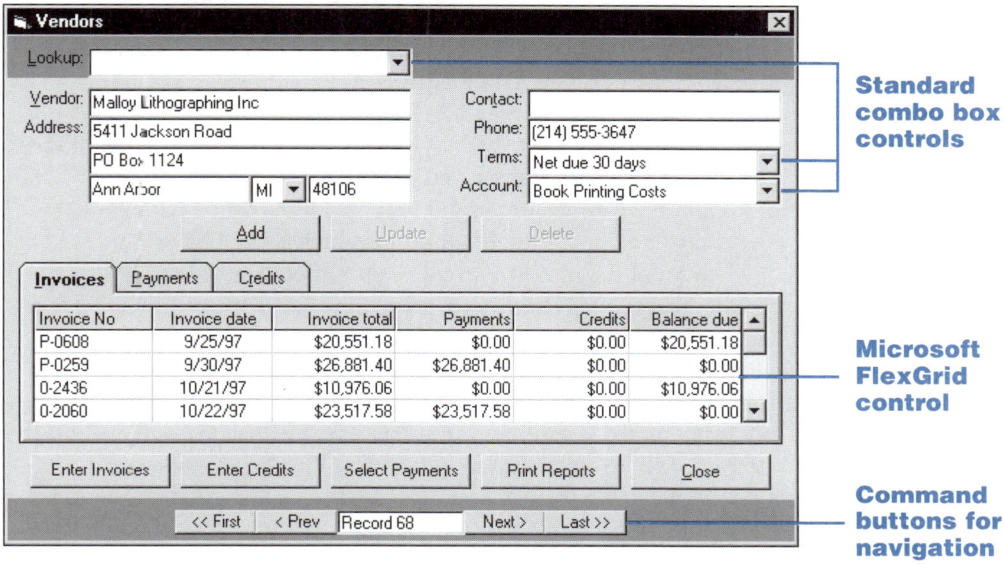

Description

- The enhanced version of the unbound Vendors form performs the same functions as the enhanced version of the bound Vendors form presented earlier in this chapter. See figure 6-6 for details.
- Because no bound controls are used on the form, each control is populated and synchronized through code. Standard combo box controls are used for the Lookup, State, Terms, and Account data. Microsoft FlexGrid controls are used to display the Invoices, Credits, and Payments associated with the current vendor. And QueryDef objects are used to define the records that are displayed in these grids.
- The navigation buttons are enhanced in this version of the program so the First and Prev buttons are disabled when the first record in the recordset is displayed and the Next and Last buttons are disabled when the last record in the recordset is displayed.
- This version of the Vendors form also updates the Lookup combo box any time a vendor is added to or deleted from the Vendors recordset.

Figure 6-15 An enhanced version of the unbound Vendors form

How to work with form events

When a form is first displayed, several events can occur before the form actually appears on the screen. These events are summarized in figure 6-16. In general, you use these events to initialize the form and its data before it's displayed.

In chapter 4, the unbound version of the Vendors form used the Load event of the form to open the AccountsPayable database and the Vendors recordset, load the values in the current record into the form controls, and initialize some of the module-level variables. For efficiency, though, you should open the database and recordsets used by the form in the procedure for the Initialize event. This is illustrated by the first procedure presented in this figure. The second procedure shows the type of code that should be included in the Load event procedure.

Although you may not use the Resize event often, it can be useful if the user is allowed to change the size of a form. Then, the Resize event procedure can be used to resize the controls based on the size of the form. This event can be also be useful if the form you're developing will be displayed on monitors with varying resolutions. Since the Resize event occurs when the form is first displayed as well as when the form is resized, you can use it to get the monitor resolution and adjust the size of the form and its controls accordingly. How you do that, though, is beyond the scope of this book.

The Activate event of a form is typically used to display custom toolbars and menus on the form. In chapter 8, you can learn how to do that.

The events that occur when you display a form

Event	Description
Initialize	Occurs when an instance of the form is created. You can use this event to initialize any data that's used by the form.
Load	Occurs when the form is loaded into memory. You can use this event to initialize controls and module-level variables.
Resize	Occurs when the form is first displayed or when its size changes. You can use this event to resize controls when a form is resized.
Activate	Occurs when the form becomes the active window. You can use this event to display custom menus and toolbars.

The code for an initialize procedure

```
Private Sub Form_Initialize()
    Dim strSQL As String
    strSQL = "SELECT * FROM Vendors ORDER BY VendorName"
    Set dbAP = OpenDatabase("AccountsPayable", 0, 0, _
        "ODBC;DATABASE=AccountsPayable")
    Set recVendors = dbAP.OpenRecordset(strSQL, _
        dbOpenDynaset, dbSeeChanges)
End Sub
```

The code for a load procedure

```
Private Sub Form_Load()
    txtVendor = recVendors!VendorName
    txtAddress1 = recVendors!VendorAddress1
    txtAddress2 = recVendors!VendorAddress2
    txtCity = recVendors!VendorCity
    cboStates = recVendors!VendorState
    txtZipCode = recVendors!VendorZipCode
    blnRecordEdited = False
    blnAddMode = False
End Sub
```

Note

- Although you can include the code for initializing data in the load procedure, it's more efficient to include it in the initialize procedure.

Figure 6-16 How to work with form events

How to work with a standard combo box control

Figure 6-17 presents some of the properties and methods of the standard combo box control. When you first create this type of control, its list is empty. Then, to populate the control, you provide the list items in the List property. To do that, you can use two different techniques.

First, you can type a list of items directly into the drop-down box for the List property. To do that, enter the first value, then press Ctrl and the Enter key together to move to the next line. (If you press just the Enter key, the drop-down list will close.) The values you enter are treated as an array of string variables with index values from 0 to the number of items minus 1.

Second, you can use the AddItem method to add items to the list. This is illustrated by the procedure in this figure. This procedure reads through the records in a recordset named recTerms and loads the value of the TermsDescription field for each record into the list. It also loads the value of the TermsID field for each record into the ItemData property of the new list item (the item identified by the NewIndex property). This property can contain a number that's associated with the list item. It is particularly useful when you need to associate the items in the list with other data in the form by a field other than the one that's displayed in the list. You'll see how this works when you see the code for this version of the unbound Vendors form later in this chapter.

Once you populate a combo box list, you can refer to a specific item in the list by using its index value. For example, the following statement assigns the value of the first item in a combo box named cboTerms to a string variable named strTerms:

```
strTerms = cboTerms.List(0)
```

To get the value of the item that's currently selected in the combo box, you can use the ListIndex property of the combo box control like this:

```
strTerms = cboTerms.List(cboTerms.ListIndex)
```

However, you can also accomplish the same thing using the Text property of the combo box:

```
strTerms = cboTerms.Text
```

Property	Description
ItemData	An array of numbers with each number corresponding to an item in the combo box list.
List	An array of text strings that define the items in the combo box list.
ListCount	The number of items in the combo box list.
ListIndex	The index of the item that's currently selected in the combo box.
NewIndex	The index of the last item that was added to the combo box.
Sorted	Determines whether or not the combo box list is sorted alphabetically.
Style	Determines whether the list portion of the combo box drops down or is fixed and whether text can be entered into the text portion of the combo box.
Text	The value of the item that's currently selected in the combo box.

Method	Description
AddItem	Adds an item to the combo box list. If the list is sorted, the item is added in the appropriate position in the list. Otherwise, it's added to the end of the list.
Clear	Clears the combo box list.
RemoveItem	Removes the item with the specified index from the combo box list.

A procedure that populates a combo box from a recordset

```
Private Sub LoadTerms()
    Do Until recTerms.EOF
        cboTerms.AddItem recTerms!TermsDescription
        cboTerms.ItemData(cboTerms.NewIndex) _
            = recTerms!TermsID
        recTerms.MoveNext
    Loop
End Sub
```

Description

- If the items that are displayed in a combo box are fixed, you can enter a list of values into the List property. Otherwise, you can use the AddItem method to add items to the list as shown in the procedure above.
- You can use the ItemData property to associate a key field with each item you add to a combo box list. This is useful if you need to synchronize the item that's displayed in the combo box with other data in the form using the key field.

Figure 6-17 How to work with a standard combo box control

How to create and work with a Microsoft FlexGrid control

The Microsoft FlexGrid (MSFlexGrid) control lets you display data in a row and column format like the one for a data-bound grid control. Unlike the data-bound grid control, though, you have to use code to populate the MSFlexGrid control. Within the code, you use the properties shown in figure 6-18.

When you first create an MSFlexGrid control, it contains two rows and two columns, and those values are stored in the Rows and Cols properties. If you will be populating the grid with data from a variable number of records as in the Vendors form, it isn't necessary to change the value in the Rows property until the form is run. Then, you can set this property based on the number of records in the recordset that's used to populate the control. In contrast, the number of columns is usually fixed so you can set the Cols property when you define the control.

When you set the Rows and Cols property, be sure to include any column or row headers displayed in the form. The Invoices grid in the Vendors form, for example, includes one row that contains the column headings. As a result, the total number of rows will be one more than the number of rows in the recordset. As you can see in figure 6-18, the number of columns and rows used for the headings are specified by the FixedCols and FixedRows properties, which are typically set when the control is defined.

The FormatString property contains a string that determines the appearance of the rows and columns in the grid. You can use this property to specify the width and alignment of each column and the text that's displayed at the top of each column. You can also use it to specify the text that's displayed to the left of each row. In figure 6-18, the FormatString property that's shown defines the columns for the Invoices grid in the Vendors form.

To refer to the value of a specific cell in a grid, you first have to make that cell the *active cell*. To do that, you set the Col property to the number of the column that the cell is in, and you set the Row property to the number of the row that the cell is in. Note, however, that the columns and rows in a grid are numbered from zero. After you set these properties, you can use the Text property to refer to the value of the active cell. To refer to the value of the cell in the second row (row number 1) of the first column (column number 0), for example, you can use code like this:

```
Dim strActiveCell As String
msgInvoices.Col = 0
msgInvoices.Row = 1
strActiveCell = msgInvoices.Text
```

You'll see a complete example of how to populate an MSFlexGrid control in the code for the unbound Vendors form.

Property	Description
Rows	The number of rows in the grid, including the header row.
Cols	The number of columns in the grid, including the header column.
FixedRows	The number of rows used for column headings. These rows do not move as you scroll.
FixedCols	The number of columns used for row headings. These columns do not move as you scroll.
FormatString	Defines the widths of the columns in the grid, the alignment of the data in each column, and the text in the column and row headers.
Col	The number of the column that contains the active cell. Columns are numbered beginning with zero.
Row	The number of the row that contains the active cell. Rows are numbered beginning with zero.
Text	The value of the cell that's defined by the current column and row.

The FormatString property for the Invoices grid in the Vendors form

```
<Invoice No   |^Invoice date   |>   Invoice total|>   Payments|>   Credits|>  Balance due
```

Description

- By default, the Rows and Cols properties provide for two columns and two rows in an MSFlexGrid control. The first column and first row are fixed and can be used for headings as indicated by the FixedCols and FixedRows properties. If the number of rows and columns are fixed, these properties can be set when you design the grid. Otherwise, they can be changed through code.
- To specify the alignment of the data in each column in the grid, you use the characters > (right-align), < (left-align), and ^ (center) in the FormatString property as shown above. You can also specify the text to be displayed in the column header for each column. And you can specify the width of the column by including spaces following the header text. To divide the column definitions, you use the pipe character: |
- If the grid includes row headers, you can also define the text to be displayed in each row of the header. To do that, follow the column definitions with a semicolon and then the text for each row separated by pipe characters. The length of the longest heading is used as the width of the column.
- You can identify a specific cell in the grid by setting the Col and Row properties. Then, you can use the Text property to refer to the value of the cell.

Figure 6-18 How to create and work with a Microsoft FlexGrid control

How to work with QueryDef objects

In the bound Vendors form in this chapter, you saw how you can change the RecordSource property of a data control and then use the Refresh method of the data control to populate the Invoices grid with the invoices for the current vendor. To accomplish this with code, you can use the OpenRecordset method to rebuild the recordset each time a different vendor record is displayed. A more efficient way to do that, though, is to use a QueryDef object as described in figure 6-19.

A QueryDef object contains the definition of a query. These objects are particularly useful for creating *parameter queries*. This type of query contains parameters that you can use to change the *criteria* for the query. For instance, the criteria for the Invoices grid in the Vendors form is that the VendorID field in an Invoice record must be equal to the VendorID field in the current vendor record. To implement this with a QueryDef object, you define a parameter that will contain the current vendor id.

Because ODBC databases don't support permanent QueryDef objects, you have to create these objects through program code each time the program is run. To do that, you use the CreateQueryDef method of the Database object as shown by the first example in figure 6-19. For this method, the first argument in parentheses is the Name argument, which is coded as a zero-length string ("") to identify the object as a temporary QueryDef. The second argument is a string variable that contains a SQL statement that includes a PARAMETERS statement that defines a parameter named Vendor. This is the parameter that will contain the current vendor id.

After the QueryDef object is created, the code in this example uses the Parameters collection of the QueryDef object to set the value of the Vendor parameter. This value is set to the value of the VendorID field in the current vendor record. Then, the OpenRecordset method is used on the QueryDef object to create a recordset based on that object and the value of the parameter.

To change the value of a parameter, you again refer to the parameter through the Parameters collection. Then, you use the Requery method of the Recordset object to update the recordset based on the new parameter. This is illustrated by the second example in figure 6-19. Note, however, that when you use the Requery method, the Recordset object isn't recreated as it is when you use the OpenRecordset method. Instead, the source of data is just requeried. That's why using a QueryDef object with a parameter is more efficient than using the OpenRecordset method.

If you're working with ODBC data, you can create a permanent QueryDef object and store it in a Jet database. You can also use QueryDef objects to implement pass-through queries, and you can use stored procedures to implement parameter queries. In chapter 7, you can learn more about those techniques.

Some of the methods you can use to work with QueryDef objects

Method	Object	Description
CreateQueryDef	Database	Creates a QueryDef object. This method includes arguments that specify the name of the QueryDef object and the SQL statements that define the query.
OpenRecordset	QueryDef	Creates a recordset from the QueryDef object.
Execute	QueryDef	Executes an action query.
Requery	Recordset	Updates the recordset based on a QueryDef object. You can use this method to re-execute a query after you change the values of the parameters in a parameter query.

Code that creates a recordset from a QueryDef

```
Dim qdfInvoices As QueryDef, recInvoices As Recordset
Dim strSQL As String
strSQL = "PARAMETERS Vendor int; " _
    & "SELECT * FROM Invoices WHERE VendorID = Vendor"
Set qdfInvoices = dbAP.CreateQueryDef("", strSQL)
qdfInvoices.Parameters!Vendor = recVendors!VendorID
Set recInvoices = qdfInvoices.OpenRecordset(dbOpenSnapshot)
```

Code that changes the QueryDef parameter and requeries the recordset

```
qdfInvoices.Parameters!Vendor = recVendors!VendorID
recInvoices.Requery qdfInvoices
```

Code that creates and executes an action query

```
Dim qdfInvoices As QueryDef, strSQL As String
strSQL = "DELETE FROM Invoices " _
    & "WHERE InvoiceTotal - PaymentTotal - CreditTotal = 0"
Set qdfInvoices = dbAP.CreateQueryDef("", strSQL)
qdfInvoices.Execute
```

Description

- A QueryDef object contains the definition of a query. To create a *parameter query*, you include the PARAMETERS statement in the query definition as shown in the first example above. Then, you use the Parameters collection of the QueryDef object to change the parameters.
- If you code the name of a QueryDef object as a zero-length string (""), a temporary QueryDef object is created. Since ODBC databases don't support permanent QueryDef objects, you should always code the name as a zero-length string when you're accessing ODBC data.

Figure 6-19 How to work with QueryDef objects

Code for the enhanced version of the unbound Vendors form

Figure 6-20 presents the code for the enhanced version of the unbound Vendors form. In general, the logic of this program is the same as the logic of the unbound Vendors form presented in chapter 4. Most of the time, the program responds to the events that occur when the user clicks on one of the command buttons on the form. However, additional coding is required to populate and work with the combo box and grid controls. Although the code in this figure shows only how to implement the Invoices grid, the code for implementing the Credits and Payments grids is so similar that you shouldn't have any trouble with it.

The Declarations section of the Vendors form (1) declares an object variable for each recordset used by the form as well as an object for the database and the QueryDef. In addition, five other variables are declared. The intLastRecord variable will hold the number of the last record and will be used to determine when to disable the Next and Last navigation buttons. The blnAddMode variable will be used to determine when records are being added. The blnRecordEdited variable will be used to determine when a record has been changed. The blnLoadControls variable will be used to determine when controls are being loaded. The blnLookup variable will be used to determine when a lookup operation should be performed. And the intKeyCode variable will hold the value of the last key to be pressed and will also be used to determine when a lookup operation should be performed.

When the Initialize event of the form occurs, the Initialize procedure (2) opens the AccountsPayable database and all of the recordsets required by the form. Notice that the recTerms and recGLAccounts recordsets are opened with the dbOpenForwardOnly recordset type since it's only necessary to make a single pass through these recordsets. This procedure also creates the QueryDef that will be used as the source of data for the Invoices grid.

When the Load event of the form occurs, the Load procedure (3) calls five or six general procedures that load values into all of the controls on the form including the combo box and grid controls. Before the sixth procedure (LoadInvoiceGrid) is called, though, the program checks the RecordCount property of the Invoices recordset to be sure that there are invoices for the current vendor. If there are, the LoadInvoiceGrid procedure is called. If there aren't, this procedure isn't called and the Rows property of the grid is set to 1 so only the header row is displayed. This Load procedure also enables the Delete command button if no invoices are found for the vendor and disables it if records are found. Notice that this procedure doesn't initialize any of the module-level variables because the initial values that are given to the variables when they're defined are what you want.

Visual Basic code for the unbound Vendors form — Page 1

1

```
Option Explicit
Dim dbAP As Database
Dim recVendors As Recordset
Dim recStates As Recordset
Dim recInvoices As Recordset
Dim recTerms As Recordset
Dim recGLAccounts As Recordset
Dim qdfInvoices As QueryDef
Dim intLastRecord As Integer
Dim blnAddMode As Boolean
Dim blnRecordEdited As Boolean
Dim blnLoadControls As Boolean
Dim blnLookup As Boolean
Dim intKeyCode As Integer
```

2

```
Private Sub Form_Initialize()
    Dim strSQL As String
    Set dbAP = OpenDatabase("AccountsPayable", 0, 0, _
        "ODBC;DATABASE=AccountsPayable")
    strSQL = "SELECT * FROM Vendors ORDER BY VendorName"
    Set recVendors = dbAP.OpenRecordset(strSQL, dbOpenDynaset, _
        dbSeeChanges)
    Set recStates = dbAP.OpenRecordset("States", dbOpenSnapshot)
    Set recTerms = dbAP.OpenRecordset("Terms", dbOpenForwardOnly)
    Set recGLAccounts = dbAP.OpenRecordset("GLAccounts", _
        dbOpenForwardOnly)
    Set qdfInvoices = dbAP.CreateQueryDef("", _
        "PARAMETERS Vendor int; " & _
        "SELECT VendorID, InvoiceNumber, InvoiceDate, " & _
        "InvoiceTotal, PaymentTotal, CreditTotal, " & _
        "InvoiceTotal-PaymentTotal-CreditTotal " & _
        "AS BalanceDue " & _
        "FROM Invoices WHERE VendorID = Vendor")
    qdfInvoices.Parameters!Vendor = recVendors!VendorID
    Set recInvoices = qdfInvoices.OpenRecordset(dbOpenSnapshot)
End Sub
```

3

```
Private Sub Form_Load()
    LoadLookup
    LoadStates
    LoadTerms
    LoadAccounts
    LoadControls
    If recInvoices.RecordCount > 0 Then
        LoadInvoiceGrid
        cmdDelete.Enabled = False
    Else
        msgInvoices.Rows = 1
        cmdDelete.Enabled = True
    End If
End Sub
```

Figure 6-20 Code for the unbound Vendors form (part 1of 10)

The general procedures that load the combo box controls (4 through 7) use a Do loop with a MoveNext method to load one item into the combo box list for each record in the related recordset. The procedures for the Lookup, Terms, and Accounts combo boxes also load a value into the ItemData property for each record. These values will be used later in the program to uniquely identify each item in the list. This property isn't used for the States combo box because the value that's displayed in the list (the state code) is the value that uniquely identifies the item.

After all of the records in the Vendors recordset have been read and the vendor names have been loaded into the Lookup combo box (4), the intLastRecord variable is initialized so it contains the number of records in the Vendors recordset. Since this variable is set after all of the records in the Vendors recordset have been accessed, the RecordCount property contains the total number of records in the recordset. (Remember, the RecordCount property indicates the number of records that have been accessed and not the number of records in the recordset.) Then, the MoveFirst method is used to move back to the first record in the recordset so that record is displayed in the form.

Visual Basic code for the unbound Vendors form — Page 2

4

```
Private Sub LoadLookup()
    Do Until recVendors.EOF
        cboLookup.AddItem recVendors!VendorName
        cboLookup.ItemData(cboLookup.NewIndex) = recVendors!VendorID
        recVendors.MoveNext
    Loop
    intLastRecord = recVendors.RecordCount
    recVendors.MoveFirst
End Sub
```

5

```
Private Sub LoadStates()
    Do Until recStates.EOF
        cboStates.AddItem recStates!StateCode
        recStates.MoveNext
    Loop
End Sub
```

6

```
Private Sub LoadTerms()
    Do Until recTerms.EOF
        cboTerms.AddItem recTerms!TermsDescription
        cboTerms.ItemData(cboTerms.NewIndex) = recTerms!TermsID
        recTerms.MoveNext
    Loop
End Sub
```

7

```
Private Sub LoadAccounts()
    Do Until recGLAccounts.EOF
        cboAccounts.AddItem recGLAccounts!AccountDescription
        cboAccounts.ItemData(cboAccounts.NewIndex) _
            = recGLAccounts!AccountNo
        recGLAccounts.MoveNext
    Loop
End Sub
```

Figure 6-20 Code for the unbound Vendors form (part 2 of 10)

The LoadControls procedure (8) begins by setting the blnLoadControls variable to True. This is necessary because when a value is loaded into a control, the Change event occurs on the control. Since the Change event procedure contains code that should only be executed when a control is changed by the user, the blnLoadControls variable is used within that procedure to prevent the code from being executed when the controls are loaded by the program.

The LoadControls procedure uses the With statement to load the fields in the Vendors recordset into the text boxes on the form. It also loads a value into the States combo box so it's displayed in the text portion of that box. This value identifies the currently selected item in the combo box list. After the With statement, this procedure calls the GetTerms and GetAccount procedures.

The GetTerms procedure (9) uses a Do loop to find a terms description in the Terms combo box that has an ItemData property that's equal to the TermsID field in the current Vendor record. After the item is found, the ListIndex property of the combo box is set to the index value for that item. That causes the item with that index to be displayed in the text portion of the combo box. Similarly, the GetAccount procedure (10) uses a Do loop to display the appropriate account description in the Accounts combo box.

After the GetTerms and GetAccount procedures are executed, the LoadControls procedure sets the value of the txtRecord text box so it displays the number of the current vendor record (this is the text box that's between the navigation buttons). To do that, it uses the AbsolutePosition property of the Vendors recordset. Because the absolute position of the first record in a recordset is zero, one is added to the AbsolutePosition value so the resulting value is the correct record number.

Visual Basic code for the unbound Vendors form **Page 3**

8

```
Private Sub LoadControls()
    blnLoadControls = True
    With recVendors
        txtVendor = !VendorName
        txtAddress1 = !VendorAddress1
        txtAddress2 = !VendorAddress2
        txtCity = !VendorCity
        cboStates = !VendorState
        txtZipCode = !VendorZipCode
        txtContact = !VendorContact
        txtPhone = !VendorPhone
    End With
    GetTerms
    GetAccount
    txtRecord = "Record " & recVendors.AbsolutePosition + 1
    blnLoadControls = False
End Sub
```

9

```
Private Sub GetTerms()
    Dim intTermsIndex As Integer
    Dim blnMatch As Boolean
    Do Until blnMatch
        If cboTerms.ItemData(intTermsIndex) _
                = recVendors!TermsID Then
            blnMatch = True
        Else
            intTermsIndex = intTermsIndex + 1
        End If
    Loop
    cboTerms.ListIndex = intTermsIndex
End Sub
```

10

```
Private Sub GetAccount()
    Dim intAccountIndex As Integer
    Dim blnMatch As Boolean
    Do Until blnMatch
        If cboAccounts.ItemData(intAccountIndex) _
                = recVendors!AccountNo Then
            blnMatch = True
        Else
            intAccountIndex = intAccountIndex + 1
        End If
    Loop
    cboAccounts.ListIndex = intAccountIndex
End Sub
```

Figure 6-20 Code for the unbound Vendors form (part 3 of 10)

The procedure that loads the Invoices grid (11) starts by getting the number of records in the Invoices recordset. It does that by moving to the last record in the recordset. Then, it moves back to the first record so the records can be loaded sequentially from the start of the recordset. It also sets the Rows property of the grid to one more than the RecordCount property since the extra row is needed for the header row.

The code that actually loads the Invoices grid uses a With statement so the name of the grid doesn't have to be repeated each time it's referred to. Then, a For...Next statement is used with the MoveNext method to load the data from each record in the Invoices recordset into a row in the grid. Since the first row of the grid contains the column headings, the counter that's used by this For...Next statement starts at a value of 1 (the second row) and is incremented by 1 until it reaches the value of the RecordCount property.

Because some of the columns in the grid need to be formatted, each column is loaded individually. To do that, the Col property is initially set to zero to indicate that the active cell is in the first column. Next, the value of the InvoiceNumber field is loaded into the cell in the current row of that column. Then, the Col property is set to one, the next field is loaded, and so on. Note that if the fields didn't need to be formatted or if all of the fields were formatted the same, you could code another For...Next statement that processes each column within the For...Next statement that processes each row. In that case, you would use a column counter variable to refer to each field in the current record by its index number rather than referring to the fields by name.

The Click event procedure for the cmdNavigate array (12) uses a Case structure to determine what Move method to use on the Vendors recordset. Notice that unlike the code for the unbound form presented in chapter 4, the code here doesn't check the BOF and EOF properties of the recordset when the user clicks on the Previous or Next navigation buttons. That's because these buttons are disabled when the first or last record is displayed, so a beginning-of-file or end-of-file condition can never occur. You'll see the procedure that disables these buttons in a moment.

After the recordset is repositioned, the LoadControls procedure (8) is called to load the values in the current record into the form. Next, the procedure named GetInvoices (13) is called. This procedure changes the Vendor parameter in the Invoices QueryDef so it contains the current VendorID. Then, it requeries the Invoices recordset using the new parameter.

Back in the cmdNavigate_Click procedure (12), if the new Invoices recordset contains at least one record, the LoadInvoiceGrid procedure (11) is called to load the data from the records into the Invoices grid and the Delete command button is disabled. Otherwise, the Rows property of the grid is set to 1 so only the header row is displayed in the Invoices grid and the Delete button is enabled. Then, this procedure calls the EnableNavigation (14) and the InitializeCommandButtons (15) procedures.

Visual Basic code for the unbound Vendors form Page 4

11

```
Private Sub LoadInvoiceGrid()
    Dim intRecordCounter As Integer
    recInvoices.MoveLast
    recInvoices.MoveFirst
    msgInvoices.Rows = recInvoices.RecordCount + 1
    With msgInvoices
        For intRecordCounter = 1 To recInvoices.RecordCount
            .Col = 0
            .Row = intRecordCounter
            .Text = recInvoices!InvoiceNumber
            .Col = 1
            .Text = recInvoices!InvoiceDate
            .Col = 2
            .Text = Format(recInvoices!InvoiceTotal, "Currency")
            .Col = 3
            .Text = Format(recInvoices!PaymentTotal, "Currency")
            .Col = 4
            .Text = Format(recInvoices!CreditTotal, "Currency")
            .Col = 5
            .Text = Format(recInvoices!BalanceDue, "Currency")
            recInvoices.MoveNext
        Next intRecordCounter
    End With
End Sub
```

12

```
Private Sub cmdNavigate_Click(Index As Integer)
    Select Case Index
        Case 0
            recVendors.MoveFirst
        Case 1
            recVendors.MovePrevious
        Case 2
            recVendors.MoveNext
        Case 3
            recVendors.MoveLast
    End Select
    LoadControls
    GetInvoices
    If recInvoices.RecordCount > 0 Then
        LoadInvoiceGrid
        cmdDelete.Enabled = False
    Else
        msgInvoices.Rows = 1
        cmdDelete.Enabled = True
    End If
    EnableNavigation
    InitializeCommandButtons
    blnRecordEdited = False
    txtVendor.SetFocus
End Sub
```

Figure 6-20 Code for the unbound Vendors form (part 4 of 10)

The EnableNavigation procedure (14) determines which navigation buttons should be enabled and which should be disabled. This code uses the AbsolutePosition property of the Vendors recordset to determine whether the first or last record in the recordset is displayed.

The InitializeCommandButtons procedure (15) disables the Update button to indicate that no changes have been made to the record and enables the Add button so a new record can be added to the recordset. It also sets the Default property of the Update button to False so the button doesn't appear with a dark border around it when it's disabled.

Visual Basic code for the unbound Vendors form Page 5

13

```
Private Sub GetInvoices()
    qdfInvoices.Parameters!Vendor = recVendors!VendorID
    recInvoices.Requery qdfInvoices
End Sub
```

14

```
Private Sub EnableNavigation()
    If recVendors.AbsolutePosition = 0 Then
        cmdNavigate(0).Enabled = False
        cmdNavigate(1).Enabled = False
        cmdNavigate(2).Enabled = True
        cmdNavigate(3).Enabled = True
    ElseIf recVendors.AbsolutePosition = intLastRecord - 1 Then
        cmdNavigate(0).Enabled = True
        cmdNavigate(1).Enabled = True
        cmdNavigate(2).Enabled = False
        cmdNavigate(3).Enabled = False
    Else
        cmdNavigate(0).Enabled = True
        cmdNavigate(1).Enabled = True
        cmdNavigate(2).Enabled = True
        cmdNavigate(3).Enabled = True
    End If
End Sub
```

15

```
Private Sub InitializeCommandButtons()
    cmdUpdate.Enabled = False
    cmdUpdate.Default = False
    cmdAdd.Enabled = True
End Sub
```

Figure 6-20 Code for the unbound Vendors form (part 5 of 10)

When the user clicks on the Add button, the Click event procedure for the button (16) is executed. First, this procedure sets the blnAddMode variable to True. Second, it calls a procedure named ClearControls (17) to clear all of the controls. Third, it sets the value of the Rows property of the Invoices grid to 1 so only the header row is displayed. Fourth, it calls a procedure named ChangeCommandButtons (18) to enable or disable the related command buttons. Fifth, it sets the focus on the first text box in the form. Sixth, it calls a procedure named DisableNavigation (19) to disable all the navigation buttons. Last, it sets the value of the txtRecord control so it displays the number of the current record (this is the text box that's between the navigation buttons).

In the ClearControls procedure (17), an empty string is assigned to each text box. In addition, each combo box is cleared by setting the ListIndex property of the control to -1. This value indicates that none of the items in the list is selected.

In the ChangeCommandButtons procedure (18), the code enables the Update button and makes it the default button. It also disables the Add button, and, if a record is being added, disables the Delete button.

In the DisableNavigation procedure (19), you can see that all four buttons in the navigation array are disabled.

Visual Basic code for the unbound Vendors form Page 6

16

```
Private Sub cmdAdd_Click()
    blnAddMode = True
    ClearControls
    msgInvoices.Rows = 1
    ChangeCommandButtons
    txtVendor.SetFocus
    DisableNavigation
    txtRecord = "Record " & intLastRecord + 1
End Sub
```

17

```
Private Sub ClearControls()
    txtVendor = ""
    txtAddress1 = ""
    txtAddress2 = ""
    txtCity = ""
    cboStates.ListIndex = -1
    txtZipCode = ""
    txtContact = ""
    txtPhone = ""
    cboTerms.ListIndex = -1
    cboAccounts.ListIndex = -1
End Sub
```

18

```
Private Sub ChangeCommandButtons()
    cmdUpdate.Enabled = True
    cmdUpdate.Default = True
    cmdAdd.Enabled = False
    If blnAddMode Then cmdDelete.Enabled = False
End Sub
```

19

```
Private Sub DisableNavigation()
    cmdNavigate(0).Enabled = False
    cmdNavigate(1).Enabled = False
    cmdNavigate(2).Enabled = False
    cmdNavigate(3).Enabled = False
End Sub
```

Figure 6-20 Code for the unbound Vendors form (part 6 of 10)

When the user clicks on the Update button, the Click event procedure for that button (20) is executed. This procedure uses an On Error statement to activate an error-handling routine named UpdateError. This routine is identical to the routine presented for the unbound form in chapter 4.

Before the changes to a record are saved, the update procedure calls a function named ValidData (22). This function checks the zip code the user entered to verify that it is valid for the state that was entered. If the zip code is valid, a True value is returned to the update procedure and the update process continues. If the zip code is not valid, an error message is displayed, a False value is returned to the update procedure, and the record is not updated.

If the zip code is valid and a record is being added to the recordset, the AddNew method is executed. Then, one is added to the intLastRecord variable so it reflects the new record count, and the record number display is updated. If a record is being edited, the Edit method is executed.

Next, a procedure named LoadBuffer (21) is called to move the data from the controls to the copy buffer. This procedure uses a With statement to process the fields in the Vendors recordset. Notice here that the TermsID and AccountNo fields are loaded with the value of the ItemData property of the currently selected item. After all of the fields are loaded, the update procedure executes the update method to save the record.

If a record was added to the recordset, the current record pointer is moved to the new record using the Bookmark and LastModified properties of the recordset. Then, the new vendor name is added to the Lookup combo box using the AddItem method and the ItemData property, and the ClearControls procedure (17) is called so another new record can be added. If a record was edited, the EnableNavigation (14) and InitializeCommandButtons (15) procedures are called and the blnRecordEdited variable is set to False. Last, the focus is moved to the txtVendor control.

Visual Basic code for the unbound Vendors form Page 7

20

```
Private Sub cmdUpdate_Click()
    On Error GoTo UpdateError
    If ValidData Then
        If blnAddMode Then
            recVendors.AddNew
            intLastRecord = intLastRecord + 1
            txtRecord = "Record " & intLastRecord + 1
        Else
            recVendors.Edit
        End If
        LoadBuffer
        recVendors.Update
        If blnAddMode Then
            recVendors.Bookmark = recVendors.LastModified
            cboLookup.AddItem recVendors!VendorName
            cboLookup.ItemData(cboLookup.NewIndex) _
                = recVendors!VendorID
            ClearControls
        Else
            EnableNavigation
            InitializeCommandButtons
            blnRecordEdited = False
        End If
        txtVendor.SetFocus
    End If
    Exit Sub
UpdateError:
    Dim strMessage1 As String, strMessage2 As String
    strMessage1 = "The record could not be updated."
    strMessage2 = "Press Esc to cancel operation."
    MsgBox strMessage1 & vbCrLf & strMessage2, vbOKOnly, _
        "Update error"
    txtVendor.SetFocus
End Sub
```

21

```
Private Sub LoadBuffer()
    With recVendors
        !VendorName = txtVendor
        !VendorAddress1 = txtAddress1
        !VendorAddress2 = txtAddress2
        !VendorCity = txtCity
        !VendorState = cboStates
        !VendorZipCode = txtZipCode
        !VendorContact = txtContact
        !VendorPhone = txtPhone
        !TermsID = cboTerms.ItemData(cboTerms.ListIndex)
        !AccountNo = cboAccounts.ItemData(cboAccounts.ListIndex)
    End With
End Sub
```

Figure 6-20 Code for the unbound Vendors form (part 7 of 10)

The ValidData function (22) checks only the zip code data to make sure that it's valid, but a function like this could also check other fields. To check the zip code, this function uses code that's similar to the code you saw for the bound form earlier in this chapter. If the zip code is valid, this function returns a value of True to the calling procedure; otherwise, it returns a value of False.

If the user clicks on the Delete button, the Delete event procedure for that button (23) is executed. This procedure is almost identical to the procedure you saw in chapter 4. The differences are that it calls a procedure named RemoveVendor to remove the deleted vendor from the Lookup combo box, and it updates the intLastRecord variable so it reflects the new record count.

The RemoveVendor procedure (24) uses a Do loop to locate the Vendor that was deleted. The vendor is found when the value of the ItemData property for an item matches the VendorID of the deleted vendor. Then, the RemoveItem method is used to remove that item from the combo box list.

Visual Basic code for the unbound Vendors form Page 8

22

```
Private Function ValidData() As Boolean
    Dim strLookupText As String
    ValidData = True
    strLookupText = "StateCode = '" & cboStates & "'"
    recStates.FindFirst strLookupText
    If Val(Left(txtZipCode, 5)) < recStates!FirstZipCode _
        Or Val(Left(txtZipCode, 5)) > recStates!LastZipCode Then
        MsgBox "The zip code is invalid for the state", , _
            "Data entry error"
        txtZipCode.SetFocus
        ValidData = False
    End If
End Function
```

23

```
Private Sub cmdDelete_Click()
    Dim strResponse As String
    strResponse = MsgBox("Delete this record?", _
        vbYesNo + vbDefaultButton2, "Delete Confirmation")
    If strResponse = vbYes Then
        RemoveVendor
        recVendors.Delete
        intLastRecord = intLastRecord - 1
        recVendors.MoveNext
        If recVendors.EOF Then recVendors.MoveLast
        LoadControls
        EnableNavigation
        InitializeCommandButtons
        blnRecordEdited = False
        txtVendor.SetFocus
    End If
End Sub
```

24

```
Private Sub RemoveVendor()
    Dim intVendorIndex As Integer
    Dim blnMatch As Boolean
    Do Until blnMatch
        If cboLookup.ItemData(intVendorIndex) = _
                recVendors!VendorID Then
            blnMatch = True
        Else
            intVendorIndex = intVendorIndex + 1
        End If
    Loop
    cboLookup.RemoveItem intVendorIndex
End Sub
```

Figure 6-20 Code for the unbound Vendors form (part 8 of 10)

By default, if the user presses an arrow key while the focus is on the Lookup combo box or types text into the combo box, the Click event procedure for the combo box is executed. As you'll see in a moment, though, this Click event procedure is the one that displays the data for the vendor that's selected in the combo box. As a result, you don't want this procedure executed every time a user presses an arrow or keyboard key. Instead, the lookup operation should be performed only when the user presses the Enter key. To get the interface to work that way, the program uses the KeyDown event of the combo box to determine what key was pressed.

This KeyDown event procedure (25) begins by setting a variable named intKeyCode equal to the KeyCode variable. The intKeyCode variable is defined as a module-level variable so it can be used by other procedures, while the KeyCode variable is defined by the event procedure and indicates which key was pressed to initiate the event. Next, this procedure initializes the blnLookup variable to a value of False. This variable is also a module-level variable, and it is used to determine whether or not the lookup function should be performed. Last, this procedure checks the value of the KeyCode variable to determine what key was pressed. If the Enter key was pressed, blnLookup is set to True and the Click event procedure for the Lookup combo box is called. This procedure must be called explicitly because it isn't called by default when the Enter key is pressed (although it is called by default when an arrow key or text key is pressed).

The Click event procedure (26) begins by checking the intKeyCode and blnLookup variables. If the blnLookup variable is True, the user has pressed the Enter key and the lookup should be performed. If the intKeyCode variable is zero, the user has clicked the mouse instead of pressing a key and the lookup should be performed. (Because this variable is initialized to zero when it's declared and set to zero at the end of this procedure, the only time it isn't zero is when the user has pressed a key.)

If a record was being added when the user selected a new vendor, the Click procedure sets the blnAddMode property to False to cancel the add operation. Then, the FindFirst method is used to locate the vendor record with the VendorID that's associated with the vendor name selected from the combo box. Since this value was stored in the ItemData property when the combo box list was loaded, the value in this property is used to locate the appropriate vendor. After the vendor record is found, the data from that record is loaded into the controls on the form, and the invoices for that vendor are retrieved and loaded into the Invoices grid.

When the user changes the text in any of the text boxes on the form, a Change event procedure like the one for the txtVendor text box (27) is executed. Although the code in this figure shows only the procedure for the Change event of one text box, the code must of course include a similar procedure for each text box.

The procedure for the Vendor text box starts by checking whether the Change event occurred as the result of the controls being loaded (blnLoadControls) rather than by the user changing a control. If so, no code is executed. In not, the procedure checks to see whether other data on the form has already been changed (blnRecordEdited). If so, no code is executed. If not, the DisableNavigation procedure is called so the user can't move to another record until the changes are saved or canceled. Then, the ChangeCommandButtons procedure is called so the appropriate command buttons are available. Last, the blnRecordEdited variable is set to True so this processing doesn't occur again when another control is changed.

Visual Basic code for the unbound Vendors form Page 9

25
```
Private Sub cboLookup_KeyDown(KeyCode As Integer, _
        Shift As Integer)
    intKeyCode = KeyCode
    blnLookup = False
    If KeyCode = vbKeyReturn Then
        blnLookup = True
        cboLookup_Click
    End If
End Sub
```

26
```
Private Sub cboLookup_Click()
    If intKeyCode = 0 Or blnLookup Then
        If blnAddMode Then blnAddMode = False
        Dim strLookupText As String
        strLookupText = "VendorID = " _
            & cboLookup.ItemData(cboLookup.ListIndex)
        recVendors.FindFirst strLookupText
        LoadControls
        GetInvoices
        If recInvoices.RecordCount > 0 Then
            LoadInvoiceGrid
            cmdDelete.Enabled = False
        Else
            msgInvoices.Rows = 1
            cmdDelete.Enabled = True
        End If
        EnableNavigation
        InitializeCommandButtons
        blnRecordEdited = False
        txtVendor.SetFocus
    End If
    intKeyCode = 0
End Sub
```

27
```
Private Sub txtVendor_Change()
    If Not blnLoadControls Then
        If Not blnRecordEdited Then
            DisableNavigation
            ChangeCommandButtons
            blnRecordEdited = True
        End If
    End If
End Sub

.
.
.
```

Figure 6-20 Code for the unbound Vendors form (part 9 of 10)

Because the State, Terms, and Accounts combo boxes on the form don't let the user enter new values (the Style property is set to Dropdown List), the Change event can't occur on these controls. Instead, the Click event occurs when the user selects an item from a list by typing into the text box portion of the combo box, presses an arrow key, or selects an item from the list portion of the combo box. Then, the event procedures for the Click event of these controls do the same processing that's done by the Change event procedures for the text box controls. In figure 6-20, you can see the procedure for the Click event for the States combo box (28), and the procedures for the other combo boxes are exactly the same.

The first four command buttons at the bottom of the Vendors form display related forms. When the user clicks on one of these buttons, the Click event procedure for that button is executed. Then, that procedure uses the Show method to display the appropriate form. In figure 6-20, you can see the procedure for the Click event of the Invoices command button (29), and the procedures for the other three buttons are similar.

The fifth command button at the bottom of the Vendors form is the Close button. When the user clicks on that button, the Click event procedure (30) executes the Unload statement to close the current form and the End statement to release the resources used by the application.

The last procedure for the Vendors form (31) detects when the user presses the Escape key. The basic logic of this procedure is similar to the logic you saw for detecting the Escape key in chapter 4. (Remember, the KeyPreview property of the form must be set to True for this to work properly.) If the Esc key was pressed, this procedure uses the Edit method of the Vendors recordset and the LoadControls procedure to redisplay the original values for the current record in the form. Then, if a record was being added, the invoices for the current vendor are retrieved, the Invoices grid is reloaded, and the blnAddMode variable is set to False. Finally, the EnableNavigation and InitializeCommandButtons procedures are called to reset the navigation and command buttons.

Now that you've browsed through all the procedures for this unbound form, you can reflect on what difficulties its code presents. In all, this code requires 17 different general procedures, including one Function procedure. In addition, it uses four Boolean variables that are defined at the module level to control the processing that's done by some of the procedures. These variables are set to True or False in some procedures and tested by If statements in other procedures. Although this use of Boolean variables (sometimes called *switches*) makes the code harder to read, debug, and maintain, this is a common requirement in the code for unbound forms.

Visual Basic code for the unbound Vendors form Page 10

28

```
Private Sub cboStates_Click()
    If Not blnLoadControls Then
        If Not blnRecordEdited Then
            DisableNavigation
            ChangeCommandButtons
            blnRecordEdited = True
        End If
    End If
End Sub

.
.
.
```

29

```
Private Sub cmdInvoices_Click()
    frmInvoices.Show
End Sub

.
.
.
```

30

```
Private Sub cmdClose_Click()
    Unload Me
    End
End Sub
```

31

```
Private Sub Form_KeyDown(KeyCode As Integer, Shift As Integer)
    If KeyCode = vbKeyEscape Then
        recVendors.Edit
        LoadControls
        If blnAddMode Then
            GetInvoices
            If recInvoices.RecordCount > 0 Then
                LoadInvoiceGrid
                cmdDelete.Enabled = False
            Else
                msgInvoices.Rows = 1
                cmdDelete.Enabled = True
            End If
            blnAddMode = False
        End If
        EnableNavigation
        InitializeCommandButtons
        blnRecordEdited = False
    End If
End Sub
```

Figure 6-20 Code for the unbound Vendors form (part 10 of 10)

Perspective

The primary goal of this chapter has been to show you how to use the controls and coding techniques that you need for developing complete business applications with a practical user interface. Now, by using the various types of combo box and grid controls that were presented, you should be able to start developing serious business applications of your own.

A second goal of this chapter has been to help you understand the advantages and disadvantages of using bound and unbound forms. Although the use of bound forms is often tempting because of the minimal coding requirements, the built-in functions of the data controls and data-bound controls limit the way the user interface can work. In addition, the relationships between the property settings and the code can be difficult to establish and maintain. That's why using unbound forms will often lead to an improved interface as well as code that's easier to debug and maintain.

A third goal of this chapter has been to give you a realistic view of the difficulties of Visual Basic programming. Simply stated, it's anything but easy, whether or not you use unbound forms. So if you had difficulty understanding the code for the bound or unbound forms in this chapter, that's to be expected. You just need to keep studying the code until you understand every line of it, even if that requires a review of some of the material in chapters 3, 4, and 5. Eventually, you will get used to the syntax of Visual Basic and the use of its objects, methods, properties, and events. But you need to work at it. Like any other skill of significance, the more time you spend doing it, the better you'll get.

Compared to this chapter, the chapters that follow should be easy for you. In the next chapter, for example, you can learn how to enhance the database programming for a project. In chapter 8, you can learn how to enhance the user interface with menus and toolbars. And in chapter 9, you can learn how to use the Visual Basic tools for testing and debugging.

Chapter 7

How to enhance the database programming

In chapter 6, you learned how to develop business applications using basic DAO techniques. Now, in this chapter, you can learn how to enhance the database programming in those applications. In particular, you'll learn three more ways for working with queries, how to work with transactions, how to handle data access errors, and how to use a Jet database to access ODBC data. By using these techniques, you can improve the efficiency of your applications and help maintain the integrity of your data.

How to work with queries

In previous chapters, you learned how to use DAO methods for adding, changing, and deleting records from a table. However, you can also do these actions by using action queries, pass-through queries, *and* stored procedures. *In the topics that follow, you'll learn how to use those techniques as well as some basic techniques for optimizing queries.*

How to execute an action query

Figure 7-1 presents two techniques for executing an *action query*. First, you can use the Execute method of a Database object to execute a SQL statement that you create through code or a SQL statement that's saved in a QueryDef object. Second, if the SQL statement is saved in a QueryDef object, you can use the Execute method of that object to execute its query.

When you execute an action query, you can specify several options that determine the characteristics of the query. The dbSeeChanges option, as you may remember, causes an error to be generated if another user is editing the same data. This option is required if you're accessing a SQL Server table that contains an identity field.

Two other options you may need are the dbSQLPassThrough option, which you'll learn to use in a moment, and the dbFailOnError option. If you use this error option, a run-time error is generated if an error occurs during the execution of the action query and any changes already made by the query are reversed. This option is necessary because, by default, a run-time error occurs only if the syntax of the SQL statement you're executing is incorrect or you don't have permission to perform the SQL operation. But that means that a run-time error does *not* occur if the execution of the action query is unsuccessful. To trap for this error, then, you need to specify the dbFailOnError option.

Figure 7-1 presents code that uses the Execute method of the Database object to delete all the records from the Invoices table that have a zero balance. Notice that both the dbFailOnError and dbSeeChanges options are specified. Also notice that these two options are concatenated by a plus (+) sign. In this case, a plus sign is required because the dbFailOnError and dbSeeChanges constants represent numeric values.

The last statement in this coding example displays the number of records that were deleted by the operation. This is accomplished by using the RecordsAffected property of the Database object. This same property is available for a QueryDef object.

In general, you should use action queries when you want to perform an operation that may affect more than one record. The alternative is to use Visual Basic code to access each record in a recordset, test for the conditions under which you want to perform the operation, and use DAO methods to perform the operation on each record that meets the conditions. This isn't as efficient as using an action query, though, because one SQL statement is sent to the server for each record that's affected. In contrast, a single statement is sent to the server for all the records that are processed when you use an action query.

The syntax of the Execute method for a Database object

```
Database.Execute source, options
```

The syntax of the Execute method for a QueryDef object

```
QueryDef.Execute options
```

Syntax item	Description
Database	An object variable that refers to the database you want to execute the query on.
Source	A string that contains the SQL statement you want to execute, or a QueryDef object variable that contains the SQL statement you want to execute.
Options	One or more constants that determine the characteristics of the query. The dbSQLPassThrough constant causes the query to be executed as a pass-through query. The dbFailOnError constant generates a run-time error and causes changes to be rolled back if an error occurs.
QueryDef	An object variable that refers to the QueryDef that contains the query you want to execute.

Code that uses the Execute method to perform a delete operation

```
Dim dbAP As Database, strSQL As String
Set dbAP = OpenDatabase("AccountsPayable", 0, 0, _
  "ODBC;DATABASE=AccountsPayable")
strSQL = "DELETE FROM Invoices " _
  & "WHERE InvoiceTotal - PaymentTotal - CreditTotal = 0"
dbAP.Execute strSQL, dbFailOnError + dbSeeChanges
MsgBox dbAP.RecordsAffected & " records deleted."
```

Concepts

- An *action query* is a query that inserts records into a table, changes records in a table, or deletes records from a table. To execute an action query, you use the Execute method shown above.
- Action queries are typically used to perform operations that affect a number of records. This is more efficient than using Visual Basic code and DAO methods to perform the same operation.
- A run-time error will occur on the Execute method only if the syntax of the SQL statement is incorrect or you don't have permission to perform the requested operation. If you want a run-time error to occur when the SQL statement fails, use the dbFailOnError option. This option also causes any changes made by the SQL statement before it failed to be reversed.

Figure 7-1 How to execute an action query

How to execute a pass-through query

By default, the queries you execute from a Visual Basic program are processed by the Jet engine before they're passed on to the database server. If the query contains features or functions that aren't supported by Jet, however, Jet isn't able to process them. To execute these types of queries, then, you need to bypass Jet by executing a *pass-through query*.

Figure 7-2 presents three techniques for executing a pass-through query. To execute a pass-through action query, you use the Execute method that's illustrated by the first example. This works like any other action query, except that you specify the dbSQLPassThrough option. You can also execute a pass-through action query by specifying this option on the Execute method for a QueryDef object that contains the action query. Note, however, that you don't have to specify other options like dbFailOnError and dbSeeChanges. That's because these options supply information to Jet, and Jet isn't used in a pass-through query.

To execute a SELECT statement as a pass-through query, you specify the dbSQLPassThrough option on the OpenRecordset method as illustrated by the second example in this figure. When you do that, though, you need to realize that the recordset that's returned is a snapshot-type recordset. This is indicated by the dbOpenSnapshot option that I've coded in this statement. Because a snapshot-type recordset can't be modified, you should use this technique only if you don't need to modify the records in the recordset using DAO methods. You can still modify them using action queries, however.

You can also execute a SELECT statement as a pass-through query when you're using a data control. To do that, you specify 64 for the Options property of the data control, which corresponds to the dbSQLPassThrough constant. Then, you choose the Snapshot option for the RecordsetType property and code a SELECT statement for the RecordSource property. Note that you can't specify a table name for the RecordSource property because Jet doesn't process a pass-through query. In contrast, when you use a normal query, Jet converts a table name to a SELECT statement for you.

Code that executes a pass-through action query

```
strSQL = "DELETE FROM Invoices " _
    & "WHERE InvoiceTotal - PaymentTotal - CreditTotal = 0"
dbAP.Execute strSQL, dbSQLPassThrough
```

Code that executes a pass-through Select query

```
strSQL = "SELECT VendorName, VendorContact, VendorPhone " _
    & "FROM Vendors"
Set recVendors = dbAP.OpenRecordset(strSQL, _
    dbOpenSnapshot, dbSQLPassThrough)
```

A data control that executes a pass-through query

Concepts

- A *pass-through query* is a query that is not processed by Jet. Instead, it is sent directly to the database server for processing.
- Pass-through queries are typically used to perform operations that can't be performed by Jet. For example, you can use them to execute a query that contains SQL syntax that's specific to the server, to execute a query that returns multiple result sets, or to execute multiple action queries. You can also use them to execute stored procedures.
- If a pass-through query returns records, the records are always returned in a snapshot-type recordset, which means that they can't be updated.
- To execute a pass-through action query, use the Execute method on a Database or QueryDef object and specify the dbSQLPassThrough option. To execute a pass-through Select query, use the OpenRecordset method with the dbOpenSnapshot and dbSQLPassThrough options or define a data control with these options. (A value of 64 in the Options property of a data control corresponds to the dbSQLPassThrough option.)

Figure 7-2 How to execute a pass-through query

How to execute a stored procedure

In chapter 2, you learned that a *stored procedure* is a series of SQL statements that have been saved as a separate object in an ODBC database. These procedures can improve the efficiency of your applications because the statements they contain are compiled and optimized when they're created. In contrast, the SQL statements that are sent from a client to the database server have to be compiled and optimized each time they're executed.

To execute a stored procedure, you specify the name of the procedure instead of a SQL statement on a pass-through query. This is illustrated by the examples in figure 7-3. In the first example, the Execute method is used to execute a stored procedure named DeleteInvoices that deletes paid invoices from the Invoices table.

The second stored procedure in this figure, named VendorInvoices, retrieves all of the records from the Invoices table for a specific vendor. To identify the vendor whose records are to be retrieved, the procedure uses a parameter named @Vendor. Then, when the procedure is executed, the value for this parameter must be sent to the procedure.

To execute a stored procedure that retrieves records, you can specify the name of the stored procedure on the OpenRecordset method or in the RecordSource property of a data control. Both of these techniques are illustrated in this figure. In both cases, the statement that's sent to the server contains the name of the stored procedure followed by a value for its parameter.

How to work with a simple stored procedure

The CREATE PROCEDURE statement for a stored procedure that deletes paid invoices

```
CREATE PROCEDURE DeleteInvoices AS
DELETE FROM Invoices
WHERE InvoiceTotal - PaymentTotal - CreditTotal = 0
```

Code that executes the DeleteInvoices stored procedure

```
dbAP.Execute "DeleteInvoices", dbSQLPassThrough
```

How to work with a stored procedure that contains parameters

The CREATE PROCEDURE statement for a stored procedure that retrieves invoices for a specified vendor

```
CREATE PROCEDURE VendorInvoices @Vendor int AS
SELECT InvoiceNumber, InvoiceDate, InvoiceTotal,
    PaymentTotal, CreditTotal,
    InvoiceTotal-PaymentTotal-CreditTotal As BalanceDue
FROM Invoices
WHERE VendorID = @Vendor
```

Code that executes the VendorInvoices procedure using the OpenRecordset method

```
strSQL = "VendorInvoices " & intVendorID
Set recVendors = dbAP.OpenRecordset(strSQL, _
    dbOpenSnapshot, dbSQLPassThrough)
```

Code that executes the VendorInvoices procedure using a data control

```
datInvoices.RecordSource = "VendorInvoices " & intVendorID
datInvoices.Refresh
```

Concepts

- A *stored procedure* is a set of SQL statements stored on the server. You execute a stored procedure using the same techniques you use to execute a pass-through query. Instead of specifying a SQL statement, though, you specify the name of the stored procedure followed by any parameters you want to pass to the procedure.
- Because stored procedures are executed as pass-through queries, a recordset that's created from a stored procedure is always a snapshot-type recordset. That means that the records in the recordset can't be updated.

Figure 7-3 How to execute a stored procedure

How to optimize queries

When you're developing client/server applications, you need to be concerned about the *network traffic*. In general, to maximize the performance of an application, you want to minimize the amount of information that's passed between the clients and the server. To accomplish that, you need to *optimize* your queries.

Figure 7-4 summarizes the basic techniques you can use to optimize queries. To start, you should retrieve only the fields and records that are needed by the application. (We haven't always followed that advice in this book, though, because we've tried to keep the examples simple.) In addition, you should use stored procedures whenever appropriate since they can be executed more quickly.

You can also optimize queries by not using features provided by Jet that aren't supported by the database server. In particular, you shouldn't use Jet features that restrict the records that are selected. If you do, all of the records that satisfy the other conditions of the query have to be returned to the client so Jet can then apply the requested feature.

To illustrate, suppose you want to retrieve the 50 invoices from the Invoices table that have the largest invoice totals. To do that, you can execute a SQL statement like this:

```
SELECT TOP 50 InvoiceNumber, InvoiceDate, InvoiceTotal
FROM Invoices
WHERE InvoiceDate >= #1/1/97# _
      And InvoiceDate <= #12/31/97#
ORDER BY InvoiceTotal Descending
```

Because TOP isn't supported by SQL Server, though, this statement will cause all of the records in the Invoices table between the specified dates to be returned to the client. Then, Jet will select the top 50 records from those returned. And that isn't an efficient way to do this.

A better way to do this is to create a QueryDef object that contains the SELECT statement shown above without the TOP restriction. Then, you can set the MaxRecords property of the QueryDef to 50 so only the first 50 records will be returned to the client. Because these records are sorted by invoice total in descending sequence on the server, those 50 records will be the top 50. This, of course, is far more efficient than the first alternative.

Techniques for optimizing queries

Technique	Notes
Retrieve only the fields that you need	Don't use a SELECT * query unless your program uses all of the fields in a table. Instead, specify only the fields that you need. This will reduce network traffic.
Retrieve as few records as possible	Use the WHERE clause whenever possible to restrict the number of records that are retrieved. This may involve rethinking the way that an application works, but it can dramatically improve the efficiency of an application.
Use stored procedures whenever that makes sense	Because a stored procedure is compiled and optimized when it's created, it executes more quickly than a SQL statement that's sent to the server.
Code your queries so as much of the query as possible can be executed on the server	If you use features and functions that can't be executed by the server, the server may have to pass more data back to the client than is necessary so the query can be completed by Jet.

Concepts

- When Jet receives a query request, it sends as much of the query as possible to the server for processing. If the query includes features not supported by the server, some or all of the query may have to be processed on the client. Then, any data that Jet needs to process the query must be sent to the client.
- Jet provides a variety of features that aren't supported by most database servers. These features include complex crosstab queries, TOP queries, multiple levels of grouping or totals, DAO functions, user-defined functions, and heterogeneous joins. If possible, you should avoid using these features when accessing ODBC data so the query can be executed on the server.

Figure 7-4 How to optimize queries

How to work with Jet transactions

When you process a group of closely-related transactions, you sometimes need to treat them as a single transaction. Then, if one of the transactions in the group fails, you can *rollback* the changes made to all of the transactions in the group. Otherwise, if all the transactions are successful, you can *commit* all the changes. This type of processing can be referred to as *transaction processing*.

To illustrate, suppose you want to save all the paid invoices from an Invoices table to an archive table, and then delete all the paid invoices from the Invoices table. However, you don't want to save an invoice unless the related delete operation was successful. To do that, you can treat all the saves and deletes as a single transaction that can be rolled back if any part of it isn't successful.

Jet implements transaction processing by saving the changes made during the group transaction to cache memory or, if no additional memory is available, to a temporary database. Then, if the transaction is committed, the changes are applied to the database. If the transaction is rolled back, the changes are discarded.

To create Jet transactions, you use the BeginTrans, CommitTrans, and Rollback methods that are illustrated in figure 7-5. As you can see, the BeginTrans method starts a transaction, the CommitTrans method commits the changes made by the statements in the transaction, and the Rollback method reverses the changes made by the statements in the transaction.

When you use these methods, they operate on a Workspace object. If you omit the reference to this workspace as in the example in this figure, the default workspace is used just as it is when you omit the workspace reference from the OpenDatabase method.

If you want to refer to the default workspace explicitly, you can do that by referring to the first workspace in the Workspaces collection like this:

```
Workspaces(0).BeginTrans
```

You can also assign the default workspace to an object variable of type Workspace and then refer to the workspace using that variable.

When you use transactions, you should be aware that a transaction is never committed unless you execute the CommitTrans method. So if you close a database that has an uncommitted transaction, the transaction is rolled back. And if you close a workspace that has an uncommitted transaction against one or more databases in the workspace, the transaction is rolled back.

If you use Jet transactions on a Jet database, you can nest the transactions up to five levels deep. But when you use Jet transactions on an ODBC database, they can't be nested. If you need to nest them, though, you can use the SQL statements for transaction processing (BEGIN TRAN, COMMIT TRAN, and ROLLBACK TRAN) in a SQL string that's executed as a pass-through query or in a stored procedure. Because stored procedures can include conditional processing, they provide the greatest flexibility for working with transactions.

A procedure that uses transactions to control processing

```
Private Sub ArchiveInvoices()
    Dim dbAP As Database, strSQL As String
    On Error GoTo ArchiveError

    Set dbAP = OpenDatabase("AccountsPayable", 0, 0, _
        "ODBC;DATABASE=AccountsPayable")
    BeginTrans
    strSQL = "INSERT INTO InvoiceArchive " & _
        "SELECT * FROM Invoices " & _
        "WHERE InvoiceTotal - PaymentTotal - CreditTotal = 0"
    dbAP.Execute strSQL, dbFailOnError + dbSeeChanges
    strSQL = "DELETE FROM Invoices " & _
        "WHERE InvoiceTotal - PaymentTotal - CreditTotal = 0"
    dbAP.Execute strSQL, dbFailOnError + dbSeeChanges
    CommitTrans
    Exit Sub

ArchiveError:
    MsgBox "The archive operation was unsuccessful", _
        vbOKOnly, "Processing error"
    Rollback

End Sub
```

Concepts

- By default, each SQL statement and each DAO method is treated by Jet as a separate *transaction*. In contrast, if you want to treat a sequence of statements or methods as a single transaction, you have to define that transaction explicitly. This is often referred to as *transaction processing*.
- You use the BeginTrans, CommitTrans, and Rollback methods of the Workspace object to implement transactions. If the name of the workspace is omitted from these methods as in the example above, the default workspace is used. You can refer to this default workspace explicitly as Workspaces(0). You can also create a separate workspace for a transaction, but that usually isn't necessary.
- The BeginTrans method starts a transaction. If the operations in the transaction complete successfully, you can use the CommitTrans method to save the changes to the database. If an error occurs during the transaction, you can use the Rollback method to discard the changes made to the database.
- The data that's affected by a transaction is typically locked for the duration of the transaction. Because of that, you should avoid lengthy transactions and transactions that require user input.
- You can also implement transactions using the SQL BEGIN TRAN, COMMIT TRAN, and ROLLBACK TRAN statements. These statements are similar to the DAO methods for transaction processing, but provide some additional flexibility.

Figure 7-5 How to work with Jet transactions

How to handle data access errors

In chapter 5, you learned the basic techniques for handling errors. Now, you'll learn specifically about handling data access errors. First, you'll learn how to handle errors when you're using data access objects through Visual Basic code. Then, you'll learn how to handle errors when you're using a data control.

When using DAO

When an error occurs in response to a DAO operation like Update or Delete, the Visual Basic Err object contains information about the last *trappable* error that occurred. (For a complete list of these errors, see the help information for the DAO Number property.) Unfortunately, the last trappable error doesn't always contain detailed information about what actually caused the operation to fail. Then, to get additional information about a DAO error, you can use the Error objects in the DAO Errors collection.

Figure 7-6 describes how to use the objects in the Errors collection. Note that each time a DAO error occurs, the Errors collection can contain one or more Error objects. If you're accessing SQL Server data, these objects can contain information about Jet errors, ODBC errors, SQL Server errors, and even network errors.

Although the Errors collection can contain several objects for a single error, the first object in the collection typically contains the most useful information. In figure 7-6, for example, you can see that the first Error object, Errors(0), contains specific information about the cause of the error, while the other two Error objects contain more general information. In this example, only the second Error object, Errors(1), is a trappable error, so if you use the Err object to handle this error, it will tell you only that the ODBC call failed.

You can use the Error objects in an error handling routine the same way you use the Err object. For instance, the error routine shown in this figure uses the MsgBox function to display the error number and description in the Errors(0) object when an error occurs. You can also test for specific errors using the Error objects, and you can reformat the error description or create your own error message.

As you're debugging a program, you may want to see all of the errors that are stored in the Errors collection. One way to do that is to code a For Each...Next statement that steps through each Error object in the Errors collection. This is illustrated by the last example in figure 5-21 in chapter 5. Another way to work with an Error object is to use the Immediate window of the Visual Basic debugger to display its contents. You can learn how to do that in chapter 9.

Some of the properties of the Error object

Property	Description
Number	The number associated with the error.
Description	Text that describes the error.
Source	The object that caused the error.

Three Error objects returned by a single DAO operation that results in an invalid field entry

Object	Number	Description	Source
0	233	[Microsoft][ODBC SQL Server Driver] [SQL Server] The column TermsID in table dbo.Invoices may not be null.	ODBC.Recordset
1	3146	ODBC—call failed.	DAO.Recordset
2	3426	This action was canceled by an associated object.	DAO.Generic Object

An error routine that displays the information in an Error object

```
DataError:
    Dim strMessage As String
    strMessage = "Error number: " & Errors(0).Number _
        & vbCrLf & Errors(0).Description
    MsgBox strMessage, vbOKOnly, "Data Access Error"
```

Concepts

- The Error objects in the DAO Errors collection contain information about the most recent errors that occurred in response to a DAO operation. You can use these objects to get more information than the Visual Basic Err object provides.
- The first object in the Errors collection usually contains the most detailed information about the error. You can use this object to display information to the user. The other objects contain higher-level information. These objects can occasionally be useful during debugging.
- To refer to a specific object in the Errors collection, use the object's index. The first Error object, for example, can be referred to as Errors(0).

Figure 7-6 How to handle data access errors when using DAO

When using a data control

When you use a data control to work with data, the data control handles Jet errors for you. It does that by displaying a dialog box like the one shown at the top of figure 7-7. Notice that the message displayed in this dialog box is the message that's stored in the Description property of the Errors(0) object (see figure 7-6).

If you want to provide additional processing when an error occurs or if you want to replace the default processing, you can respond to the Error event of the data control. This event occurs whenever an error occurs on an operation that's performed by the data control. In other words, it only occurs when you perform an operation by clicking on one of the navigation buttons in the data control. It does *not* occur when you execute a method on the recordset object that's associated with a data control.

The procedure shown in figure 7-7 shows one way to use the Error event. This procedure displays the error number, which is not displayed by default, and formats the error message so that only the text that follows "[SQL Server]" is displayed. To extract this text, the code uses the Mid and InStr functions. In this example, the code gets the error number from the Errors(0) object, but it could also get the number from the DataErr argument that's passed to the Error procedure.

The Response argument of the Error event indicates whether or not the default message is displayed. This argument's default value is vbDataErrDisplay, which causes the default message to be displayed. If you replace this message with your own, though, you should change the value of this argument to vbDataErrContinue as shown in this figure. Otherwise, both messages will be displayed.

A sample dialog box that shows a data access error on a data control

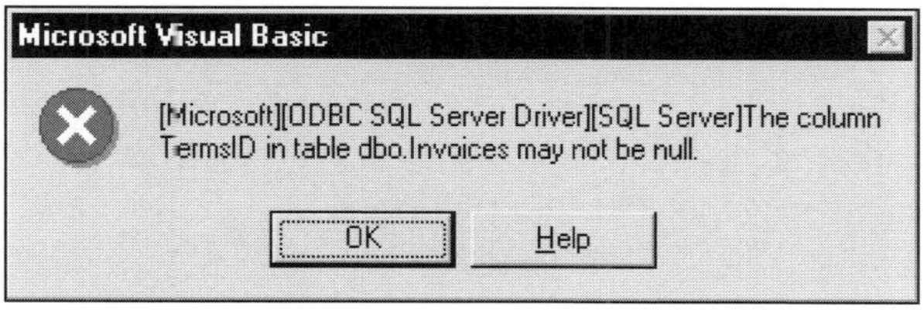

A procedure that responds to an error on a data control

```
Private Sub datVendors_Error(DataErr As Integer, _
        Response As Integer)
    Dim strMessage As String
    strMessage = Errors(0).Description
    strMessage = Mid(strMessage, InStr(strMessage, _
        "[SQL Server]") + 12)
    strMessage = "Error number: " & Errors(0).Number _
        & vbCrLf & strMessage
    MsgBox strMessage, vbOKOnly, "Update error"
    Response = vbDataErrContinue
End Sub
```

Concepts

- When a data access error occurs on an operation that's done automatically by a data control, the data control displays a dialog box that describes the error in the Errors(0) object. In most cases, this message provides sufficient information for the user.
- If you want to display a different message or if you want to perform additional processing when an error occurs, you can respond to the Error event of the data control.
- Two arguments are passed to the Error procedure when the Error event occurs. The DataErr argument contains the number of the error that occurred. You can use this argument to test for specific errors. The Response argument determines whether the default message is displayed. If you display a different message, change this argument to the vbDataErrContinue constant so the default message isn't displayed.

Note

- The Error event is *not* triggered when you issue a method on the recordset associated with a data control. It's triggered only when an operation is done automatically by the data control.

Figure 7-7 How to handle data access errors when using a data control

How to use a Jet database to access ODBC data

Every time you create a recordset based on one or more tables in an ODBC database, information about the structure of those tables has to be sent from the database server to Jet. Jet then uses that information to perform operations on the tables. As you can imagine, this requires some additional overhead.

One alternative is to open a Jet database with *links* to the ODBC tables. The links then contain the information about the structure of the table and how to connect to the table. That way, the table information doesn't have to be downloaded to Jet every time you create a recordset from the table, and you don't have to supply connection information for the database. Figure 7-8 summarizes how this works.

To link an ODBC table to a Jet database, you can use several techniques. The easiest way is to use Access to create the database and the links. If you don't have Access, though, you can use the Visual Data Manager that's presented in chapter 10. Finally, you can use SQL data definition statements from a Visual Basic application to create the database and the linked tables. In most cases, though, there's no need to use that technique.

After you create a Jet database and link its tables to ODBC tables, you can use the Jet tables to work with the ODBC tables. For instance, when you create a recordset based on the linked tables, Jet connects to the ODBC tables for you. And when you change the data in a linked table, Jet applies the changes to the ODBC tables.

You can't, however, use this technique to change the structure of the ODBC tables. To do that, you have to access the tables directly. In most cases, though, structural changes are done by the database administrator so you won't have to make them at all.

In addition to linking ODBC tables to a Jet database, you can link ODBC views. When you link a view to a Jet database, you can retrieve data from the view just as if you were working with a table. By default, however, you can't change the data in the view because it doesn't contain a unique index that Jet can use to identify its records. To get around this limitation, though, you can create a pseudo index by using the SQL CREATE INDEX statement. For more information about this statement, you can refer to its help information.

You can also use Jet to create permanent QueryDef objects for working with ODBC databases. These queries, called *saved queries*, let you get beyond the limitations of the temporary QueryDef objects that you had to create when using the techniques of chapter 6. Within the saved queries, you can use Jet SQL statements or SQL statements that are specific to a database server. And to run the queries that contain SQL-specific statements, you can use pass-through queries.

A Jet database with linked tables displayed in Access

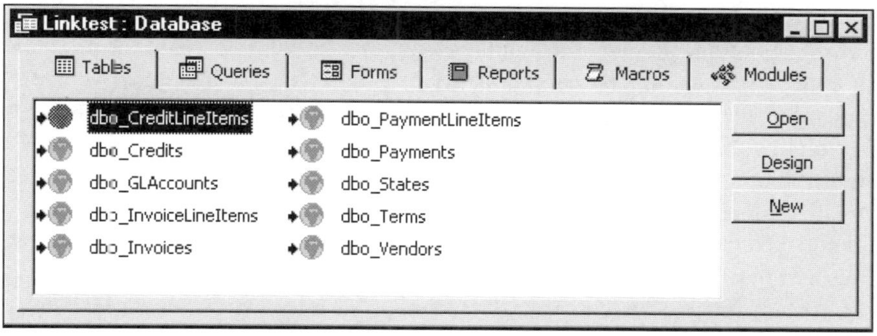

How to use linked tables

- When you link an ODBC table to a Jet database, you can work with the data in the ODBC table using the linked table. This is more efficient than accessing the table directly because information about the structure of the table is stored in the linked table and doesn't have to be retrieved from the ODBC table each time it's accessed.
- You can use Jet and DAO to work with a linked table just like any other Jet table. Because information about connecting to the ODBC table is stored with the linked table, the connection is made automatically when you access the linked table.
- If you change the structure of the underlying ODBC table or move the database that contains the table, you have to relink the table to the Jet database to update the table information.
- You can't use a linked table to change the structure of the ODBC table. To do that, you have to access the ODBC table directly. You can change the name of the linked table, however.
- You can also link views to a Jet table and work with them just like a linked table. You can't update the data using the linked view, however, unless you create a pseudo index for it. To do that, you use the SQL CREATE UNIQUE INDEX statement to identify the field or fields you want to use as the unique key.

How to use permanent QueryDef objects

- You can store permanent QueryDef objects in a Jet database (called *saved queries*) and refer to them by name in a Visual Basic application. That way, you don't have to create the query in code each time you use it.
- A saved query can contain any of the SQL statements supported by Jet. In addition, it can contain SQL statements that are specific to the ODBC database server, which can then be executed as pass-through queries.

How to work with linked tables and QueryDef objects

- You can work with linked tables and QueryDef objects using (1) the Access interface shown above, (2) the Visual Data Manager (see chapter 10), or (3) DAO methods like CreateQueryDef and SQL statements like CREATE TABLE.

Figure 7-8 How to use a Jet database to access ODBC data

Perspective

This chapter has presented techniques that you can use to increase the efficiency of your applications and improve the integrity of your data. Now that you've completed this chapter, you should be able to use these techniques to enhance the database programming of any application that you develop. Often, though, you won't apply these techniques until after you develop a working version of the application. Then, you will apply these techniques as you fine-tune the application.

In the next chapter, you can learn how to enhance the user interface by adding menus, toolbars, and help information to a form. Then, if you haven't already read it, you can read chapter 9 to learn the best techniques for testing and debugging an application. When you finish these chapters, you'll have all of the essential skills that you need for developing complete client/server applications with DAO.

Chapter 8

How to enhance the user interface

Once you have the forms of an application working right, you can enhance the user interface by adding a startup form, menus, toolbars, and help information. You may also want to add a splash form to the application or change from a single-document interface to a multiple-document interface. By making these additions and changes, you improve the appearance of the application at the same time that you make it easier to use.

An introduction to user interfaces

When you develop business applications with Visual Basic 5, you normally use either a single-document or a multiple-document interface. In the topics that follow, you'll learn about these two interfaces and about the use of startup forms and splash forms with either type of interface.

Single-document and multiple-document interfaces

Figure 8-1 shows the primary user interfaces when applied to the Accounts Payable application. The first interface is known as the *single-document interface*, or *SDI*, while the second one is known as the *multiple-document interface,* or *MDI.*

In a single-document interface, each form runs in its own application window, and this window is usually shown in the Windows 95 taskbar. Then, you can click on the buttons in the taskbar to switch between the open forms. When you use this interface, each form can have its own menus and toolbars.

In a multiple-document interface, a container form called a *parent form* contains one or more *child forms*. Then, the menus and toolbars on the parent form contain the commands that let you open and view forms, and you can use the Window menu to switch between the open forms. When you close the parent form of an MDI application, all of the other forms are closed and the application ends. If you've used a Windows application like Word and Excel, you're already familiar with the multiple-document interface.

The main advantage of a multiple-document interface is that the parent form keeps all of the child forms organized and provides a central location for storing the objects that are common to the entire application such as menus and toolbars. However, the multiple-document interface also adds a level of complexity to the application for both the user and the programmer. As a result, a well-designed SDI application is often easier to use and to code than a comparable MDI application.

When you work with more than one form in an application, whether SDI or MDI, you can use the Form Layout window to set the initial positions of the forms. As you drag the forms to new positions in this window, the Top and Left properties are automatically adjusted to the new positions. Of course, you can also adjust these properties with code as you'll see in figure 8-3.

Since the amount of space each form takes on a user's monitor depends on the resolution of that monitor, you usually design all forms for the lowest common resolution, which today is 640 by 480. That way, you can design the forms to fit on the user's screen without scrolling. To make it easy to design for that resolution when you're working on a monitor with a higher resolution, the Form Layout window shows you the size of each form as it will appear in all resolutions lower than your monitor's.

Incidentally, you can also develop an *explorer-style interface* with Visual Basic 5, but this interface isn't usually used with business applications. As you might guess, the Windows Explorer is an example of this type of interface.

Single-document interface (SDI)

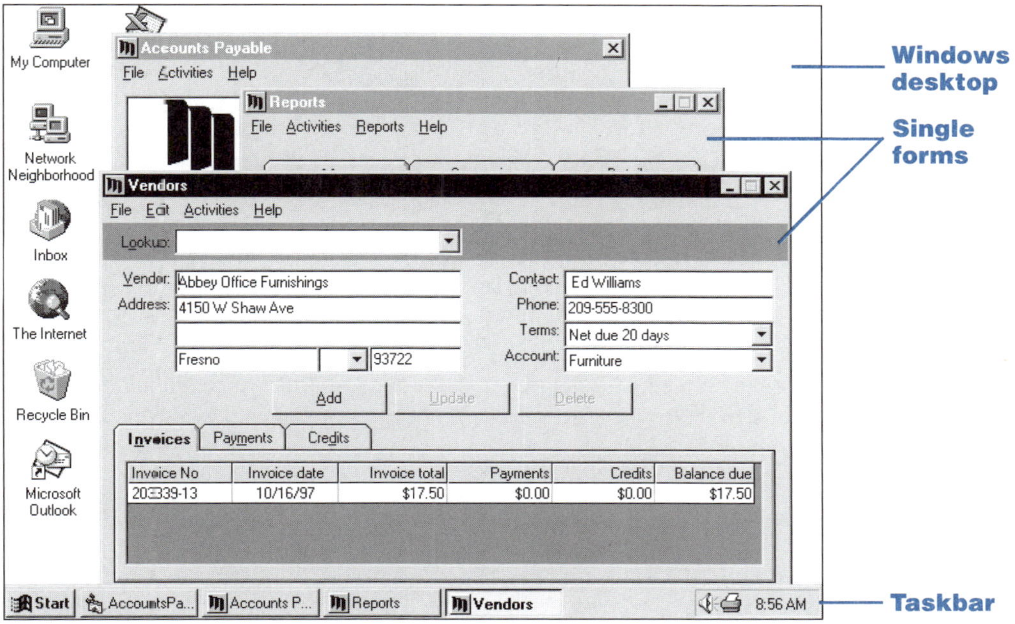

Multiple-document interface (MDI)

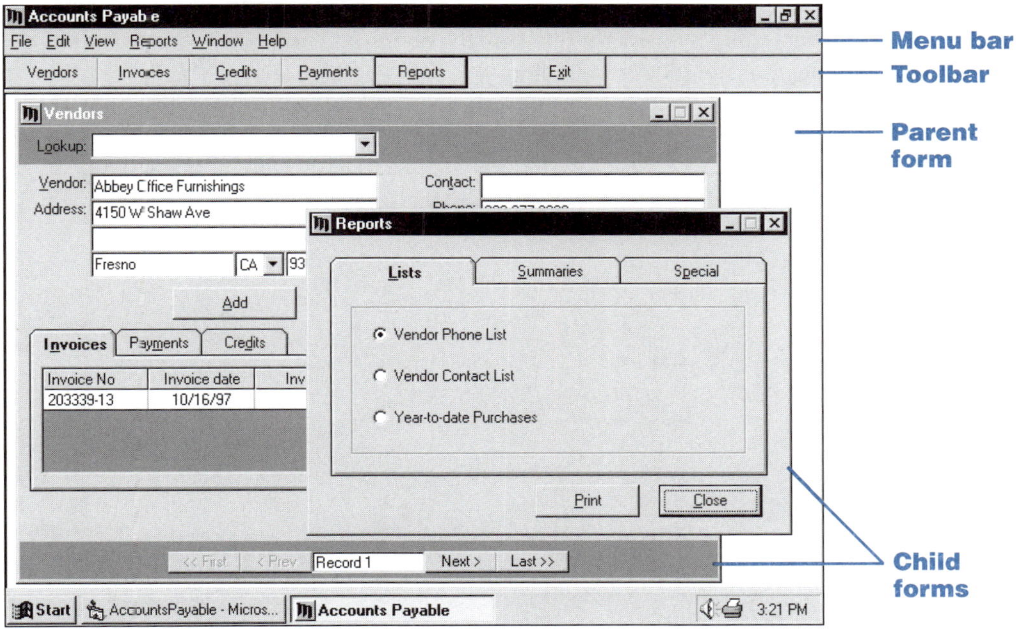

Figure 8-1 Single-document and multiple-document interfaces

Splash forms and startup forms

When your application consists of more than one form, you usually need to provide a *startup form* that directs the user to the other forms of the application. This is illustrated by the second form in figure 8-2, which is the first form in an SDI application. In an MDI application, the parent form can be used as the startup form, but often a special child form is used within the parent form to provide information about the application.

When you start an application, you may want to load all of the forms of the application, but show only the startup form. Then, you can show the other forms as they are required by the user. Although this takes the application longer to start up, the forms appear quickly once the startup procedure has been completed. An alternative is to load each form as it is required by the user. Another alternative is to load the primary forms when the application starts and the other forms as they are needed.

If there is a significant delay before the first screen is displayed by an application, you may want to start the application by displaying a *splash form* (or *splash screen*) like the one in figure 8-2. This type of screen shows the user that the startup procedure is in progress. Then, to show the user that progress is being made, you can change the caption of a label on the splash form as you move through the startup procedure, or you can change the Value property of a progress bar like the one shown in this figure.

Incidentally, a ProgressBar control is one of eight controls that are included in the Microsoft Windows Common Controls 5.0. To add these controls to the Visual Basic toolbox, you use the Components command in the Project menu. Three of the other controls in this group that are useful when you're enhancing the user interface are the Toolbar, ImageList, and StatusBar controls.

A splash form for the Accounts Payable application

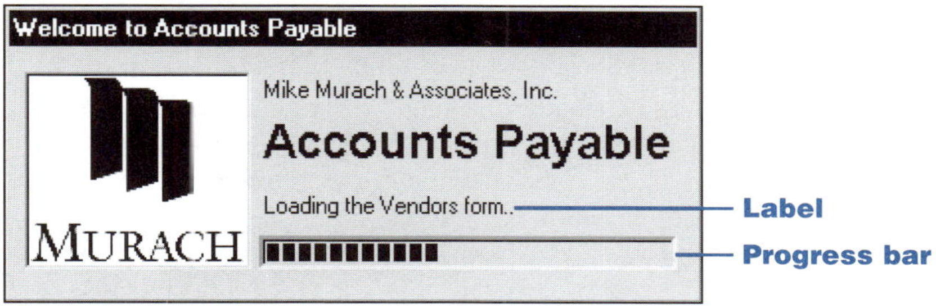

A startup form for the SDI version of the Accounts Payable application

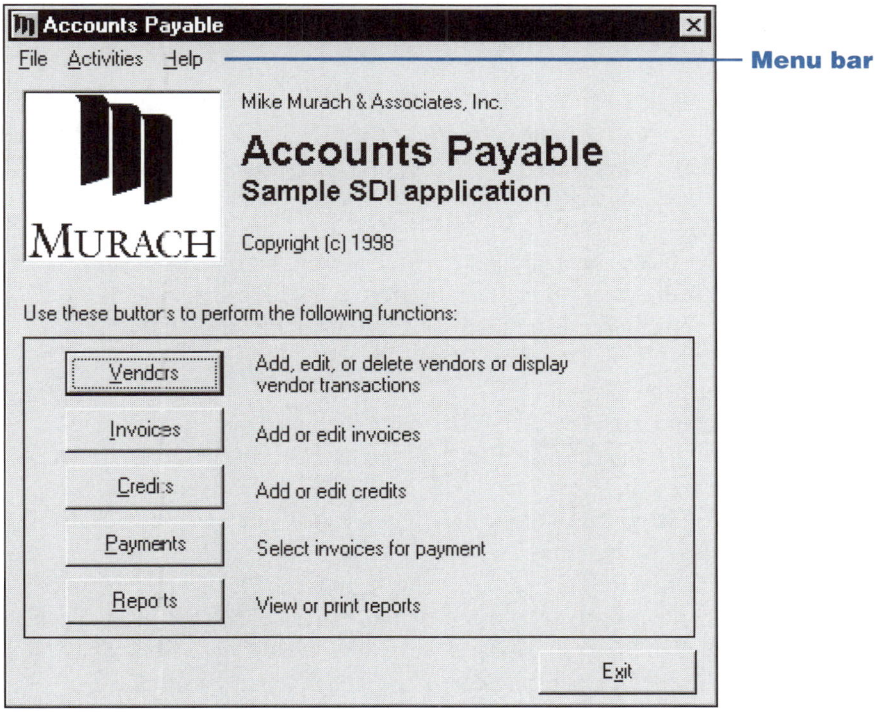

Notes

- If you set the Screen.MousePointer property to vbHourglass for a splash form, the mouse pointer appears as an hourglass when it's positioned over the form.
- You can change the caption for a label on the splash form to tell the user what tasks the application is performing.
- You can use the ProgressBar control to show what portion of the startup procedure has been completed. You can add this control and seven others to the toolbox by choosing the Components command in the Project menu, and then checking the Microsoft Windows Common Controls 5.0.

Figure 8-2 A splash form and a startup form

How to start an application with a splash form

After you add a startup form or splash form to an application, you need to change the properties of the application so it starts by loading the right form. To do that, you access the Project Properties dialog box that's shown in figure 8-3 and change the Startup Object property. In this example, the startup object is a form named frmSplash, which is the splash form for the application.

The code in this figure shows how you can use the Load event procedure for the splash form to load the primary forms of the application and to show the progress of this startup procedure. The first two statements in this procedure set the Top and Left properties for the form to center the form on the screen. It does this by subtracting the form height and width from the screen height and width and dividing by 2. In both of these statements, the object name is omitted from the property reference so Visual Basic assumes that Top, Left, Height, and Width refer to those properties of the current form.

The next two statements assign a message to the Caption property of the Label control and a value of zero to the Value property of the ProgressBar control. In later statements, the procedure displays three more progress messages in the Label control and three updated values in the ProgressBar control to show the user how the startup procedure is progressing.

Although Visual Basic automatically loads and shows the form that's designated as the startup object, the fifth statement in this procedure is the Show method for the form. Here again, the object name is omitted. This statement forces Visual Basic to show the form for the first time. Otherwise, the form won't be displayed until the entire procedure is finished.

After the Show method and after each updating of the Label and ProgressBar controls, a DoEvents function is issued. This function passes control to the Windows operating system so it does the events that are already in its queue. Otherwise, Windows decides what the priorities of the events in its queue are and executes them based on those priorities. But that may mean that the form isn't displayed with appropriate delays each time the controls are updated. In fact, if the DoEvents functions are removed from the procedure in this example, the Label control never appears to get updated, even though the ProgressBar control does get updated. Each time Windows finishes the queued events, control is passed back to the Visual Basic application so the procedure continues. The DoEvents function is useful whenever you want to make sure that all the commands in the queue are executed before the procedure continues.

The last two statements in this procedure unload the splash form and show the startup form. The Show method for the startup form is required because loading a form doesn't also display it.

If you use an MDI interface, you may want to use the parent form as the startup form and display the splash form over the MDI form. Then, you can use the Load event procedure of the MDI form to display the splash form. At the end of the procedure, you can unload the splash form and show the first child form that you want displayed.

The Project Properties dialog box that sets the startup form

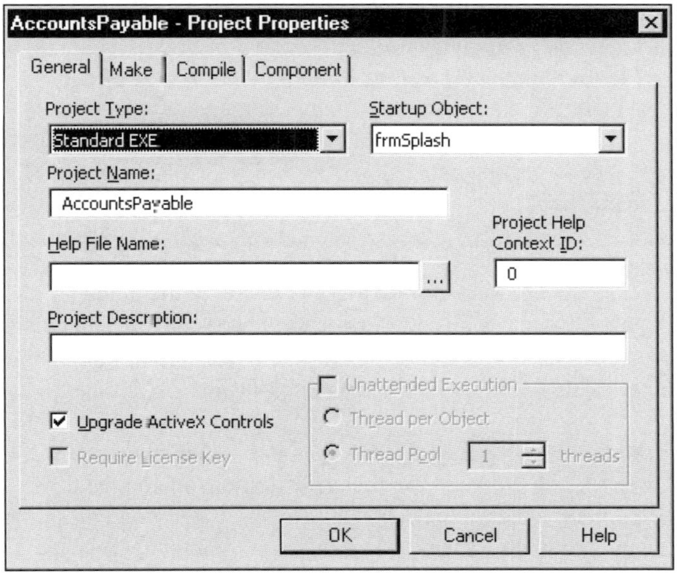

Code for the Load event procedure of the splash form

```
Private Sub Form_Load()
    Top = (Screen.Height - Height) / 2
    Left = (Screen.Width - Width) / 2
    lblStatus.Caption = "Loading the Startup form.."
    prbProgressBar.Value = 0
    Show
    DoEvents
    Load frmAPmain
    lblStatus.Caption = "Loading the Vendors form.."
    prbProgressBar.Value = 40
    DoEvents
    Load frmVendors
    lblStatus.Caption = "Loading the Invoices form.."
    prbProgressBar.Value = 80
    DoEvents
    Load frmInvoices
    lblStatus.Caption = "All forms loaded.."
    prbProgressBar.Value = 100
    DoEvents
    Unload frmSplash
    frmAPmain.Show
End Sub
```

Figure 8-3 How to start an application with a splash form

How to add menus, toolbars, and help

Menus and toolbars let the user access the functions of an application in familiar ways, while help information can answer some of the questions that the user has. In the topics that follow, you'll learn how to add menus, toolbars, and help to an application.

How to create menus

Figure 8-4 shows how to use the Menu Editor dialog box to create the menus for a form. Since each form can have its own menus, the first step in accessing the Menu Editor dialog box is to display the form you want to work with. Then, you open the Menu Editor dialog box by clicking on its toolbar button or choosing it from the Tools menu.

Within the Menu Editor dialog box, you use the Caption and Name boxes to set those properties for each object. Then, you can use the arrow buttons to change the level of indentation for each object, which identifies it as a menu title, menu command, or submenu. You can also provide a shortcut key for each menu object. When you're done with an object, you can click on the Next button. And to insert an object between existing objects, you can use the Insert button.

The check boxes for each menu object correspond to the properties of the object. If, for example, you remove the check from the Visible check box, that menu object won't be displayed when the application starts. Similarly, if you remove the check from the Enabled check box, the menu object won't be enabled. And if you add a check to the Checked box, a check mark will appear before the menu object. These, of course, are only the starting properties for a menu object, and you can use code to change these properties while an application is running.

When you create the menus for a form, you should try to follow the conventions that are used by other Windows applications. For instance, you'll want to keep the File menu on the far left (at the top of the Menu Editor list), the Help menu on the far right (at the bottom), and the other menus in a consistent sequence between the File and Help menus. Similarly, if a menu command leads to a dialog box, you should include an ellipsis (...) at the end of the Caption property for the object.

In addition, most programmers follow some conventions for naming menu objects. If, for example, you use *mnu* as the prefix for menu objects, mnuFileExit is a standard way to name the Exit command of the File menu.

After you use the Menu Editor dialog box to add the menus to a form, the menu bar appears on your form in the Design window, and you can pull down its menus to make sure they're set up right. Then, to provide the code for a menu object, you can click on the object, which switches you to the Code window and starts the Click event for the menu object. In figure 8-6, you can see some typical code for these events.

You can also use the Menu Editor to create *popup menus* that are activated when the user clicks the right mouse button on a form. If these menus are different than the pull-down menus, you need to turn their Visible properties off so they aren't displayed with the pull-down menus. However, you can also use the menus in the menu bar as popup menus. In figure 8-6, you can see the coding requirements for a popup menu.

The Menu Editor dialog box

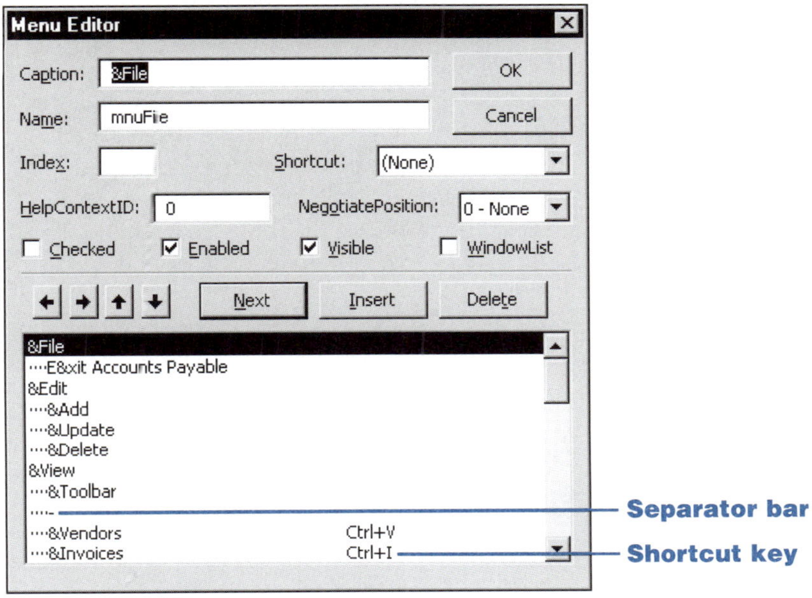

Drop-down menus

- To access the Menu Editor dialog box, display the form and click on the Menu Editor icon in the toolbar or choose Menu Editor from the Tools menu. The entries that you make in this dialog box are for the starting properties of each menu object. However, you can also set these properties with code.
- The Caption and Name properties are required for all menu objects, and the prefix *mnu* is commonly used in the name of a menu object.
- You can use the ellipsis (…) at the end of the Caption property to identify menu commands that lead to dialog boxes. And you can use a single hyphen (-) in the Caption property to display a separator bar between menu commands.

Popup menus

- You can also use the Menu Editor to create a *popup* (or *shortcut*) *menu* that's different from one of the other menus. In that case, you don't want the Visible property checked. Then, you can use code to test whether the right mouse button has been clicked and, if so, to display the popup menu (see figure 8-6).
- Some controls provide built-in popup menus. If, for example, you right-click on any masked edit or text box control, a popup menu is displayed with these standard Windows commands: Undo, Cut, Copy, Paste, Delete, and Select All.

Figure 8-4 How to create menus

How to create a toolbar

Figure 8-5 shows how to create a simple toolbar by placing command buttons on a PictureBox control. The only trick here is to set the Align property of the picture box to Align Top. Once you do that, the picture box automatically extends from the left side of the form to the right side. Then, you can adjust the Height property of the picture box so it's just slightly larger than the height of the command buttons. Since toolbar buttons often duplicate functions that are already available from other controls on the form or from the menu system, you'll often code a toolbar button so it calls an existing procedure.

If you want to create toolbar buttons that have icons on them, you can add graphic images to the command buttons. Or, you can use the Toolbar and ImageList controls that are part of the Microsoft Windows Common Controls 5.0. In this case, you use the properties of an invisible ImageList control to build a list of images that can be used on toolbar buttons. Next, you add a Toolbar control to the form and relate it to the ImageList control. Then, you add buttons to the toolbar, and you use the Image property of each button to relate it to the index number of an image in the image list.

Whether you add grapic images to command buttons or use a Toolbar control in combination with an ImageList control, you'll probably need to get or create some images for use on the toolbar. The preferred format for this purpose is the icon format, which is designed for small graphic files. All icon files have a small number of pixels (usually 32 by 32 or 16 by 16) and have ico as the extension. Although the Professional and Enterprise editions of Visual Basic include many common icons, they don't include icons for specialized functions like the ones you're likely to need for business applications. In that case, you may be able to buy the icons you need from another source, or, if you have the Windows 95 resource kit, you can use the Image Editor that comes with that kit to design your own icons.

From a practical point of view, though, it's usually best to avoid the use of icons when you're developing business applications. After all, it's easier to understand the words on a command button than it is to guess what an icon represents. And if you avoid the use of icons, you also eliminate the need to provide ToolTips for the icons. On the other hand, the Toolbar and ImageList controls make it relatively easy to create a toolbar with ToolTips, as long as you're satisfied with the icons that are already available on your PC.

A toolbar in the parent form of the Accounts Payable application

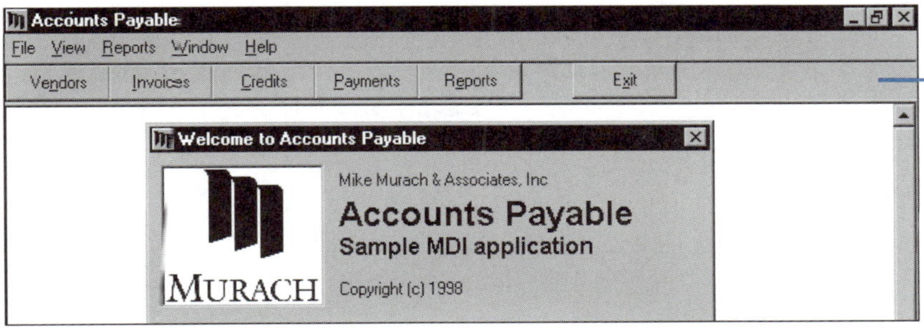

Picture box

How to create a simple toolbar

- Add a PictureBox control as a toolbar area as shown above. If you set the Align property for this control to Align Top, it automatically reaches across the width of the form. Then, add command buttons to this toolbar area, and write the code for the Click event of each command button.
- To place a graphic image on a command button, change the Style property for the command button to Graphical and then use the Picture property for the button to select a graphic file, preferably one with the ico (icon) extension.
- To create a ToolTip for the button, use its ToolTip property (see figure 8-7).

How to create a toolbar with the Toolbar and ImageList controls

1. Add an ImageList control to the form, which will be invisible when the form is displayed, and use the Images tab of its Property Pages dialog box to add images to the list that this control represents. As you add each image, an Index number is assigned to it.
2. Add a Toolbar control to the form and use the General tab of its Property Pages dialog box to point to the ImageList control that contains the images you want. Then, use the Buttons tab to add buttons to the toolbar. For each button, set the Image value to the Index number for the image that you want from the image list.
3. You can also use the Buttons tab for the Toolbar control to add a Caption to the button, to set Key or Tag properties that can be referred to by code later on, and to set other properties like the ToolTipText for each button.
4. Write the code for the ButtonClick event of the Toolbar control, which passes a Button object to the procedure. To determine which button has been clicked, you can refer to the Index, Key, or Tag property of the Button object.

Figure 8-5 How to create a toolbar

How to write the code for menus and toolbars

Figure 8-6 shows some typical procedures for working with menu commands and toolbar buttons. The first procedure is for the Click event of the Update command in the Edit menu. However, since the update function has already been provided for by the Click event procedure for the Update command button, the menu command procedure simply calls the command button procedure: cmdUpdate_Click.

Similarly, the second procedure in this figure is for the Click event of a toolbar button that switches to the Vendors form. But since that function is already provided for by the Vendors command in the View menu, the procedure just calls the procedure for that menu command.

The third procedure in this figure is for the ButtonClick event of a Toolbar control that's related to an ImageList control (there is no Click event for a Toolbar control). For the ButtonClick event, Visual Basic passes a Button object to the procedure. Then, the code can refer to the Index, Key, or Tag property that was set when the button was defined to determine which button was clicked. In this example, the Key property is used, and the code for each button calls an existing procedure.

The fourth procedure shows or hides a toolbar when the Toolbar command on the View menu is clicked. This code uses the Checked property to display a check mark on the menu command when the toolbar is shown and to remove the check property when the toolbar is hidden. It also uses the Visible property to show and hide the toolbar. At the bottom of this figure, you can see another way to code this function in just two statements by using the Not operator to reverse the value of the Checked and Visible properties.

The fifth procedure is the event procedure for the MouseUp event for a form, but similar code can be used for a control (and the MouseDown event can be used instead of the MouseUp event). When the MouseUp event occurs, four arguments are passed to the procedure. Then, an If statement uses the button argument to determine whether the right mouse button (2) has been clicked. If it has, the code uses the PopupMenu method of the form to display the View menu, which is one of the menus in the menu bar. Of course, this method can also be used to display a hidden menu that isn't one of the menus that's available from the menu bar.

To pop up different menus when the user right-clicks on different portions of a form, the procedure can use the X and Y arguments to first determine where the mouse pointer was when the click event occurred. This, of course, makes the coding more difficult, although it may improve the usefulness of the popup menu. From a practical point of view, though, providing popup menus for must business applications usually isn't worth the effort, and some of the most useful editing commands are provided automatically for text boxes and masked edit controls.

Code for the Click event of a menu object

```
Private Sub mnuEditUpdate_Click()
    cmdUpdate_Click
End Sub
```

Code for the Click event of a toolbar button

```
Private Sub cmdVendors_Click()
    mnuViewVendors_Click
End Sub
```

Code for the ButtonClick event of a Toolbar control

```
Private Sub Toolbar1_ButtonClick(ByVal Button As _
        ComctlLib.Button)
    If Button.Key = "Update" Then
        cmdUpdate_Click
    ElseIf Button.Key = "Add" Then
        cmdAdd_Click
    End If
End Sub
```

Code that shows or hides a toolbar

```
Private Sub mnuViewToolbar_Click()
    If mnuViewToolbar.Checked = True Then
        mnuViewToolbar.Checked = False
        pbxToolbar.Visible = False
    Else
        mnuViewToolbar.Checked = True
        pbxToolbar.Visible = True
    End If
End Sub
```

Code for a popup menu

```
Private Sub Form_MouseUp(Button As Integer, _
        Shift As Integer, X As Single, Y As Single)
    If Button = 2 Then
        PopupMenu mnuView
    End If
End Sub
```

Another way to write the code that shows or hides a toolbar

```
mnuViewToolbar.Checked = Not mnuViewToolbar.Checked
pbxToolbar.Visible = Not pbxToolbar.Visible
```

Figure 8-6 How to write code for menus and toolbars

How to add help information

Because Visual Basic 5 applications use the standard Windows interface, users who are already familiar with other Windows applications should quickly adapt to Visual Basic applications. In addition, you should try to design and develop each application so it is as easy to use as is practical. Nevertheless, almost all applications can benefit from the addition of at least a minimum amount of help information.

In figure 8-7, you can see two quick ways to add help information to an application. To provide a ToolTip for a control, for example, you just add the tip to the ToolTipText property of the control. And to provide help information that's available from the Help menu, you can develop a simple form that displays the information.

Another way to provide help information is to add a StatusBar control (one of the Microsoft Windows Common Controls 5.0) to the bottom of a form. Then, you can display descriptive information in the status bar from the event procedure for the MouseMove or GotFocus event of another control. This, however, is more time-consuming than providing ToolTips for the controls.

Beyond that, you can build a complete context-sensitive help system for an application that's comparable to one for a commercial application. To do that, you can use a Help editor or compiler from a third-party vendor to create the help topics. Then, you can use the HelpFile property for the application to set the path and file name for the help file, and you can use the HelpContextID property of a form or control to point to the related help topic. This is the topic that's displayed when the user presses the F1 key while the form or control is active. Once you've developed the help file, you can also provide "What's This?" help by providing a way for the user to switch to WhatsThis mode and by using the WhatsThisHelpID property of an object to point to the related help topic.

Providing this level of help, though, goes well beyond the normal duties of a Visual Basic programmer and the scope of this book. In fact, this type of work is often done by a person who specializes in performance tools.

The good news is that a well-designed business application doesn't require that much online help. In fact, you can usually get by with ToolTips for those controls that are likely to be confusing, plus a few Help menu topics that are implemented as separate forms. In addition, it's often useful to provide a short printed overview of how the application works and what the critical operational issues are.

A ToolTip for a toolbar button

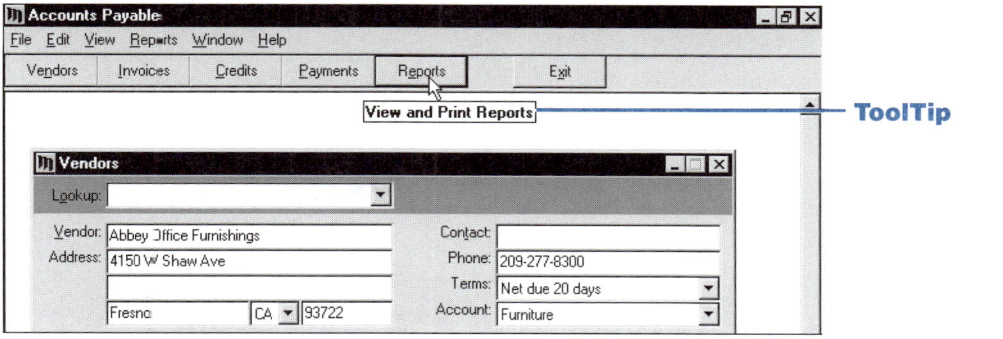

Description

- To provide a ToolTip for any control on a form, enter the tip into its ToolTipText property. This tip is automatically displayed when you position the mouse pointer over the control.

A form used to display help information

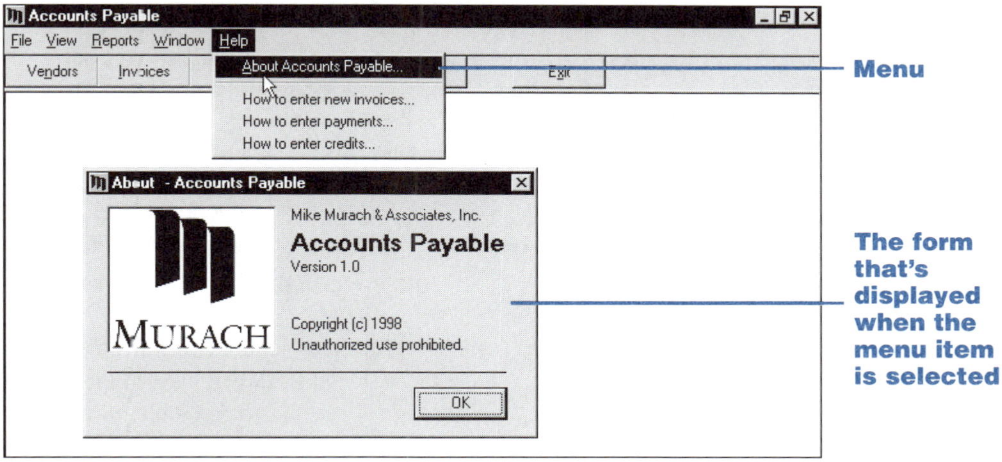

Description

- To display help information for a menu selection, you can develop a form that provides the information.

Figure 8-7 Two quick ways to add help information to a form

How to develop a multiple-document interface

The multi-document interface is especially useful for office applications like Word or Excel so two or more documents can be opened at the same time. Nevertheless, the MDI interface can also be useful for business applications. In particular, this interface establishes a parent form that can be used for the common elements of an application like the menus and toolbars.

How to create the parent and child forms

In figure 8-8, you can see the design time view of the parent form for the Accounts Payable form that's shown in figure 8-1. This parent form provides menus and a toolbar, and its Window menu lets the user switch from one child form to another.

To create a parent form, you use the Add MDI Form command in the Project menu. If you always want the form maximized when it is displayed, you can then set the WindowState property to Maximized.

To create a child form or to change a regular form to a child form, you just set the MDIChild property of the form to True. After that, the child form will always be displayed within the interior of the parent form. To make sure that a child form is always sized appropriately for the interior of the form, you usually set the BorderStyle property to Single Fixed so the form can't be resized.

If you look at the Project Explorer window, you can see that Visual Basic uses a different icon to identify the parent form and the child forms for a project. In addition, you should notice that the frmAboutAP and frmIntro forms are neither parent nor child forms so they can be displayed in modal form (a form that has to be closed before the application can continue).

When you work with a parent form, you can't place any visible controls on the parent form that aren't aligned along the edge of the form. In this figure, for example, the parent form contains a PictureBox control that's aligned to the top edge of the form, right below the menu bar. Then, the child forms are displayed in the open area of the form.

When you unload the parent form, all of the child forms are unloaded first. If one of the child forms has a task in progress, though, this can cause problems. If, for example, a user has made changes to one of the child forms but the related database hasn't been updated, the child form shouldn't be unloaded without asking the user whether the changes should be saved. To provide for situations like this, you can code a procedure for the QueryUnload event of each child form. Within this procedure, you can cancel the unloading events if that is necessary.

The IDE for an MDI application

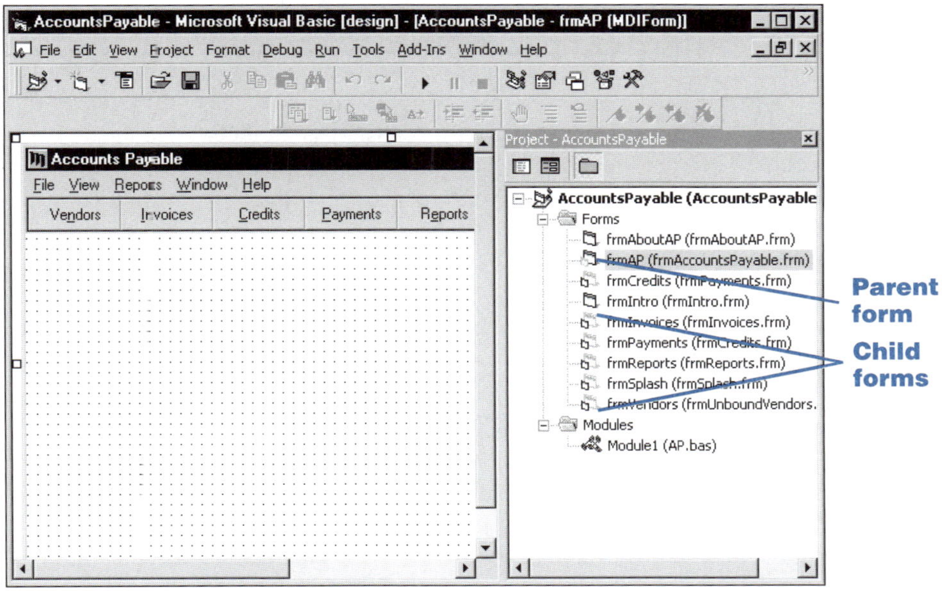

Description

- To create the parent form, pull down the Project menu and select the Add MDI form command. To create a child form, set the MDI Child property for a form to True.
- In general, you should set the BorderStyle property for each child form to Fixed Single and the MaxButton property to False so its size can't be changed. You may also want to set the WindowState property for the parent form to Maximized so the form is always maximized.
- If you want to display a modal form, you have to create it as a regular form that is neither parent nor child. This is illustrated by the frmAboutAP and frmIntro forms in the example above. Then, to display a form as modal, you use the Show method with 1 as the argument.
- When you unload the parent form, all child forms are automatically unloaded. When you load a child form, the parent form is automatically loaded.
- When the parent form is unloaded, the QueryUnload event occurs first for the parent form and then for each of the child forms. If none of the procedures for the QueryUnload events of the child forms cancels the QueryUnload event, the Unload events occur first for the child forms, last for the parent form.
- You can use the QueryUnload event for each child form to make sure that the related database tables have been updated properly. If you set the Cancel argument in one of these procedures to True, the UnLoad events for all of the forms are canceled.

Figure 8-8 How to create parent and child forms for an MDI application

Other information for working with an MDI application

Figure 8-9 presents some properties and coding examples that may help you work with the forms in an MDI application. To start, you can use the ActiveForm and ActiveControl properties of the MDI parent form to identify the active form and the active control on that form. For instance, you can use the ActiveForm property to unload the active child form as illustrated by the first coding example. You can use code like this for the Close command of the File menu on the parent form when that menu is used for all forms.

If you want to center a child form in the interior area of a parent form, you can use the ScaleHeight and ScaleWidth properties of the parent form in a formula that sets the Top and Left properties that position the child form when it is displayed. This is illustrated by the second example in this figure. Here, the Height property of the child form is subtracted from the ScaleHeight property of the parent form and divided by 2 to set the Top property for the child form. A similar formula is used to set the Left property for the child form.

When you develop the menus for an MDI application, one alternative is to develop one set of menus for the parent form that work for all of the child forms. Then, if necessary, you can use code to modify the menus at run time so they're appropriate for the active child form. This is illustrated by the third coding example in figure 8-9. The other alternative is to include a separate menu system for the parent form and each child form. Then, if the active child form has menus, the menus for that form replace the menus of the parent form. But if the active child form doesn't have menus or if no child form is active, the menus of the parent form are displayed.

To let the user switch from one open child form to another, the menus for a parent form usually include a Window menu like the one in figure 8-1. To create a menu like this, just use the Menu Editor and check the WindowList property for the menu; no coding is required. However, you may also want to add a Cascade, Tile, or Arrange command by coding the Arrange method for these menu objects with one of the arguments shown in this figure.

Properties for working with the MDI parent form

Property	Description
ActiveForm	Identifies the active child form.
ActiveControl	Identifies the active control on the active child form.
ScaleHeight	The height of the form between the borders, title bar, menu bar, and other controls aligned on the top or bottom of the form.
ScaleWidth	The width of the form between the borders and any controls aligned on the left or right sides of the form.

Code that unloads the active child form

```
Unload frmAP.ActiveForm
```

Code in the Load event procedure for a child form that centers the form within the interior of the parent form

```
Private Sub Form_Load
    Top = (frmAP.ScaleHeight - Height) / 2
    Left = (frmAP.ScaleWidth - Width) / 2
    Show
End Sub
```

Code that modifies the menus on the parent form when a child form becomes active

```
Private Sub Form_Activate()
    With frmAP
        .mnuEdit.Visible = True
        .mnuEditAdd.Caption = "&Add Vendor"
        .mnuEditUpdate.Caption = "&Update Vendor"
        .mnuEditDelete.Caption = "&Delete Vendor"
    End With
End Sub
```

How to create a Window menu for a parent form

- Use the Menu Editor dialog box to create a Window menu with the WindowList property checked. This menu will automatically provide for switching from one open child form to another. You can also add commands like Cascade, Tile, or Arrange to this menu.
- To code the click event procedure for the Cascade, Tile, or Arrange command, use the Arrange method for the MDIForm object with one of the arguments shown in these examples:

```
frmAPMain.Arrange vbCascade
frmAPMain.Arrange vbTileHorizontal
frmAPMain.Arrange vbArrangeIcons
```

Figure 8-9 Properties and code for working with an MDI application

Perspective

If you take an hour or two to experiment with the features presented in this chapter, you'll see that they're all relatively easy to use. Nevertheless, they can significantly improve the impression that an application makes on its users. And they can help the users of the application work more efficiently.

If you've read the other chapters in this section, you should now be able to develop business applications that do everything but prepare reports. In chapter 11, though, you can learn how to use an add-in program called Crystal Reports to generate the reports that an application requires. Then, after you define the reports for an application, you can set up menus, toolbars, or other Visual Basic controls that let the user view and print those reports.

Chapter 9

How to test and debug an application

If you've done much programming, you know that testing and debugging a program is both difficult and time-consuming. Fortunately, though, Visual Basic provides some excellent tools for finding errors. In this chapter, you'll learn how to use those tools.

An overview of testing and debugging

To start, this chapter introduces you to the different types of errors that can occur when you're testing a Visual Basic program. It also shows you how Visual Basic handles these errors and what you can do to control the way Visual Basic handles them.

An introduction to testing and debugging

Figure 9-1 summarizes the three types of errors you'll encounter when testing Visual Basic programs. The most common and easiest to fix is a *compile*, or *compile-time*, *error*. This type of error can occur as you type in code or as a program executes and is usually caused by incorrect syntax or a misspelled keyword or name.

In contrast, a *run-time error* always occurs as a program executes. This type of error occurs when a statement compiles cleanly, but its operation can't be performed. For instance, a run-time error occurs when a statement tries to divide a value by zero or when a statement refers to an object whose value hasn't been set.

The third type of error is a *logic error*. This type of error can be difficult to identify and correct because it doesn't cause an error message to be displayed. Instead, it causes unexpected results that aren't always immediately apparent. To identify logic errors, you need to test a program thoroughly by trying every possible combination of events.

In figure 9-1, you can also see a summary of the Visual Basic options that control the way it identifies and deals with errors. To review or change these options, you use the Options command in the Tools menu. In particular, you may want to make sure that the Auto Syntax Check and Auto Data Tips options are on, although they should be on by default.

By default, the Break in Class Mode option is also on, which means Visual Basic traps any error that occurs in a class module if an On Error statement hasn't been coded to handle the error. Although this option will work for most of the applications you develop, you can change to one of the other Break options whenever that's appropriate. If you choose the Break on All Errors option, Visual Basic traps all errors even if an error handler is active. If you choose the Break on Unhandled Errors option, Visual Basic traps unhandled errors, but not within class modules. (For more information about class modules, please read chapter 12.)

Incidentally, the Break option you choose is saved from one Visual Basic session to another. So if you want to change this option just for the current session, use the Toggle command in the shortcut menu for the Code window.

Another option you need to be familiar with is the Compile On Demand option. If this option is selected, as it is by default, program statements are compiled as they're executed. But if this option isn't selected, every module in the project is compiled before the application is executed. Because this can cause problems as you're developing an application, you'll want to make sure that the Compile On Demand option is on until you're ready to test the entire application.

Three types of programming errors

Error type	Description
Compile error	Occurs when the compiler detects code that isn't constructed correctly. Most compile errors are caused by incorrect syntax like a missing parentheses or a misspelled keyword.
Run-time error	Occurs when a compiled instruction can't be executed like when an instruction tries to divide a value by zero.
Logic error	Occurs when an application doesn't produce the intended results even though the code compiles correctly and runs without errors.

Visual Basic options for testing and debugging

Option	Tab	Description
Auto Syntax Check	Editor	Checks the syntax of statements as you enter them in the Code window.
Auto Data Tips	Editor	Displays the value of a variable or property in break mode when the mouse pointer is positioned over the variable or property.
Break on All Errors	General	Causes the project to enter break mode any time an error occurs.
Break in Class Mode	General	Causes the project to enter break mode if an error occurs in a class module and no error handler is active. The project breaks at the line of code that caused the error.
Break on Unhandled Errors	General	Causes the project to enter break mode if no error handler is active. If the error occurs in a class module, the project breaks at the line of code that referenced the class module.
Compile On Demand	General	Compiles the project as it executes.
Background Compile	General	Finishes compiling the project during any idle time as the project executes.

Notes

- Choose the Options command from the Tools menu to display the options shown above.
- Even if the Auto Syntax Check option isn't selected, Visual Basic identifies syntax errors by displaying the incorrect code in a different color.

Figure 9-1 An introduction to testing and debugging

How to handle compile errors

If the Auto Syntax Check option is selected, Visual Basic checks the syntax of the statements in the Code window as you enter them. If it detects an error, Visual Basic displays a dialog box that describes the error and the statement that caused the error is highlighted in the Code window as shown in figure 9-2. Then, if you need more information about the error, you can click on the Help button. In most cases, though, you can tell from the error message what the cause of the problem is. Then, you can click on the OK button to return to the Code window and correct the statement.

Although syntax errors are the most common cause of compile errors, other types of compile errors can occur when you run a program. When that happens, a dialog box similar to the one shown in figure 9-2 is displayed. Then, if you click on the OK button, the program enters *break mode*. This is a special state that lets you fix errors and modify code without having to cancel execution of the program.

To start and compile a program, you can use the two commands shown in figure 9-2. If you use the Start command and the Compile On Demand option is on, the program is compiled as it's executed. If this option is off, all of the modules in the program are compiled before the program is executed. To access the Start command, you can use the Run menu, the Standard toolbar, the Debug toolbar, or the shortcut key shown in the Run menu (F5).

Another way to compile all the modules of a program before the program is run is to use the Start with Full Compile command. You can use this command, which overrides the setting of the Compile On Demand option, when you complete an application and want to make sure that all of the modules have been compiled since they were last changed. After the modules have been compiled without error, the program is run.

Two commands for starting and compiling a program

Menu	Command	Toolbar	Function
Run	Start (F5)		Run the application. Changes to Continue when the project is in break mode.
	Start with Full Compile (Crtl+F5)		Compile all statements, then run the application.

The type of message that's displayed when a compile error occurs at design time

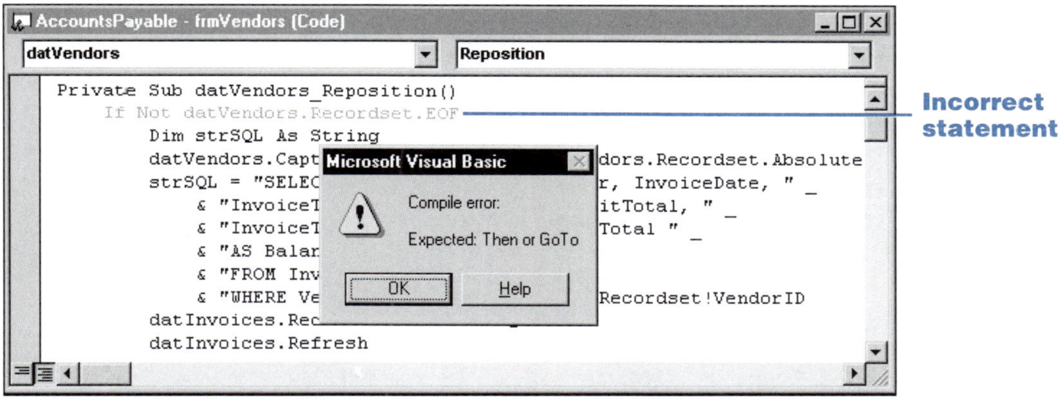

Description

- If you enter code with incorrect syntax and the Auto Syntax Check option is on, Visual Basic displays a compile error message and highlights the incorrect statement. Then, you can click on the Help button in the dialog box to get additional information about the error. Or, you can click on the OK button to return to the Code window where you can correct the error.
- If a compile error occurs as you run a program, a message like the one above is displayed and the project enters *break mode* when you click on the OK button. Then, you can view and modify the values of properties and variables used by the program, and you can view and edit the program code. When you're done, you can continue the execution of the program.
- To compile and run a program, you can click on the Start button in the Standard or Debug toolbar, or you can select the Start command from the Run menu or use its shortcut key. If the Compile On Demand option is on, the program is compiled as it's executed; otherwise, it's compiled completely before it's executed. To compile a program completely when this option is on, use the Start With Full Compile command.

Figure 9-2 How to handle compile errors

How to handle run-time errors

If a run-time error occurs as a program executes, Visual Basic displays a dialog box like the one shown in figure 9-3. From this dialog box, you can enter break mode by clicking on the Debug button. In break mode, the Code window is displayed and the statement that caused the error is highlighted.

If you can determine the cause of an error, you can make the appropriate change in the Code window while the program is in break mode. Then, if you continue executing the program, the statement that caused the error is executed again so you can see immediately if the change you made corrected the problem.

In many cases, though, you need to do more than just change program code to correct a problem. For example, you may need to change the value of a property or variable to determine if that's what caused the problem. Or, you may need to rerun lines of code that have already been executed. To perform these functions, you can use the debugging tools that are presented in this chapter, and many of these tools are available from the Debug toolbar shown in this figure.

Although you can change the code any way you want to when a program is in break mode, you can't always continue executing the program from the point where the error occurred. That's because some coding changes can't be applied while the application is executing. For example, the data type of a variable can't be changed once it's declared. So if you try to make this type of change, Visual Basic displays a dialog box indicating that the project will be reset. Then, if you accept the change from this dialog box, Visual Basic ends the execution of the program. Or, if you cancel the change, the change is reversed and you are returned to break mode where you can continue debugging the program.

The type of message that's displayed for a run-time error

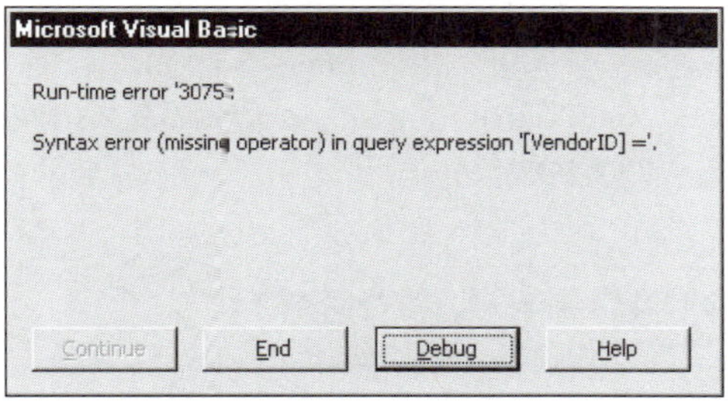

How an application looks in break mode

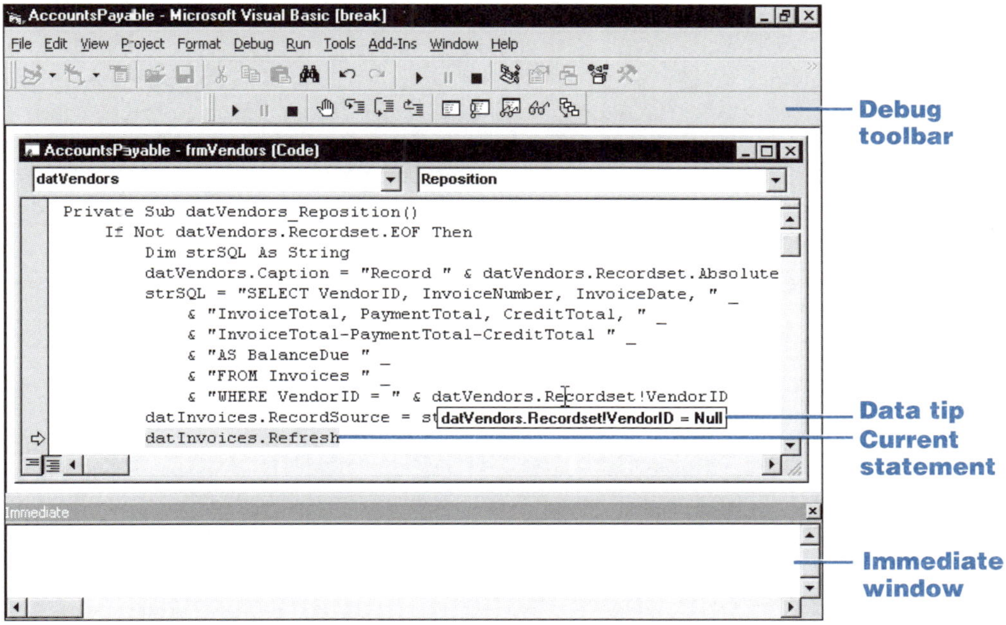

Description

- From a dialog box like the one above, you can click on the Help button to display additional information about the error, click on the End button to end program execution, click on the Continue button (if it's available) to continue execution, or click on the Debug button to enter break mode.
- In break mode, the Code window is displayed and the statement that caused the error is highlighted. Then, you can use the debugging tools to determine the cause of the problem, correct it, and continue processing.
- Some coding changes that you make in break mode can't be applied unless the program is restarted. In those cases, a dialog box says the action will reset your project and asks if you want to proceed.
- If the Auto Data Tips option is on, you can display the value of a variable or property by positioning the mouse pointer in its code as shown above. You can also display the values of variables and properties in the Immediate window.

Figure 9-3 How to handle run-time errors

Basic debugging skills

Now that you have an idea of what's involved in debugging an application, you're ready to learn some debugging skills. To start, you'll learn how to use all of the Visual Basic commands and windows for debugging an application.

How to control the execution of a program

Figure 9-4 presents the commands that you can use to control the execution of a program. As you can see, some of these commands are in the Run menu and others are in the Debug menu. The Break and End commands are not only available from the Run menu, but also from both the Standard and the Debug toolbar.

To execute one statement of a program at a time, you use the Step Into command. Then, the program enters break mode before each statement is executed so you can test the values of properties and variables and perform other debugging functions. Similarly, the Step Over command executes one statement at a time, except that the statements in a called procedure are executed without interruption (they are "stepped over"). You can use either of these commands to start program execution or to restart execution when a program is in break mode.

You can use the Step Out command to execute the remaining statements in the current procedure without interruption. After that, the program enters break mode before the next statement in the calling procedure is executed.

One of the disadvantages of the Step commands is that they can't skip over looping statements like those in a For..Next or Do loop. For those situations, though, you can use the Run To Cursor or Set Next Statement command to skip over code that you know is working properly. You can also use the Set Next Statement command to rerun lines of code that were executed before an error occurred. And if you're not sure what line of code will normally execute next, you can use the Show Next Statement command to highlight it.

The commands for controlling program execution

Menu	Command	Toolbar	Function
Run	Break (Ctrl+Break)		Suspend execution of the program.
	End		End execution of the program.
	Restart (Shift+F5)		Restart the program.
Debug	Step Into (F8)		Execute one statement at a time.
	Step Over (Shift+F8)		Execute one statement at a time except for called procedures.
	Step Out (Ctrl+Shift+F8)		Execute the remaining lines in the current procedure.
	Run to Cursor (Ctrl+F8)		Execute the program until it reaches the statement that contains the cursor.
	Set Next Statement (Ctrl+F9)		Set the statement that contains the cursor as the next statement to be executed.
	Show Next Statement		Highlight the next statement that's going to to be executed.

Description

- If you use the Step Into or Step Over command to start the execution of a program, the program will enter break mode before the first statement is executed. If you use Run to Cursor, the program will enter break mode when it reaches the statement where the cursor is positioned. In either case, the statement currently being executed will be highlighted in the Code window.
- Another way to enter break mode during the execution of a program is to use the Break command. This is useful when you need to stop the execution of a program that's caught in a loop. Then, if a statement is being executed, it will be highlighted.
- From break mode, you can use the Step Into, Step Over, Step Out, and Run To Cursor commands to execute one or more statements and return to break mode. You can also set breakpoints at specific lines as described in the next figure.
- To alter the normal execution sequence of the program, you can use the Select Next Statement command. Just place the cursor in the statement you want to execute next, issue this command, and click on the Continue (Start) button to continue program execution. To determine what statement will normally be executed next, you can issue the Show Next Statement command.

Figure 9-4 How to control the execution of a program

How to use breakpoints to suspend program execution

Although the Step commands are powerful tools for reviewing the way a program works and for finding the bugs in a program, you usually don't want to step through an entire program. Instead, you want to step through just those portions of the program that are likely to contain the bugs. To do that, you can set a *breakpoint* at a statement. Then, the program executes without interruption until it reaches that breakpoint.

To set breakpoints, you use the commands presented in figure 9-5. You can set them either before you begin the execution of a program or while the program is in break mode. Then, when the program is run, it enters break mode whenever it reaches a breakpoint but before the statement at the breakpoint is executed.

Once you set a breakpoint, it remains active until you remove it or close the project. To remove a breakpoint, you use the same techniques that you use to set a breakpoint. And to remove all of the breakpoints in a program at once, you use the Clear All Breakpoints command.

Commands for working with breakpoints

Menu	Command	Toolbar	Function
Debug	Toggle Breakpoint (F9)		Set or remove a breakpoint.
	Clear All Breakpoints (Ctrl+Shift+F9)		Clear all breakpoints.

How a breakpoint appears in the Code window

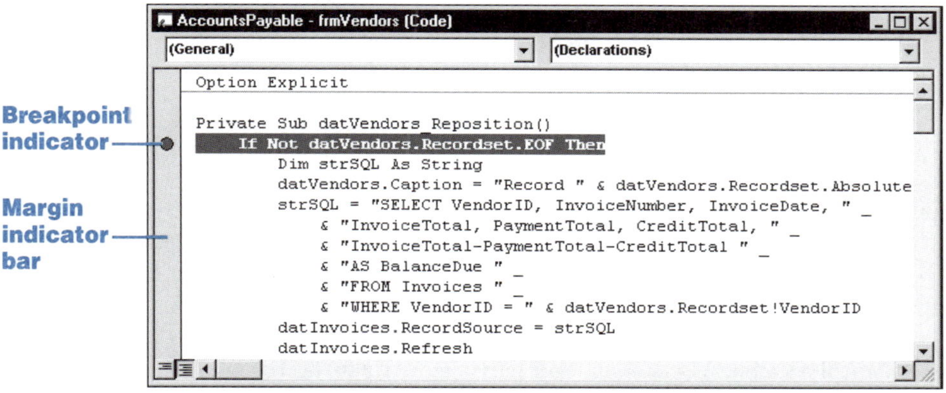

Description

- A *breakpoint* is used to suspend the execution of an application. You can set a breakpoint before you run an application or while the application is in break mode.
- To set a breakpoint, move the cursor to the statement where you want the breakpoint and issue the Toggle Breakpoint command. You can also set a breakpoint by clicking in the margin indicator bar to the left of the statement where you want the breakpoint. To remove a breakpoint, use the same techniques.
- You can set a breakpoint only on a line that contains an executable statement. You cannot set breakpoints on blank lines, comments, or declarative statements.
- When you start or continue program execution, the program enters break mode before the statement that contains the next breakpoint is executed. Then, you can use other debugging tools to work with the program.

Figure 9-5 How to use breakpoints to suspend program execution

How to use the Immediate window to work with program values

Figure 9-6 shows how to use the Immediate window. This window should be displayed by default whenever a program enters break mode. Otherwise, you can open it by using the Immediate Window command in the View menu or the Immediate Window button in the Debug toolbar.

One use of the Immediate window is to display the values of variables, properties, and fields as shown in this figure. If the Auto Data Tips option is on, however, you can also do this using that feature. However, if the variable, property, or field you want to display doesn't appear in the portion of code that's currently displayed, it is often easier to display it in the Immediate window. In addition, you can use this window to change values.

You can also use the Immediate window to execute a Sub procedure or function or to display the value returned by the execution of a function. This can be useful for testing the result of a procedure with different arguments. When you do this, you can execute built-in functions as well as user-defined functions.

When you enter statements in the Immediate window, you should know that they're executed in the same context as the program that's running. That means that you can't display the value of a variable that's out of scope and you can't execute a private procedure that's in a module that isn't currently executing. If you try to do that, Visual Basic displays a blank line or an error message. You can, however, display the value of a property of another form in the project or a property of one of its controls. To do that, just include the name of the form in the reference. Then, if you refer to a form that isn't currently loaded, it will be loaded.

You should also know that the statements you enter into the Immediate window remain there until you exit from the Visual Basic program or explicitly delete them. That way, you can use the same statements from one execution of a program to another without having to re-enter them. To execute a statement you've already entered in the Immediate window, just place the cursor in it and press the Enter key.

Command for displaying the Immediate window

Menu	Command	Toolbar	Function
View	Immediate Window (Ctrl+G)		Display the Immediate window

How to work in the Immediate window

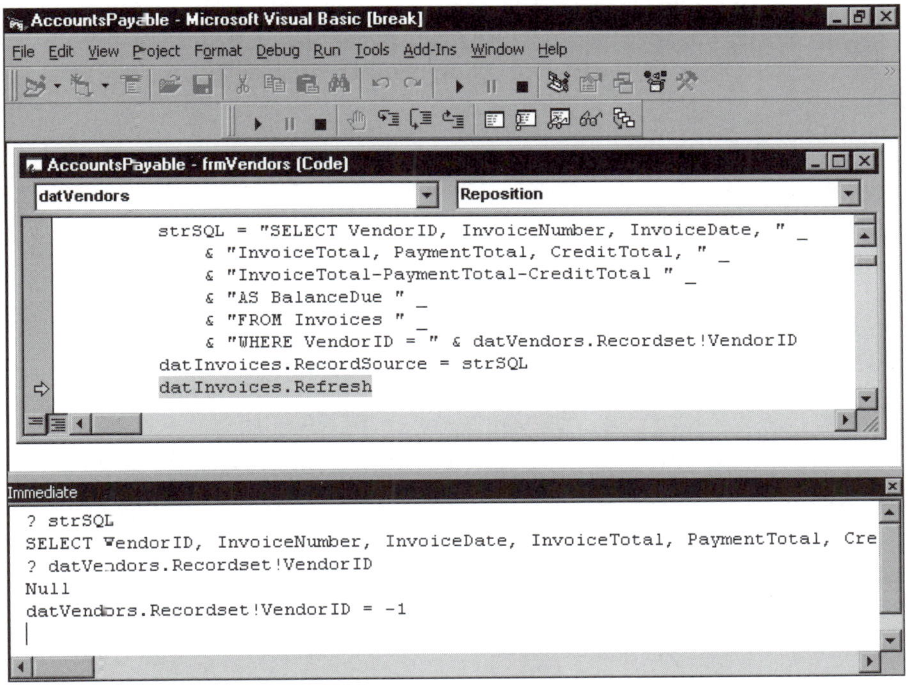

Description

- To display a value in the Immediate window, enter the Print method or a question mark followed by the expression whose value you want to display. Then, press the Enter key. (The question mark is a shorthand for the Print method.)
- To assign a different value to a variable, property, or object, enter an assignment statement in the Immediate window and press the Enter key.
- You can also use the Print method in your program code to display values in the Immediate window as the program executes. When used in program code, though, the Print method must be preceded by the object it belongs to like this:

  ```
  Debug.Print
  ```

  In the Immediate window, the Debug object is assumed.
- You can also execute functions and Sub procedures from the Immediate window. To do that, just enter the name of the function or procedure followed by any arguments it requires and press the Enter key. If you want to display the result of a function, precede the function call with a question mark.

Figure 9-6 How to use the Immediate window to work with program values

How to use the Watch window to monitor expressions

Although you can display the values of expressions in the Immediate window, those values aren't updated automatically when they change. In contrast, the Watch window lets you monitor the value of an expression so you know when it changes.

The use of this window is summarized in figure 9-7. As you can see, this window is displayed automatically when you add a *watch expression* to a project. If you close this window, though, you can reopen it using the Watch Window command in the View menu or the Watch Window button in the Debug toolbar.

To add a watch expression, you use the Add Watch dialog box shown in this figure. This expression can be any valid Visual Basic expression, and it doesn't have to exist in the program. For instance, the first expression in the Watch window in this figure checks to see if the RecordCount property of the datInvoices.Recordset object is equal to zero. For this expression, I specified the Break When Value is True option so the program will enter break mode whenever the expression evaluates to a true value.

You can tell which Watch Type option is used for an expression by the icon that's displayed to the left of the expression in the Watch window. The second expression in this figure, for example, uses the Break When Value Changes option. And the third expression uses the Watch Expression option, which simply displays the value of the expression in the Watch window whenever the program enters break mode.

If the expression you add to the Watch window is an object, a plus sign is displayed to the right of the Watch Type icon for the expression. This is illustrated by the second watch expression in this figure. Then, if you click on the plus sign, the properties of the object are displayed.

The Context options in the Add Watch dialog box determine when the value of the expression is displayed in the Watch window. In general, you should keep this context as specific as possible. Although the smallest context is a specific procedure in a specific module, you can also choose a context that consists of all the procedures in a module or all the modules in a project. If you add too many watch expressions with module-level or project-level contexts, though, the execution speed of your program could be noticeably affected.

If you select an expression in the Code window before you display the Add Watch dialog box, that expression is displayed in the Expression text box and Visual Basic chooses the context that's appropriate for the expression. If, for example, you select a variable that's declared at the procedure-level, the context is that procedure in the current module. Similarly, if you select a module-level variable, the context is all the procedures in the current module. If necessary, though, you can change the context using the Procedure and Module drop-down lists. You may want to do that, for example, if a variable is defined at the module-level but you only need to watch its value during the execution of a specific procedure.

Commands for working with the Watch window

Menu	Command	Toolbar	Function
Debug	Add Watch		Add an expression to the Watch window.
	Edit Watch		Edit or delete a watch expression.
View	Watch Window		Display the Watch window.

The Add Watch dialog box

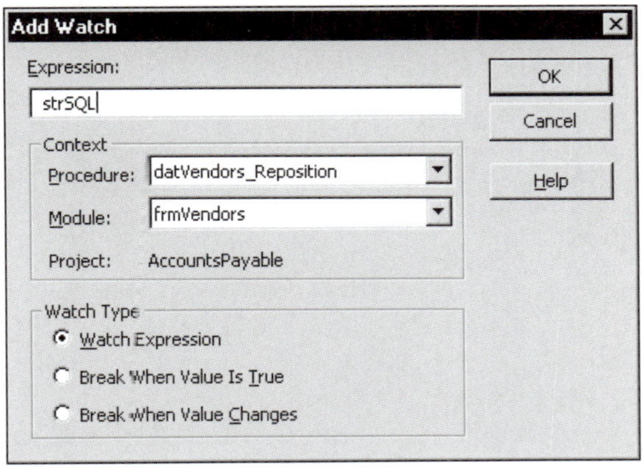

The Watch window

Description

- The Watch window lets you view the values of watch expressions while a program is in break mode. A *watch expression* can be any valid Visual Basic expression.
- To add an expression to the Watch window, complete the Add Watch dialog box. If a valid expression is selected in the Code window when this dialog box is displayed, it will be displayed in the Expression text box.
- The Context options determine the scope of a watch expression. If an expression is out of scope, a message is displayed in the Watch window instead of a value.
- The Watch Type option determines when the value of an expression is displayed. The first option displays the value whenever the program enters break mode. The second option causes the program to enter break mode whenever the expression is true. The third option causes the program to enter break mode whenever the expression changes. The icon to the left of a watch expression in the Watch window indicates the watch type.

Figure 9-7 How to use the Watch window to monitor expressions

How to use the Quick Watch feature to monitor an expression

Figure 9-8 shows you how to use the Quick Watch feature. This feature lets you display the value of an expression that exists in your program whenever you're in break mode. After you select the expression and start the Quick Watch command, its dialog box is displayed along with the value and context of the expression. Then, if you want to continue monitoring the value of the expression, you can click on the Add button to add the expression to the Watch window.

Here again, if the Auto Data Tips option is on, you can use that feature instead of the Quick Watch feature to display a value. Then, the primary benefit of using the Quick Watch feature is that it provides another way to add items to the Watch window.

Command for displaying the Quick Watch dialog box

Menu	Command	Toolbar	Function
Debug	Quick Watch (Shift+F9)		Display the value of the expression highlighted in the Code window.

The Quick Watch dialog box

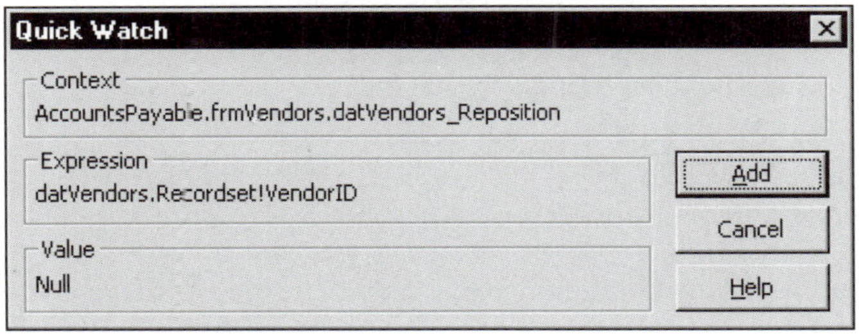

Description

- You can use the Quick Watch feature to display the value of an expression that exists in your program code. However, you can't create a new expression when you use this feature like you can when you use the Watch window.
- To display the Quick Watch dialog box, highlight the expression whose value you want to display and select the Quick Watch command from the Debug menu or Debug toolbar.
- To add an expression to the Watch window from the Quick Watch dialog box, click on the Add button.
- Remember that you can display the value of a property, variable, or field by positioning the mouse pointer over it when the Auto Data Tips option is on. As a result, you usually don't need to use the Quick Watch feature to perform that function.

Figure 9-8 How to use the Quick Watch feature to monitor an expression

How to use the Locals window to monitor variables

The Locals window shown in figure 9-9 displays the values of all the variables that are in scope when a program enters break mode. At the top of this window, the name of the procedure that's currently executing is displayed. In this example, the Locals window displays the values of all variables in the datVendors_Validate procedure in the frmVendors module of the AccountsPayable project.

The Locals window is useful when you need to see the values of several variables that are used within the same procedure. Then, you can set a breakpoint at that procedure and display the Locals window to see those values. This is usually easier than displaying each variable in the Immediate window or adding each variable to the Watch window.

In the Locals window in this figure, you'll notice that only the variables that are declared within the current procedure are displayed. If any variables are declared at the module level, the values of those variables are displayed under a special module variable that's included at the top of the Locals window. For a form module, this variable is the system variable Me. For a standard module, this variable is the name of the module. In either case, if you click on the plus sign to the left of this variable, you can see the module-level variables defined in the module along with the properties of the module and its controls.

Besides displaying variables, you can use the Locals window to change the values of those variables. To do that, you simply highlight the value you want to change and enter a new value. You can then continue the execution of the program.

Command for displaying the Locals window

Menu	Command	Toolbar	Function
View	Locals Window		Display the Locals window.

How to use the Locals window for debugging

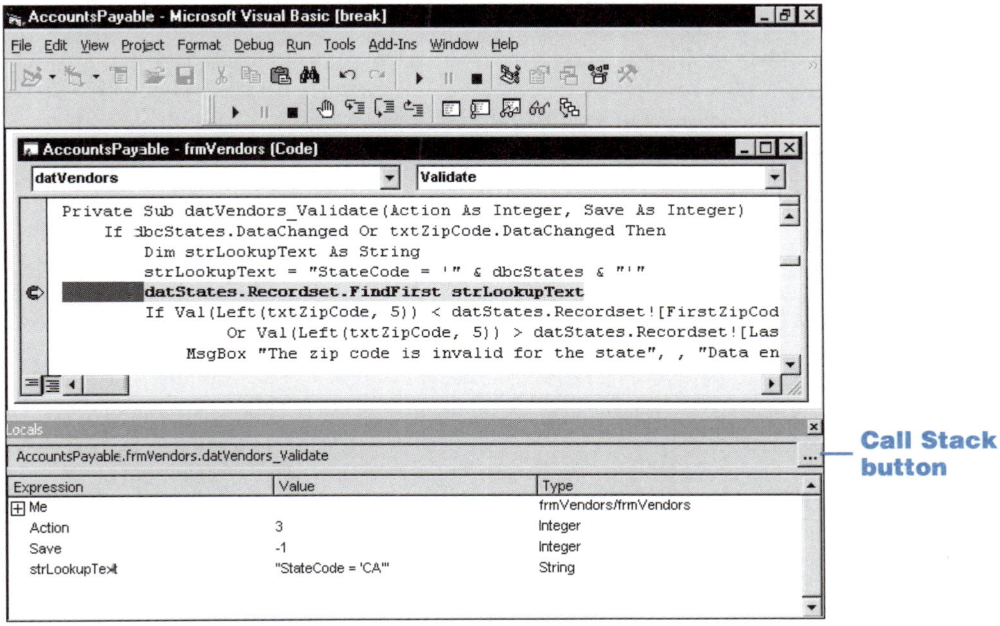

Description

- The Locals window displays information about the variables within the scope of the procedure that's current when a program enters break mode. That includes module-level variables, but not global variables defined in other modules.
- Module-level variables are displayed under a special module variable at the top of the Locals window. For a form module, that variable name is Me. For a standard module, that variable name is the module name. To display the variables declared in the module, click on the plus sign to the left of the special variable name. Then, the properties of the module and any controls it contains are displayed.
- You can also use the Locals window to change the value of a property or variable. To do that, click on the line that contains the property or variable, click on its value to highlight it, and enter its new value. If the value you enter isn't appropriate for the data type, an error message is displayed and the value isn't changed.
- To display the Call Stack dialog box shown in the next figure from the Locals window, click on the Call Stack button.

Figure 9-9 How to use the Locals window to monitor variables

How to use the Call Stack to monitor program execution

Figure 9-10 shows you how to use the Call Stack dialog box to monitor the execution of a program. When you display this dialog box from break mode, it lists all of the procedures that are currently active. That can help you trace the execution of a program from one procedure to another.

The procedures listed in the Call Stack dialog box appear in reverse order from the order that they were called. So in this example, the Form_Load procedure called the LoadControls procedure, which called the GetTerms procedure. To locate the statement in one procedure that called the next procedure, you can highlight the calling procedure in the Call Stack and click on the Show button. The calling statement in that procedure is then highlighted in the Code window.

Because the Call Stack dialog box shows only active procedures, you can't use it to trace the execution of all the procedures in a program from beginning to end. But fortunately, that usually isn't necessary when you're developing event-driven programs. If you do need to do that, though, one alternative is to place a MsgBox function that displays the name of the procedure at the start of each procedure that you want to trace. Then, a message is displayed each time a procedure is called. Another alternative is to place a breakpoint at the start of each procedure that you want to trace. Once you've solved the debugging problem, you can remove the MsgBox functions or breakpoints.

Command for displaying the Call Stack dialog box

Menu	Command	Toolbar	Function
View	Call Stack (Ctrl+L)		Display the Call Stack dialog box.

The Call Stack dialog box

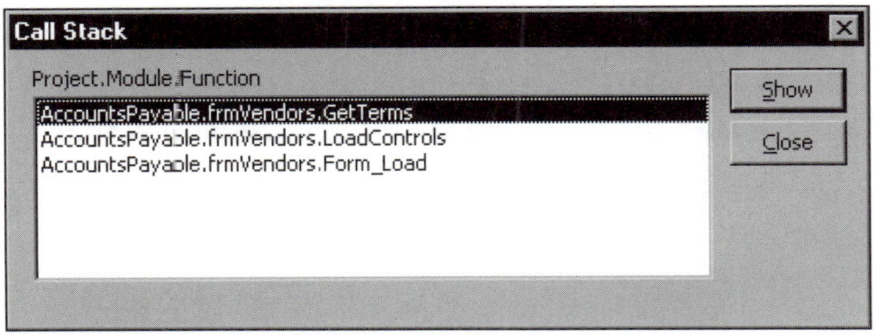

Description

- The Call Stack dialog box lists all of the procedures that are active when a program enters break mode. To display this dialog box, you can use the Call Stack command or toolbar button, or you can click on the Call Stack button in the Locals window.
- If more than one procedure is listed in the Call Stack dialog box, it means that one procedure called another procedure, and so on, in the reverse order from the sequence shown.
- You can use the Show button in the Call Stack dialog box to display the statement that passed control from the procedure that's highlighted to the next procedure. If, for example, you highlight the LoadControls procedure in the dialog box above and click on the Show button, the statement that called the GetTerms procedure is displayed in the Code window.

Figure 9-10 How to use the Call Stack to monitor program execution

Other debugging techniques

In addition to the debugging commands and features presented so far in this chapter, you should know about two other techniques for debugging Visual Basic programs. First, you should know how to test an error-handling routine so you can be sure that it works the way you want it to. Second, you should know how to use compiler directives to control the statements that are included when you compile a project.

How to test an error-handling routine

In figure 5-20 of chapter 5, you learned how to use the On Error and Resume statements to develop an error-handling routine. One way to test a routine like that is to set up the conditions that force an error. Because that can be time-consuming, a better way to test an error-handling routine is to use the Raise method of the Err object as shown in figure 9-11.

In this example, the Raise method causes error number 91 to occur and Visual Basic sets the other properties of the Err object based on that error number. In the dialog box that's displayed by the error-handling routine in this example, you can see that the Number property has been set to 91 and the Description property has been set to the description associated with that error number.

In addition to coding the error number with the Raise method, you can code arguments that Visual Basic can use to set the other properties of the Err object. If, for example, you include the description argument, Visual Basic uses the value you specify for the Description property instead of the description associated with the error number. Unless the error number you specify isn't a valid error number, though, you usually specify just the error number.

To make it easy to find and remove debugging statements like this, you can code them at the left margin of the Code window as shown in this figure. Since you indent the other statements of a procedure, this makes the debugging statements easy to spot. Another way to handle debugging statements, though, is to use compiler directives as shown in the next figure.

The syntax of the Raise method

```
Err.Raise number[, source][, description]
              [, helpfile][, helpcontext]
```

A procedure that use the Raise method to test an error-handling routine

```
Private Sub cmdUpdate_Click()
    On Error GoTo UpdateError
    .
    .
Err.Raise 91
    .
    .
UpdateError:
    MsgBox "Error no: " & Err.Number & vbCrLf _
        & "Source: " & Err.Source & vbCrLf _
        & "Description: " & Err.Description
End Sub
```

The error message that's displayed when the code above is executed

Description

- You can use the Raise method of the Err object to generate a run-time error during the execution of a program. This is useful when you want to test an error-handling routine.
- The only required argument of the Raise method is the number argument. This number indicates the Visual Basic error that you want to generate, and this number is assigned to the Number property of the Err object.
- The other arguments of the Raise method correspond to other properties of the Err object. If you don't specify these arguments, Visual Basic uses the values associated with the error number you specify. Or, if the number you specify isn't a valid error number, Visual Basic uses default values for these arguments.
- To get a list of valid error numbers, see the "Trappable errors" topic in Visual Basic online help.
- You can also use the Error statement to generate a run-time error, but this statement is provided only for backward compatibility with earlier releases of Visual Basic. Its only argument is the error number.

Figure 9-11 How to test an error-handling routine

How to use compiler directives with debugging statements

If you use debugging statements like Debug.Print and Err.Raise in a program, you'll want to be sure that these statements aren't included when you compile the program for distribution to its users. One way to do that is to delete these statements from the program. Another way is to use compiler directives as described in figure 9-12.

You use *compiler directives* to tell Visual Basic what statements to include in the compiled program. During debugging, for example, you want any debugging statements to be compiled and executed. Otherwise, you want these statements omitted from the compilation.

To determine what statements are included in the compiled program, you use the #If...Then...#Else directive. Although the syntax of this statement is similar to the syntax of the normal If statement, the conditions you specify must be based on one or more *conditional compiler constants*. In other words, you can't use regular program constants or variables in the conditions.

To declare a conditional compiler constant, you use the #Const directive as shown in this figure. However, the expression that you assign to a constant like this can consist only of a literal value or another conditional compiler constant. In addition, you can't specify a data type for a compiler constant. Instead, Visual Basic uses the data type that's most appropriate for the value that's assigned to the constant.

In the example in this figure, you can see a typical use of compiler directives. Here, the compiler constant is assigned a value of True so the Err.Raise method is executed during debugging. Then, when the program is ready for production, you can assign a value of False to this constant so the debugging statements will be excluded and the normal statements will be included in the compiled program. In this example, the coding for the compiler directives starts at the left margin so you can easily spot them.

When you use compiler directives, you normally declare the compiler constants in the Declarations section of a module; you don't code them in a procedure as shown in this figure. However, even if they're coded in a procedure, they're treated as module-level constants so they're available to all the procedures in the module.

If you use the same compiler constants throughout the modules in a project, you can also define them as public constants. To do that, you specify the constants and their values in the Make tab of the Project Properties dialog box. To define the constant shown in figure 9-12 as public, for example, you enter

```
bDebug = True
```

in the Conditional Compilation Argument text box. To define more than one constant, you separate them with colons.

The syntax of the #If..Then..#Else conditional directive

```
#If condition Then
    statements
[#ElseIf condition-n Then
    statements] ...
[#Else
    statements]
#End If
```

The syntax of the #Const directive

```
#Const constantname = expression
```

A procedure that uses compiler directives

```
Private Sub cmdUpdate_Click()
#Const bDebug = True
    On Error GoTo UpdateError
#If bDebug Then
    Err.Raise 91
#Else
    If ValidData Then
    .
    .
#End If
UpdateError:
    MsgBox "Error no: " & Err.Number & vbCrLf _
        & "Source: " & Err.Source & vbCrLf _
        & "Description: " & Err.Description
End Sub
```

Description

- A *compiler directive* tells Visual Basic whether or not to compile blocks of code. Compiler directives can be used to omit debugging statements from a compiled application without removing them from the source code.
- The #If…Then…#Else directive tells the compiler what statements to include based on the specified conditions. The conditions in this statement can include one or more *conditional compiler constants*, literals, and operators. To declare a conditional compiler constant, you use the #Const directive.
- Conditional compiler constants are always private to the module in which they're declared and are always evaluated as module-level variables even if they're declared within a procedure. However, you can also define public conditional compiler constants by specifying them in the Make tab of the Project Properties dialog box.

Figure 9-12 How to use compiler directives with debugging statements

Perspective

If you have much debugging experience in other programming environments, you should now realize that Visual Basic provides a powerful set of debugging tools. By using them, you can set breakpoints at the start of critical portions of code. Then, you can step through the statements that follow each breakpoint, and you can review the values of the related variables and properties after each step. If necessary, you can also change values and alter the execution sequence of the statements. With tools like these, an inherently difficult job becomes manageable.

Now, if you've completed all of the chapters in this section of this book, you have all the programming skills you need to develop client/server applications with Visual Basic. You know how to use the syntax, statements, and functions of Visual Basic. You know how to build forms using DAO. You know how to enhance the database programming. You know how to add menus, toolbars, and help to forms and how to create a multiple-document interface. And no matter what features you use, you should be able to find and correct any errors.

SECTION THREE 3

Other development skills

As in section 2, you can read the chapters in this section in whatever sequence you prefer. In chapter 10, you can learn how to use the Visual Data Manager for working with Jet databases and for creating queries. And in chapter 11, you can learn how to use Crystal Reports for generating the reports that an application requires.

Chapter 12 takes you deeper into object-oriented programming. Here, you can learn how to create class modules to define your own objects with their own properties and methods. Then, you can learn how to use those class modules by including them in a standard project or by deploying them as ActiveX components. Because ActiveX components can be stored on a component server and can be modified without changing the client software, they can make application maintenance easier.

The last chapter in this section shows you how to deploy a completed application on the clients of a system. This includes creating a setup program and all the files that are needed by the clients. Then, you can run the setup program to install the application on each client.

Chapter 10

How to use the Visual Data Manager to work with databases

Visual Basic 5 includes an add-in program called the Visual Data Manager that lets you work with the objects and data in a variety of databases. Because it isn't able to handle some of the complexities of working with ODBC databases, though, the Visual Data Manager is more useful for working with Access databases than it is for working with ODBC databases. In particular, the Visual Data Manager can be useful when you're learning because it lets you create Access test databases that you can experiment with, even if you don't have Access on your system.

Basic skills for working with the Visual Data Manager

Before you can work with a database using the Visual Data Manager, you have to open an existing database or create a new one. You'll learn how to do that in a moment. But first, I want to present some basic techniques for working in the Visual Data Manager's application window.

An overview of the Visual Data Manager

Figure 10-1 shows the Visual Data Manager with an existing Access database displayed. As you can see, all of the tables and queries in the database are listed in the Database window. To expand and collapse the display of these tables and queries, you can use standard Windows techniques. When you expand a table, its fields, indexes, and properties are displayed as shown in the figure. When you expand a query, only its properties are displayed.

You use the shortcut menus that are available in the Database window to perform most functions related to tables and queries. To create a new table or query, for example, you can right-click anywhere in the Database window and choose the New Table or New Query command from the shortcut menu that's displayed. And to change the design of an existing table, you can right-click on the table name and choose the Design command.

If you use the New Query command to create a query, a utility called the Query Builder is started. This utility lets you create Select queries using a graphical interface. You can also create a query by typing it into the SQL Statement window. This is useful for creating queries that aren't supported by the Query Builder, and it's useful for editing an existing query.

The Visual Data Manager with an open database

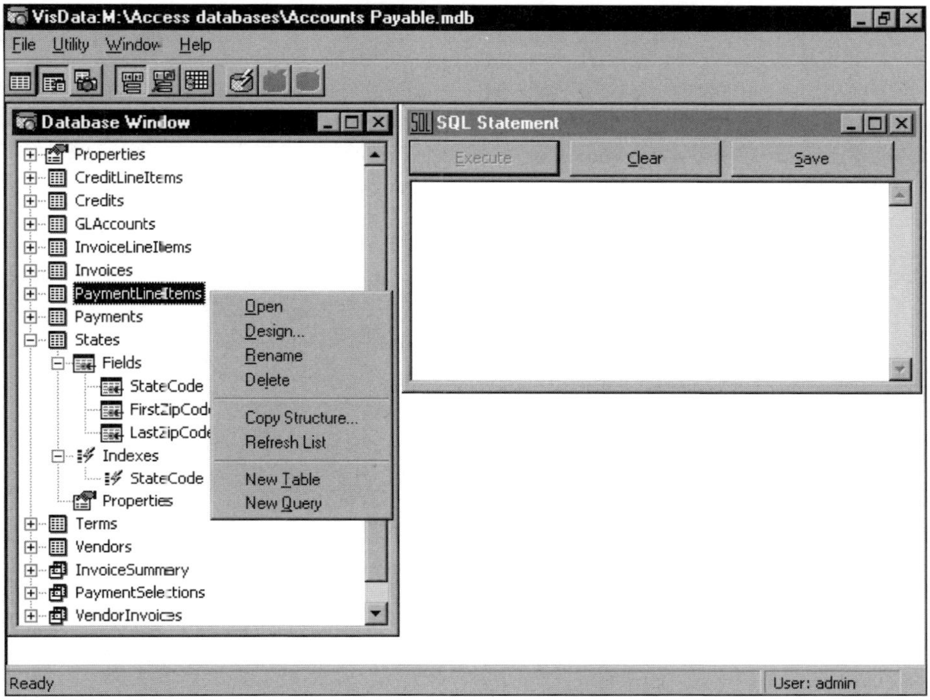

Description

- The Visual Data Manager is an add-in program that comes with Visual Basic 5. To access this program, choose the Visual Data Manager command from the Add-ins menu.
- The Visual Data Manager lets you work with a variety of databases, including Access and ODBC databases. You can also create a new Access database, and you can create a data source that defines the connection to an ODBC database.
- The Database window shows all of the objects in the current database. You'll use shortcut menus like the one shown above to work with these database objects.
- The SQL Statement window lets you enter and issue SQL statements to the current database. You can also create queries using the Query Builder utility.
- The Data Form Designer utility lets you build a form based on a table or query. Because the Visual Basic Data Form Wizard gives you more flexibility, though, you probably won't use the Data Form Designer.
- You can also import and export tables from one database to another. And you can link (or attach) tables in another database to an Access database.

Figure 10-1 An overview of the Visual Data Manager

How to open or create an Access database

Figure 10-2 shows you how to open an existing Access database or create a new Access database. To open an existing database, you locate the folder that contains the database and then select the database. Then, all of the tables and queries in the database are displayed in the Database window. To create a new database, you identify the folder where you want to save the database and then specify the name for the database. Then, you can use the shortcut menu in the Database window to create tables and queries for the new database.

The dialog box for opening an Access database

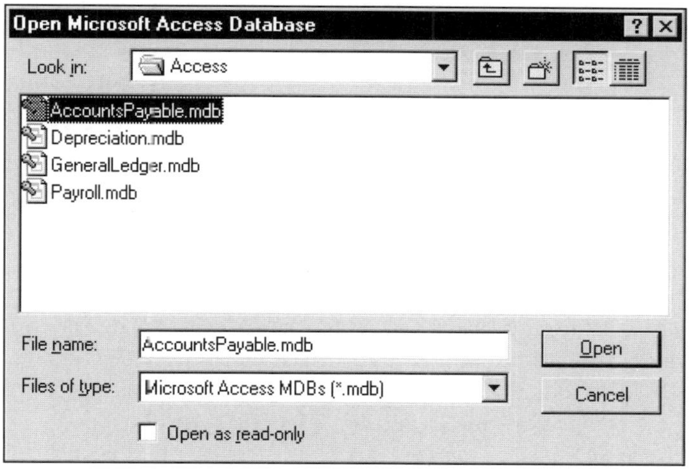

The dialog box for creating an Access database

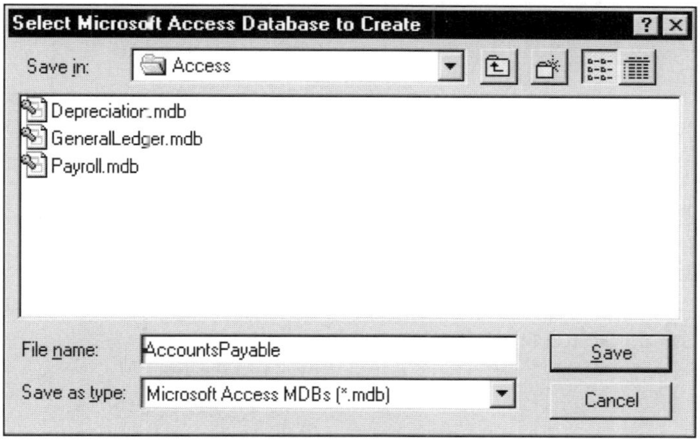

Description

- To open an Access database, choose the Open Database command from the File menu and select the Microsoft Access option to display the first dialog box shown above. Use this dialog box to locate the folder that contains the database you want to open, then highlight the database and click on the Open button.
- To create a new Access database, select the New command from the File menu, select Microsoft Access from the list of database types that's displayed, and select the Version 2.0 MDB or the Version 7.0 MDB option to display the second dialog box shown above. Then, use this dialog box to identify the folder where you want to save the new database, enter the name of the database in the File Name text box, and click on the Save button to create the database.

Figure 10-2 How to open or create an Access database

How to open an ODBC database or create an ODBC data source

To open an ODBC database, you have to specify the name of the *data source*, or the *DSN*, that describes the connection to the database. To do that, you use the ODBC Logon dialog box shown at the top of figure 10-3. This dialog box also lets you enter a user id and password that the database server uses to verify that you have access to the server and the database. You can also enter the name of the database you want to connect to in the ODBC Logon dialog box. However, because the database is typically identified in the DSN, that's usually not necessary.

You can also create a new data source using the Visual Data Manager if one doesn't already exist for the database you want to access. To do that, you start by selecting the (None) option from the DSN list in the ODBC Logon dialog box. When you select this option, the Driver list becomes available so you can select the type of database you want to connect to. To create the data source, click on the Register button and complete the ODBC SQL Server Setup dialog box that's displayed. When you click on the OK button, the data source is created and you're returned to the ODBC Logon dialog box. Unfortunately, if you display the DSN list in this dialog box, you'll see that it hasn't been updated to include the DSN you just created. To use the new DSN, you have to close this dialog box and then open it again.

You can also create a new data source using the New command in the File menu. When you use this technique, though, you have to type in the name of the ODBC driver you want to use. Since you're not given a list of drivers to choose, it's usually easier to create a data source using the ODBC Logon dialog box.

When you use the Visual Data Manager to create a data source, a user data source is created. A *user data source* can be used only by the user who creates it, and it can be used only on the machine where it's created. If you need to create a data source that can be used by any user on a machine, called a *system data source*, you can use the 32bit ODBC application in the Windows Control Panel. You can also use this application to create a *file data source*, which can be used by any user on any machine that has the appropriate driver installed. To find out more about using this application, see the Windows help.

The dialog box for opening an ODBC database

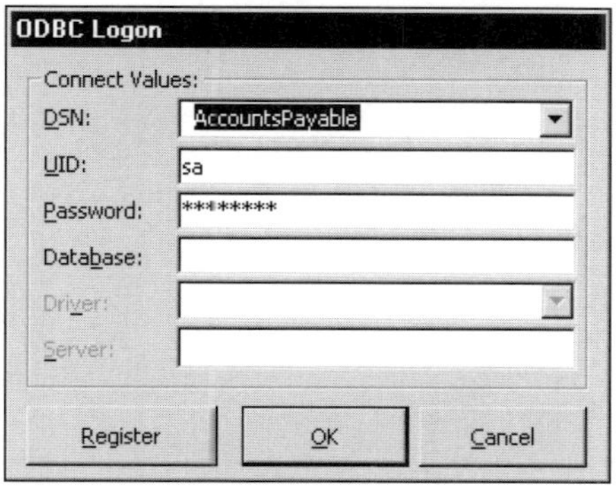

The dialog box for creating an ODBC data source

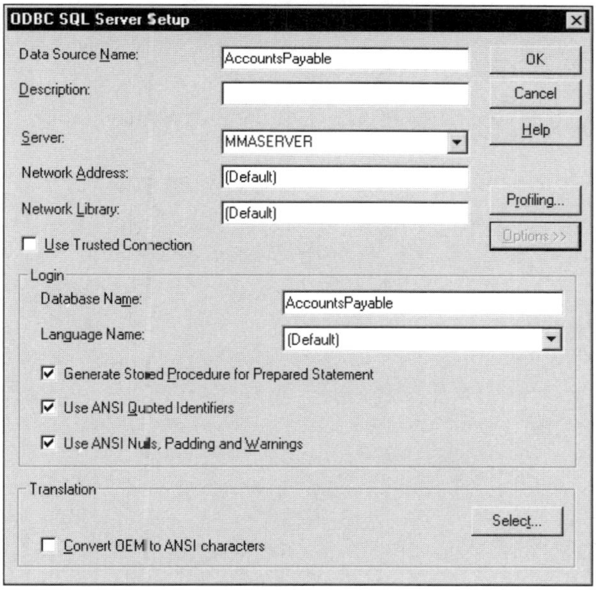

Description

- To open an ODBC database, choose the Open Database command from the File menu and select the ODBC option to display the ODBC Logon dialog box. Then, select a data source from the DSN list, enter a valid user id and password, enter the database name if the DSN doesn't identify one, and click on the OK button.
- To create a new data source, select (None) from the DSN list in the ODBC Logon dialog box, and select the type of database you want to connect to from the Driver list. Then, click on the Register button to display the ODBC SQL Server Setup dialog box, enter a data source name and a server name, click on the Options button and enter the name of the database you want to connect to, and click on the OK button.

Figure 10-3 How to open an ODBC database or create an ODBC data source

How to create and work with database tables

After you open an existing database or create a new database, you can use the Visual Data Manager to work with the tables in the database. Specifically, you can use the Visual Data Manager to create a new table or edit an existing table, add fields and indexes to a table, and enter and manipulate data.

How to define a table

Figure 10-4 presents the dialog box that lets you work with a table from the Visual Data Manager. This dialog box lets you add and remove fields and indexes from a table. (You'll see the specifics for adding a field or index in just a moment.) It also lets you edit an existing field or index. Note, however, that you can't change all of the properties for an existing field or index. For example, you can't change a field's data type once you've created it. To do that, you have to remove the field and then add it back with the new data type.

After you define all of the fields and indexes for a new table, you enter a name for the table and then click on the Build the Table button to create the table. If you're editing an existing table, this button isn't available. Instead, any changes you make to the table are saved as they're made.

The Table Structure dialog box for a new table

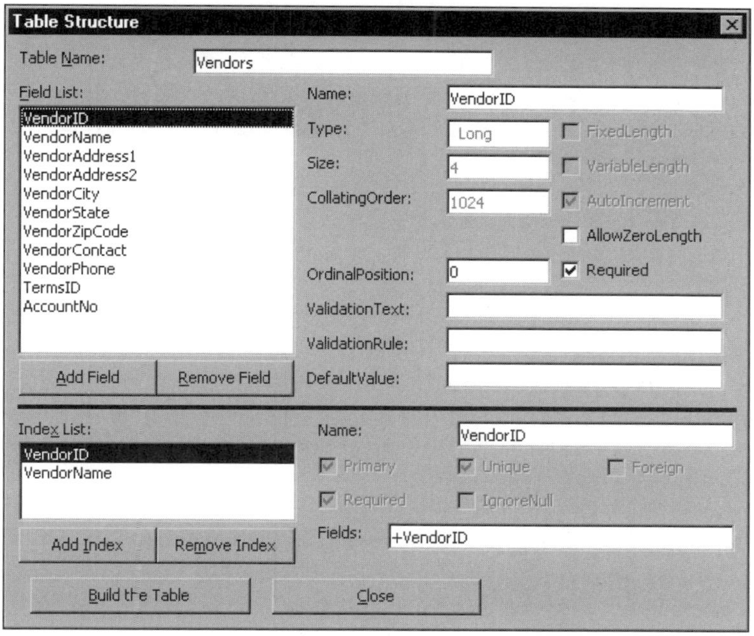

Description

- The Table Structure dialog box lets you add, modify, and delete the fields and indexes in a table. To display this dialog box for an existing table, right-click on the table in the Database window and choose the Design option from the shortcut menu. To display this dialog box for a new table, right-click anywhere in the Database window and choose the New Table option.
- When you click on the Add Field button, the first dialog box in figure 10-5 is displayed. After you add fields and close this dialog box, the new fields are displayed in the Field list in the Table Structure dialog box as shown above.
- When you click on the Add Index button, the second dialog box in figure 10-5 is displayed. After you add indexes and close this dialog box, the indexes are displayed in the Index list in the Table Structure dialog box as shown above.
- To modify a field or an index in the Table Structure dialog box, highlight the field or index and change the appropriate options. Not all of the options can be modified, though.
- After you define the fields and indexes for the table, enter a name for the table and click on the Build the Table button to create the table.
- The Table Structure dialog box for an existing table includes a Print Structure button. This button prints basic information for each field and index in the table.

Figure 10-4 How to define a table

How to add fields and indexes to a table

Figure 10-5 presents the dialog boxes you use to add a field or an index to a table. To add a field, you specify the name of the field along with a variety of other options that define the properties of the field. Note that if you're working with an ODBC database, some of these options aren't available.

Most of the field properties, like data type and size, are self-explanatory. Some of the others, though, may not be so obvious. If you select the AutoIncrField option, for example, the field will contain a number that is generated automatically by the database server. In SQL Server, this is called an *identity column*. In Access, it's called an *autonumber field*. To use the AutoIncrField option, you have to select the Long data type as shown in the figure.

Another property you might not be familiar with is OrdinalPosition. This property indicates where the field occurs in the table. By default, the fields occur in the order that you enter them. To change this order, change the OrdinalPosition properties of the affected fields.

To add an index to a table, you use the second dialog box shown in figure 10-5. This dialog box lets you specify a name for the index, the fields that make up the index, whether the index is the primary key for the table, whether the index is unique, and whether null values should be ignored and not included in the index. Again, some of these options aren't available for ODBC databases.

The dialog box that lets you add fields to a table

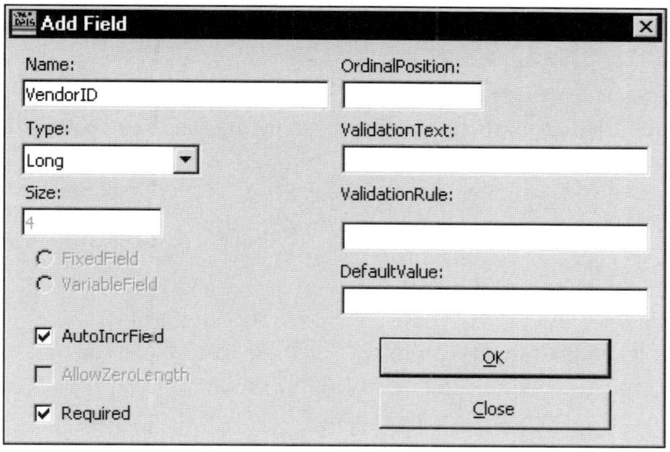

The dialog box that lets you add indexes to a table

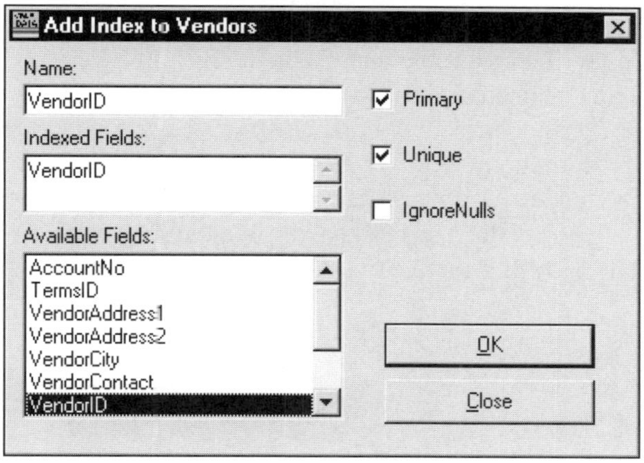

Description

- The Add Field dialog box lets you add new fields to a table. It provides a variety of options for defining the characteristics of the field. To define a field, enter the name of the field into the Name text box, set the other options as appropriate, and click on the OK button.
- The Add Index dialog box lets you define the primary key and other indexes for the table. To do that, enter the name you want to use for the index in the Name text box, select the fields that make up the index from the Available Fields list, set the other options as appropriate, and click on the OK button.
- When you click on the OK button from either dialog box, the dialog box remains open so you can define another field or index. To return to the Table Structure dialog box, click on the Close button.

Figure 10-5 How to add fields and indexes to a table

How to enter and manipulate data

Figure 10-6 illustrates and describes how to work with the data in a table. To start, you should know that the data is displayed in a form like the one shown at the top of the figure. The exact layout of this form, though, depends on the buttons you select in the Visual Data Manager's toolbar.

The first set of three buttons in the toolbar determines the type of recordset that's created. For an Access database, you can create a table-type recordset, a dynaset-type recordset, or a snapshot-type recordset. Unlike the dynaset-type and snapshot-type recordsets that you should already be familiar with, a table-type recordset is a special type of recordset that can only be used with Access databases. It is similar to a dynaset-type recordset, but it can include data from only a single table. The type of recordset you choose determines the buttons that are available on the form and the operations you can perform.

The second set of three buttons determines how the data is displayed and manipulated on the form. The options are to display one record at a time using a data control, display one record at a time without using a data control, and display as many records as will fit on the form at one time using a data control and a DBGrid control. If you've read chapters 4 and 6, you shouldn't have any trouble understanding how this works.

If you display data in a form with a data control, you should know that you can change some of the properties of the data control so it works the way you want it to. For example, you can change the EOFAction property to AddNew so that you can use it to add new records. To change the properties of the data control, just right click on it so the Data Control Properties dialog box is displayed. Then, change the properties the way you want them and click on the Refresh Data Control button to apply the changes.

A form with a data control that displays a dynaset-type recordset

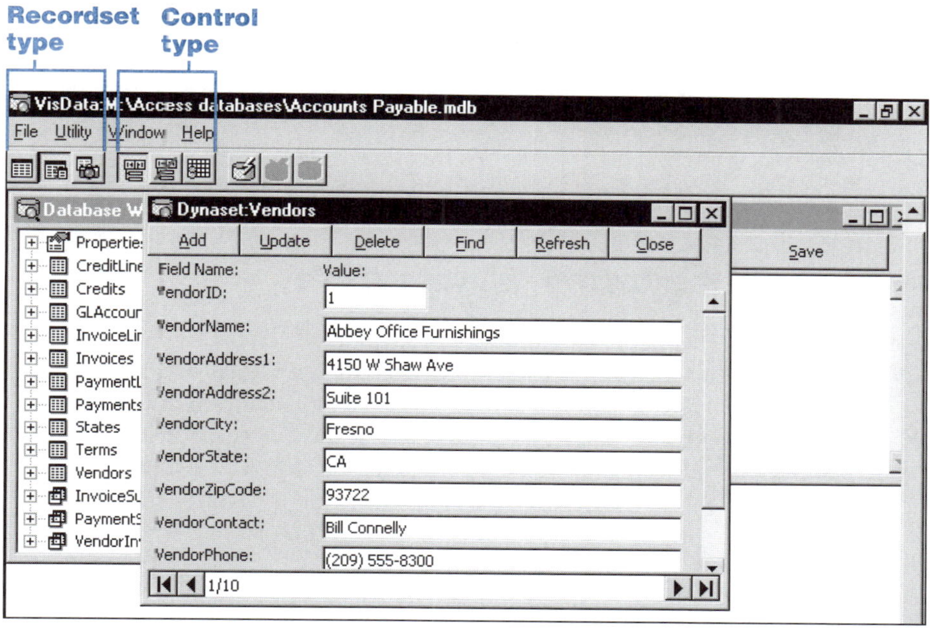

Button	Description
Table type Recordset	Creates a table-type recordset that you can use to add, modify, and delete records from a table.
Dynaset type Recordset	Creates a dynaset-type recordset that you can use to add, modify, and delete records from a table or a query.
Snapshot type Recordset	Creates a snapshot-type recordset that you can use to display the records in a table or query.
Use Data Control on New Form	Creates a form with a data control that you can use to move from one record to another (shown above).
Don't Use Data Control on New Form	Creates a form without a data control but with command buttons that provide the functions that are appropriate for the recordset type.
Use DBGrid Control on New Form	Creates a form with a DBGrid control that contains one row for each record in the table or query.

Description

- To access the dialog box shown above, right-click on the table or query whose data you want to display and choose the Open command from the shortcut menu. The type of recordset that's created and the layout of the form that's displayed depend on the toolbar buttons that are selected as described above.

Figure 10-6 How to enter and manipulate data

How to create and work with database queries

The Visual Data Manager that comes with Visual Basic 5 provides a graphical tool called the Query Builder that you can use to create typical Select queries. If you need to create more complex Select queries or if you need to create other types of queries, you can enter the SQL statement into the SQL Statement window. After you create a query, you can execute it to display and work with the results.

How to use the Query Builder utility

Figure 10-7 presents the Query Builder dialog box. To create a query from this dialog box, you select the tables and fields that you want to include in the query from the Tables and Fields to Show lists. If you select two or more tables, you can specify how they're related by clicking on the Set Table Joins button and choosing the related fields from each table. Note that even if you're working with a database that already has table relationships defined, these relationships are not carried over to the Query Builder.

To specify the criteria for the query, you use the Field Name, Operator, and Value controls at the top of the dialog box. Then, you click on the And into Criteria or Or into Criteria buttons to add the criteria to the Criteria box at the bottom of the dialog box. You can also edit the criteria directly in this box.

The Order By option buttons and list let you specify how the records in the query results are sorted. Note that you can only sort by a single field using the Query Builder. If you specify a sort order, you may also want to use the Top N Value and Top Percent controls to return a specific number or percent of the records. The Group By list lets you choose a field that's used to group the records in the query results.

After you create a query, you can click on the Run button at the bottom of the dialog box to display and work with its results. You can also copy the SQL statement created by the Query Builder into the SQL Statement window so you can edit it. If you're working with an Access database, you can also save the query.

The Query Builder dialog box

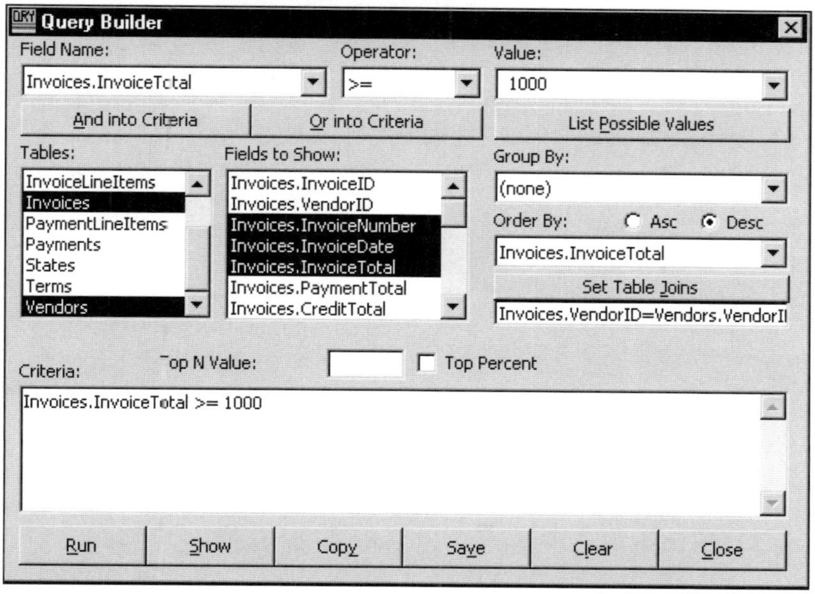

Description

- The Query Builder lets you create queries against the current database. To display its dialog box, choose the Query Builder command from the Utility menu or the New Query command from the Database window shortcut menu.
- You begin a query by choosing the tables you want to include in the query from the Tables list. Then, the fields in those tables are displayed in the Fields to Show list so you can select the ones you want to include.
- You can filter a query by selecting a field, operator, and value from the lists at the top of the dialog box. To list the values that occur in a selected field, click on the List Possible Values button. Otherwise, you can enter a value into the Value text box. Then, click on the And into Criteria or Or into Criteria button to add the criteria to the Criteria box at the bottom of the dialog box. You can also enter criteria directly into the Criteria box.
- To join data from two or more tables, click on the Set Table Joins button and choose the tables and fields for the join from the dialog box that's displayed. The Query Builder doesn't recognize established relationships between tables.
- You can use the Group By and Order By lists to group and sort query results. You can also use the Top N Value and Top Percent boxes to return a specific number or percent of the records.
- The buttons at the bottom of the dialog box let you run the query or show the resulting SQL statement (see figure 10-8), copy the SQL statement to the SQL Statement window (see figure 10-9), save the query (Jet only), clear the dialog box, and close the dialog box. If you save a query, it appears in the Visual Data Manager's Database window.

Figure 10-7 How to use the Query Builder utility

How to work with query results

Figure 10-8 shows how you can work with the results of a query that you create with the Query Builder. The first dialog box shows how the results are displayed in a DBGrid control. To change the way results are displayed and the type of recordset that's created by a query, you can use the buttons in the Visual Data Manager's toolbar. These buttons work the same way that they do for displaying the data in a table.

The second dialog box in figure 10-8 shows the SQL statement that's generated by the Query Builder. You should notice in this example that the join relationship between the Invoices and the Vendors table is included in the WHERE clause of the SELECT statement instead of the FROM clause. Because of that, the recordset that's created by this query is not updateable. If you want to create an updateable query, you have to copy the SELECT statement to the SQL Statement window and edit it.

Query results displayed in a DBGrid control

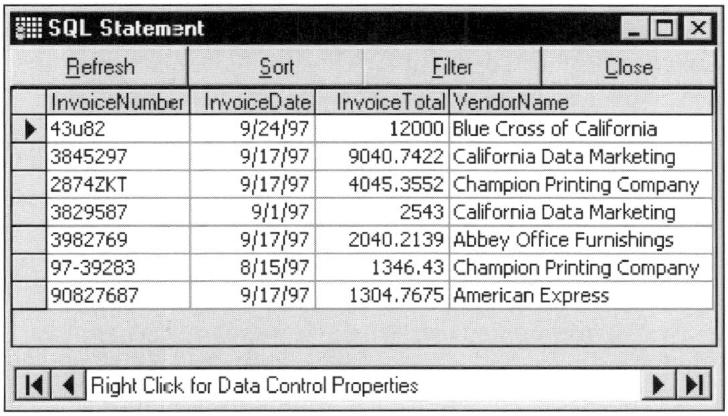

InvoiceNumber	InvoiceDate	InvoiceTotal	VendorName
43u82	9/24/97	12000	Blue Cross of California
3845297	9/17/97	9040.7422	California Data Marketing
2874ZKT	9/17/97	4045.3552	Champion Printing Company
3829587	9/1/97	2543	California Data Marketing
3982769	9/17/97	2040.2139	Abbey Office Furnishings
97-39283	8/15/97	1346.43	Champion Printing Company
90827687	9/17/97	1304.7675	American Express

The dialog box that displays the SQL statement

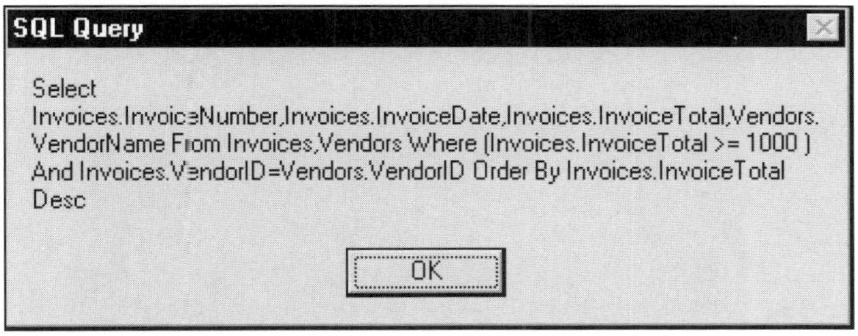

Description

- To display the results of a query, click on the Run button at the bottom of the Query Builder dialog box. When you do, another dialog box is displayed that asks if the query is a pass-through query. Click on the Yes or No button as appropriate to execute the query.
- The form that the query results are displayed in depends on the buttons that are selected in the Visual Data Manager's toolbar. See figure 10-6 for a description of these buttons.
- To display the SQL statement that's generated by the Query Builder, click on the Show button at the bottom of the Query Builder dialog box. The SQL statement is displayed in a dialog box as shown above.
- The Query Builder always joins tables by including the join relationship in the WHERE clause of the SELECT statement it generates, as you can see in the SQL statement shown above. When you join tables this way, however, the resulting recordset can't be updated. To create an updateable recordset, you have to edit the SELECT statement so the join relationship is specified in the FROM clause (see figure 10-9).

Figure 10-8 How to work with query results

How to work in the SQL Statement window

If you click on the Copy button at the bottom of the Query Builder dialog box, the SELECT statement generated by the current query is copied to the SQL Statement window as shown in figure 10-9. Then, you can use this window to edit the statement. In figure 10-9, for example, I edited the query so the join relationship is specified on the FROM clause instead of the WHERE clause. That way the result set will be updateable.

You can also use the SQL Statement window to enter, run, and save queries that you can't create using the Query Builder. For example, you can use this window to create append, update, and delete queries. You can also use it to create data definition queries or any other queries that are supported by the current database, and you can use it to edit queries that have been saved in the database. Unfortunately, you can't edit an existing query using the Query Builder.

After you run a query to make sure that it works right, you can copy it from the SQL Statement window to the clipboard and paste it into your Visual Basic code. That way you can be sure that the syntax of the SQL statement is correct.

The SQL Statement window with a query copied from the Query Builder and edited

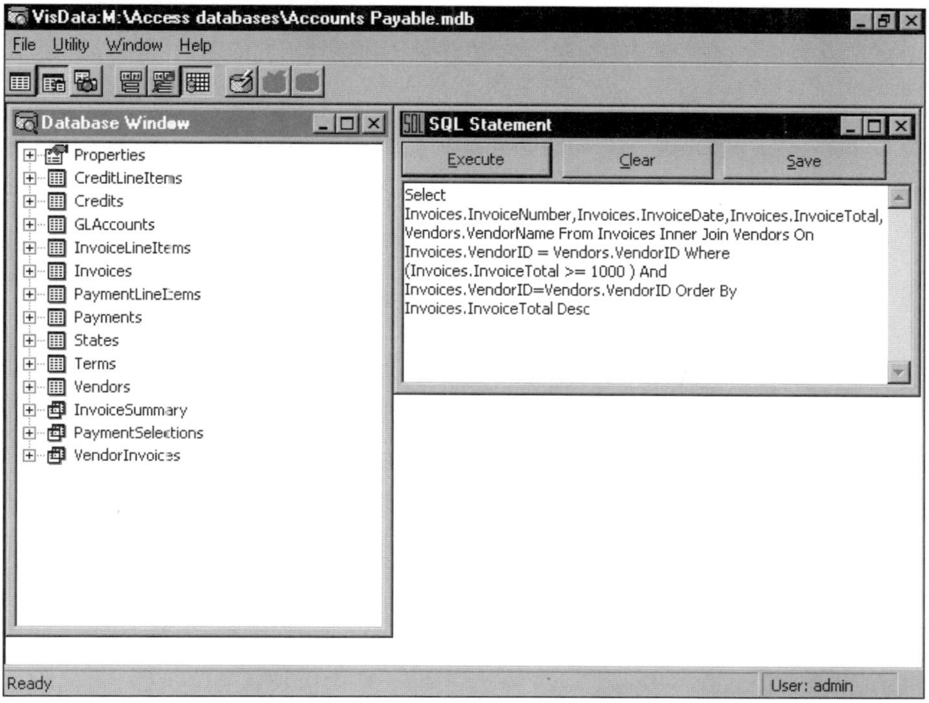

Description

- To copy a query from the Query Builder to the SQL Statement window, click on the Copy button at the bottom of the Query Builder dialog box. Then, you can edit the query in the SQL Statement window any way you like. You can also enter a SQL statement directly into the SQL Statement window.
- The buttons at the top of the SQL Statement window let you execute the query, clear the SQL Statement window, and save the query. If you save the query, it appears in the Database window with the name you specify.
- To edit an existing query, right-click on it in the Database window and select the Design command from the shortcut menu. The query then appears in the SQL Statement window where you can edit or execute it. You can also execute an existing query without opening it in the SQL Statement window. To do that, select the Open command from the query's shortcut menu.
- To copy a statement from the SQL Statement window to the clipboard, just highlight the statement and press Ctrl+C. Then, you can paste the statement into your Visual Basic application.

Figure 10-9 How to work in the SQL Statement window

Other skills for working with databases

In addition to what you've learned so far in this chapter, the Visual Data Manager provides some additional features for working with databases. Two features that you may want to use from time to time are the one that lets you import and export tables and the one that lets you attach (or link) tables to an Access database.

How to import and export tables

If a table you want to work with already exists in another database or file, you can *import* that table into the current database instead of recreating it. When you import a table, both the table definition and the table data are imported. Similarly, you can export a table from one database or file to another.

Figure 10-10 summarizes how you import and export tables using the Visual Data Manager. Note that this figure focuses on importing and exporting tables from Access and ODBC databases. If you work with other types of databases, the dialog boxes that are displayed may be different from the ones shown here. Also note that when you work with an ODBC database, you are usually required to enter a valid user id and password before you can access the database.

The dialog boxes for importing tables

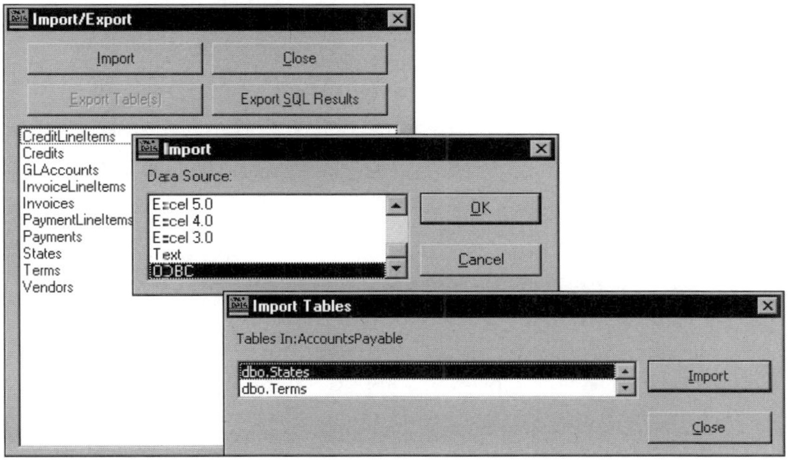

How to import tables

1. Open the database you want to import the tables into and select the Import/Export command from the File menu. From the Import/Export dialog box that's displayed, click on the Import button to display the Import dialog box.
2. Select the type of database that contains the table you want to import and click on the OK button. If you select the ODBC option, you will be asked to select the data source name for the database. Otherwise, you will be asked to select the file that contains the database. After you select a DSN or file name, the Import Tables dialog box is displayed.
3. Select the tables you want to import and click on the Import button to import the tables into the current database.

How to export tables

1. Open the database you want to export tables from and select the Import/Export command from the File menu to display the Import/Export dialog box.
2. Select the tables you want to export and click on the Export Table(s) button. An Export dialog box like the Import dialog box shown above is displayed for each table you selected.
3. Select the type of database you want to export the table to and click on the OK button. Select the DSN or file name that identifies the database, and another dialog box is displayed that lets you change the name that will be used for the table. Change the name if necessary, then click on the OK button to export the table.

Note

- You can also export the results of the query in the SQL Statement window by clicking on the Export SQL Results button in the Import/Export dialog box. The results are saved as a table.

Figure 10-10 How to import and export tables

How to attach tables to an Access database

In chapter 7, you learned the benefits of accessing ODBC tables by *linking* them to an Access database rather than accessing the ODBC tables directly. Specifically, the ODBC table information doesn't have to be downloaded to Jet every time you create a recordset from the table, and you don't have to supply connection information for the database every time you use it. When you use the Visual Database Manager, this is referred to as *attaching* tables to an Access database.

In figure 10-11, you can see how to use the Visual Data Manager to attach tables to an Access database. After you attach a table, the connection information is saved with the table as indicated in the Attachments dialog box. That way, you don't need to specify this information when you access the ODBC table through the attached table.

Figure 10-11 also shows how an attached table appears in the Database window. Except for the icon for the table and the additional item that indicates the type of table that's attached, the table looks just like any other table. Because the data is stored in another database, though, you can't change the definition of an attached table, although you can display the definition in the Table Structure dialog box. When you try to do that, however, you get an error message indicating that the operation can't be performed on a linked table. If you continue, the Table Structure dialog box is displayed anyway, but an error message will be displayed if you try to change any of the options in the Table Structure dialog box.

Although you can work with the data in an attached table using the Visual Data Manager, there are some restrictions you should be aware of. First, you can't create a table-type recordset from an attached table, even if it's an Access table. Second, if the attached table is an ODBC table that contains an identity field, you can't create a dynaset-type recordset for it, which means that you can't modify the data in the table, although you can view the data by creating a snapshot-type recordset. This is just one of many limitations when working with ODBC databases.

The dialog boxes for attaching tables

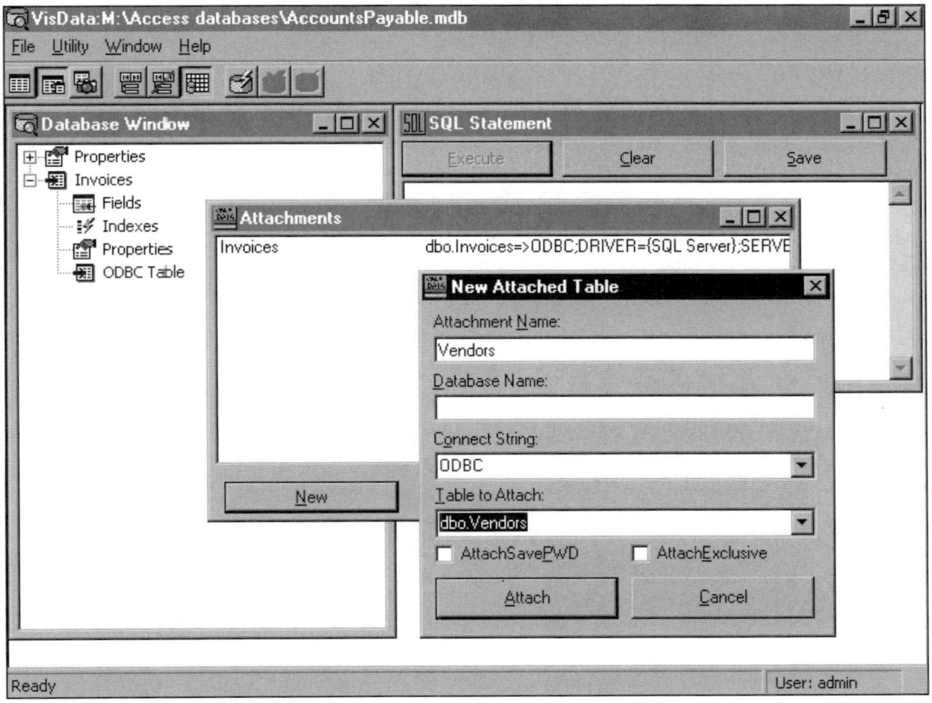

Procedure

1. Open the Access database that you want to attach (or link) tables to, and select the Attachments command from the Utility menu to display the Attachments dialog box. This dialog box lists the tables that are already attached to the database.
2. Click on the New button to display the New Attached Table dialog box. Enter the name you want to use for the attached table in the Attachment Name box. Then, for an Access database, enter the name and location of the database that contains the table you want to attach in the Database Name box. For an ODBC database, enter the name of the database if it's not specified by the DSN for the database.
3. Select the type of database that contains the table from the Connect String drop-down list. Then, select the table you want to attach from the Table To Attach list. (If you're connecting to an ODBC database, you will be asked to specify the DSN for the database before the table names can be displayed.)
4. Click on the Attach button to attach the table to the current database. (If you're attaching tables from an ODBC database, you will again be asked to select the DSN for the database.) The attachment will appear in the Attachments dialog box and the attached table will appear in the Database window.

Note

- The AttachSavePWD and AttachExclusive options let you save a password with the attachment and open the attached table for exclusive use.

Figure 10-11 How to attach (or link) tables to an Access database

Perspective

If you need to create an Access database, the best way to do it is to use Access itself. If you don't have it on your system, though, the next best choice is to use the Visual Data Manager. Although it has some limitations, it provides most of the features you need for creating tables that you can use for testing an application.

If you need to create an ODBC database, however, we don't recommend the use of the Visual Data Manager. Instead, you should use the tools that come with the DBMS for the database. For a SQL Server database, for example, you can use the SQL Enterprise Manager. Once you've done that, you can use the Visual Data Manager to display the data in an ODBC table or to attach an ODBC table to an Access database.

If you have the Enterprise Edition of Visual Basic, another option for creating and working with an ODBC database is to use the Visual Database Tools add-in program that comes with that edition. This program is specifically designed to be used with ODBC databases and provides much more functionality than the Visual Data Manager. For more information on this program, see the Visual Basic help under "Visual Data Tools."

Chapter 11

How to use Crystal Reports to develop reports

Crystal Reports is an add-in program made by Seagate Software that ships with both the Professional and Enterprise editions of Visual Basic. You can use it to develop the reports for a business application. Then, you can print the reports from the forms of your application by using the CrystalReport control that comes with Crystal Reports.

How to use an Expert to design a standard report

When you use Crystal Reports to develop reports, you can design custom reports or you can use one of the Experts to step you through the design of a report. Since using an Expert is a quick way to see what Crystal Reports can do, this chapter starts by showing you how to use an Expert for designing a standard report.

How to start a new report

If Crystal Reports has been installed with Visual Basic and added to the Add-Ins menu, you start Crystal Reports from Visual Basic by choosing Report Designer from the Add-Ins menu. Then, when you select the New command from the File menu, the dialog box shown in figure 11-1 is displayed. As you can see, you can use this box to start a new report from an Expert; to start a new report based on another report; or to start a custom report. Although you may decide later that you prefer to start custom reports or reports that are based on other reports, you should at least experiment with the Experts to see what they can do.

For business applications, the most commonly-used Experts are the Standard, Listing, and Summary Experts. When you use the Standard Expert, you develop a report that prints one *detail line* for each record in the result set along with *group totals*. For instance, an invoice summary by vendor report shows the detail for each invoice row and a group total for all the invoices for each vendor. A report like this also has grand totals at the bottom of the report. In contrast to the Standard Expert, the Listing Expert develops a report with just detail lines, and the Summary Expert develops a report with group totals but no detail lines.

Four of the other Experts offer some other reporting capabilities for business applications. The Cross-Tab Expert lets you develop a report that presents data in a row and column format like a spreadsheet. The Mail Label Expert lets you prepare mailing labels. The Graph Expert lets you prepare a graph or chart from a result set. The TopN Expert is like the Standard or Summary Expert, but it prepares a report that includes the data for only a specific number (N) of groups at the top or bottom of the sort sequence.

In contrast, the Drill Down Expert is for end users who are using Crystal Reports to extract reports directly from a database without going through Visual Basic. Then, after a summary report is extracted, the user can *drill down* into the detail data that the group totals are derived from.

To start a report from one of the Experts, you just click on the Expert. The Expert then displays a dialog box that walks you through three or more steps as you design the form. When you click on the Standard Expert, for example, the Expert starts with a dialog box like the one shown in the next figure.

The dialog box for starting a new report

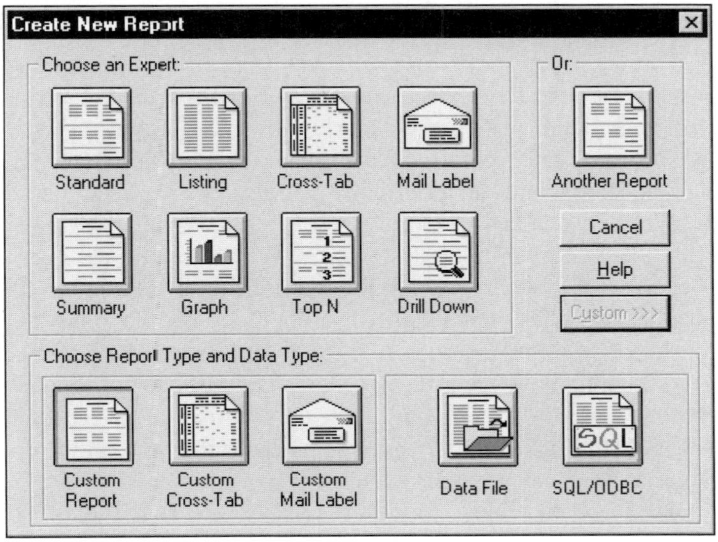

Description

- To start Crystal Reports, choose Report Designer from the Add-Ins menu. If this choice isn't available, choose Add-In Manager from this menu and check Crystal Reports to add it to the menu (you may have to install Crystal Reports on your system before you can do this).
- To start a new report, choose Create New Report from the File menu. This displays the top portion of the dialog box shown above. Then, to display the lower portion of this dialog box, click on the Custom button.
- To start a new report from one of the eight Experts, click on the Expert. The three most common types of business reports are (1) Standard, which prints both detail lines and summary lines; (2) Listing, which prints just the detail lines; and (3) Summary, which prints just the summary lines.
- To start a new report based on an existing report, click on the Another Report option and use the resulting dialog box to choose the other report.
- To start a custom report, click on one of the three types of custom reports. Then, to get the data for the report from a database server, click on the SQL/ODBC button.
- Crystal Reports is designed to work with three file types: columnar reports (*.rpt), label reports (*.rpl), and cross-tab reports (*.rpc).

Figure 11-1 How to start a new report

Step 1: Tables

Part 1 of figure 11-2 shows the dialog box for the Standard Expert. When it is first displayed, it has six tabs representing six steps. Then, after you click on the SQL/ODBC button, the Choose SQL Table dialog box is displayed, which lets you choose the tables that you want to extract data from. If you choose two or more tables, the Expert dialog box adds a Links step and changes from the original six steps to seven. In the dialog box in this figure, two tables have been chosen (Vendors and Invoices) so seven steps are indicated by the tabs.

The first time you start a new report in a Crystal Reports session, a Log On Server dialog box is displayed when you click on the SQL/ODBC button. This dialog box lets you choose the data source that you're going to use. Then, if you choose a SQL Server data source, a SQL Server Login dialog box is displayed, which forces you to enter a user id and password before you can access data from the data source. By the time you read this chapter, you should already be familiar with the process for connecting with a SQL Server data source so these dialog boxes shouldn't give you any trouble.

After you connect, you choose the tables you want to use from the SQL Tables list in the Choose SQL Table dialog box. Each time you add a table to the report, it is added to the list in the Step 1 tab of the Create Report Expert dialog box (the two dialog boxes are overlapped as you work). When you've added all the tables that you need, you click on the Done button to return to the Create Report Expert dialog box, then click on the Next button to move to the next tab.

Step 2: Links

The Links step isn't illustrated in this chapter because the smart linking feature of Crystal Reports normally determines the correct links or relationships between the tables that you've chosen. As a result, you just look at the links that are shown to make sure they're correct, then click on the Next button to continue with step 3.

If the links aren't the way you want them, though, you can easily adjust them. To establish a link that isn't shown, just drag a key field in one table to the related key field in another table. To delete a link that shouldn't be there, click on the line that represents the link and press the Delete key.

Step 1: Tables

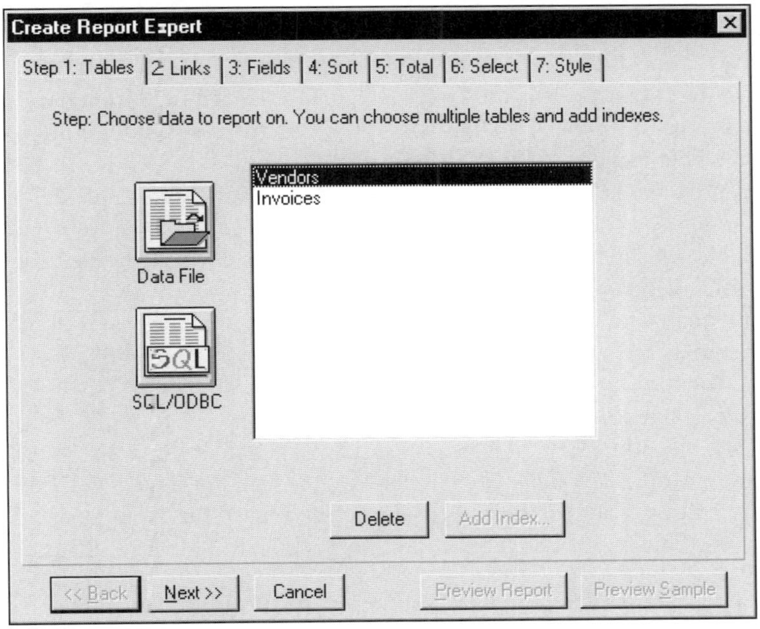

The Choose SQL Table dialog box

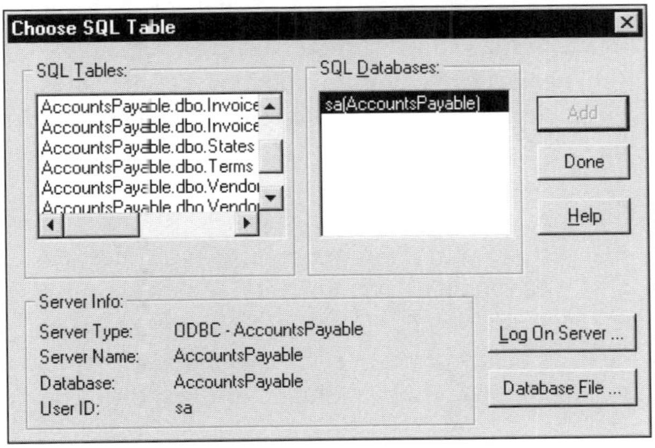

Notes

- When you click on the SQL/ODBC button for the first time in a session, the first dialog box asks you to choose the data source that the report will be derived from. You may then be asked to enter a user id and password to gain access to that data source. After that, the Choose SQL Table dialog box is displayed.
- You can use either the Data File or the SQL/ODBC button to select an Access database. If you use the SQL/ODBC button, Crystal Reports communicates with the database using SQL and the Access ODBC driver. If you use the Data File button, Crystal Reports communicates with the database directly. For client/server applications, you should use the SQL/ODBC button.

Figure 11-2 How to use the Expert for preparing a standard report (part 1 of 4)

Step 3: Fields

Part 2 of figure 11-2 shows the Fields tab of the Create Report Expert dialog box. It lets you select the fields that you want to get data from. To select a field from the Database Fields list, you can double-click on it or highlight it and click on the Add button. This adds the field name to the Report Fields list.

Since the order of the fields in the Report Fields list is the order in which the fields will appear on the report, you need to get these fields in the proper sequence. To adjust the position of a field, you can highlight it and click on the up or down arrow above the Report Fields list.

By default, a title for each field column is added to the report, and the title is the same as the field name. If you want to change that title, though, you can modify the name shown in the Column Heading text box.

If you want to create a report column for data that is derived from a formula, you can click on the Formula button. Crystal Reports then displays a dialog box that asks you to provide a name for the new field. Next, it displays the Edit Formula dialog box shown in this figure. In this example, the name BalanceDue is used for the field, and the formula creates the field by subtracting the PaymentTotal and CreditTotal fields from the InvoiceTotal field.

To distinguish a formula field from a database field, Crystal Reports precedes the field name you supply with this sign: @. If, for example, you name the field BalanceDue, Crystal Reports refers to it as @BalanceDue. When you finish the Edit Formula dialog box, you are returned to the Create Report Expert dialog box so you can add the new field to the Report Fields list as shown in this figure.

If you've read chapter 5, you should already be familiar with the types of expressions that are created in the Edit Formula dialog box. Then, to create an expression in this dialog box, you can double-click on a report field, database field, function, or operator to add it to the expression. If parentheses are necessary, you can type them wherever needed. When you're done, you click on the Accept button.

If you scroll through the functions and operators, you'll see that Crystal Reports provides rich sets of both. As a result, you should be able to create whatever formulas you need. If, for example, you want to create formulas that print the invoice amounts in four different columns of the report depending on how old the date of each invoice is (called an *aged* report), you can use an If statement like this for the first formula:

```
If {Invoices.InvoiceDate} in Aged0To30Days Then
     {Invoices.InvoiceTotal} Else 0
```

Then, the value of the formula is the invoice total if the invoice date is aged from 0 to 30 days when compared with the current date. Otherwise, the value is zero. Later on, you can format this field so a zero value isn't printed.

To create a formula like this, you can find the If..Then..Else structure in the operators list, the word *in* also in the operators list, and the Aged0To30Days function in the functions list. For the other columns of the report, you can use the same basic code with these functions: Aged31To60Days, Aged61To90Days, and Over90Days.

Step 3: Fields

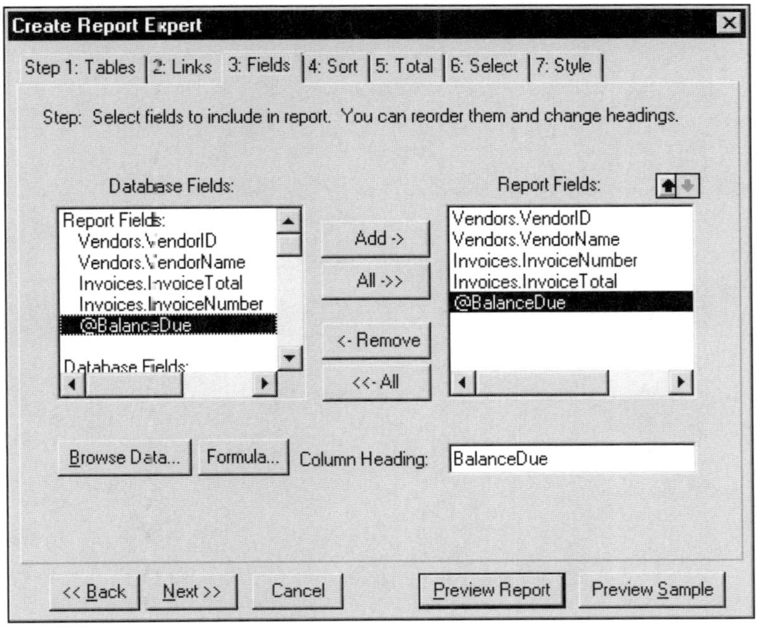

The Edit Formula dialog box

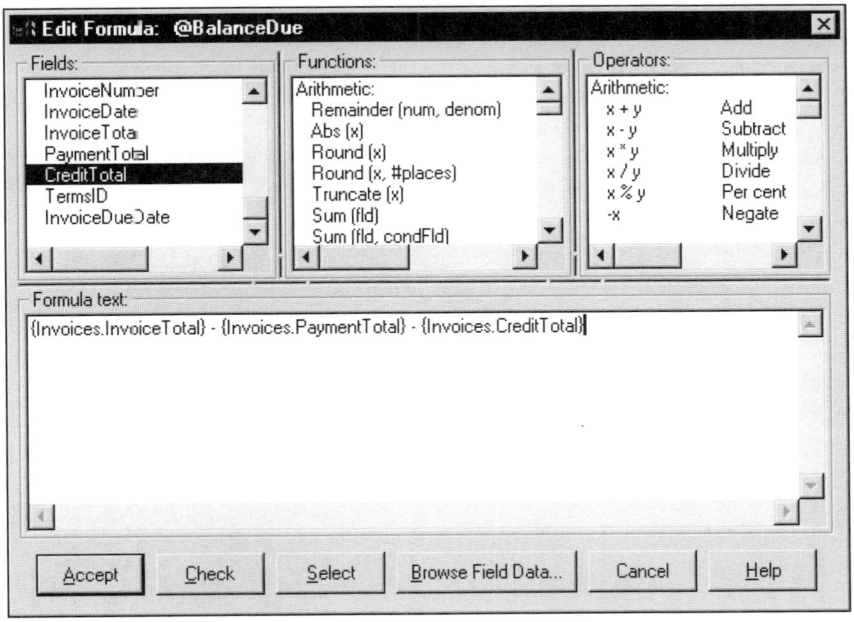

Note

- When you click on the Formula button, the first dialog box asks you to provide a name for the field that will be created by the formula. Then, the Edit Formula dialog box is displayed.

Figure 11-2 How to use the Expert for preparing a standard report (part 2 of 4)

Step 4: Sort

In step 4, you choose the field or fields that you want the report to be in sequence by and whether you want them in ascending order, descending order, the original order, or an order that you specify. These sort fields are also used to group the fields in the report so group totals can be printed for each group. In the example in this figure, the records will be sorted and grouped by VendorID so group totals will be printed each time the number in the VendorID field changes. If, for example, the first vendor has five invoices, group totals will be printed after the detail lines for those five invoices.

When more than one field is added to the Group Fields list, the report is sorted and can be grouped by each of the fields. If, for example, a sales report is sorted by salesperson number within branch number, the report can print group totals for each salesperson as well as group totals for each branch number. Note, however, that you don't have to include group totals for each field that you're sorting by.

You can also sort and group based on date fields or Boolean fields. Then, you can use a drop-down Break list that's available for these fields to choose when you want group totals prepared. For a date field, you can choose from items like Weekly, For Each Month, and For Each Quarter. For a Boolean field, you can choose from items like On Change to Yes, On Change to No, and On Every Yes.

Step 5: Total

In step 5, the dialog box includes one tab for each field that you've chosen to sort by in step 4. Then, for each tab, you choose the fields that you want to print group totals for. When the tab for each sort field is first displayed, the Total Fields list includes all of the numeric fields that you've selected for the report. As a result, you may have to remove one or more of the fields from this list. In this example, the VendorID field is included as a total field when the tab is first displayed so you have to remove it, although you do want group totals for both the InvoiceTotal and BalanceDue fields.

By default, the sum function is used to total each of the fields in the Total Fields list. However, you can use the drop-down function list to choose another function for each field like the average or count function. Also by default, the Add Grand Totals box is checked so grand totals are printed for each column that has group totals, which is the standard practice for any business report.

Step 4: Sort

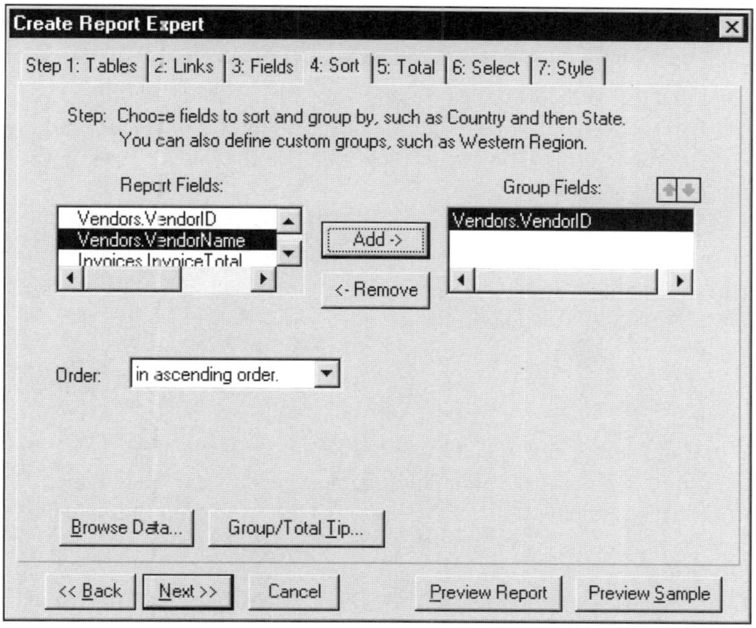

Step 5: Total

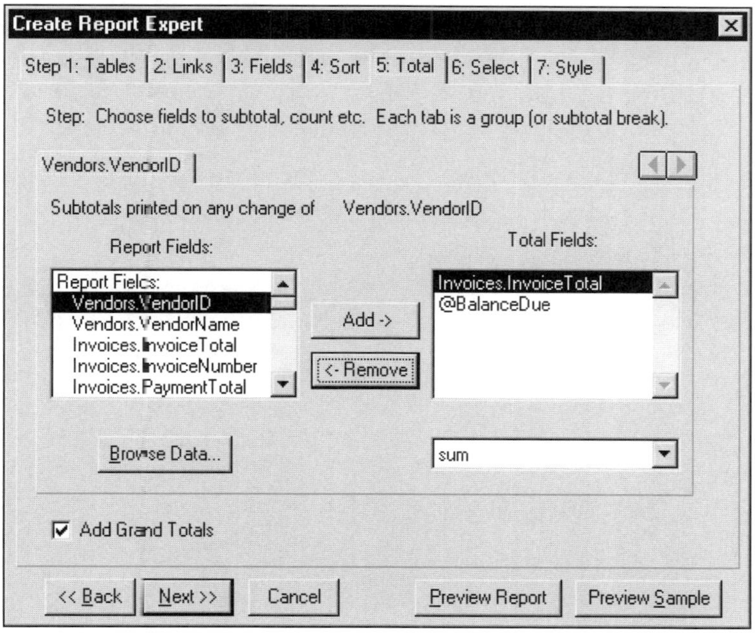

Figure 11-2 How to use the Expert for preparing a standard report (part 3 of 4)

Step 6: Select

In step 6, you can reduce the amount of data that the report prepares by selecting one or more fields and creating conditional expressions for them. In the example in this figure, the report will include only those records in which the BalanceDue value is greater than zero. In other words, the report won't include data for invoices that have already been paid.

If you create more than one select field, all of the conditions must be satisfied before the related data is included in the report. If, for example, you add the state field to the report, you can select data for just the vendors in a specific state like California. Then, the report will include only the unpaid invoices for vendors in that state. If necessary, you can modify the way the selection conditions work after the Expert creates the initial version of the report. For instance, you can change an *and* relationship to an *or* relationship.

By creating one or more select fields, you make the report more focused. This can make the report easier to read and more valuable to management. It can also reduce the amount of data that has to be passed from the server to the client, but that depends on the SQL statement that's created by Crystal Reports (see figure 11-7).

Step 7: Style

In the last step, you can add a title to the report and choose a style for the report. You can also add a picture like the company logo to the report. Although the report image to the right of the Style list gives you a rough idea what the style will look like when the report is displayed, you usually have to experiment with the various styles to find the ones that you like the best. However, you can easily change the style after you finish using the Standard Expert.

To end the Expert and display the report, you normally click on the Preview Report button. If the report is going to be large, however, you can click on the Preview Sample button. This lets you specify the number of records that are used to create the report preview. Either way, the report is displayed in the two windows that are shown in the next figure. That report will automatically include the current date and a page number for each page.

Step 6: Select

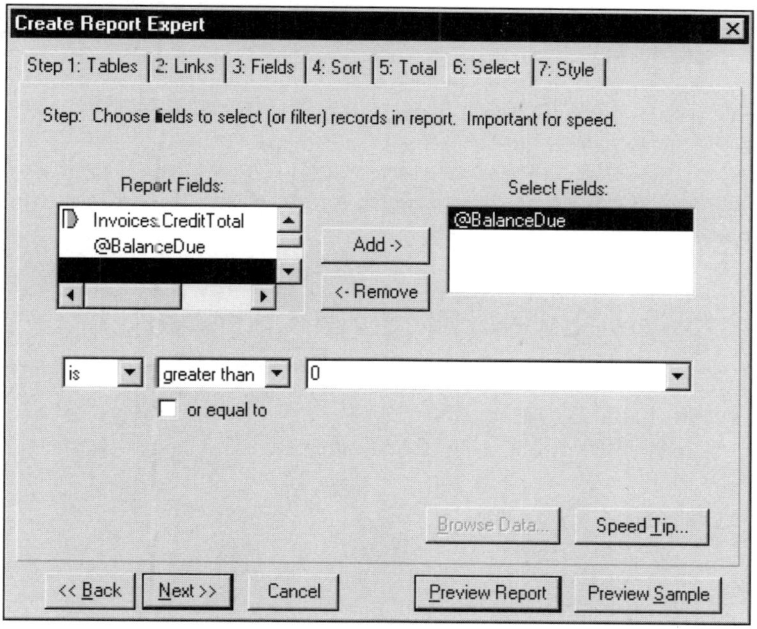

Step 7: Style

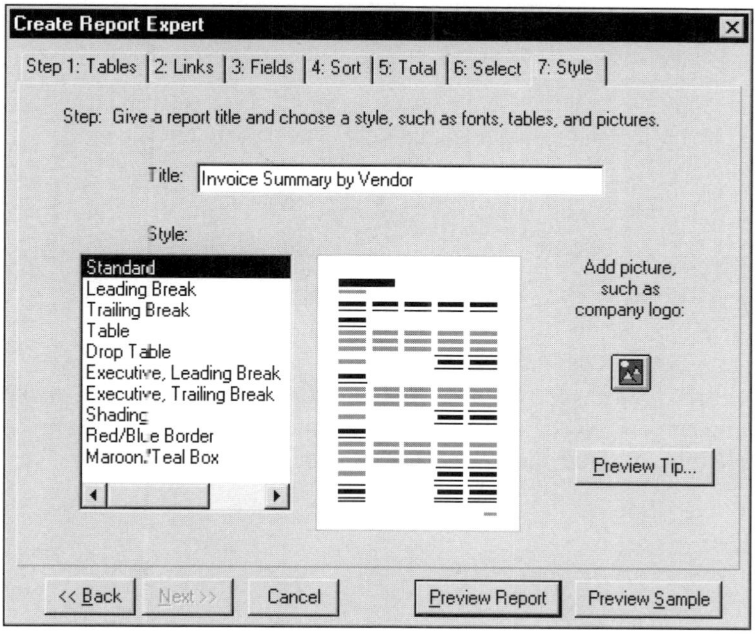

Figure 11-2 How to use the Expert for preparing a standard report (part 4 of 4)

How to modify a report or create a custom report

When you use an Expert to create a report, you usually need to spend some time modifying it because it doesn't come out the way you want it to. For that reason, you may prefer to create custom reports instead of using an Expert to create new reports. In the topics that follow, you'll see that the techniques for modifying an existing report or creating a custom report are similar.

The two windows for working with a report

Figure 11-3 shows the two windows you can use for working with a report. In the Design window, the names of the database fields and other items are shown on the report. In the Preview window, the actual report is shown. To switch from one window to another, you just click on the appropriate tab at the top of the report.

On the left side of the Design window, you can see the *sections* that the report is divided into. At the least, a columnar report usually includes three sections: Page header, Details, and Grand total. In addition, a report can have a Title section that's only printed on the first page, a Page footer section, and a Summary section that's only printed on the last page. A report also has one section for each group with the Group header above the detail lines for the group and a Group footer below the detail lines.

The report shown in this figure is a modified version of the report prepared by the Expert steps in figure 11-2. To modify it, I reduced the width of the left margin, the width of the VendorName field, and the widths between fields so more of the report shows in this example. I also deleted an unwanted field, and expanded some of the group and sum field names in the Design window so they're easier to interpret.

As you work with a report in either the Design or Preview window, you can use the buttons in the Button bar and the Format bar. For instance, to change the formatting for a field in the Preview window, you can select the field and click on one or more buttons in the Format bar. Or, to add a new database field to the report in the Design window, you can click on the Add Database Field button in the Button bar.

To scroll through the data in the Preview window, you can use the buttons above the preview to move from one page to another. (The report in this example consists of a single page so these buttons are dimmed.) And you can use the horizontal and vertical scroll bars to move through the data on one page in either the Design or Preview window.

The finished report in the Design window

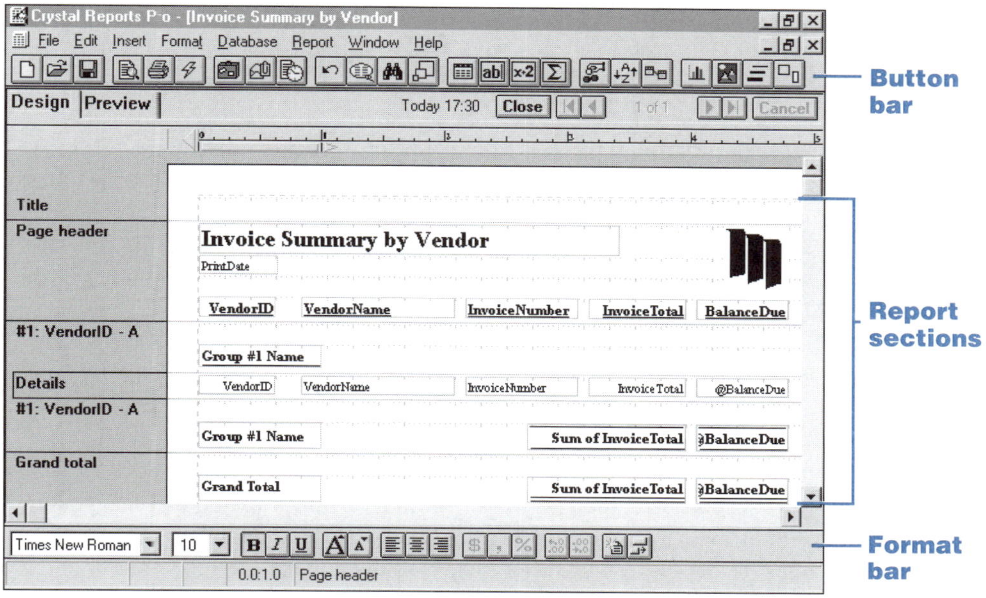

The finished report in the Preview window

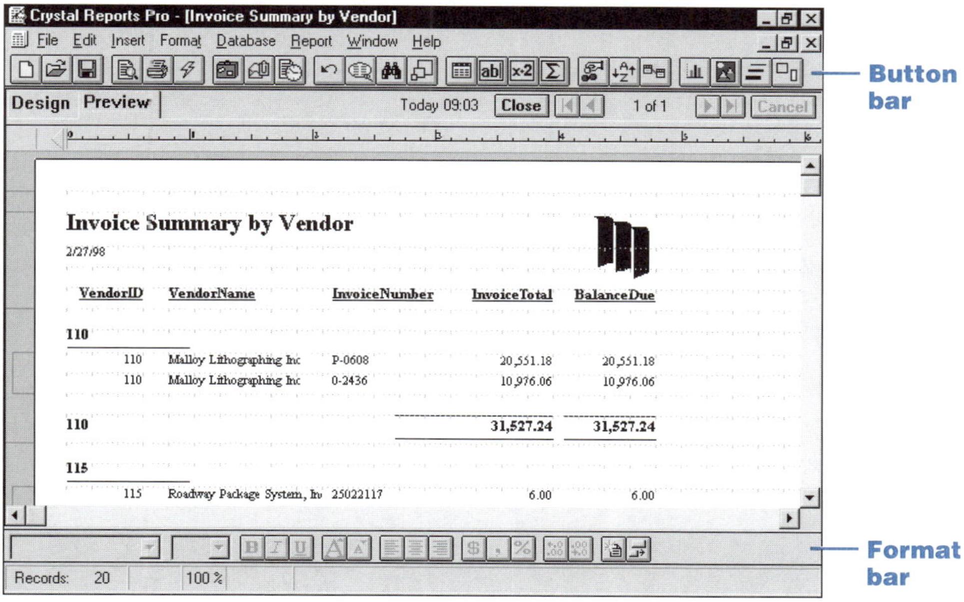

Figure 11-3 The Design and Preview windows

The primary commands and buttons

Figure 11-4 is a two-part summary of the primary commands for designing a report that's going to be part of a Visual Basic application. As a result, it doesn't include commands for using Crystal Reports as an end-user. This summary also indicates whether a button in the Button bar is available for the command. If you read through this summary, you'll get a quick idea of what capabilities Crystal Reports offers, but some highlights follow.

If you choose the Save Data with Report command in the File menu, the data that's used for the report preview is saved with the report definition and the menu command is checked to indicate that this option is on. Then, if you want the preview to show any updates to the data, you can choose the Refresh Report Data command in the Reports menu. *You don't, however, want this option on when you save the final version of a report that's going to be prepared from Visual Basic.*

The Options command in the File menu lets you set a variety of options for working with Crystal Reports, so you should take the time to set these options the way you want them. For instance, the Fonts tab in the File Options dialog box lets you choose the default fonts for each section of a report, the Layout tab lets you specify that field names (rather than codes) should be displayed in the Design window, and the New Report tab lets you set the directory (folder) that you want the reports saved in. In contrast, the Report Options command isn't as useful because it lets you change only a few options for an existing report.

Before you use most of the commands in the Edit menu, you need to select the field or fields that you want to edit. To edit a summary (or total) field, for example, you select the field and choose the Summary Field command. Then, you can change the function that's used to derive the value for the summary field.

To add more fields to a report, you use the commands in the Insert menu. For instance, you can use the Summary command to add another summary field as a group total. Then, for example, you can have one group total that gets the sum of the data in the group and another that gets the average of the data.

You can also use the commands in the Insert menu to add a group section based on another field, to add a group section name, or to add a line, box, or picture. Instead of adding independent lines to a report, though, it's often better to use the Borders and Colors command in the Format menu to add borders to selected fields.

Menu	Command	Button	Description
File	New, Open, Save, Print	Yes	Standard Windows commands
	Save Data with Report		Determines whether the preview data is saved with the report definition
	Print Preview	Yes	Switch to the Preview window
	Print	Yes	Change the number of records used for the print preview
	Printer Setup		Change the printing orientation (Portrait or Landscape)
	Page Margins		Change the page margins
	Options, Report Options		Set the default options for Crystal Reports or the current report
Edit	Undo	Yes	Standard Windows command
	Select Fields	Yes	Select two or more fields
	Formula, Text Field		Edit the selected formula or text field
	Summary Field		Change the function (like sum, count, or average) that's used for the selected field
	Delete Section		Delete a report section
Insert	Database Field	Yes	Insert a database field (like step 3 for the standard Expert in figure 11-2)
	Text Field	Yes	Insert a text field
	Formula	Yes	Insert a formula (like step 3 for the standard Expert in figure 11-2)
	Special Field		Insert a page number, record number, group number, or print date field
	Subtotal, Grand Total		Insert a subtotal or grand total field
	Summary	Yes	Insert a summary field
	Group Section		Insert a group section
	Group Name Field		Insert a name field for a group
	Line, Box, Picture	Yes	Insert a line, box, or picture

Figure 11-4 The primary commands and buttons (part 1 of 2)

In the Format menu, the Report Style Expert command lets you choose another style for the report. That makes it easy to change a report that you've created from an Expert from one style to another until you find one you like. In addition, the Auto Arrange Report command can sometimes remove some of the unnecessary space between the fields of the report. These commands can be started by the two buttons on the far right of the Format bar.

To suppress the duplication that occurs when a field like vendor number or description is printed in each line of a report, you can use the Field command in the Format menu. You can also use this command to print a long field like vendor name on more than one line so you can shorten the column width for the field.

The Borders and Colors command in the Format menu is useful when you want to add line borders or colors to a field like a summary field. The Section command is useful when you want to apply special formatting to a section like skipping to a new page before each section starts.

In the Database menu, you can use the Show SQL Query command when you want to review or modify the SQL statement that the report is based on. This is illustrated by figure 11-7.

In the Report menu, you can use the Select Records Expert command to add or modify the fields and conditional expressions that are used to select the records for the report. Then, if you want to see the complete selection expression, you can use the Edit Selection Formula command to review or modify the expression. You can use this command, for example, if you want to change the expressions for two fields from an *and* relationship to an *or* relationship.

The Top N/Sort Group Expert command in the Report menu lets you select one of the report fields, then choose the top (or bottom) N records for the report based on the values in that field. For instance, you can use this Expert to choose the top 5 vendors based on the value in the Sum of the InvoiceTotal field. This is a valuable command that can help put the emphasis on the data that matters most.

Menu	Command	Button	Description
Format	Report Style Expert	Yes	Start the Expert that lets you choose a style for a report (like step 7 for the Expert in figure 11-2)
	Auto Arrange Report	Yes	Remove unnecessary space in a report
	Field		Format the selected field by suppressing the duplication of data or by allowing a field to be printed on more than one line
	Borders and Colors		Apply borders or colors to the selected field
	Line, Box, Picture		Format a line, box, or picture
	Section		Format the selected section by adding page breaks before or after, suppressing blank lines, etc.
Database	Visual Linking Expert		Start the Expert that lets you set the links between the tables of a report
	Add Database to Report		Add database tables to a report (like step 1 for the Expert in figure 11-2)
	Remove from Report		Delete database tables from a report
	Show SQL Query		Review or modify the SQL statement for the report
Report	Select Records Expert		Start the Expert that lets you select the records you want used in the report (like step 6 for the Expert in figure 11-2)
	Edit Selection Formula		Edit the formula used for selecting the records for a report or a group
	Change Group Expert		Start the Expert that lets you change the way the records sort and group
	Top N/Sort Group Expert		Start the Expert that lets you select N records from the top or bottom of a report
	Sort Records		Add or remove sort fields for the report (like step 4 for the Expert in figure 11-2)
	Search		Search the selected field for a specific value
	Zoom	Yes	Set the preview magnification level
	Refresh Report Data	Yes	Refreshes the report data that's used in the Preview window

Figure 11-4 The primary commands and buttons (part 2 of 2)

How to modify a report

With the command summary behind you, figure 11-5 presents some of the basic techniques for modifying a report. Many of these techniques work in both the Design and Preview windows so be sure to experiment in both windows.

In either window, the best way to change the font or format of a field is to select the field and use the buttons in the Format bar. Although a description isn't displayed for the buttons in this bar when you point to a button, most of them are standard buttons that are used with programs like Word or Excel. The exceptions are the two buttons on the right of this bar, which activate the first two commands in the Report menu.

Besides using the menu commands and buttons, you use standard windows techniques to work in the either window. Right-click on an item to display a shortcut menu of context-sensitive commands. Drag a line between sections to add or reduce space. Drag a field to move it. Drag a sizing handle to change the size of a field or drag a line or corner to change the size of a graphic box. And if you don't like the change, press Ctrl+Z or click on the Undo button to undo the last change (but only the last change).

The Design window

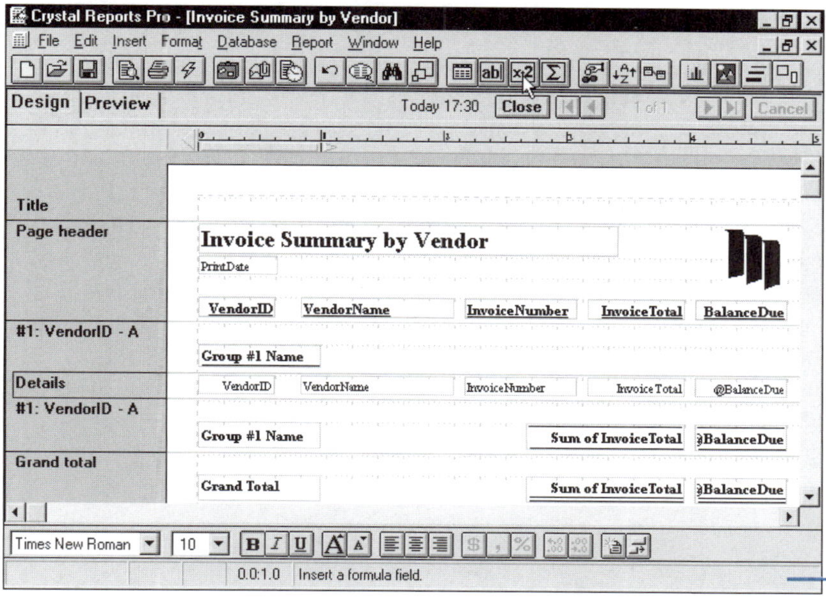

Description

- To find out what a button in the Button bar does, point at a button so its description is displayed in the status bar.
- To adjust the height of a section, drag the line between sections up or down. To delete a blank line within a section, move the insertion point into it and press the Backspace or Delete key. To add a line to a section, press the Enter key.
- To move a field, drag it to a new location. To change the size of a field, drag one of its sizing handles.
- To insert text fields or database fields, click on the Insert Text Field or Insert Database Field button on the Button bar.
- To change the font, font size, alignment, and formatting of the selected field, use the buttons in the Formatting bar. To select more than one field for formatting, hold down the Ctrl key as you click on the fields, or click on the Select Fields button and then drag a rectangle around the fields.
- To insert a graphic, click on the Insert Picture button and select the image. To size the graphic, drag a border or corner.
- To get a context-sensitive list of the commands that are available for a field or section, right-click on the field or the section name.
- To undo your most recent changes, use the Undo button or press Ctrl+Z.
- When you add fields to a report, Crystal Reports automatically assigns a default font for each section. To change these and other defaults, you can choose the Options command in the File menu.

Figure 11-5 How to modify a report

How to create a custom report

If you don't like using the Experts because you spend too much time modifying the reports that you create, you may prefer to create custom reports. Figure 11-6 shows how. After you choose a report type (usually, Custom Report) and click on the SQL/ODBC button in the Create New Report dialog box in figure 11-1, you use the Insert Database Field dialog box to add fields to the report. By default, a column title is also added to the report each time you add a database field, but you can use the Options command in the File menu to change that.

Once you've inserted all of the database fields, you can close that dialog box. Then, you can use the commands and buttons summarized in figure 11-4 to perform the other functions normally done by the Expert. For instance, you can use the commands in the Insert menu to insert a title, the current date, page numbers, a logo, formula fields, subtotals, and grand totals. And you can use the commands in the Report menu to sort the data for the report and to select records for the report.

The Insert Database Field dialog box in the design window

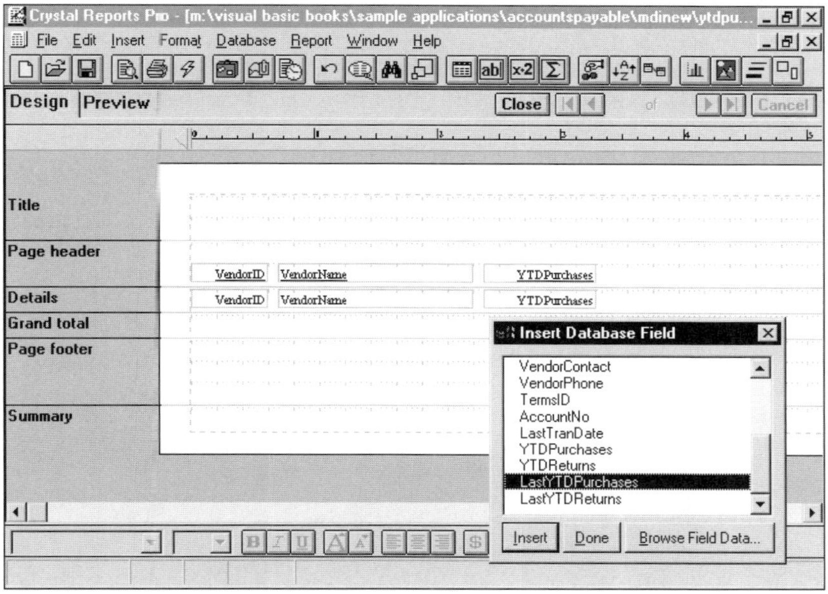

Description

- To start a custom report, click on the Create New Report button in the button bar; click on the Custom button; click on one of the three custom report buttons; and click on the SQL/ODBC button.
- If the Log On Server dialog box is displayed, choose a server type. Then, when the Choose SQL Table dialog box is displayed, choose the tables you want to extract the report from. This returns you to the Design window with the Insert Database Field dialog box displayed.
- To add a field to the report, double-click on the field name in the Insert Database Field dialog box or highlight the name and click on the Insert button. Then, drag the field image to the Details section of the report. If the option is set right, this automatically adds a text field to the Header section too.
- After you add the database fields to the report, you can use the commands in the Insert menu to add other fields to the report. To add a formula field to the report, for example, you can use the Formula command. To add a section and a subtotal to a report, you can select a database field and choose the Subtotal command. To add a grand total, you can select a database field and choose the Grand Total command. To add a report title, a logo, the current date, and the page number to the report, you can use the Text Field, Picture, and Special Field commands.
- After you add all the fields to the report, you can further enhance the report. To sort the data for the report, for example, you can use the Sort Records command in the Report menu. And to select the records for the report, you can use the Select Records Expert command in the Report menu.

Figure 11-6 How to create a custom report

How to work with the SQL statement that gets the data

After you create a report, you can review the SQL statement that's used to get the data for the report by choosing the Show SQL Query command from the Database menu. In figure11-7, for example, you can see the SQL statement for the standard report developed by the Expert in figure 11-2. Note that this statement is formatted specifically for a SQL Server database. If a different type of database was being accessed, the statement would be formatted according to the SQL dialect of the DBMS for that database.

For most reports, the SQL statement will work the way you expect it to. In this example, though, the WHERE clause in this statement gets the data from all the Invoice records that match the Vendor records on the VendorID field, even though the report prints data for only those invoice records with a balance due that's greater than zero. This means that far more data is going to be passed from server to client than is necessary. This problem exists because the selection is based on a formula field, which can't be included in the query.

To correct this problem, you can modify the WHERE clause of the SELECT statement as shown in this figure. Here, the formula used for the selection is included in the query. Then, when you click on the OK button, Crystal Reports recreates the report using the modified SQL statement. Or, if the modified statement has a syntax error, Crystal Reports displays an appropriate error message.

If your database supports stored procedures, you may also be able to change the SQL statement so it calls a stored procedure. Normally, though, it doesn't make sense to set up a stored procedure for each report that's used in a business application so you probably won't ever need to do that.

The Show SQL Query dialog box

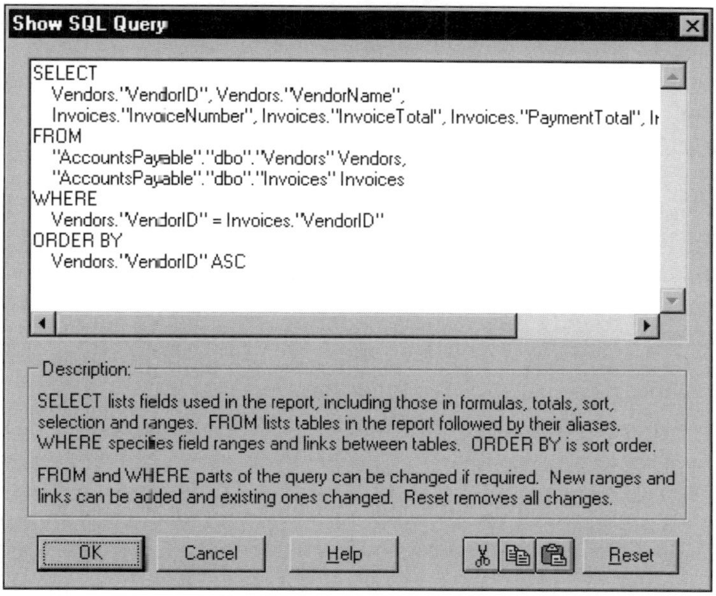

An improved query for database efficiency

```
SELECT
    Vendors."VendorID", Vendors."VendorName",
    Invoices."InvoiceNumber", Invoices."InvoiceTotal",
    Invoices."PaymentTotal", Invoices."CreditTotal"
FROM
    "AccountsPayable"."dbo"."Vendors" Vendors,
    "AccountsPayable"."dbo"."Invoices" Invoices
WHERE
    Vendors."VendorID" = Invoices."VendorID" AND
    Invoices."InvoiceTotal" - Invoices."PaymentTotal"
        - Invoices."CreditTotal" > 0
ORDER BY
    Vendors."VendorID" ASC,
    Invoices."InvoiceNumber" ASC
```

Description

- To display the SQL statement that gets the data for a report, choose the Show SQL Query command from the Database menu.
- The format of the SQL statement the Expert creates conforms to the SQL dialect of the DBMS. The SQL statement shown above is for SQL Server. The SQL statement for an Access database would be formatted differently.
- Sometimes, you can improve the efficiency of the SQL statement by modifying or adding to its WHERE clause. This is illustrated by the example above.

Figure 11-7 How to work with the SQL statement that gets the data for a report

How to run a report from Visual Basic

To this point, you've seen Crystal Reports used as an independent tool for designing reports and previewing data. In fact, many people use Crystal Reports for just that purpose. In the context of a client/server system, though, you need to be able to print the reports that you design from the Visual Basic application.

How Crystal Reports works with Visual Basic

Figure 11-8 presents one type of Visual Basic form that can be used for printing reports that have been designed by Crystal Reports. Here, the user clicks on the option button that identifies the report and clicks on the Print command button to print the report. Normally, this causes the report to be displayed in a Preview window like the one shown. Then, the user can use the scroll bars and the buttons at the bottom of the window to scroll through the data.

To change the magnification in the Preview window, the user clicks on the Zoom button to cycle through three levels of magnification. To print the report, the user clicks on the Print button. The other two buttons let the user save the report to a file or e-mail the report to someone. To close the Preview window, the user clicks on the Close button.

The Reports form in this figure, of course, illustrates just one way that the reports of an application can be organized and printed. Another way is to use a Report menu and appropriate submenus. A third way is to use one or more forms for the reports of an application with one command button for each report. No matter how you design the user interface for printing the report, though, you need to add the CrystalReport control to at least one form.

A Visual Basic form for printing reports

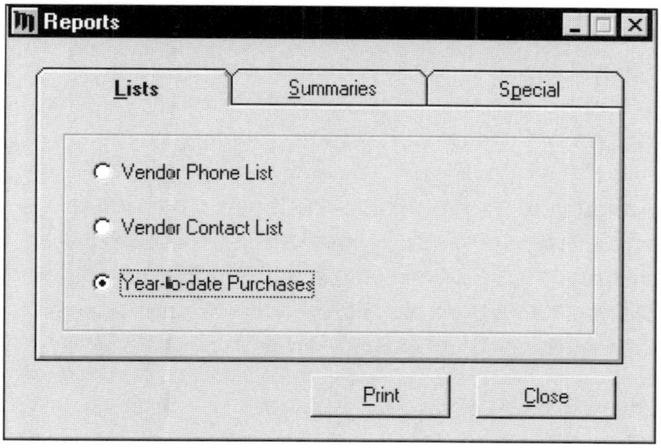

The Crystal Reports Preview window

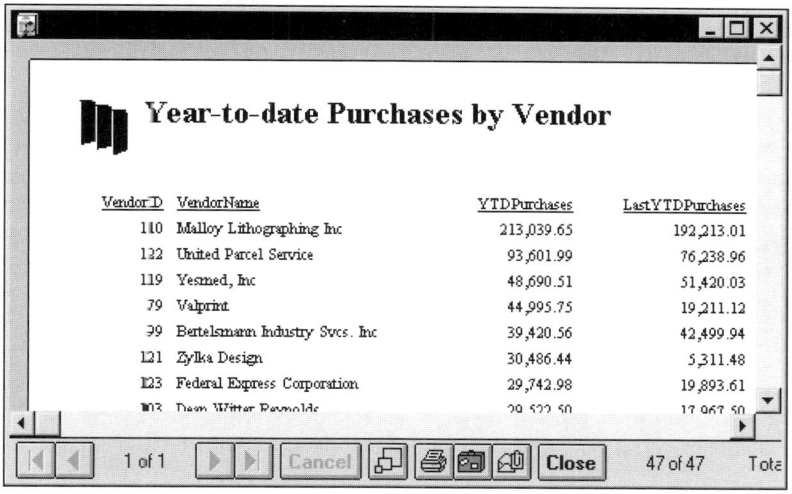

Description

- When a user clicks on the Print button in the Reports form, the report indicated by the option button is printed. Most of the time, however, the reports are set up so they are displayed in the Preview window before printing.
- To change the magnification of the report in the Preview window, click on the Zoom button. To go to another page, use the navigation buttons. To scroll through a page, use the scroll bars.
- To print the report in the Preview window, click on the Print button. To save the report to a file, click on the Save to File button. And to e-mail the report, click on the Email button.

Figure 11-8 How Crystal Reports works with Visual Basic

How to use the CrystalReport control

Figure 11-9 shows how to add the CrystalReport control to the toolbox and to a form. Once it has been added to a form, you can move it or size it just like any other control. You can also set its properties. When the application is run, however, this control is always hidden.

If you want to use a CrystalReport control to print just one report, you need to set its Name property to an appropriate name and set its ReportFileName property so it gives the path and filename for the report. Then, you can use the PrintReport method to print the report. If, for example, the Name property is crptInvoiceSummary, this code will print the report identified by the ReportFileName property:

```
crptInvoiceSummary.PrintReport
```

If you use this technique for printing reports, you need to add one CrystalReport control to a form for each report printed by the application. Since that's inefficient, you usually use code to set the ReportFileName property before printing the report. That way, you can use just one control for printing all the reports of an application, which is illustrated in the next figure.

Whether you print one report or many from a single control, you may also need to set the Connect and Password properties for the database you're using. Otherwise, an error will occur when you try to run a report from the control. When you access a SQL Server database, for example, you need to set the Connect property so it gives the data source name, the user id, and the user password.

By default, the Destination property directs the report to the Preview window, which is usually what you want for business reports. However, you can change this property so the report will be sent to a printer, exported as a file, or sent as e-mail.

Depending on the database you're accessing, you may be able to use the SQLQuery property to override the SQL query created by the report definition (see figure 11-7). For instance, you may be able to use this method to call a stored procedure. If you do that, of course, the resulting query must be compatible with the report definition.

The CrystalReport control on a form in the Design window

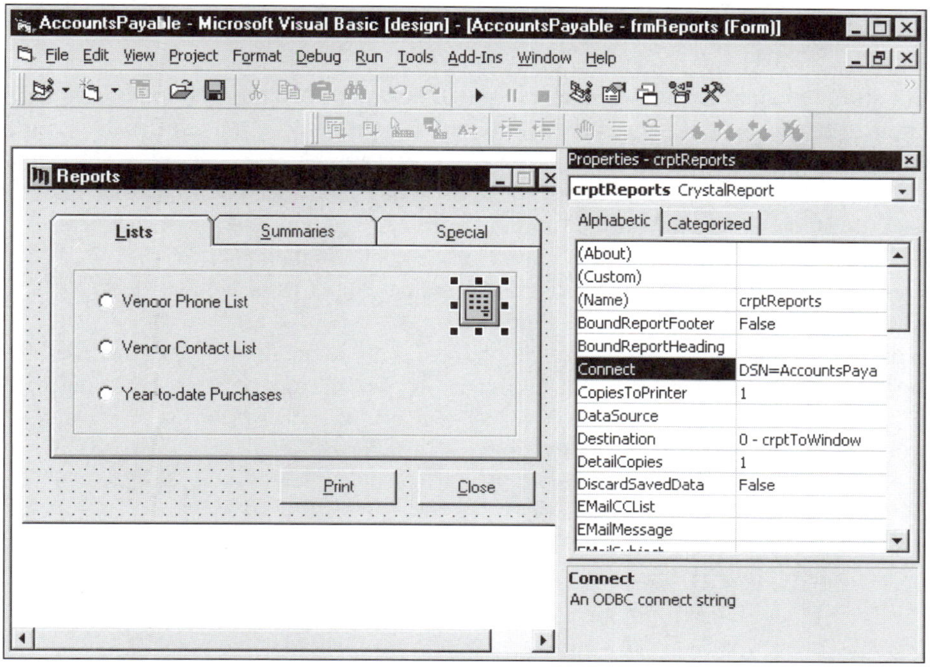

The critical properties

Property	Description
Name	Names the control (*crpt* is the recommended prefix).
Connect	Identifies the data source, user id, and user password for an ODBC database.
Password	Supplies the password for accessing an Access database.
ReportFileName	Identifies the path (drive and folder) and filename for the report.
SQLQuery	Can be used to override the SQL statement for the report.

Description

- To add the CrystalReport control to the toolbox for a project, use the Components command in the Project menu. Once you've done that, you can work with the control and its properties and methods just as you would any other control.
- To access a tabbed dialog box that lists all of the properties for the control, right-click on the control and choose Crystal Properties from the shortcut menu.
- For Visual Basic applications to use the Preview window, the Crystal Reports Engine DLL (CRPE.DLL) must be installed on each system. If you are a licensed user of Crystal Reports, you receive royalty-free rights to ship the Report Engine DLL with any applications you create.

Figure 11-9 How to use the CrystalReport control

How to use code to print reports

Figure 11-10 shows three ways to use code to print reports from a single CrystalReport control. The first example shows how to print a report from a command button. Here, the code changes the ReportFileName property so it identifies the report, then uses the PrintReport method to print the report.

The second example shows how to print the reports for three option buttons like those shown on the first tab of the form in figure 11-8. As you can see, this code uses an If statement to determine which option button is on. Then, it sets the ReportFileName property to identify the report that should be printed and uses the PrintReport method to print that report.

In this example and in the third example, you should note the way the path and file name for the report are specified each time the ReportFileName property is changed. Here, App is a global object available for all projects that keeps information about the application's title, version, and paths for executable files. Then, its Path property gives the path for the application. As a result,

```
App.Path & "ytdpurchases.rpt"
```

refers to the file named *ytdpurchases.rpt* in the same folder as the project.

When you use the PrintReport method to print a report, any errors that occur aren't trappable. Then, you're left to figure out what the problem is without any help. Another way to print a report from a CrystalReport control, though, is to set its Action property to a value of 1. Strangely enough, that actually causes the report to be printed. It also generates trappable errors so you can use code like that for the third example in this figure to print the reports and trap any errors. This is useful when you're debugging an application, but shouldn't be necessary in the final code for an application.

Code that uses the PrintReport method to print a report

```
Private Sub cmdVendorPhoneList_Click()
    crptReports.ReportFileName = _
        "c:\VBApps\vendorphonelist.rpt"
    crptVendorPhoneList.PrintReport
End Sub
```

Code that uses the PrintReport method to print the reports identified by the Lists tab in figure 11-8

```
Private Sub cmdPrintReports_Click()
    If optVendorPhoneList Then
        crptReports.ReportFileName = App.Path & _
            "\vendorphonelist.rpt"
    ElseIf optVendorContactList Then
        crptReports.ReportFileName = App.Path & _
            "\vendorcontacts.rpt"
    ElseIf optYTDPurchases Then
        crptReports.ReportFileName = App.Path & _
            "\ytdpurchases.rpt"
    End If
    crptReports.PrintReport
End Sub
```

Code that uses the Action property to print the reports

```
Private Sub cmdPrintReports_Click()
    On Error GoTo ErrorHandler
    If optVendorPhoneList Then
        crptReports.ReportFileName = App.Path & _
            "\vendorphonelist.rpt"
    ElseIf optVendorContactList Then
        crptReports.ReportFileName = App.Path & _
            "\vendorcontacts.rpt"
    ElseIf optYTDPurchases Then
        crptReports.ReportFileName = App.Path & _
            "\ytdpurchases.rpt"
    Else
        MsgBox "Invalid report identification"
    End If
    crptReports.Action = 1
    Exit Sub
ErrorHandler:
    Dim strMessage As String
    strMessage = "Error Number = " & Err.Number & vbCrLf
    strMessage = strMessage & Err.Description
    MsgBox strMessage, vbOKOnly, "Print Error"
End Sub
```

Figure 11-10 Typical code for printing reports from a CrystalReport control

Perspective

Although this chapter has introduced you to the primary commands and features of Crystal Reports, it will take you a few hours of experimentation to get comfortable with this product. In particular, you should experiment with some of the other Experts and with the techniques for developing custom reports. Then, you can decide for yourself whether you prefer to use the Experts or work without them.

As you experiment, you should keep in mind that the goal of this chapter has been to present the best Crystal Reports techniques for developing reports for client/server systems. As a result, you may discover some features that aren't presented in this chapter. For instance, Crystal Reports has some end-user features that can't be used through Visual Basic. Crystal Reports can be used to prepare reports from files (not databases). And Crystal Reports can be used to prepare reports from result sets that are bound to data controls.

You should also be aware that other products are available for developing the reports for Visual Basic applications. So if you don't like the way Crystal Reports works, you may want to review one or more of them. On the other hand, Crystal Reports comes with Visual Basic; it has some powerful features with a manageable interface; and the CrystalReport control does an adequate job of integrating the reports with Visual Basic.

Chapter 12

How to create and use class modules and ActiveX components

Class modules are the basis of object-oriented programming. They define the objects that you can use to build an application. Although many objects are available to you when you develop applications in Visual Basic, you can also define new objects by creating your own class modules.

The first part of this chapter shows you how to create and use class modules. These techniques are the same whether the class module is part of a standard project, like those you've seen so far in this book, or an ActiveX project. After you learn how to create and use class modules, you can learn the concepts and techniques for implementing class modules as ActiveX components.

How to create and use class modules

The potential benefits of using class modules include faster development, easier maintenance, and the ability to reuse code. Class modules also make it possible to hide implementation details from the other modules that use them. That makes it easier for one programmer to use class modules developed by other programmers.

The first few times you use class modules, though, you probably won't get all these benefits. That's because using class modules requires you to think about program development in a new way. So after mastering the concepts and techniques presented in this topic, you need to figure out how you can make productive use of class modules in your own development efforts.

An overview of class modules

In chapter 3, you learned that an *object* is based on an *object class* that defines the object's properties, methods, and events. These definitions are stored in a *class module* as illustrated in figure 12-1. Here, you can see that the public code and data define the *properties* and *methods* of the object. These properties and methods are *exposed* to the other modules in the application and form the *default interface* of the object.

This interface is used by the other modules in a project to access the properties and methods of the class module (or object). In contrast, the private code and data in a class module can be accessed only from within the class module. (You can also create events within a class module, but that's beyond the scope of this book.)

For the most part, the code you use to create class modules is the same code you use within form modules and standard modules. To define a method within a class module, for example, you code public Sub procedures and functions. And to define a property within a class module, you can declare public variables.

Although you can define a property using a public variable, you may not always want to do that. That's because the value of a public variable can be retrieved and changed by anyone who has access to it. To protect a variable from unwanted access, you can declare it as a private variable and use *property procedures* to provide access to it. A property procedure can contain code that restricts access to the variable or that performs additional processing when a variable is accessed. You'll learn how to code property procedures in figure 12-4.

After you create a class module, you use it in the other modules of the project by creating an *instance* of it. When you create an instance of a class module, you create an object that contains the properties, methods, and events defined by the class module. If you create more than one instance of a class module within an application, each instance is a separate object that contains its own data (although most business applications don't require more than one instance of a class module).

How you use a class module in a standard project

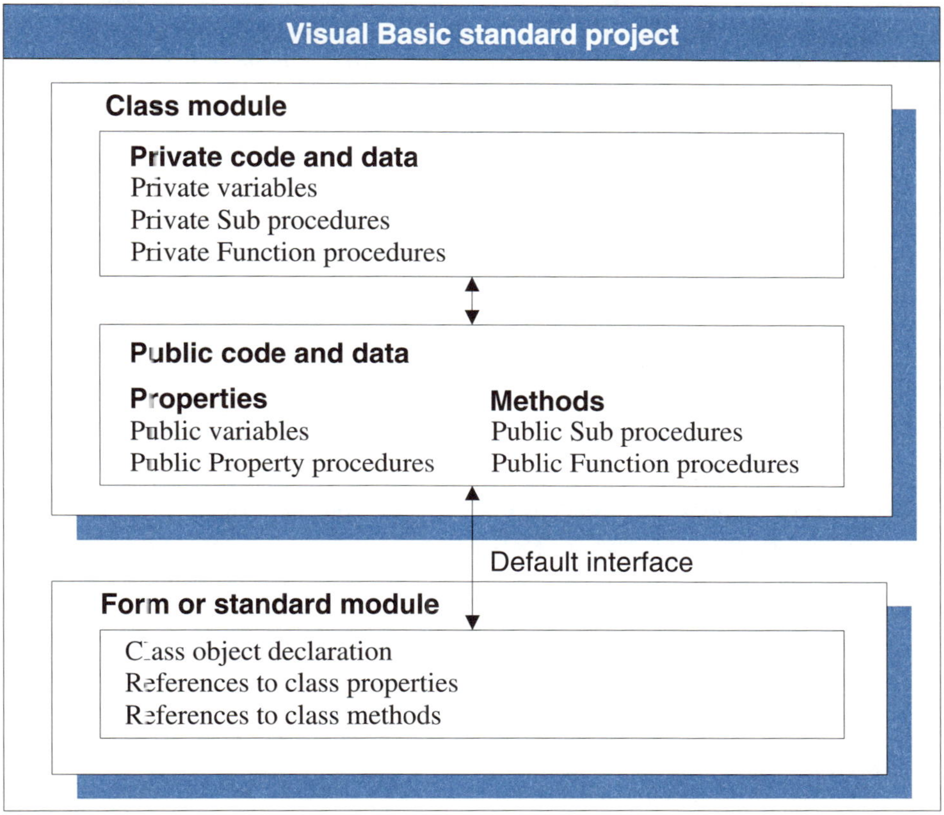

Concepts

- A *class module* contains the definition of an object class. The public variables that are defined within the class module are the properties of the object. And the public procedures that are coded within the class module are the methods of the object.
- By defining variables and procedures within a class module as Public, they're exposed to other modules. These exposed variables and procedures form the *default interface* of the object. You refer to class modules from an application through this interface.
- You can also expose private variables within a class module using *property procedures*. Property procedures provide a means of protecting the variables defined within a class module from unwanted changes.
- To use a class module, you create an *instance* of the class within your application called a *class object*. If you create more than one instance of a class, each will contain its own data.
- If a class module is created within a standard project, it can be accessed only from within that project. However, you can add an existing class module to any number of projects.

Figure 12-1 An overview of class modules

When you create a class module within a standard project as shown in figure 12-1, it is available only to the other modules in the project. Because of that, you may think that class modules have limited use. Like the other modules in a project, though, class modules are stored in separate files with the extension *cls*. That means that once you create a class module, you can use it in other projects by adding it to that project. Then, if necessary, you can modify its code and save it as a new class module.

If you want to share a class module with other applications without including it in each application, you can include the class module in an ActiveX project. You'll learn how to do that later in this chapter.

A book order application that uses a class module

Figure 12-2 presents the book order application that I'll use throughout this chapter to illustrate class modules. This application calculates the total amount due for a book order that consists of from one to five books. The order total is based on the books that are ordered, the number of each book that is ordered, the shipping method that will be used, and the state that the book will be shipped to.

The Visual Basic project for this application consists of two modules: a form module and a class module. As in the other applications shown in this book, the form module provides the user interface. In this application, though, all the processing for the application is done by the class module. Besides doing all of the calculations required by this application, the class module does all of the database processing that's required to get the data that's displayed in the combo boxes on the form and to get the book prices, shipping costs, and sales tax for each order.

The Book order form

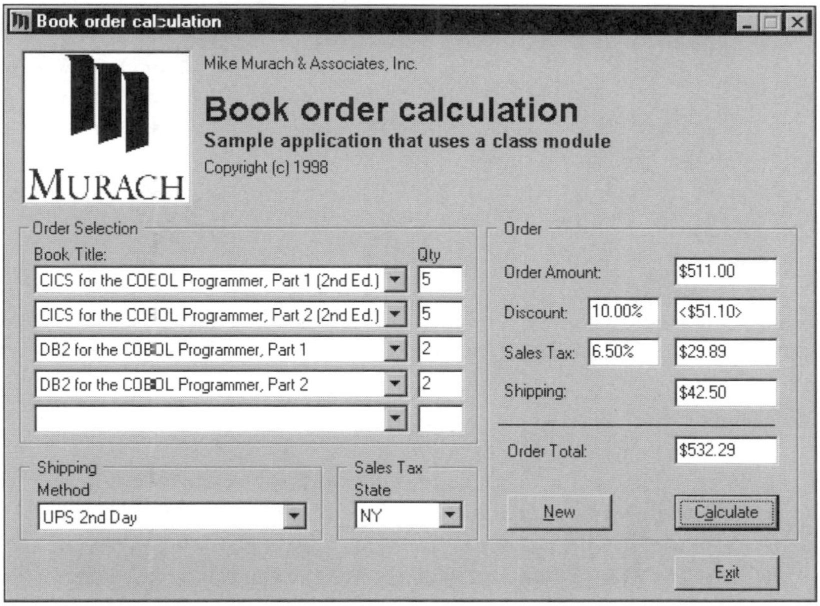

Description

- The book order application calculates order totals based on the books, quantities, shipping method, and state selected by the user. After entering these values, the user clicks on the Calculate button to calculate the order total. The user can also click on the New button to clear the form before entering a new order.
- This project consists of a form module and a class module. The form module provides the user interface that's represented by the form above. The class module does all of the processing that goes on behind this form. Later on, if you need to change the way discounts, sales tax, or shipping are calculated, you need only modify the code in the class module.
- Besides doing all of the necessary calculations, the class module for this application does all of the database processing required by the application. For example, it retrieves the data that's displayed in all of the combo boxes on the form, and it retrieves the price of each book that's selected by the user. To keep this example simple, though, this form doesn't actually process the orders that are entered.

Figure 12-2 A book order application that uses a class module

How to create a class module

You can use two techniques to create a class module. First, you can add a new, blank class module to your project and then use standard techniques to add code to that module. To create a new class module, choose the Class Module option from the Add Class Module dialog box shown in figure 12-3. Second, you can use the VB Class Builder to help you create the properties, methods, and events for the class module. To do that, choose the VB Class Builder option from the Add Class Module dialog box.

The VB Class Builder provides a simple graphical interface that you can use to define the properties, methods, and events for a class. When you use this tool, it creates a framework for the properties, methods, and events you define, but you still have to add the specific code to implement these elements. Nevertheless, you may want to use this tool the first few times you create a class module to help you understand the coding that's required. After that, though, it's just as easy to enter the code yourself.

Like form modules, class modules include Initialize and Terminate events. The Initialize event occurs whenever you create an instance of the class module. You'll typically use this event to initialize any data used by the object as shown in the class module in figure 12-3. The Terminate event occurs when the last reference to an object created from the class module is removed or when the object goes out of scope. You can use this event to perform any necessary housekeeping tasks.

When you name a class module, you should know that it can't have the same name as the project that it's in. In fact, none of the modules in a project can have the same name as the project. With form modules, that's not a problem if you use the *frm* prefix that we recommend. And that's usually not a problem with standard and class modules because they'll have names specific to their functions while the project will have a more general name. For instance, the name of the project in figure 12-3 is MurachBooks, while the name of the class module is BookOrder. This can be a problem, however, when you create an ActiveX project that contains a single class module that performs the main function of the project. Then, you have to work around this naming restriction as you'll see later in this chapter.

How to create a class module

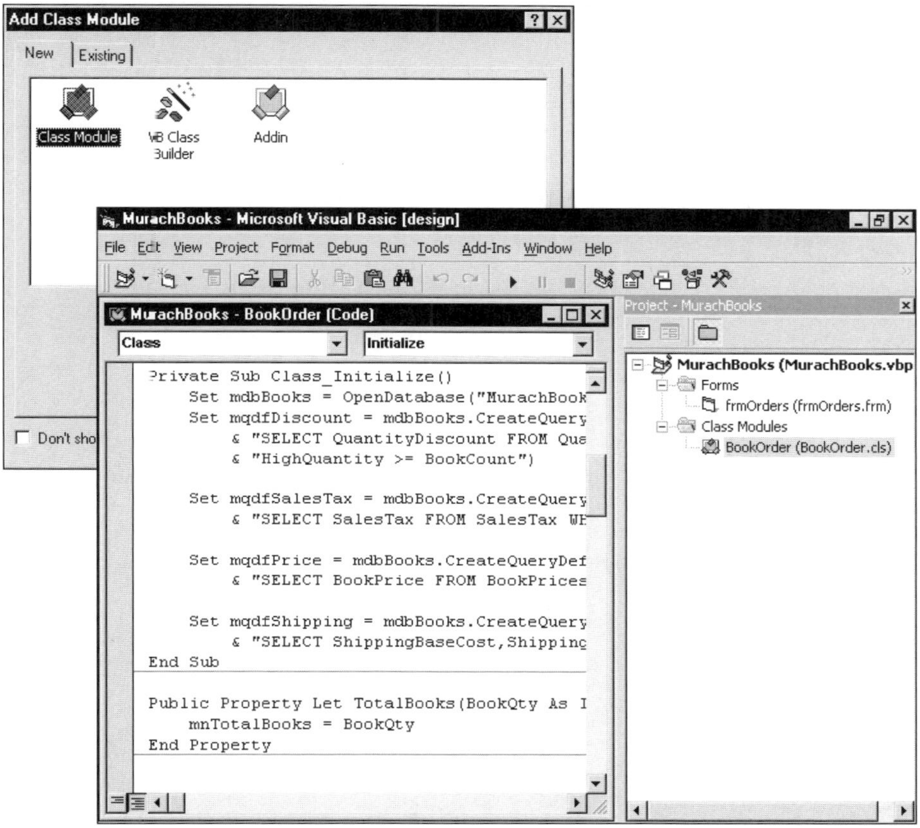

Description

- To add a class module to a project, choose the Add Class Module command from the Project menu to display the Add Class Module dialog box shown above. Then, select the Class Module or VB Class Builder option from the New tab. You can also add an existing class module to a project by selecting the module from the Existing tab.
- The VB Class Builder lets you create and define new classes using a simple graphical user interface. You can use it to create the code framework for the properties, methods, and events to be included in the class module. In most cases, though, it's just as easy to write your own code.
- To enter the code for a class module, you use the Code window and the Add Procedure command in the Tools menu. This works the same as it does for a form or standard module.
- When you create an instance of a class module, the Initialize event of the module occurs. You can use this event to initialize any data used by the class as shown above.

Figure 12-3 How to create a class module

How to code property procedures

If you want to expose a variable in a class module to other modules in the project, you can declare the variable as Public or you can code *property procedures* that provide access to the variable. Even if you don't need to use property procedures to restrict access to a variable or to perform additional processing when a variable is accessed, you may still want to use property procedures to expose private variables. Then, you can easily add code to the procedures later if you need to.

You can code three different types of property procedures that are started by three different Visual Basic statements. The Property Let and Property Set statements let you assign values to private variables. Like the Set statement, the Property Set statement is used with object variables. Usually, a Let or Set procedure receives a value from the procedure that calls it and assigns that value to a private variable. This is illustrated by the Property Let procedure in figure 12-4. Here, the value passed to the procedure is stored in a variable named BookQty, which is then assigned to the private variable named mnTotalBooks. (The letter *m* used in the prefix of this variable identifies it as a module-level variable, the letter *n* as an integer variable.)

The Property Get statement lets you retrieve the value of a private variable as illustrated by the two procedures in figure 12-4. In the first procedure, the value of the private variable named mfSalesTaxPercent is assigned to the name of the procedure, SalesTaxPct. Then, that value is passed back to the calling procedure. In that way, the Property Get procedure works just like a Function procedure.

The second Property Get procedure in this figure does more than just retrieve the value of a private variable. It changes the value of a QueryDef parameter, and then opens a recordset based on that value. In this case, it returns a single record for the book specified by the parameter. Then, it assigns the value of the BookPrice field in that record to the name of the function.

Keep in mind when you use property procedures that you don't have to code procedures to both retrieve and assign values. So if you don't want to allow the value of a private variable to be changed, you can code just a Get procedure. And if you don't want to allow the value of a variable to be retrieved, you can code just a Let or Set procedure. These are other ways you can use property procedures to restrict access to private variables.

How to expose private variables using property procedures

```
Private mnTotalBooks As Integer
Private mfSalesTaxPercent as Single
Private mqdfPrice As QueryDef
Private mrecPrice as Recordset

Public Property Let TotalBooks(BookQty as Integer)
    mnTotalBooks = BookQty
End Property

Public Property Get SalesTaxPct() As Single
    SalesTaxPct = mfSalesTaxPercent
End Property

Public Property Get BookPrice(BookDesc as String) _
        As Currency
    mqdfPrice.Parameters!BookDesc = BookDesc
    Set mrecPrice = mqdfPrice.OpenRecordset(dbOpenSnapshot)
    BookPrice = mrecPrice!BookPrice
End Property
```

Description

- If a variable in a class module is defined as Public, it can be accessed directly by any other module in the project. If you want to protect a variable from direct access, or if you want to perform some additional processing when a variable is accessed, you can code *property procedures* to provide that access.
- To code a property procedure, you use the three Property statements. The Property Let statement assigns a value to a private variable. The Property Get statement gets the value of a private variable. And the Property Set statement assigns a value to a private object variable.
- You code a Property Get procedure the same way that you code a Function procedure. Within the procedure, you assign a value to the procedure name. Usually, that value is retrieved from a private class variable. Then, that value is passed back to the calling procedure.
- You code a Property Let or Property Set procedure like a Sub procedure. Since the purpose of the procedure is to assign a value to a private class variable, the procedure must accept at least one argument that contains the value to be assigned. Then, that value is assigned to a private variable within the procedure.
- You refer to a property procedure by name, just as you do other procedures. You'll see how that works in the next figure.

Figure 12-4 How to code property procedures

How to use class modules

To use a class module in a project, you create an instance of it. You can do that using any of the three techniques shown at the top of figure 12-5. With the first technique, you declare an object variable using the generic Object data type. Then, you set that variable equal to an instance of the class module. Notice that you use the New keyword and the name of the class module to create an instance of the class module.

When you use this first technique, you are using what's called *late binding*. With late binding, Visual Basic can't determine what type of object will be referred to until the program is executed. When you compile the project, then, it has no way to determine if the properties, methods, and events you use actually exist in the object. Because of that, Visual Basic must check the properties, methods, and events at run-time, which makes the code run slower. As a result, you should use late binding only if you don't know what type of object you'll be working with until the application is run.

The preferred way to declare a class object is to use *early binding*. With early binding, you declare an object variable with a specific class type as illustrated by the second example in this figure. Then, Visual Basic can resolve references to the object when the project is compiled, which makes the application run faster.

Another way to use early binding is illustrated by the third example in this figure. Instead of declaring the object variable and assigning a value to it in separate statements, though, it accomplishes this in one statement. It does that by including the New keyword within the Dim statement.

After you create an instance of a class module, you can refer to any of its properties and methods. You do that the same way that you refer to the properties and methods of other objects. Just code the name of the object, followed by a period, followed by the name of the property or method you want to use. This too is illustrated by the code in this figure.

If you're not sure what properties and methods are available for an object that you create from a class module, you can use the Object Browser to find out. To do that, select the project name from the Object Browser's Project/Library list, then click on the name of the class module in the Classes box. This displays the object's properties, methods, and events in the Members box. If the Auto List Members option of Visual Basic is on, you will also see the available properties and methods when you enter the name of the object variable followed by a period in the Code window. This works the same as it does for other objects.

When you're done using an object, you should remove any references to it so the memory it uses is freed. To do that, you set the value of the variable that refers to the object to the keyword Nothing. If more than one variable refers to the same object, be sure to set each one to Nothing.

Three ways to create a class object

```
Dim mclsBookOrder As Object
Set mclsBookOrder = New BookOrder

Dim mclsBookOrder As BookOrder
Set mclsBookOrder = New BookOrder

Dim mclsBookOrder As New BookOrder
```

How to refer to a class property

```
For nIndex = 0 To Ubound(mnBookQty)
    cBookTotal = cBookTotal + mnBookQty(nIndex) * _
                 mclsBookOrder.BookPrice(cboBooks(nIndex).Text)
Next nIndex

mclsBookOrder.OrderAmount = cBookTotal
```

How to execute a class method

```
TxtOrderTotal = Format(mclsBookOrder.OrderTotal(cboShipping.Text, _
                       cboStates.Text), "Currency")
```

How to disassociate an object variable from an object

```
Set mclsBookOrder = Nothing
```

Description

- To create a class object, you declare an object variable and set it equal to an instance of the class module. You can do that using any one of the three techniques shown above.
- You can declare an object using either *late binding* or *early binding*. With late binding, the object is declared with the generic Object data type as shown in the first example above. With early binding, the object is declared with the data type of the class module as shown in the second example. Early binding is the preferred method because it requires fewer resources and Visual Basic knows what kind of object you want to create prior to run-time.
- To create an instance of a class module, you use the *New* keyword and the name of the class module as shown above. You can do that in a Set statement or combine it with the variable declaration.
- You refer to a property or method of a class object the same way that you refer to a property or method of any other object. Just precede the name of the property or method with the name of the object variable that refers to that object as shown above.
- When you're done using an object variable, you should disassociate it from the object to free up the memory it uses. To do that, you set the object variable to *Nothing*.

Figure 12-5 How to use class modules

Code for the book order application

Figure 12-6 presents the code for the two modules of the application shown in figure 12-2. The form module for this project provides the user interface for the application, and the class module provides the required calculations and database access. If you study this code, you should get a good feel for how you can use class modules. Keep in mind, though, that our intent in developing and coding this application was to illustrate all of the basic techniques for working with class modules, not to build a production application.

Code for the class module

The first three parts of figure 12-6 present the code for the BookOrder class module. This code starts by declaring all of the variables used within this module (1). Notice that all of these variables are declared as Private so none of them can be accessed directly by the form module. Instead, Property Let and Get procedures are used to expose some of these variables to the form module.

The Initialize procedure for the module (2) establishes a connection to the database and defines the QueryDefs used by the class module. The first QueryDef retrieves the quantity discount from the QuantityDiscounts table depending on the number of books that are purchased. The second QueryDef retrieves the sales tax from the SalesTax table depending on the state that the books are being shipped to. The third QueryDef retrieves the price of a book from the BookPrices table depending on the book that's purchased. And the last QueryDef retrieves the base shipping cost and the unit cost to ship each additional book from the ShippingCosts table depending on the shipping method to be used.

The Property Let procedures (3 and 4) assign values to two of the private variables defined in the module. These values are passed from the form module as you'll see in a minute, and they are stored in the class module because they are used by more than one procedure in this module. Another way to accomplish this would be to pass the value to each procedure that uses it.

Visual Basic code for the class module — Page 1

1

```
Option Explicit
Private mnTotalBooks As Integer
Private mcOrderAmount As Currency
Private mfDiscountPercent As Single
Private mcDiscountTotal As Currency
Private mfSalesTaxPercent As Single
Private mcSalesTaxTotal As Currency
Private mcShippingAmount As Currency
Private mdbBooks As Database
Private mqdfDiscount As QueryDef
Private mqdfSalesTax As QueryDef
Private mqdfPrice As QueryDef
Private mqdfShipping As QueryDef
Private mrecDiscount As Recordset
Private mrecSalesTax As Recordset
Private mrecPrice As Recordset
Private mrecShipping As Recordset
```

2

```
Private Sub Class_Initialize()
    Set mdbBooks = OpenDatabase("MurachBooks", 0, 0, _
                             "ODBC;DATABASE=MurachBooks")
    Set mqdfDiscount = mdbBooks.CreateQueryDef("", _
        "PARAMETERS BookCount int; SELECT QuantityDiscount " _
        & "FROM QuantityDiscounts WHERE LowQuantity <= BookCount " _
        & "AND HighQuantity >= BookCount")
    Set mqdfSalesTax = mdbBooks.CreateQueryDef("", _
        "PARAMETERS State Char; SELECT SalesTax FROM SalesTax "_
        & "WHERE StateCode = State")
    Set mqdfPrice = mdbBooks.CreateQueryDef("", _
        "PARAMETERS BookDesc Char; SELECT BookPrice FROM " _
        & "BookPrices WHERE BookDescription = BookDesc")
    Set mqdfShipping = mdbBooks.CreateQueryDef("", _
        "PARAMETERS ShipMethod Char; SELECT ShippingBaseCost, " _
        & "ShippingUnitCost FROM ShippingCosts " _
        & "WHERE ShippingMethod = ShipMethod")
End Sub
```

3

```
Public Property Let TotalBooks(BookQty As Integer)
    mnTotalBooks = BookQty
End Property
```

4

```
Public Property Let OrderAmount(BookTotal As Currency)
    mcOrderAmount = BookTotal
End Property
```

Figure 12-6 Code for the book order application (part 1 of 6)

The next procedure (5) is a Property Get procedure that gets a book description value from a private variable and then does some processing. Since this procedure was presented in figure 12-4, you should already understand how it works. The five procedures after that (6) are also Property Get procedures that get values from private variables, but they don't do any processing.

The next procedure (7) is a public function named OrderTotal that calculates the total amount of the order. As you can see, this function receives the shipping method and state as arguments. The other values needed to perform this calculation, the number of books ordered and the total amount of the books ordered, were previously stored in private variables using Let procedures (3 and 4).

The OrderTotal function begins by calling a private function named DiscountPercent (8). This function assigns the value of the mnTotalBooks variable, which contains the total numbers of books ordered, to the BookCount parameter of the mqdfDiscount query created in the Initialize procedure (2). Next, a recordset is opened based on that query and the record that contains the discount for that quantity is retrieved. Then, the value of the QuantityDiscount field in that record is assigned to the name of the function, and that value is passed back to the OrderTotal function where it is assigned to the variable named mfDiscountPercent. The next line of code in the OrderTotal function then calculates the discount by multiplying the order amount by the discount percent.

The OrderTotal function calculates the sales tax and shipping costs in a similar manner. First, it calls the StateTax function (9) to get the sales tax percent based on the state that is passed to the function, and it uses that value to calculate the sales tax total. Then, it calls the ShippingCost function (10) to get the shipping costs based on the shipping method value that it passes to the function. After that, the OrderTotal function calculates the total amount of the order and assigns it to the name of the function (OrderTotal) so this value is passed back to the calling procedure in the form module.

Visual Basic code for the class module **Page 2**

5
```
Public Property Get BookPrice(BookDesc As String) As Currency
    mqdfPrice.Parameters!BookDesc = BookDesc
    Set mrecPrice = mqdfPrice.OpenRecordset(dbOpenSnapshot)
    BookPrice = mrecPrice!BookPrice
End Property
```

6
```
Public Property Get SalesTaxPct() As Single
    SalesTaxPct = mfSalesTaxPercent
End Property

Public Property Get SalesTaxAmount() As Currency
    SalesTaxAmount = mcSalesTaxTotal
End Property

Public Property Get DiscountPct() As Single
    DiscountPct = mfDiscountPercent
End Property

Public Property Get DiscountAmount() As Currency
    DiscountAmount = mcDiscountTotal
End Property

Public Property Get ShippingAmount() As Currency
    ShippingAmount = mcShippingAmount
End Property
```

7
```
Public Function OrderTotal(ShipMethod As String, _
                State As String) As Currency
    mfDiscountPercent = DiscountPercent
    mcDiscountTotal = mfDiscountPercent * mcOrderAmount
    mfSalesTaxPercent = StateTax(State)
    mcSalesTaxTotal = (mcOrderAmount - mcDiscountTotal) * _
                      (mfSalesTaxPercent / 100)
    mcShippingAmount = ShippingCost(ShipMethod)
    OrderTotal = mcOrderAmount - mcDiscountTotal + mcSalesTaxTotal + _
                 mcShippingAmount
End Function
```

8
```
Private Function DiscountPercent() As Currency
    mqdfDiscount.Parameters!BookCount = mnTotalBooks
    Set mrecDiscount = mqdfDiscount.OpenRecordset(dbOpenSnapshot)
    DiscountPercent = mrecDiscount!QuantityDiscount
End Function
```

9
```
Private Function StateTax(StateCode As String) As Single
    mqdfSalesTax.Parameters!State = StateCode
    Set mrecSalesTax = mqdfSalesTax.OpenRecordset(dbOpenSnapshot)
    StateTax = mrecSalesTax!SalesTax
End Function
```

Figure 12-6 Code for the book order application (part 1 of 6)

The last three procedures in the BookOrder class module (11-13) are public functions. The BookDescriptions function (11) opens a recordset that retrieves the descriptions of all the books in the BookPrices table. This recordset is then passed back to the form module where it's used to populate the Book Title combo boxes.

The second and third procedures are similar. The StateCodes function (12) opens a recordset that contains all the state codes in the SalesTax table, and this recordset is used in the form module to populate the State combo box. The ShippingMethods function (13) opens a recordset that contains all the shipping methods in the ShippingCosts table, and this recordset is used in the form module to populate the Shipping Method combo box.

Visual Basic code for the class module — Page 3

10

```
Private Function ShippingCost(ShippingMethod As String) _
                As Currency
    mqdfShipping.Parameters!ShipMethod = ShippingMethod
    Set mrecShipping = mqdfShipping.OpenRecordset(dbOpenSnapshot)
    If mnTotalBooks > 1 Then
        ShippingCost = mrecShipping!ShippingBaseCost + _
                     ((mnTotalBooks - 1) * _
                     mrecShipping!ShippingUnitCost)
    Else
        ShippingCost = mrecShipping!ShippingBaseCost
    End If
End Function
```

11

```
Public Function BookDescriptions() As Recordset
    Set BookDescriptions = mdbBooks.OpenRecordset("SELECT " _
        & "BookDescription FROM BookPrices ORDER BY BookDescription", _
        dbOpenSnapshot)
End Function
```

12

```
Public Function StateCodes() As Recordset
    Set StateCodes = mdbBooks.OpenRecordset("SELECT StateCode " _
        & "FROM SalesTax ORDER BY StateCode", dbOpenSnapshot)
End Function
```

13

```
Public Function ShippingMethods() As Recordset
    Set ShippingMethods = mdbBooks.OpenRecordset("SELECT " _
        & "ShippingMethod FROM ShippingCosts " _
        & "ORDER BY ShippingBaseCost", dbOpenSnapshot)
End Function
```

Figure 12-6 Code for the book order application (part 3 of 6)

Code for the form module

The code for the form module of this project starts by declaring three private variables used within the module (14). The first variable, mclsBookOrder, contains a reference to the BookOrder object, which is created using the New keyword on the declaration. You'll see how the other variables are used in later procedures.

The Load procedure of the form (15) calls three procedures that populate the combo boxes used on the form. The LoadcboBooks procedure (16) starts by using the BookDescriptions method of the class module (11) to get a recordset that contains the descriptions of all of the books to be included in the Book Title combo boxes. It stores this recordset in the variable named mrecTemp. The LoadcboBooks procedure then retrieves each of the records in the recordset and adds the book description to each of the five combo boxes (index numbers 0 to 4).

The LoadcboShipping procedure (17) uses the ShippingMethods method of the class module (13) to retrieve the descriptions of all the shipping methods that are available. It too stores this recordset in the variable named mrecTemp. The shipping methods are then used to populate the Shipping Method combo box.

The LoadcboStates procedure (18) is similar. It uses the StateCodes method of the class module (12) to retrieve the state codes that are used to populate the State combo box.

The last procedure in this part of the figure (19) is the GotFocus event procedure for the Quantity text boxes. Because these boxes are designed as an array, the Index argument indicates which text box received the focus. This procedure then uses the SelStart and SelLength methods of a text box control to select the quantity in that box if one has already been entered. This lets the user enter a new value in a text box without first deleting the old one.

Visual Basic code for the form module **Page 1**

14
```
Option Explicit
Private mclsBookOrder As New BookOrder
Private mnBookQty() As Integer
Private mrecTemp As Recordset
```

15
```
Private Sub Form_Load()
    LoadcboBooks
    LoadcboShipping
    LoadcboStates
End Sub
```

16
```
Private Sub LoadcboBooks()
    Set mrecTemp = mclsBookOrder.BookDescriptions
    Do Until mrecTemp.EOF
        cboBooks(0).AddItem mrecTemp!BookDescription
        cboBooks(1).AddItem mrecTemp!BookDescription
        cboBooks(2).AddItem mrecTemp!BookDescription
        cboBooks(3).AddItem mrecTemp!BookDescription
        cboBooks(4).AddItem mrecTemp!BookDescription
        mrecTemp.MoveNext
    Loop
End Sub
```

17
```
Private Sub LoadcboShipping()
    Set mrecTemp = mclsBookOrder.ShippingMethods
    Do Until mrecTemp.EOF
        cboShipping.AddItem mrecTemp!ShippingMethod
        mrecTemp.MoveNext
    Loop
End Sub
```

18
```
Private Sub LoadcboStates()
    Set mrecTemp = mclsBookOrder.StateCodes
    Do Until mrecTemp.EOF
        cboStates.AddItem mrecTemp!StateCode
        mrecTemp.MoveNext
    Loop
End Sub
```

19
```
Private Sub txtQty_GotFocus(Index As Integer)
    txtQty(Index).SelStart = 0
    txtQty(Index).SelLength = Len(txtQty(Index).Text)
End Sub
```

Figure 12-6 Code for the book order application (part 4 of 6)

When the user clicks on the Calculate button on the form, the Click event procedure for that button (20) is executed. This procedure calculates the total amount of the order based on the books, quantities, shipping method, and state selected by the user. It does this by using several properties and methods of the BookOrder object.

After declaring two local variables, this Click event procedure calls the ValidOrder function (21) to make sure that the user has selected a shipping method, a state, and at least one book and has entered a quantity for that book. If not, an error message is displayed. If so, this procedure changes the mouse pointer to an hour glass to indicate to the user that the request is being processed.

Next, the Click procedure calls the GetBookTotals procedure (22) to calculate the total number of books that were ordered. This procedure uses a variable array, mnBookQty, to save the order quantity for each book that was ordered. To start, this array is redimensioned with a value of 5 since the user can order a maximum of five different books (that was one of the application specifications). Then, a Do loop is used to get the order quantity for each book and accumulate the total quantity ordered. The code within this loop is performed for each book that was selected (a value of –1 in the ListIndex property of a combo box indicates that a selection wasn't made). When this loop is complete, the variable array is redimensioned so it contains the number of variables that correspond to the number of books that were ordered. To retain the values in this array when it is redimensioned, the Preserve keyword is used in the Redim statement. Then, the procedure sets the value of the TotalBooks property of the class module (3) to the calculated value.

Back in the Click event procedure for the Calculate button (20), the For loop calculates the total cost of the books ordered. It does that by multiplying the quantity of each book ordered by the price of each book, and it gets the book prices by referring to the BookPrice property of the BookOrder object (5). (The Ubound function used in the For statement retrieves the highest index used by the mnBookQty array.) After this loop calculates the total cost, this procedure assigns the value to the OrderAmount property of the BookOrder object (4).

The remaining statements in this Click even procedure format and display values in the other controls on the form. These statements refer to several properties of the BookOrder object. When this procedure is done, the mouse pointer is returned to its default shape.

Visual Basic code for the form module Page 2

20

```
Private Sub cmdCalculate_Click()
    Dim nIndex As Integer
    Dim cBookTotal As Currency
    If ValidOrder Then
        Screen.MousePointer = vbHourglass
        GetBookTotals
        For nIndex = 0 To UBound(mnBookQty)
            cBookTotal = cBookTotal + mnBookQty(nIndex) * _
                        mclsBookOrder.BookPrice(cboBooks(nIndex).Text)
        Next nIndex
        mclsBookOrder.OrderAmount = cBookTotal
        txtOrderTotal = Format(mclsBookOrder.OrderTotal _
                       (cboShipping.Text, cboStates.Text), "Currency")
        txtOrderAmount = Format(cBookTotal, "Currency")
        txtDiscountPct = Format(mclsBookOrder.DiscountPct, "Percent")
        txtDiscountAmount = "<" & Format(mclsBookOrder. _
                            DiscountAmount, "Currency") & ">"
        txtSalesTaxPct = Format(mclsBookOrder.SalesTaxPct, _
                         "#.#0") & "%"
        txtSalesTaxAmount = Format(mclsBookOrder.SalesTaxAmount, _
                            "Currency")
        txtShippingAmount = Format(mclsBookOrder.ShippingAmount, _
                            "Currency")
        Screen.MousePointer = vbDefault
    Else
        MsgBox "Data validation error." & vbCrLf _
            & "Please check all field entries.", _
            vbOKOnly + vbCritical, "Mike Murach & Associates"
    End If
End Sub
```

21

```
Private Function ValidOrder() As Boolean
    Dim nIndex As Integer
    ValidOrder = True
    If cboShipping.ListIndex = -1 Or cboStates.ListIndex = -1 Then
        ValidOrder = False
    Else
        Do Until nIndex >= 4 Or ValidOrder = False
            If cboBooks(nIndex).ListIndex <> -1 _
                    And txtQty(nIndex) = "" Then
                ValidOrder = False
            Else
                nIndex = nIndex + 1
            End If
        Loop
    End If
End Function
```

Figure 12-6 Code for the book order application (part 5 of 6)

If the user clicks on the New button in the form, the Click event procedure for that button (23) is executed. This procedure clears all of the controls on the form and sets the focus to the first Book Title combo box. Then, the user can enter a new order.

Finally, if the user clicks on the Exit button, the Click event procedure for that button (24) is executed. This procedure sets the object variable that refers to the BookOrder object to a value of Nothing so the memory it occupied is freed. Then, it unloads the form and ends the program.

The benefits of using class modules

Now that you've seen how a form module can use a class module, you can reflect on the benefits that you can gain from using class modules in your projects. To start, let's assume that someone else has already developed the class modules that you need for an application. That certainly should make it easier for you to develop the application because all you have to do is use the properties and methods of the available objects just as you use the properties and methods of objects that come with Visual Basic.

A second benefit is improved maintenance of an application because all of the business processing can be done in class modules, including the database processing, while the user interface processing is done in form modules. That should make it easier to find the code that needs to be changed. In addition, you should be able to change the code without affecting the operation of the user interface.

If you can design objects that can be used by more than one application, a third benefit is reusability, which in turn can lead to improved programmer productivity. An object that provides methods for calculating freight charges, for example, could be used by both accounts payable and order processing applications. The trick here, though, is designing objects that are generic enough to be used in two or more applications without making them so simple that they aren't that useful.

Perhaps the most important benefit, though, is that the use of class modules represents an improved way of thinking about application development. Instead of thinking of subprograms and paragraphs that perform a single function as you would in COBOL, for example, you start thinking in terms of objects with clearly established properties and methods. Then, you use the appropriate property or method whenever it's needed. In the long run, that is the factor that's most likely to improve programmer productivity and program reliability.

The downside to the use of class modules is the complexity that it adds to the jobs of project managers and lead programmers. First, someone has to plan the class modules for the applications that they're going to be used by. Second, someone has to develop these modules, which some managers think is too difficult for the average programmer. Third, once the class modules have been developed, the programmers who are going to use them need to get full information about the objects, properties, and methods so they can use them effectively. In short, getting the potential benefits from the use of class modules presents some planning and management difficulties that are well beyond the scope of this book.

Visual Basic code for the form module **Page 3**

22

```
Private Sub GetBookTotals()
    Dim nIndex As Integer
    Dim nTotalBooks As Integer
    ReDim mnBookQty(5)
    Do Until cboBooks(nIndex).ListIndex = -1
        mnBookQty(nIndex) = Val(txtQty(nIndex).Text)
        nTotalBooks = nTotalBooks + mnBookQty(nIndex)
        nIndex = nIndex + 1
    Loop
    ReDim Preserve mnBookQty(nIndex - 1)
    mclsBookOrder.TotalBooks = nTotalBooks
End Sub
```

23

```
Private Sub cmdNew_Click()
    Dim nIndex As Integer
    For nIndex = 0 To 4
        cboBooks(nIndex).ListIndex = -1
        txtQty(nIndex).Text = ""
    Next nIndex
    cboShipping.ListIndex = -1
    cboStates.ListIndex = -1
    txtOrderAmount = ""
    txtDiscountPct = ""
    txtDiscountAmount = ""
    txtSalesTaxPct = ""
    txtSalesTaxAmount = ""
    txtShippingAmount = ""
    txtOrderTotal = ""
    cboBooks(0).SetFocus
End Sub
```

24

```
Private Sub cmdExit_Click()
    Set mclsBookOrder = Nothing
    Unload Me
    End
End Sub
```

Figure 12-6 Code for the book order application (part 6 of 6)

An introduction to ActiveX components

Once you know how to create class modules, you're just one step away from learning how to create ActiveX components. Before I show you how to do that, though, I want to present some basics concepts related to ActiveX and ActiveX components. I also want to show you how to use existing ActiveX components in an application. After that, you'll be ready to learn how to create your own ActiveX components.

An overview of ActiveX components

An ActiveX component is the executable form of an ActiveX project, and an ActiveX project can contain one or more class modules just like a standard project. When you create a class module within an ActiveX project, though, its properties and methods are exposed at a global level. In other words, any project that has access to the component can use its class modules. In contrast, a class module that's stored within a standard project exposes its properties only to the other modules in that project.

Figure 12-7 illustrates the difference between using class modules created in a standard project and class modules created in an ActiveX project. As you can see, a class module that's created in a standard project must be included in every project that uses it. In contrast, a class module in an ActiveX project exists separately from any project that uses it. One of the benefits of using ActiveX components, then, is that the size of each project that uses them is reduced.

Another benefit of using ActiveX components is that they're easy to maintain. To change a class module in a standard project, you have to change each project that contains that module. In contrast, since an ActiveX component is stored in its own project, its code can be changed without affecting any projects that use it. Also, the changes you make to the component are immediately available to those projects.

A third benefit of using ActiveX components is that they don't have to reside on the same machine as the client applications that use them. Although they can reside on the local machine, they can also reside on the another user's machine on the same network or on a network server called a *component server*.

To use an ActiveX component, you create an instance of one of its class modules in your application. Then, you have access to all of the properties, methods, and events defined by that class module. In other words, you can work with a class module in an ActiveX component just as if it's a class module in the client project. Before you can access a class module in an ActiveX component, though, the component must be registered on your system, which you'll learn how to do in figure 12-9.

Although this chapter focuses on ActiveX components, you should know that you can also create two other types of ActiveX objects with Visual Basic called *ActiveX controls* and *ActiveX documents*. An ActiveX control is a customized control that you can use in any project, and many of the controls that come with Visual Basic are ActiveX controls. In contrast, an ActiveX document is an application object that you can add to an ActiveX document container. For instance, Word, Excel, and Access can be used as ActiveX documents, and the Microsoft Internet Explorer can be used as an ActiveX document container.

Two projects that use the same class modules

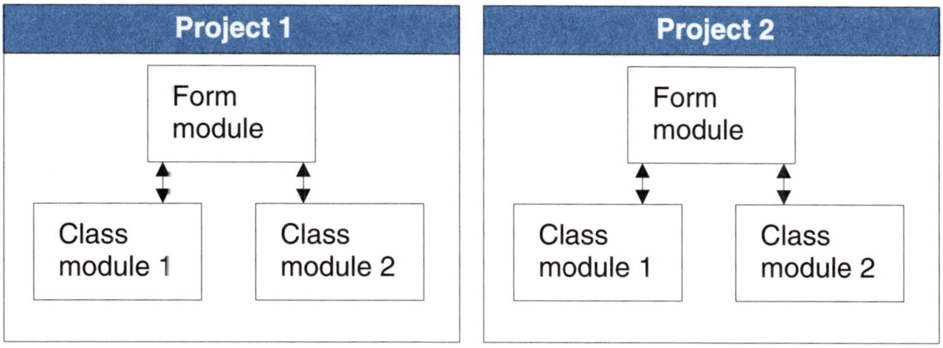

Two projects that use the same ActiveX component

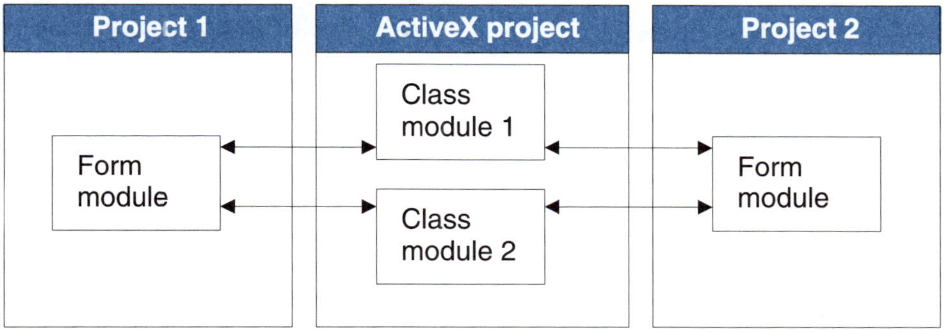

Description

- *ActiveX components* are stand-alone units of executable code that you can be used by any application that supports ActiveX technology. An ActiveX component can contain one or more class modules that expose the component to other projects.
- To use an ActiveX component, you create an instance of one of its class modules within a client application. Then, you can use standard techniques to refer to the properties and methods of the class. For this to work, the client application must include a *reference* to the component so it knows how to get to it (see figure 12-9).
- ActiveX components let you access the same code from more than one application. Unlike class modules in standard projects, you don't have to include the code in each application that uses it.
- ActiveX components can also make program maintenance easier because there's only one copy of the code. If you modify that code, the changes are immediately available to all the applications that use it.
- ActiveX components can reside on the same machine as the applications that use them, or they can reside on another machine on the network. A machine that hosts ActiveX components is typically called a *component server*.

Figure 12-7 An overview of ActiveX components

How an application communicates with ActiveX components

Microsoft developed ActiveX technology based on its *Component Object Model*, or *COM*. This model specifies the low-level functionality and interface needed for objects and programs that support ActiveX to communicate with each other. As shown in figure 12-8, a program interacts with ActiveX components through the COM interface. With COM, an application can communicate only with ActiveX components that reside on the same machine as the application, and these components can be referred to as *local components*.

If an application needs to communicate with components on other machines, which are called *remote components*, it uses another interface called the *Distributed Component Object Model*, or *DCOM*. Notice in figure 12-8, though, that an application doesn't communicate directly with DCOM. Instead, all requests for ActiveX components go through COM. Then, if COM determines that the component is on a remote machine, it passes the request on to DCOM.

COM keeps track of ActiveX components through the use of a unique id that's given to each component when it's created. This unique id is commonly referred to as the *Class Identifier*, or *CLSID*. However, it can also be referred to as the *Globally Unique Identifier* (*GUID*) or the *Universally Unique Identifier* (*UUID*). No matter what you call it, though, no two components anywhere will have the same id. That way, COM always knows which component to use and where to find it.

Before you can use an ActiveX component from an application you're developing, you must first *register* it on your machine. When you register a component, information about the component, including its unique id, is placed in the system registry. To register a component on your machine, you include a reference to it in a project as explained in the next figure.

ActiveX technology

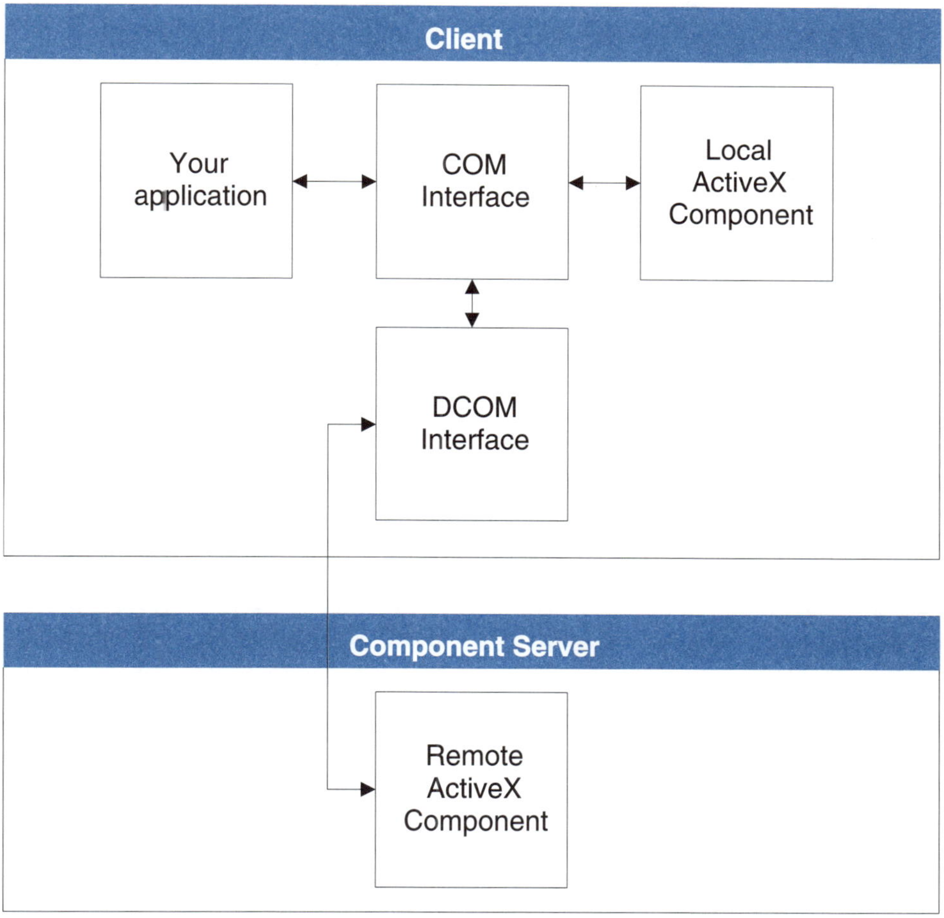

Description

- If an ActiveX component resides on the same machine as the application that uses it, the application communicates with the component using the *Component Object Model*, or *COM*. This model keeps track of ActiveX components using the unique id that's assigned to each component when it's registered.
- If an ActiveX component resides on a machine other than the one where the application that uses it resides, COM passes the request on to the *Distributed Component Object Model*, or *DCOM*. With DCOM, you can access components that reside on a local network, an intranet, or the Internet.
- The COM and DCOM interfaces are transparent to your Visual Basic programs. That means that you can work with ActiveX components the same way you work with class modules.
- The current build of Windows 95 doesn't support DCOM by default. To use DCOM, you can download the file named DCOM95.EXE from the Microsoft web site and run it on your Windows 95 machine.

Figure 12-8 How an application communicates with ActiveX components

How to use existing ActiveX components

Before you can use an ActiveX component from a client application, you must add a *reference* to it in the client application. To do that, you use the References dialog box shown in figure 12-9, which is accessed by choosing the References command from the Project menu. If you try to create an instance of a class module in a component that's not referenced by the client application, Visual Basic will display a compile error stating that the user-defined type isn't defined.

The References dialog box includes all components that have been registered on the local machine. To use one of these components, just click on it to select it. To use a component that has not been registered on the local machine, click on the Browse button to locate the component. After you locate and select the component you want, it's added to the Available References list and registered on your machine.

When you click on the Browse button in the References dialog box, you'll notice that Visual Basic looks for type library files by default. When a component resides on a remote server, the Object Browser and client applications can use the component's type library to get information about the component. (As you'll see in chapter 13, the type library file is included in the setup program for a client that accesses the remote component.) For program development purposes, though, you usually select the executable file for the component since it provides all the information you need.

After you add a reference to an ActiveX component to a project, you can use any of the class modules it contains. To do that, just create an instance of the class module, and then refer to its properties and methods as described earlier in this chapter. If you don't know what properties and methods a class module defines, you can use the Object Browser to find out. A list of properties and methods will also be displayed in the Code window if you enter the name of the object variable that refers to the class object followed by a period.

The dialog boxes for adding a reference for an ActiveX component

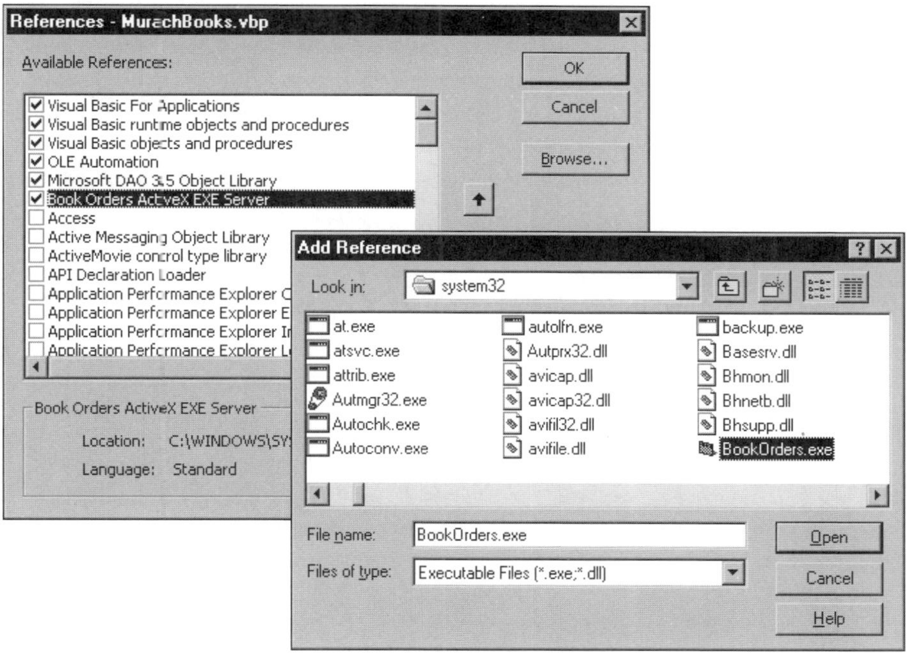

Description

- To use an ActiveX component in a client application, you select it from the References dialog box shown above. If the component has been registered on the local machine, it will already be included in the Available References list, so all you have to do is select it.
- If the component has not been registered on the local machine, you have to click on the Browse button in the References dialog box to locate the component and add it to the Available References list. When you do that, the component is automatically registered on the machine so you will have access to it from other applications.
- By default, Visual Basic displays files with type library information (file extensions OLB, TLB, or DLL) in the Add Reference dialog box. So to locate an executable file (file extensions EXE or DLL), you need to select that option from the Files of Type drop-down list.

Figure 12-9 How to use existing ActiveX components

How to create ActiveX components

If you understand how to create and work with class modules, you won't have any trouble creating ActiveX components. You can run into problems, though, if you don't set the properties for an ActiveX project correctly or you don't use the Setup Wizard that's described in the next chapter to deploy the ActiveX project and any project that uses it. Before I show you how to create an ActiveX component, then, I'll present a general procedure you can use to create and test ActiveX components that will help you avoid these problems.

A general procedure for creating and testing an ActiveX component

Figure 12-10 presents a general procedure you can use to create and test ActiveX components. In general, you create the server project that contains the component (steps 1-3), you create the client project (steps 4-5), and you test the two together on your local machine (step 6). Then, if the component will reside on a local machine, you're done. Otherwise, you can deploy the component on the remote server where it will reside (step 7), deploy the client application on a local machine (step 8), and test the two together (step 9).

Although you can start by creating a separate project for an ActiveX component as indicated by this figure, you may want to start by creating a class module within the project that contains the code for the client application. In fact, we recommend that you do that if you haven't worked with class modules before. Then, when you get the class module working the way you want it, you can start an ActiveX project, add the class module to it, and delete the class module from the client project. If you do that, though, you need to be sure to change the Instancing property of the class module to MultiUse as shown in the next figure. That's necessary because the Instancing property of a class module that's created in a standard project is Private.

Figure 12-10 also describes the four types of files that you can create for an ActiveX component. The name of each file that's created is the name of the project, and the extension is the file type shown in the figure. All of these files can be created when you build the project in step 3 of the procedure.

The main file that's created for a component, and the only one that's required for all components, is the EXE or DLL file. This file contains the executable code for the component. You'll learn about the difference between these two types of files and when you use them in the next figure.

If a component will reside on a remote machine, you also need to create TLB and VBR files for the component. These files provide information that client applications use to communicate and work with the remote component. As you'll see in the next chapter, these files must be installed on the client machine along with the client application that uses the component.

How to create and test an ActiveX component

1. Create the server project and enter the code for the ActiveX component (see figure 12-11).
2. Set the project properties and save the project (see figure 12-12).
3. Use the Make command on the File menu to build the project. This compiles the project and creates the DLL or EXE and the TLB and VBR files for the component.
4. Create the client project and select the component from the References dialog box (see figure 12-9).
5. Enter the required code, set the project properties, and save the project.
6. Run the client project and test the component. If you make changes to the component, use the Make command again to recreate the VBR, TLB, and DLL or EXE files for the component.
7. If the component will reside on a remote server, use the Setup Wizard to create a setup program for the component as described in chapter 13. Then, run the setup program to install the component on the server.
8. Use the Setup Wizard to create a setup program for the client project as described in chapter 13. Be sure to include a reference to the VBR file for the remote component (see figure 13-5). Then, run the setup program to install the client on your machine.
9. Run the client application and test the component.

Types of files that are created for a component

File type	Description
EXE or DLL	Contains the executable code for the component. Also contains information about the component's properties, methods, and events that's used by the Object Browser and client applications when the component resides on the local machine.
TLB	Contains information about the component's properties, methods, and events. This file is used by the Object Browser and client applications when the component resides on a remote server.
VBR	Contains information that's used by client applications to locate the component when it resides on a remote server.

Figure 12-10 A general procedure for creating and testing an ActiveX component

How to create an ActiveX project

Figure 12-11 shows you how to create an ActiveX project. To start, you need to decide whether to create an EXE or DLL project. In general, you create a DLL if the component will reside on the same machine as the client application because a DLL runs *in-process*, or in the same address space, as the client application. If the component will run on a remote server, though, you create an EXE, which runs *out-of-process*, or in its own address space.

After you select the type of project you want to create, Visual Basic creates the project with a single class module. Then, you can create the code for that class module just as you would for any other class module. You can also add existing class modules to the project or create additional class modules, since an ActiveX component isn't limited to a single class module. That makes sense if you remember that you refer to a class by the name of the class module that defines it, not by the name of the project that contains it.

You can also include standard modules and form modules in an ActiveX project. These modules, of course, can be referred to only from the other modules in the project. They can't be referred to from outside the project like the class modules can.

Before you save a project, you should make sure that the Instancing property of each class module in the project is set the way you want. By default, this property is set to MultiUse for a class module you create in an ActiveX project, which is usually what you want. (This property is set to Private for a class module that's created in a standard project and can't be changed.) In addition, you should be sure that the Name property is set the way you want it since this will be the name you use to access the class module.

How to create an ActiveX project

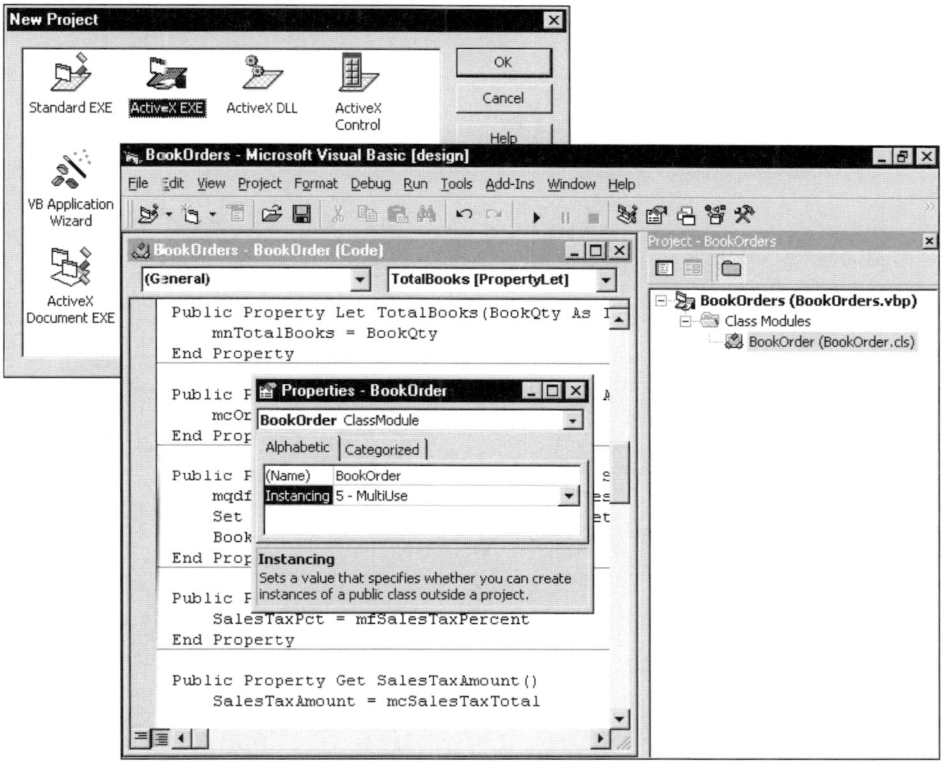

Description

- To create an ActiveX project, choose the ActiveX EXE or ActiveX DLL option from the New Project dialog box shown above. The type of ActiveX project you create depends mostly on where the component will reside.
- If the component will reside on the same machine as the application that uses it, you usually create it as a DLL (*dynamic link library*). Since a DLL runs *in-process*, which means that it runs in the same address space as the application that uses it, it's usually faster than an EXE.
- If the component will reside on a remote server, you usually create it as an EXE. This type of component is an executable program that runs *out-of-process*, which means that it runs in its own address space.
- When you start an ActiveX DLL or EXE project, a single class module is created by default. However, you can create other class modules for the project, and you can add standard or form modules to the project.
- By default, the Instancing property of a class module in an ActiveX project is set to MultiUse, which is the option you want for most DLL and EXE projects.

Figure 12-11 How to create an ActiveX project

How to set the properties for an ActiveX project

After you enter the code for an ActiveX project, but before you save or build the project, you need to set the project properties as described in figure 12-12. Three of these properties are available from the General tab of the Project Properties dialog box, and three others are available from the Component tab. To display the Project Properties dialog box, select the Properties command from the Project menu.

Although you've already seen the three properties in the General Tab, they're particularly important when used in an ActiveX project. The name you specify in the Project Name property is the name that you'll see in the Object Browser's Project/Library list. If other programmers will be using the component, then, you should be sure to give the project a meaningful name.

The Project Description property is also used by the Object Browser. It's displayed in the Details pane when you select the project from the Project/Library list. In addition, this property is used to describe the project in the References dialog box you saw in figure 12-9.

The Startup Object property typically identifies the first module that's executed when an application starts. For an ActiveX component, this is the module that's executed when the first instance of a class module in the component is created. In most cases, there's no reason to execute any code at that time. If for some reason you do need to execute code when the first instance of a class module is created, though, you can code a Sub Main procedure and choose the Sub Main option for the Startup Object property. Note, however, that you can't select a form module for the Startup Object property of an ActiveX project. (Remember that if you want to execute code each time an instance is created, you can use the Initialize event of the class module.)

If you open the Project Properties dialog box, you'll see that you can also change the type of a project using the Project Type property. You may want to do that, for example, if you start a DLL project and then decide you want to create an EXE instead. If you change the project type, Visual Basic makes any necessary changes automatically and warns you if any properties in the current project won't be valid with the new project type. This shouldn't be a problem if you're just switching between a DLL and an EXE, but it can cause problems when switching to other project types.

The Start Mode, Remote Server Files, and Version Compatibility properties are specific to ActiveX projects. Except for the Remote Server Files property, these properties are usually set the way you want them by default. If you're creating a remote component, though, you'll want to turn on the Remote Server Files property, which isn't set by default. This will create the VBR and TLB files that are needed for a client application to communicate and work with a remote component. These files aren't needed for a local component because the client has direct access to the EXE or DLL file for the component.

Once you have the properties for an ActiveX project set properly, you can save and build the project. Then, you can use it from any application on the same machine. If you want to deploy the component on a remote machine, though, you need to create a setup program as described in chapter 13.

Project properties for an ActiveX component

Tab	Property	Description
General	Project Name	The name of the type library for the component. Used to identify the project in the Object Browser.
	Project Description	The text that's displayed for the component in the Details pane of the Object Browser and in the References dialog box.
	Startup Object	For an ActiveX component, this option is usually set to (none), which is the default.
Component	Start Mode	Determines whether the application is started as a standalone application or as an ActiveX server (component) when it's run within Visual Basic. By default, the ActiveX Component option is on.
	Remote Server Files	Creates VBR and TLB files for the project when it's built. These files are used by client applications to access and use remote components, and this option isn't selected by default.
	Version Compatibility	Determines the level of compatibility between different versions of a component. Project Compatibility is the default.

Notes

- You can also specify Sub Main for the Startup Object option. If you do, the code in the Sub Main procedure will be executed when the first instance of the component is created. This code is executed before the code in the object's Initialize procedure.
- If you display the Project Properties dialog box after you build a component with the Project Compatibility option selected, you'll see that the name of the executable file you just created is displayed in the text box below the compatibility options. Then, if you change the component and build it again, Windows will use the same unique id number for the new version of the component that it used for the original version. That way, the change will not affect any applications that already refer to the component.

Figure 12-12 How to set the properties for an ActiveX project

Perspective

The goal of this chapter has been to introduce you to class modules and ActiveX components and to present the basic coding skills that are required to create and work with them. Beyond that, I hope that this chapter has helped you begin to see how you can use class modules and ActiveX components in your own development efforts. If you understand the class module that was presented in this chapter and can visualize it as an object, then this chapter has succeeded.

Now, it's worth taking the time to experiment with the use of class modules. To start, try to design and develop a simple class module or two that you can use for the development of one or more new applications. In most cases, you will have to establish the requirements of the applications that are going to use the class modules before you can design the class modules. After you've planned the class modules, code one or more of them and code a simple form module that uses the properties and methods of your class modules. Then, if you like what you've got at that point, try converting the class modules to local ActiveX components and see how that works.

One of the benefits that you'll get from this experimentation is that you'll take another step toward thinking in terms of objects. The more you think that way, the more you'll be able to take advantage of object-oriented technology, which is clearly the way applications are going to be developed in the foreseeable future. In the long run, we believe learning to think in terms of objects will help you work faster at the same time that it helps you improve the maintainability and reliability of your applications.

Chapter 13

How to deploy an application

After you complete a project, you need to *deploy* it on the machines that will run the application. Because a typical Visual Basic application requires numerous files, the easiest way to deploy it is to use the Setup Wizard that comes with Visual Basic to create a setup program for it. Then, you can run that setup program to install the application and all of the files it requires on each of the client machines. Although you can deploy an application without using the Setup Wizard, that can be quite tedious.

How to use the Setup Wizard to create a setup program for a standard project

When you start the Setup Wizard program, it leads you through a series of dialog boxes that help you configure the setup program for your application. To help you understand this process, this topic starts by describing how the Wizard works. Then, it shows you how to use the Wizard to create a setup program for the MurachBooks application presented in chapter 12. Because this application uses an ActiveX component, it will give you a realistic view of what's involved when you install a business application. Keep in mind, though, that this process is simpler for projects that don't use ActiveX components.

How the Setup Wizard works

Figure 13-1 illustrates the input files that are required by the Setup Wizard and the output files that it creates. As you can see, both the input and output files can be extensive. Fortunately, though, the Setup Wizard determines most of the files that are required for an application by analyzing its project file. For example, the Wizard identifies the ActiveX components that are required by an application by analyzing the references you selected for the project. And it identifies the controls used by the application by analyzing the components you selected for the project.

If you include an ActiveX component in a project (see chapter 12), the Setup Wizard can get additional information about the files required by that component by looking at the component's *dependency file*. This file has the same name as the executable file for the component, but with DEP as the file extension. Although dependency files are usually created for components that require other files, that's not always the case. So if a dependency file isn't available for a component and you know that it requires other files, you can select those files manually during the setup process.

A Visual Basic application also requires some Visual Basic files before it can run on a client machine. The Setup Wizard gets information about these files from the Visual Basic dependency file, named Vb5dep.ini. The only other input required by the Setup Wizard is the Setup Toolkit project file. The Setup Wizard uses this file as a template for the setup program that it creates. If you want to, you can customize this Setup Toolkit file, but the details of doing that are beyond the scope of this book.

The output of the Setup Wizard includes the setup program that you use to install the application, all of the files that will be installed in a compressed format, and a setup list that includes information about how each file will be installed and registered. Then, to install these files on a client machine, you run the setup program on that machine.

If the application you're distributing includes any third party files or components, you should be sure to check their license agreements. That's because some manufacturers require a royalty fee each time the file or component is distributed to a new user. If you're not sure whether you can distribute a file or component without paying a royalty fee, be sure to contact the manufacturer. Note, however, that you can freely distribute files in the Visual Basic Graphics, ODBC, Samples, and Icons directories.

How to create a Setup program

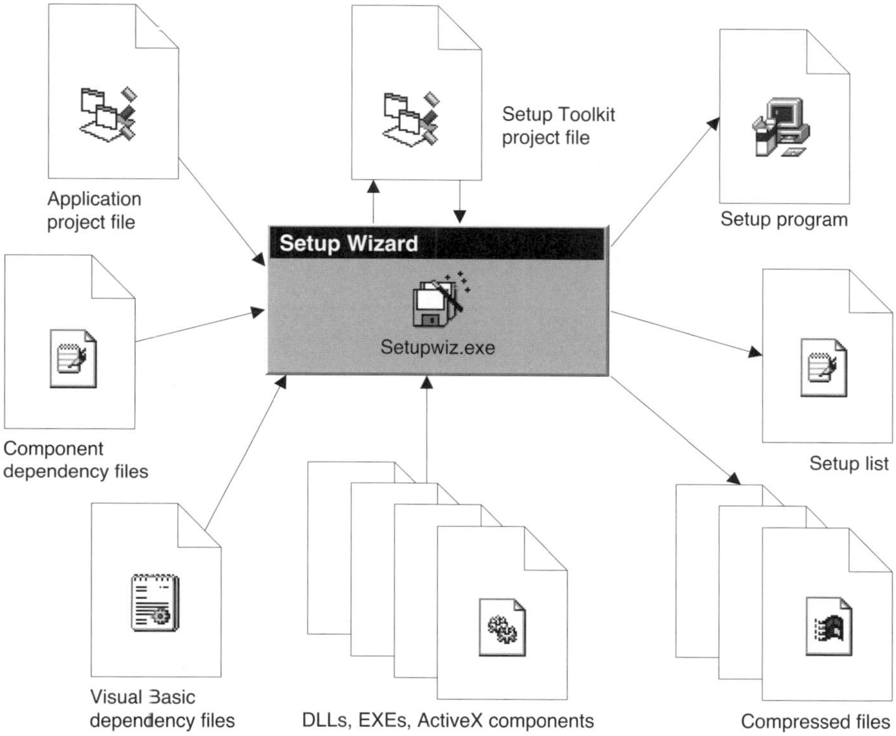

Description

- The Setup Wizard is a Visual Basic utility that you can use to create a setup program for a Visual Basic application. Then, you can use that setup program to install the application on one or more clients.
- The Setup Wizard uses a project called the Setup Toolkit as a template for the setup program it creates. The information you supply to the Setup Wizard is used to customize the Setup Toolkit project for a specific application.
- The Setup Wizard analyzes the project file you specify to determine what additional files are required by the application. These files can include DLLs and EXEs, including ActiveX components and ActiveX controls.
- The Setup Wizard uses the Visual Basic dependency file, named Vb5dep.ini, to get information about the Visual Basic files that are required by the application. It also uses *dependency files* to get information about the files required by any ActiveX components that are used by the application.
- The Setup Wizard stores information about all the required files in a file named Setup.lst. Then, when you execute the setup program for the project, it uses the Setup.lst file to determine how each file is registered and installed.
- Besides creating the setup program and Setup.lst file, the Setup Wizard compresses all the files required by the application and saves them to the location you specify. These files include the executable file for the project.

Figure 13-1 How the Setup Wizard works

How to select a project and the setup options

Although the Setup Wizard comes with Visual Basic, you can't run it from within the Visual Basic IDE. In fact, you should close Visual Basic before running the Setup Wizard so you can be sure that none of the files you need are in use. Then, you can run the Setup Wizard by using the Programs menu of the Windows Start button. By default, the Setup Wizard program is located on the same submenu as Visual Basic.

After you start the Setup Wizard, it asks you to identify the project you want to create a setup program for as shown in figure 13-2. Here, I selected the MurachBooks client application that's presented in chapter 12. I also checked the Rebuild the Project box so the project will be recompiled and the executable for the project will be rebuilt.

Although you don't normally need to build a project as you develop and test it, the Visual Basic online help says you must build and save a project at least once before you run the Setup Wizard. If you don't, the help information says that the setup program you create may not work properly. Although we haven't found that to be the case for the applications in this book, you may want to use the Make command in the Visual Basic File menu to create an executable file for a project before you create a setup program for that project. Then, you can check the Rebuild the Project box to make sure that the project doesn't contain any errors and that the executable for the project reflects the most current code for the project.

The options you choose in this dialog box determine the files that are generated by the Setup Wizard. For most projects, you'll select the Create a Setup Program option to generate the files shown in figure 13-1. In this case, you can also select the Generate Dependency File option if you want the Setup Wizard to create a dependency file that contains information about all of the files required by the application. That's only necessary, though, if the application will be used as a component by another project, which isn't usually the case.

The other two options provide special features for working with ActiveX components. Later in this chapter, for example, you'll learn how to use the Generate Dependency File Only option to create a dependency file for an ActiveX component that will reside on the local machine.

When you click on the Next button in this dialog box, the Setup Wizard compiles the project if you checked the Rebuild the Project option and displays an error message if any errors are encountered. If the project contains errors, you need to exit from the Setup Wizard, correct the errors, and run the Setup Wizard again.

If no errors are found, the Setup Wizard creates the executable for the project and then analyzes the project to determine its dependencies and the dependencies of any components included in the project. Then, if the project includes a reference to a component, the Wizard attempts to locate the component and its dependency file. If it can't find the component, the Wizard asks you to locate it, which you have to do if the component will be deployed on each client as a *local component*. If you can't locate it at this point, though, you can add it from the ActiveX Server Components dialog box later in the setup process. In contrast, if the component will be deployed as a *remote component*, you can continue without ever locating the component.

The Select Project and Options dialog box

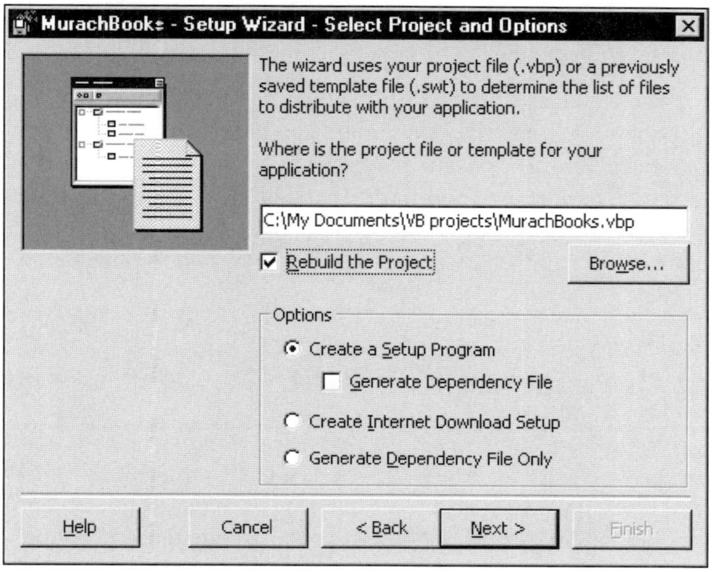

Description

- To start the Setup Wizard, choose Application Setup Wizard from the Visual Basic 5.0 submenu in the Programs menu that you access from the Windows Start button. If the Wizard displays an Introduction dialog box, click on the Next button to display the dialog box shown above.
- To identify the project you want to create a setup program for, enter its name and location in the text box or click on the Browse button and locate the project. Or, if you are recreating a setup program for a project that you created a template for, you can specify that template.
- To make sure that the Setup Wizard recompiles your project and rebuilds the executable for the project before continuing, select the Rebuild the Project option.
- For most projects, you'll use the Create a Setup Program option to create a standard setup program, and you won't need to check the Generate Dependency File box. You only need to create a dependency file for a project when it will be used as a component of another project.
- The Create Internet Download Setup option creates a setup package for an ActiveX component so it can be downloaded from the World Wide Web.
- The Generate Dependency File Only option creates a dependency file for the specified project. You use this option most often when you want to create dependency files for the ActiveX components you create.

Figure 13-2 How to select a project and the setup options

The Setup Wizard may also display an error message if the project uses a component but no dependency file is found for it. Then, if this component will be deployed as a local component and you know that it requires additional files, you can correct this problem in one of two ways. First, you can exit from the Setup Wizard, create a dependency file for the component as described later in this chapter, and run the Setup Wizard again. Second, if you know what files are required by the component, you can continue with the setup process and add those files to the File Summary dialog box that's displayed later in the setup process. On the other hand, if the component with the missing dependency file will be deployed as a remote component, you can ignore this error since the required files will be included in the setup program for the component.

How to select the distribution method

The next dialog box that's displayed by the Setup Wizard is the Distribution Method dialog box shown in figure 13-3. As you can see, you have three options for distributing an application. The Floppy disk option lets you distribute the application using floppy disks. The Single Directory option lets you distribute the application from a network server. And the Disk Directories option lets you distribute the application from floppy disks or a network server.

If you select the Floppy disk option, the Setup Wizard copies all of its output files to floppy disks on the drive you specify with the capacity you specify. By knowing the disk capacities, the Wizard can determine how many disks will be required and will prompt you to insert them in the last phase of this process.

If you select the Single Directory option, all of the output files are copied to a single directory (folder). Usually, you want to store the files this way on a network server so all the clients on the network have access to them. To start, though, you may want to store the files on your local machine, and then test the setup program to be sure that it works. Once you're sure it works, you can copy the files to a network server.

If you select the Disk Directories option, the output files are copied to directories that simulate a floppy disk layout. In this case, the Setup Wizard determines the number of directories that are required by the disk capacity you specify. Then, you have two options for distributing the application. Either you store the files on a network server so everyone on the network has access to them, or you copy the files in each directory to a floppy disk so they can be installed on machines that don't have access to the network.

The Distribution Method dialog box

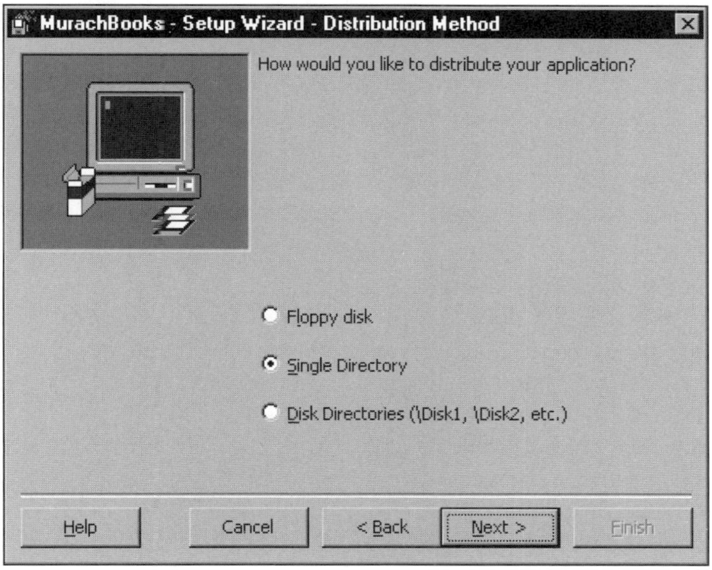

Description

- The Setup Wizard gives you three options for distributing an application as shown in the dialog box above. The option you choose determines the additional information that's required.
- If you choose the Floppy Disk option, the Setup Wizard will copy all of the setup files for the application to floppy disks. After you choose this option, the Setup Wizard will ask you to identify the drive letter for the disks and the capacity of the disks you will use (360KB, 720KB, 1.2MB, or 1.44MB).
- If you choose the Single Directory option, the Setup Wizard will copy the setup files to the single directory you specify. After you choose this option, the Setup Wizard will ask you to specify a destination for the files.
- If you choose the Disk Directories option, the Setup Wizard will copy the setup files to directories that simulate a floppy disk layout (\DISK1, \DISK2, etc.). After you choose this option, the Setup Wizard will ask you to specify a destination for the files and the disk capacity to be used.

Figure 13-3 How to select the distribution method

How to include data access support

If your application includes a reference to DAO, the Setup Wizard displays the Data Access dialog box shown in figure 13-4. This dialog box lets you select any Indexed Sequential Access Method (ISAM) file types that are used by the application (not covered in this book). If you select any of these file types, the appropriate ISAM engine files will be included with the output files.

The Data Access dialog box also lets you select the type of workspaces used by the application. By default, the dbUseJet option is selected so the required Jet engine files are included with the output files, and that's what you want if your application uses DAO. (If your application uses any of the ISAM file types, this option cannot be changed since the Jet engine is also required with those files.)

If your application uses ODBCDirect, though, you'll want to select the dbUseODBC option instead. Then, the RDO files will be used instead of the Jet files. (ODBCDirect and RDO aren't covered in this book.)

If you selected one of the DAO references in your project, the Setup Wizard assumes that the application uses DAO even if it doesn't. Because of that, it won't let you continue until you select either the dbUseJet or the dbUseODBC option. Then, if your application doesn't need the Jet or RDO files that are included when you select these options, you can correct this situation in one of two ways. First, you can cancel out of the Setup Wizard, return to Visual Basic, remove the DAO reference from this project, and start the Setup Wizard again. Second, you can wait until the Setup Wizard displays a summary of the files to be included in the output (see figure 13-7) and remove the check marks from the files you don't want to include. If you're not sure what files to remove, though, your best bet is to remove the unwanted references from the project.

The Data Access dialog box

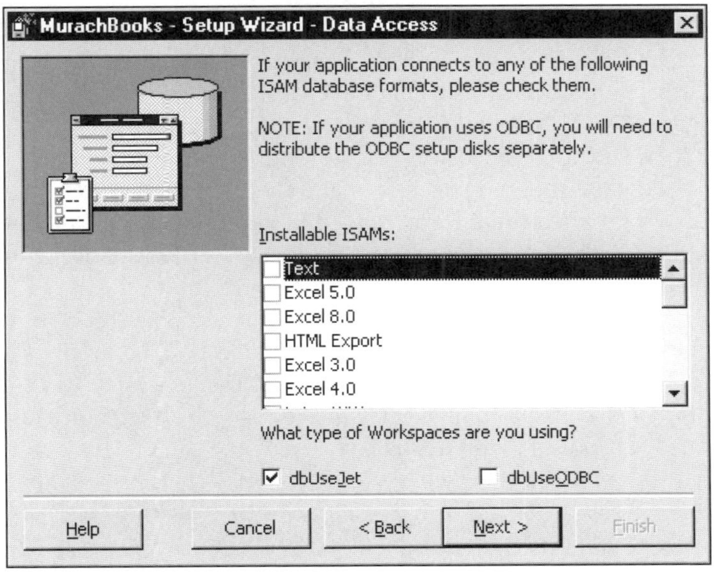

Description

- If your program uses Data Access Objects (DAO), the Setup Wizard displays the dialog box shown above. From this dialog box, you can choose the types of ISAM files and workspaces used by your application.
- If your application uses Jet workspaces to access data like the applications presented in this book, choose the dbUseJet option. Then, the Jet engine files are included with the other setup files. (This option is selected automatically if you select any of the ISAM database formats.)
- If your application uses ODBCDirect to access data, choose the dbUseODBC option. Then, the Remote Data Objects (RDO) files are included with the other setup files.
- If your application uses both Jet and ODBC workspaces, select both the dbUseJet and the dbUseODBC options.
- If you select any of the ISAM database formats, the appropriate ISAM engine files are included with the other setup files.
- If your application accesses ODBC data, you must install the appropriate ODBC driver on all the clients that will use the application (see figure 13-10).

How to include ActiveX components

If your project contains references to any ActiveX components and the Setup Wizard is able to locate them, they will be listed in the ActiveX Server Components dialog box shown in figure 13-5. If the Wizard isn't able to locate a component, though, and you didn't locate it earlier in the setup process, the component will not be listed. Then, if you want to include the component with the client application so it's distributed to each client, you need to add the executable file for the component to this dialog box. To do that, click on the Add Local button, then locate and select the DLL or EXE file for the component.

In figure 13-5, you can see that the EXE file for the BookOrders component has been included in the dialog box. Here, however, the check mark has been removed from this file so it won't be included with the client application. That's because this component will be deployed as a remote component, which is also why a reference to the remote component has been added to this dialog box.

To include a reference to a remote component, you click on the Add Remote button and select the VBR file for the component. Then, the Setup Wizard checks to be sure that a TLB file is available for the component. (If you've read chapter 12, you may remember that the VBR and TLB files are created when you build the component project if the Remote Server Files option is selected for the project.) If the Setup Wizard doesn't find a TLB file in the same folder as the VBR file, though, the Wizard displays an error message and doesn't add the remote component. That's because both the VBR and TLB files are required for an application to access and use a remote component.

If both the VBR and TLB files for a component are located, the Setup Wizard displays another dialog box that asks you to specify some connection information for the component. If you will be using DCOM to access the component, which is the default, you only need to specify the network address of the machine where the component will reside, and the network address is usually just the name of the computer. Although you can also use Remote Automation to access a remote component, it's an older technology that's provided only for backwards compatibility.

The ActiveX Server Components dialog box

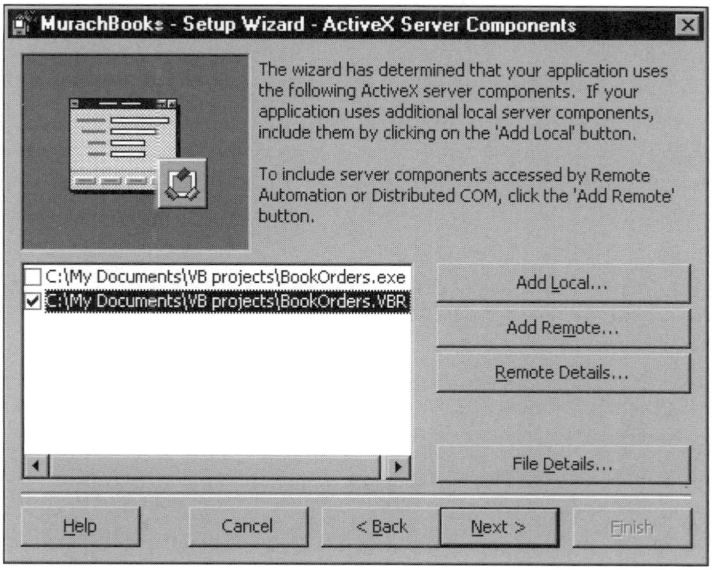

Description

- The ActiveX Server Components dialog box lists the files for all ActiveX components referenced in your project that the Setup Wizard is able to locate. If you want a component to reside on the local machine along with the client application, make sure that the executable file for that component is included in this list. If it's not, you can click on the Add Local button to add it.
- If you included a *local component* in a project but you want it used as a *remote component*, be sure to remove the check mark from the executable file for the local component. Then, click on the Add Remote button and add the VBR file for the remote component.
- When you add a remote component, the Setup Wizard will ask you to specify some connection information. This information includes whether you will be using DCOM or Remote Automation to access the component and the name of the machine where the component resides. After you specify this information, the VBR file is included in the dialog box as shown above.
- After identifying a remote component, you can redisplay its connection information by highlighting the component and clicking on the Remote Details button. You can also click on the File Details button to display information about the currently highlighted component, including its size, when it was created, and its detailed version information.

How to confirm file dependencies

The next dialog box that's displayed by the Setup Wizard is the Confirm Dependencies dialog box shown in figure 13-6. This dialog box lists all of the files required by the project other than the component files that were already identified. In this example, the Setup Wizard determined that three files are required for the MurachBooks project. The first one is the DLL that's required for DAO. The second two are the OCX files for the Microsoft Tabbed Dialog control and the Microsoft FlexGrid control.

Note, however, that the check marks have been removed from the two OCX files. That's because these two controls were added to the toolbox for the project, but were never used. As a result, they don't have to be included with the application.

If you know that some of the files already exist on the machines where the application will be installed, you can remove the check marks from those files too. However, it's usually best to include these files just in case one of the client machines doesn't include them. And even if these files are on the client machine, the files that are used by the application may be newer versions.

The Confirm Dependencies dialog box

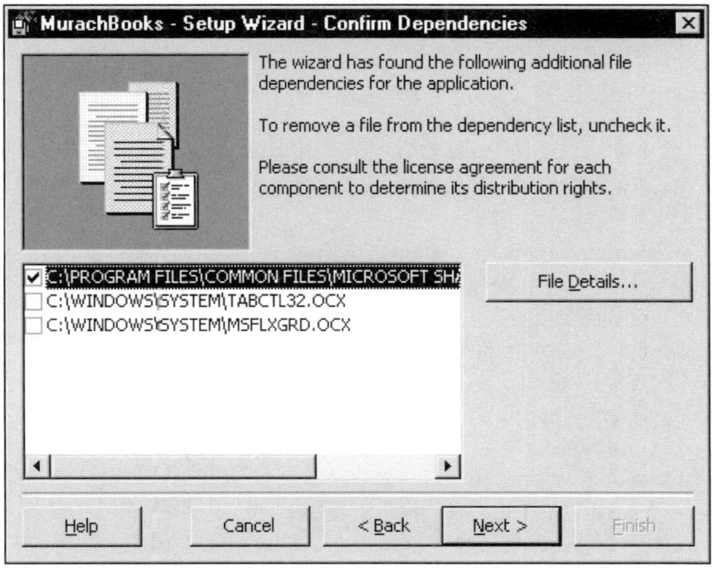

Description

- The Confirm Dependencies dialog box lists all the file dependencies identified by the Setup Wizard other than the ActiveX components. These dependencies include ActiveX controls used by your application or files referenced by your application.
- If any ActiveX controls or file references are included in the project but aren't used, you can remove the check marks from them so they're not included with the setup files. If, for example, you add an ActiveX control to the project's toolbox but don't use it, the control will be included in the file dependencies as shown above. Then, you can remove its check mark.
- You can also remove the check marks from any files that you know already exist on the clients where the application will be installed. And you must remove the check marks from files that you don't have the appropriate distribution rights for.
- The File Details button displays information about the currently highlighted file, including its size, when it was created, and its detailed version information.

How to confirm the files to be distributed

When you click on the Next button in the Confirm Dependencies dialog box, the Setup Wizard compiles a list of all the files that need to be included as output files. These include the Visual Basic run-time files that are needed for running the application and the setup program; the database drivers required by the application; the objects and references used by the application such as DAO and ActiveX controls; the ActiveX components and any files required by those components; and the executable file for the project. When it's done, the Setup Wizard displays a list of those files in the File Summary dialog box shown in figure 13-7.

You can use the File Summary dialog box to confirm that all of the files that are required by the application have been identified. You can also use it to add files that have not been identified. If, for example, you included a component that requires additional files but no dependency file was available for the component, you can add the required files from this dialog box. You can also add other files that you want to distribute with the client application such as a ReadMe file or help files.

If you're not sure why a particular file is included, you can highlight it and look in the Dependency Of box near the bottom of the dialog box. Then, if the file is a dependency of Visual Basic, the project, or a component, that information will be displayed. The file that's highlighted in this figure, for example, is a dependency of Visual Basic. In other words, it's required for running either the application or the setup program.

If you need additional information about a file, you can highlight it and click on the File Details button. Then, a dialog box is displayed that contains detailed information about the file as well as the location in which the file will be installed on the client. This location is specified as a system variable, which means that the actual location will be determined by the value of that variable on the system where the file is installed. For instance, the executable file for the application will be installed in the directory specified by the variable $(AppPath). Although you can change the variable that's specified, the default is usually what you want.

When you click on the Next button from the File Summary dialog box, the Setup Wizard displays a final dialog box that lets you save the setup information you just entered in a *template*. Then, if you have to recreate the setup program for the project later on, you can use the template file as input to the Setup Wizard as described in figure 13-2. When you click on the Finish button in this dialog box, the Setup Wizard compiles and creates the Setup.exe and Setup.lst files and compresses all of the other files that will be distributed. These files are then copied to the location you specified when you selected a distribution method.

The File Summary dialog box

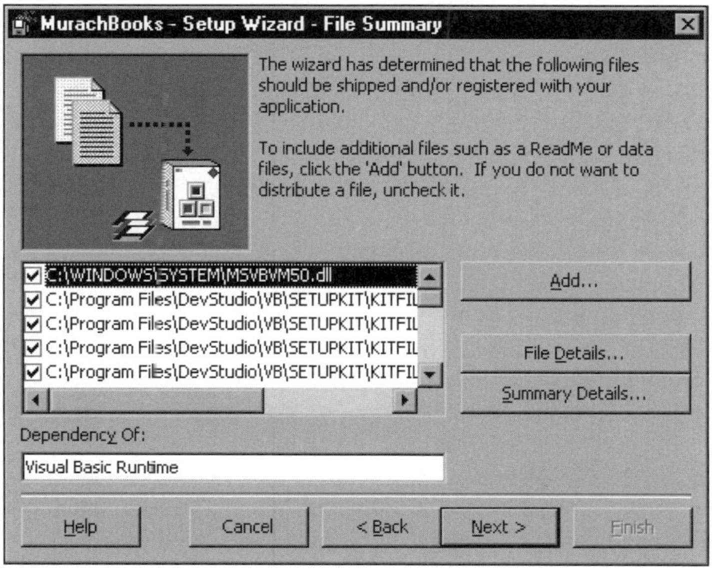

Description

- The File Summary dialog box lists all of the files that are needed by the application, including those needed to run the setup program for the application. You can use this dialog box to confirm that all required files have been identified.
- If a required file isn't included in the list of files, you can add it by clicking on the Add button. For instance, you may need to do this if you include an ActiveX component that has dependencies, but a dependency file hasn't been created for it. You can also do this if you want to include supporting files like a Readme file.
- The Dependency Of box at the bottom of the dialog box indicates the program, file, or component that requires the file that's currently highlighted. You can use this information to confirm that the dependencies for specific components are included in the list of files.
- The File Details button displays information about the currently highlighted file, including its size, when it was created, where it will be installed, and its detailed version information. The Summary Details button displays summary information about the files, including the total number of files and their size.

How to install the application

Once you've successfully created a setup program for an application, you need to run it on a client to make sure that it installs the application properly and that the application runs without any problems. Before you do that for an application that gets data from an ODBC database, though, you need to be sure that the required ODBC driver is installed on the client. If it isn't installed, you need to install it as shown in figure 13-10. You also need to define a data source on each client machine.

Assuming that the required ODBC driver is installed and the data source has been defined, figure 13-8 shows you how to install an application using its setup program. Note that the technique you use depends on the distribution method you selected when you created the setup program and on the location of the setup files. In particular, you should note that if the setup program and files are stored on a network server, you can install the application from any client on the network by running the setup program from that client.

Although you can test an application by installing and running it on your own machine first, you should also consider testing it on other machines. That's particularly true if the clients have a variety of hardware and software configurations.

When you start the setup program, it begins by copying some temporary files to the client. Then, it displays a dialog box warning that the setup program can't install system files or update shared files if they are currently in use, and it recommends that you close any applications that are currently running before you continue. To do that, you have to exit from the setup program, in which case the temporary files that were copied to the machine when the program started are removed.

If you continue with the setup process, the dialog box in figure 13-8 is displayed. This dialog box lets you confirm the location where the application will be installed. Here, the default location is determined by the value of the system variable that was specified for the application's files by the Setup Wizard. In this example, the application will be installed in a directory with the same name as the application within the Program Files directory on the C drive. If that's what you want, you can click on the large button to install the application. Otherwise, you can click on the Change Directory button to select a different location before you continue.

If an error occurs during the installation process, you can exit from the setup program and any files that were installed will be removed. Before any shared files are removed, though, you will be prompted so you can confirm their removal. After the setup program has been canceled, you can view the log file that was created to try to determine the cause of the problem. This file is named ST5UNST and is given a consecutive numeric extension beginning with 000. If necessary, you can then recreate the setup program and try running it again.

After the setup program runs without errors, you can run the installed application to be sure that it works properly. If it doesn't, you need to determine the cause of the error, make the necessary corrections, and recreate the setup program. Before you do that, though, you need to uninstall the current version of the application. To do that, you can use the Add/Remove Programs program in the Windows Control Panel. Or, you can run the ST5UNST.EXE program that's in the Windows directory. If you don't remove a program before installing it again, serious errors can occur and the installed program may not work properly.

The dialog box that's displayed by an application's setup program

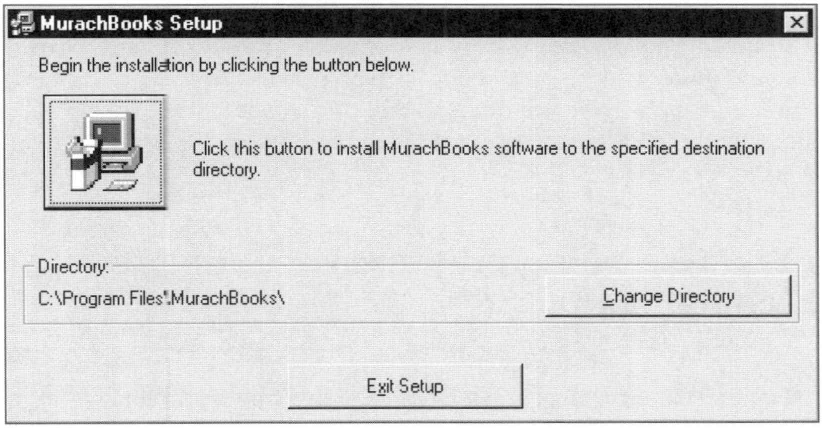

Description

- To install an application, run the Setup.exe file that was created by the Setup Wizard. The location of this file depends on the distribution method you selected when you ran the Setup Wizard to create the setup program.
- If the setup files were copied to floppy disks, the setup program will be located on the first disk in the set. If the setup files were copied to disk directories, the setup program will be located in the DISK1 directory of the path you specified. And if the setup files were copied to a single directory, the setup program will be in that directory.
- If you saved the setup files on a network server, you can run the setup program from any machine that has access to that server. Then, the setup program installs the necessary files on the client machine.
- When the setup program starts, you'll see a dialog box like the one shown above. To install the application, click on the indicated button. To change the directory where the application will be installed, click on the Change Directory button. To exit from the setup program, click on the Exit Setup button.
- If the application you install doesn't work properly, you need to uninstall it and then run the Setup Wizard again to create a new setup program that corrects the problem. To uninstall the application, use the Add/Remove Programs application in the Windows Control Panel.

Figure 13-8 How to install the application

Other deployment issues

If you follow the techniques and recommendations for using the Setup Wizard presented so far in this chapter, you should be able to create setup programs for most of the applications you develop. If you develop ActiveX components, though, you need some additional information about working with those components. And if an application accesses an ODBC database, you need to know how to install the ODBC driver on the client machines.

How to create a setup program for a remote ActiveX component

The procedure for creating a setup program for an ActiveX project is almost identical to the procedure that you use to create a setup program for a standard project. The biggest difference is that the dialog box shown in figure 13-9 is displayed after you confirm the dependencies for the application. This dialog box lets you determine whether the component is installed as a stand-alone application or as a shared component and whether it will be accessed using DCOM or Remote Automation. In general, though, you install components like the one presented in chapter 12 as shared components so they can be accessed by your client applications. You also use DCOM if it's supported by your client machines.

Note, however, that you only need to create a setup program for an ActiveX project if you want to deploy it as a remote component. If it will be deployed as a local component, you can simply include it in the setup programs for the applications that use it. Then, it will be distributed along with those applications and installed on the client machines.

How to create a dependency file for an ActiveX component

Although you don't need to create a setup program for a local ActiveX component, you may want to create a dependency file for it if it requires additional files and if it will be used by more than one client application. That way, when you create a setup program for one of those applications, you can be sure that all of the required files will be included.

To create a dependency file for an ActiveX project, you run the Setup Wizard with the Generate Dependency File Only option on (see figure 13-2). Then, because the Setup Wizard requires most of the same information to create a dependency file that it needs to create a setup program, it will lead you through many of the same dialog boxes you saw earlier in this chapter. The biggest difference is that the output will be a single DEP file.

The Shared ActiveX Application dialog box

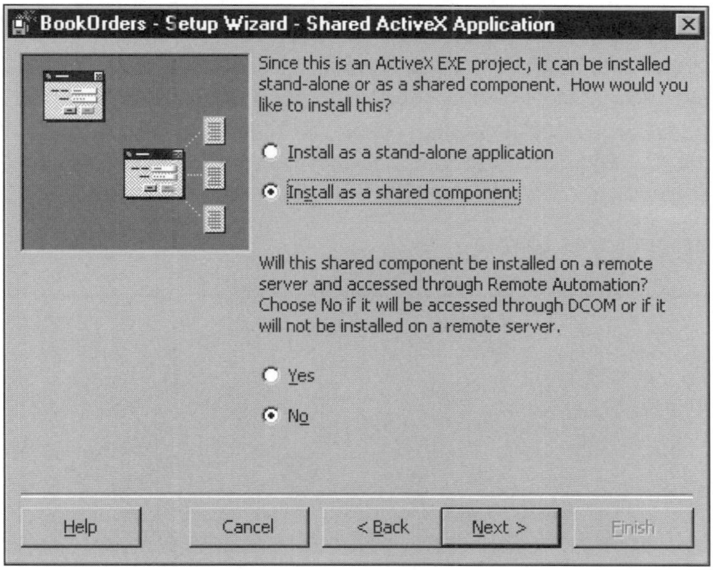

Description

- To create a setup program for an ActiveX component, you use the same basic techniques that you use for a standard project. Then, after you confirm the dependencies for the component, the dialog box shown above is displayed.
- You can install an ActiveX EXE component as either a stand-alone application or as a shared component. If you want to be able to access the component from your client applications, though, you need to install it as a shared component.
- You can use either DCOM or Remote Automation to access a remote ActiveX component, although Remote Automation is provided only for backwards compatibility with 16-bit systems. To use DCOM, select the No option.
- To install an ActiveX component, run its setup program on the machine where it will reside. In this case, the setup program doesn't let you change the directory where the component is installed. Instead, it's installed in a system directory.

Note

- By default, Windows 95 doesn't support DCOM. To use it, you can download and run the DCOM95.EXE file from the Microsoft web site.

Figure 13-9 How to create a setup program for a remote ActiveX component

You may also want to create a dependency file for some of the remote ActiveX components you create. In particular, you should create a dependency file for a remote component if it will be used by other components. Then, when you create a setup program for a component that uses the remote component, you can be sure that all of the required files are included. To create a dependency file for a remote component at the same time that you create its setup program, you can check the Generate Dependency File box under the Create a Setup Program option (see figure 13-2).

How to install ODBC drivers

Before you install an application that accesses ODBC data on a client machine, you need to be sure that ODBC and the required ODBC drivers have been installed on that machine. To find out if ODBC has been installed, look in the Windows Control Panel. If the 32bit ODBC program is available, then ODBC has been installed. To find out if the required ODBC drivers have been installed, start the 32bit ODBC program, then click on the Add button to display a list of the available drivers.

If ODBC or the required ODBC drivers haven't been installed, you can use the ODBC files that come with Visual Basic to install them as explained in figure 13-10. First, you copy the files in the ODBC directory to diskettes or to a network directory. These files include a file named Setup.exe. Then, you run the Setup.exe program on the client machine so the first dialog box in figure 13-10 is displayed. This dialog box lets you specify the folder where ODBC will be installed, and it lets you select whether you want to perform a typical or a custom installation. If you click on the Typical button, all of the ODBC files and drivers are installed. If you click on the Custom button, all of the ODBC files, but only the drivers you select, are installed.

Two of the dialog boxes from the ODBC setup program

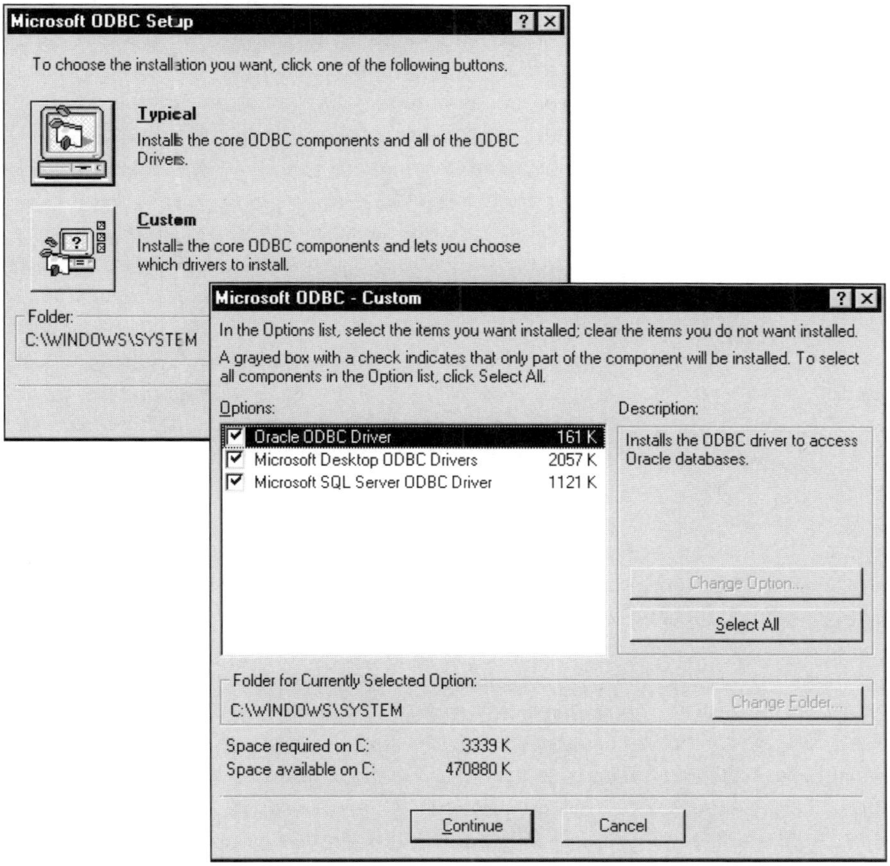

Description

- To install the appropriate ODBC drivers on a client machine, copy the files in the ODBC directory that comes with Visual Basic to a diskette or a network directory. Then, run the Setup.exe program in that directory on the client machine.
- The ODBC setup program lets you perform a typical or a custom installation as shown in the Setup dialog box above. If you choose the custom option, you can select the ODBC drivers that are installed as shown in the Custom dialog box above.
- Although you can change the default folder that is used for the ODBC files, the default is usually what you want.
- When you click on the Typical button in the Setup dialog box or on the Continue button in the Custom dialog box, the ODBC drivers are copied to the client.
- If ODBC hasn't been installed on the client machine, the setup program also copies the necessary ODBC files to that machine. If ODBC has been installed, the setup program overwrites those files with the files that come with Visual Basic if the Visual Basic files are newer.

Figure 13-10 How to install ODBC drivers

Perspective

Although the basic procedure for deploying an application using the Setup Wizard is straightforward, you can see from this chapter that there's a lot of room for error. So before you create a setup program for an application, you want to be sure that the project includes only the controls and components it needs and that all the files that need to be included in the setup program are available. If you do that, there's a much better chance that the setup process will go smoothly.

To make sure that a project doesn't include any unnecessary files, use the References and Components commands in the Project menu to display the related dialog boxes. Then, remove the check marks from any items that aren't required. That way, the Setup Wizard won't include these files when it analyzes the project.

If the application uses any ActiveX components, you also need to make sure that the required files for those components are available. For each local component, you need an EXE or DLL file. In addition, if the component has dependencies, you need a DEP file, and you can create that file yourself if you were the developer of the component. For each remote component, you need a TLB and a VBR file, and you can create those files yourself when you build the project if you were the developer of the component. On the other hand, if you didn't develop the components that your application uses, you need to find out where any required EXE, DLL, and DEP files are for local components and where the required TLB and VBR files are for remote components.

To get a better understanding for how the deployment process works, you can now experiment with one of the applications that you developed for earlier chapters. To start, for example, you can create a setup program for the chapter 4 application that uses a bound form. Then, you can use that setup program to install the application on your own machine, and you can test the application to make sure it works. Because this application doesn't use ActiveX components, this deployment process is simpler than the example used throughout this chapter. Once you get that application to work, you can deploy the chapter 12 application on your own machine so you can see how this process changes when the application uses ActiveX components.

Appendix

Applications and databases on our web site

To get the most from this book, you'll want to develop applications that are like those illustrated in the chapters of this book. After you read chapter 3, for example, you should develop a Calculate Investment application. After you read chapter 4, you should develop bound and unbound versions of the Vendors form that's part of an Accounts Payable application. After you read chapter 6, you should develop bound and unbound versions of the enhanced Accounts Payable application. After you read chapter 8, you should develop SDI and MDI versions of the Accounts Payable application. And after you read chapter 12, you should develop a Book Order application.

If you have trouble developing any of these applications, though, you may wish that you could review a working version of the application. That's why all nine of these applications are available from our web site. After you download these applications, you can review the forms, controls, and code for each application, which is a quick way to see how these elements work together. You can also use the techniques of chapter 9 to step through the code as you test each application to see how each statement works.

Because all but the first application get data from a database, you can also download Access versions of the databases that are required by these applications. You can use those databases whether you're developing the applications on your own or testing the applications that you download. Then, if you want to test the applications using SQL Server, you can use the Access Upsizing Wizard to upsize the Access databases to SQL Server databases. Or, if you prefer, you can create the SQL Server databases on your own and then export the tables from the Access to the SQL Server databases.

On the next two pages of this appendix, you can learn how to download the applications and databases from our web site to your system. After that, you'll find the specifications for the Access databases as well as the specifications for SQL Server versions of the databases. We hope that these specifications will make it easier for you to understand and use the Access databases and, if necessary, to convert the Access databases to SQL Server.

Unfortunately, if you don't have access to the Internet, you'll have to create the required databases and enter your own test data. But here again, the database specifications in this chapter should come in handy.

How to download the applications and databases

Figure A-1 shows how to download the nine applications and two databases from our web site. In brief, one Zip file is available for each of the five chapters in this book that present complete applications (chapters 3, 4, 6, 8, and 12). A sixth Zip file is available for the databases that you need for running those applications.

In case you aren't familiar with this type of file, a Zip file is a compressed, executable file that expands into the uncompressed versions of all the folders and files that it represents. To expand the file after you've downloaded it to your system, you just double-click on its file name in the Explorer window. If, for example, you double-click on the Zip file for chapter 6 (Chapter6.exe), it expands itself into the Murach folder, the Chapter6 folder, the Bound and Unbound folders, and all the files that are needed for the bound and unbound versions of the chapter 6 application. Similarly, if you double-click on the Zip file for the databases (Databases.exe), it expands itself into the Murach folder, the AccountsPayable folder, the MurachBooks folder, and the Access files for the two databases.

If you want to download all of the applications and databases at once, you can download and expand the file named AllFiles.exe. Depending on your system, though, this may take longer than you expect. As a result, you may want to start by downloading one of the other files.

Once you have the applications and files on your system, you may have to modify the Visual Basic applications so they will work on your system. In particular, if you're going to use Access databases, you need to change the connection information from the SQL Server databases that we used to the Access databases on your system. If you're going to use SQL Server databases, though, the applications will work without any changes as long as the data sources you create to connect to those databases have the same names as the data sources we use in the applications.

The folder layout for the applications and databases

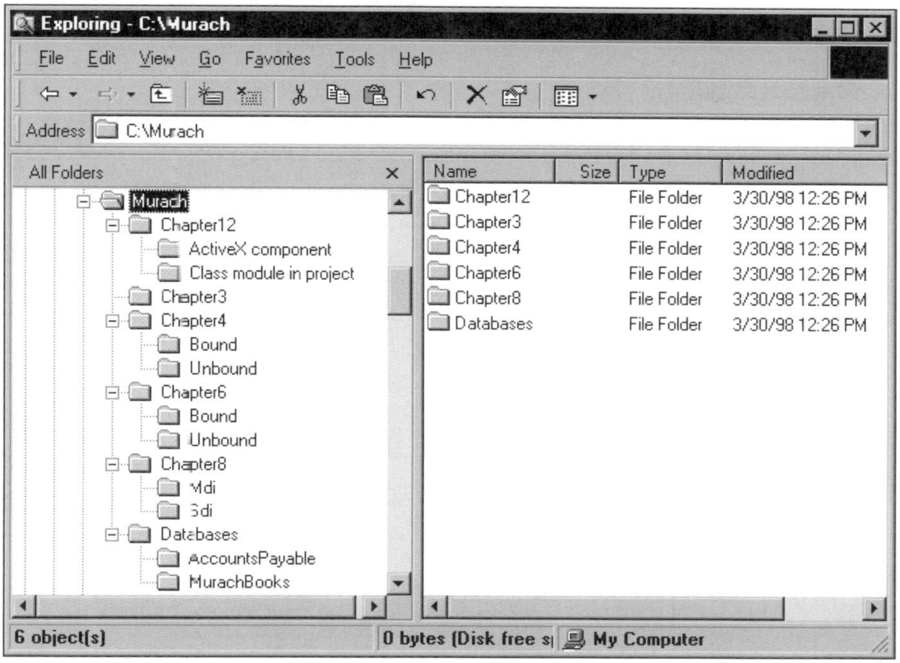

Available applications and databases

- The folders above show the available applications. As you can see, chapter 3 contains only one application, while chapters 4, 6, 8 and 12 contain two applications.
- The folders above also show the available databases. The AccountsPayable database can be used by the applications in chapters 4, 6, and 8. The MurachBooks database can be used by the applications for chapter 12. And no database is required for the application in chapter 3.

How to download the applications and databases

1. Start your Internet browser and go to *www.murach.com*. Then, select Book Catalog followed by Downloads at the Murach site.
2. Choose the Zip file that you want to download. To download all the applications and databases, choose AllFiles.exe. To download just the databases, choose Databases.exe. To download the application or applications for just one chapter, choose the Zip file for that chapter (like Chapter6.exe). When the file is downloaded, it is saved in the default folder on your system.
3. From the Explorer, double-click on the name of the downloaded file. This expands the single file into the Murach folder (C:\Murach) plus all the subfolders and files that the Zip file represents.

Figure A-1 How to download the applications and databases

The AccountsPayable database for Access

The Vendors table

Field name	Data type	Field size	Notes
VendorID	AutoNumber	Long integer	Key field
VendorName	Text	50	Required
VendorAddress1	Text	50	Allow zero length
VendorAddress2	Text	50	Allow zero length
VendorCity	Text	50	Required
VendorState	Text	2	Foreign key of States table; required
VendorZipCode	Text	10	Required
VendorContact	Text	50	Allow zero length
VendorPhone	Text	50	Allow zero length
TermsID	Number	Long integer	Foreign key of Terms table; default is 3; required
AccountNo	Number	Long integer	Foreign key of GLAccounts table; default is 570; required
LastTranDate	Date/Time		
YTDPurchases	Currency		Default is zero
YTDReturns	Currency		Default is zero
LastYTDPurchases	Currency		Default is zero
LastYTDReturns	Currency		Default is zero

The Terms table

Field name	Data type	Field size	Notes
TermsID	AutoNumber	Long integer	Key field
TermsDescription	Text	50	Required
TermsDueDays	Number	Integer	Required

The GLAccounts table

Field name	Data type	Field size	Notes
AccountNo	Number	Long integer	Key field; required
AccountDescription	Text	50	Required

The States table

Field name	Data type	Field size	Notes
StateCode	Text	2	Key field; required
FirstZipCode	Number	Long integer	Required
LastZipCode	Number	Long integer	Required

The Invoices table

Field name	Data type	Field size	Notes
InvoiceID	AutoNumber	Long integer	Key field
VendorID	Number	Long integer	Foreign key of Vendors table; required; index with duplicates
InvoiceNumber	Text	10	Required
InvoiceDate	Date/Time		Required
InvoiceTotal	Currency		Default is zero
PaymentTotal	Currency		Default is zero
CreditTotal	Currency		Default is zero
TermsID	Number	Long integer	Foreign key of Terms table; required
InvoiceDueDate	Date/Time		Required

The InvoiceLineItems table

Field name	Data type	Field size	Notes
InvoiceID	Number	Long integer	Key field; foreign key of Invoices table; required
InvoiceSequence	Number	Integer	Key field; required
AccountNo	Number	Long integer	Foreign key of GLAccounts table; required
InvoiceLine-ItemAmount	Currency		Default is zero
InvoiceLine-ItemDescription	Text	100	Allow zero length

The AccountsPayable database for SQL Server

The Vendors table

Column name	Datatype	Size	Notes
VendorID	int	4	Key field; identity field
VendorName	varchar	50	No nulls
VendorAddress1	varchar	50	No nulls; default is space
VendorAddress2	varchar	50	No nulls; default is space
VendorCity	varchar	50	No nulls
VendorState	char	2	No nulls; foreign key of States table
VendorZipCode	varchar	10	No nulls
VendorContact	varchar	50	No nulls; default is space
VendorPhone	varchar	50	No nulls; default is space
TermsID	int	4	No nulls; foreign key of Terms table; default is 3
AccountNo	int	4	No nulls; foreign key of GLAccounts table; default is 570
LastTranDate	datetime	8	No nulls; default is space
YTDPurchases	money	8	No nulls; default is zero
YTDReturns	money	8	No nulls; default is zero
LastYTDPurchases	money	8	No nulls; default is zero
LastYTDReturns	money	8	No nulls; default is zero

The Terms table

Column name	Datatype	Size	Notes
TermsID	int	4	Key field; identity field
TermsDescription	varchar	50	No nulls
TermsDueDays	smallint	2	No nulls

The GLAccounts table

Column name	Datatype	Size	Notes
AccountNo	int	4	Key field
AccountDescription	varchar	50	No nulls

The States table

Column name	Datatype	Size	Notes
StateCode	char	2	Key field
FirstZipCode	int	4	No nulls
LastZipCode	int	4	No nulls

The Invoices table

Column name	Datatype	Size	Notes
InvoiceID	int	4	Key field; identity field
VendorID	int	4	No nulls; foreign key of Vendors table; index with nonunique keys
InvoiceNumber	varchar	10	No nulls
InvoiceDate	datetime	8	No nulls
InvoiceTotal	money	8	No nulls; default is zero
PaymentTotal	money	8	No nulls; default is zero
CreditTotal	money	8	No nulls; default is zero
TermsID	int	4	No nulls; foreign key of Terms table
InvoiceDueDate	datetime	8	No nulls

The InvoiceLineItems table

Column name	Datatype	Size	Notes
InvoiceID	int	4	Key field; foreign key of Invoices table
InvoiceSequence	smallint	2	Key field
AccountNo	int	4	No nulls; foreign key of GLAccounts table
InvoiceLine-ItemAmount	money	8	No nulls; default is zero
InvoiceLine-ItemDescription	varchar	100	No nulls; default is space

The MurachBooks database for Access

The BookPrices table

Field name	Data type	Field size	Notes
BookID	Text	4	Key field; required
BookDescription	Text	50	Required
BookPrice	Currency		Required

The QuantityDiscounts table

Field name	Data type	Field size	Notes
QuantityDiscount	Number	Single	Key field; required
LowQuantity	Number	Integer	Required
HighQuantity	Number	Integer	Required

The SalesTax table

Field name	Data type	Field size	Notes
StateCode	Text	4	Key field; required
SalesTax	Number	Double	Required

The ShippingCosts table

Field name	Data type	Field size	Notes
ShippingMethod	Text	50	Key field; required
ShippingBaseCost	Currency		Required
ShippingUnitCost	Currency		Required

The MurachBooks database for SQL Server

The BookPrices table

Column name	Datatype	Size	Notes
BookID	varchar	4	Key field
BookDescription	varchar	50	No nulls
BookPrice	smallmoney	4	No nulls

The QuantityDiscounts table

Column name	Datatype	Size	Notes
QuantityDiscount	real	4	Key field
LowQuantity	smallint	2	No nulls
HighQuantity	smallint	2	No nulls

The SalesTax table

Column name	Datatype	Size	Notes
StateCode	varchar	4	Key field
SalesTax	decimal	4, 2	No nulls

The ShippsingCosts table

Column name	Datatype	Size	Notes
ShippingMethod	varchar	50	Key field
ShippingBaseCost	smallmoney	4	No nulls
ShippingUnitCost	smallmoney	4	No nulls

Index

A

B

C

E

I

J

K

L

O

P

Q

R

S

T

W

Client/Server Programming: Access 97

Scheduled to be off-press in October 1998

Check our web site (www.murach.com) for price and availability

Access 97 is designed to be used in conjunction with Visual Basic, and we believe that every client/server developer should be familiar with it. In particular, it often makes sense to prototype an application in Access before you do the final development in Visual Basic. And for small systems with fewer than 100 users, Access may be the preferred development environment for client/server applications.

With those considerations in mind, our next client/server book will teach you how to develop client/server systems using Access 97 and Visual Basic for Applications (VBA), a variation of Visual Basic that's built into Access. It will start off by covering the basic concepts of client/server programming and database processing, just as this book does, so that newcomers to the client/server environment can use it as their first book. Then, it covers the same basic programming skills as this book, but using Access instead of Visual Basic 5.

So if you liked this book and now need Access training, *Client/Server Programming: Access 97* is the book you'll want to get next (you can skip the parts you already know and go directly to the material that's new to you). And if you don't need Access training yourself, but you know of others who do, you can recommend the Access book without reservation; I promise you it will take the same practical, example-packed approach that this Visual Basic book has.

Mainframe Classics

More than just a JCL book, *MVS JCL* is a complete guide to your MVS system. Yes, you'll learn how to code JCL for everyday functions like allocating data sets, compiling programs, handling tapes, and using procedures. But you'll also learn how MVS works so you'll know *why* you code the JCL the way you do for any given job.

17 chapters, 496 pages, 227 illustrations, **$42.50**
ISBN 0-911625-85-2

The DB2 books written from the programmer's point of view. *Part 1* teaches you the essentials of designing and coding DB2 programs using embedded SQL. Then, *Part 2* covers all the subjects that you're going to want to know about as you continue working in DB2, including advanced data manipulation and error handling techniques, dynamic SQL, distributed data, DB2 processing in CICS, DBA tools and techniques that help with testing and debugging, and QMF.

Part 1: 11 chapters, 371 pages, 175 illustrations, **$36.50**
ISBN 0-911625-59-3

Part 2: 15 chapters, 393 pages, 164 illustrations, **$36.50**
ISBN 0-911625-64-X

Join the more than 100,000 programmers who have learned CICS using these practical books alone. *Part 1* teaches you all the basics that apply to *any* CICS program. Then, *Part 2* covers the advanced features you'll use regularly, though you won't need them all in every program. That includes browse commands, DB2 and DL/I processing in CICS, BMS page building, terminal control, temporary storage, transient data, distributed processing features like Distributed Program Link and APPC, and more!

Part 1: 12 chapters, 409 pages, 168 illustrations, **$36.50**
ISBN 0-911625-60-7

Part 2: 12 chapters, 352 pages, 168 illustrations, **$36.50**
ISBN 0-911625-67-4

Shove all those IBM manuals off your desk! This one book contains everything you need at your side when you're doing CICS work. BMS macros...CICS commands...AMS commands...JCL setups...ISPF editing commands...model programs...program design techniques...testing and debugging. It's the one book you won't want to be without!

12 sections, 507 pages, **$42.50**
ISBN 0-911625-68-2

Short books for instant results on the job

That's what you get in the Murach Crash Courses.

Whether you're completely new to the software, converting from another system or program, or upgrading, you can use each *Crash Course* as your own personal software consultant:

- to get you going FAST
- to answer your questions, on demand
- to point out shortcuts
- to reduce the woes of upgrading
- to get you through your workload without being bogged down by your software

So if you already have more than enough to do at work, don't waste time struggling with your software. Let the *Crash Courses* be your easy-to-use software guides, starting TODAY!

2 chapters
53 pages
$10
ISBN 0-911625-97-6

Contents

Chapter 1
Essential Windows skills
The desktop • Program and document windows • Menus and commands • Using the Open and Save As commands • Managing folders and files • Windows Explorer

Chapter 2
More useful Windows skills
Shortcuts • Customizing your Start menu • Controlling the view in folder windows • The Control Panel • Local and network drives • Printers and print queues • Online help

3 chapters
83 pages
$15
ISBN 0-911625-95-X

3 chapters
83 pages
$15
ISBN 0-911625-98-4

Contents

Chapter 1
How to create, print, and save a document

Chapter 2
Essential word processing skills
Edit a document • Format characters, paragraphs, and pages • Prepare multi-page documents

Chapter 3
3 features that help you work like a PRO
Templates and wizards • Styles • Tables

3 chapters
83 pages
$15
ISBN 0-911625-96-8

3 chapters
83 pages
$15
ISBN 0-911625-99-2

Contents

Chapter 1
How to create, print, and save a worksheet

Chapter 2
Essential worksheet skills
10 essential editing skills • 10 essential formatting skills • 9 essential skills for working with larger worksheets

Chapter 3
2 features that help you work like a PRO
Working with more than one worksheet at a time • Charts

They're faster than asking anyone.

Comment Form

Your opinions count

If you have any comments, criticisms, or suggestions for us, I'm eager to hear from you. Your opinions today will affect our products of tomorrow. And if you find any errors in this book, typographical or otherwise, please point them out so we can correct them in the next printing.

Thanks for your help.

Book title: Client/Server Programming: Visual Basic 5

Dear Mike: ____________________

Name ____________________

Company (if company address) ____________________

Address ____________________

City, State, Zip ____________________

Fold where indicated and tape closed.
No postage needed if mailed in the U.S.

NO POSTAGE
NECESSARY
IF MAILED
IN THE
UNITED STATES

BUSINESS REPLY MAIL

FIRST-CLASS MAIL PERMIT NO. 3063 FRESNO, CA

POSTAGE WILL BE PAID BY ADDRESSEE

Mike Murach & Associates, Inc.

2560 W SHAW LN STE 101
FRESNO CA 93711-9866

Order form

Our Unlimited Guarantee

To our customers who order directly from us: You must be satisfied. Our books must work for you, or you can send them back for a full refund...no questions asked.

Name ______________________________

Company (if company address) ______________________________

Street Address ______________________________

City, State, Zip ______________________________

Phone number (including area code) ______________________________

Fax number (if you fax your order to us) ______________________________

Qty	Product code & title		*Price
Client/Server books			
____	VB50	Client/Server Programming: Visual Basic 5	$40.00
____	AC97	Client/Server Programming: Access 97 (Scheduled for October 1998; check web site for availability)	TBA
PC books			
____	C95N	Crash Course: Windows 95 & NT 4.0	10.00
____	CCW8	Crash Course: Word 97	15.00
____	CCX8	Crash Course: Excel 97	15.00
____	CCW7	Crash Course: Word 95	15.00
____	CCX7	Crash Course: Excel 95	15.00
Mainframe books			
____	MJLR	MVS JCL (Second Edition)	42.50
____	CC1R	CICS for the COBOL Programmer, Part 1	36.50
____	CC2R	CICS for the COBOL Programmer, Part 2	36.50
____	CRFR	The CICS Programmer's Desk Reference	42.50
____	DB21	DB2 for the COBOL Programmer, Part 1	36.50
____	DB22	DB2 for the COBOL Programmer, Part 2	36.50

❑ Bill my company for the books plus UPS shipping and handling (and sales tax within California).
P.O.# ______________________________

❑ I want to **SAVE 10%** by paying in advance. Charge to my ___Visa ___MasterCard ___American Express:

Card number ______________________________

Valid thru (mo/yr) ______________________________

Cardowner's signature ______________________________

❑ I want to **SAVE 10% plus shipping and handling**. Here's my check or money order for the books minus 10% ($__________). California residents, please add sales tax to your total. (Offer valid in U.S.)

***Prices are subject to change. Please call for current prices.**

To order more quickly,

Call **toll-free** 1-800-221-5528
(Weekdays, 8 to 5 Pacific Time)

Fax: 1-209-440-0963

Web: www.murach.com

MURACH

Mike Murach & Associates
2560 West Shaw Lane, Suite 101
Fresno, California 93711-2765
(209) 440-9071
E-mail: murachbooks@murach.com

NO POSTAGE
NECESSARY
IF MAILED
IN THE
UNITED STATES

BUSINESS REPLY MAIL

FIRST-CLASS MAIL PERMIT NO. 3063 FRESNO, CA

POSTAGE WILL BE PAID BY ADDRESSEE

Mike Murach & Associates, Inc.

2560 W SHAW LN STE 101
FRESNO CA 93711-9866

Order form

Our Unlimited Guarantee

To our customers who order directly from us: You must be satisfied. Our books must work for you, or you can send them back for a full refund…no questions asked.

Name ______________________________

Company (if company address) ______________________________

Street Address ______________________________

City, State, Zip ______________________________

Phone number (including area code) ______________________________

Fax number (if you fax your order to us) ______________________________

Qty	Product code & title		*Price
Client/Server books			
____	VB50	Client/Server Programming: Visual Basic 5	$40.00
____	AC97	Client/Server Programming: Access 97 (Scheduled for October 1998; check web site for availability)	TBA
PC books			
____	C95N	Crash Course: Windows 95 & NT 4.0	10.00
____	CCW8	Crash Course: Word 97	15.00
____	CCX8	Crash Course: Excel 97	15.00
____	CCW7	Crash Course: Word 95	15.00
____	CCX7	Crash Course: Excel 95	15.00
Mainframe books			
____	MJLR	MVS JCL (Second Edition)	42.50
____	CC1R	CICS for the COBOL Programmer, Part 1	36.50
____	CC2R	CICS for the COBOL Programmer, Part 2	36.50
____	CRFR	The CICS Programmer's Desk Reference	42.50
____	DB21	DB2 for the COBOL Programmer, Part 1	36.50
____	DB22	DB2 for the COBOL Programmer, Part 2	36.50

❑ Bill my company for the books plus UPS shipping and handling (and sales tax within California).
P.O.# ______________________________

❑ I want to **SAVE 10%** by paying in advance. Charge to my ___Visa ___MasterCard ___American Express:

Card number ______________________________

Valid thru (mo/yr) ______________________________

Cardowner's signature ______________________________

❑ I want to **SAVE 10% plus shipping and handling**. Here's my check or money order for the books minus 10% ($_________). California residents, please add sales tax to your total. (Offer valid in U.S.)

***Prices are subject to change. Please call for current prices.**

To order more quickly,

Call **toll-free** 1-800-221-5528
(Weekdays, 8 to 5 Pacific Time)

Fax: 1-209-440-0963

Web: www.murach.com

MURACH

Mike Murach & Associates
2560 West Shaw Lane, Suite 101
Fresno, California 93711-2765
(209) 440-9071
E-mail: murachbooks@murach.com

NO POSTAGE
NECESSARY
IF MAILED
IN THE
UNITED STATES

BUSINESS REPLY MAIL

FIRST-CLASS MAIL PERMIT NO. 3063 FRESNO, CA

POSTAGE WILL BE PAID BY ADDRESSEE

Mike Murach & Associates, Inc.

2560 W SHAW LN STE 101
FRESNO CA 93711-9866